The best of **Britain**

Cornwall

and the Isles of Scilly

Lesley Gillilan

Contents

Themed Maps

Town/City Centre Maps

The Guide

Introduction

Here's a word of warning: Cornwall is addictive. And it doesn't take much to get you hooked. It starts, perhaps, with a whiff of salt air, the ruffle of an Atlantic breeze on a lofty granite headland, a dash of gold on a distant lighthouse in the midst of a Far West sunset – and before you know it, you've got the makings of a Cornwall habit. Once addicted, you will return year after year, possibly for life; many fall so in love with the place, they stay for good. There is a magnetism, a magic, that gets under the skin, leaving everyone wanting more.

For generations of artists, it's all about the light and the landscapes; a vivid palette of pink sea thrift, mauve heathers and coppered heaths splashed with yellow gorse. Writers are inspired by the brooding hills of Cornwall's rugged moorland core, by tales of smugglers, shipwrecks and hidden creeks. Romantics love the drama of winter's wild Atlantic storms, the haunted ruins of Celtic castles, where history and mythology are intertwined.

For most Cornwall addicts, the seaside is the thing. On a tapering finger of granite heading west from the Tamar Valley all the way to Land's End, the coast is never much more than 15 miles away. From bold stretches of surfy sand to tiny, rocky inlets, there are some 300 glorious beaches to choose from. And where else in England can you travel from north to south coast within an hour or less? Off the west coast, on the brink of England, you can be on the white-sand shores of the sub-tropical Isles of Scilly in more or less the same time.

Tourism is relatively new to Cornwall, having emerged as an antidote to the collapse of the region's global mining industry. By the 1960s, it was enjoying its first taste of the mass tourism that turned fishing ports like Newquay and Bude into busy holiday resorts. Back then it was all fish and chips, caravans and gift-shop Cornish Pixies, and in the years of decline that followed, very little changed. Then, in the mid 1990s, Cornish tourism bounced back with new vigour. Now, it's one of the most visited and most fashionable holiday regions in the British Isles.

With regular services flying in and out of Newquay Airport, and a widened A30 that reaches all the way to Penzance, Cornwall is much easier to get to these days. Since the opening of landmark visitor centres like Tate St Ives and the Eden Project, there is more to do. There is also a greater emphasis on real Cornish culture: its history, traditions and, of course, its real food. With tourism helping to underpin a revival of the once moribund farming and fishing industries, Cornwall's larder of local produce is now one of its main attractions. Even the ruined mining industry has undergone a revival of sorts. The scattered relics of Cornish tin and copper mining were awarded World Heritage status in 2006, generating fresh interest in the industries that shaped the region's fortunes for centuries.

If all you know of Cornwall is the Rick Stein effect, the Jamie Oliver factor, the crowds of beach-party surfers who beat a path to Fistral Bay and the staggering price of real estate, then you could be forgiven for thinking that Cornwall has been discovered to the point of overkill. And it's true, there are crowded places; in high season, the roads can get grid-locked and you can hardly move for people in, say, Padstow. But this is a difficult place to spoil. Much of the coastline is protected by the National Trust, many of is towns and seaside villages lie in conservation areas, and there is a pride, a passion, among Cornish folk that helps retain a strong sense of identity. The cool Cornwall of contemporary tourism has brought a wave of hip hotels and foodie fish restaurants; it's brought literally millions of visitors – but even in high summer, you can still find an empty beach, a lonely cliff-top footpath. Nature, after all, is the main attraction.

In the following pages, we have tried our utmost to help you get the best out of the rich and varied landscapes of this proudly independent county. It's not been easy – at times, we feel we've merely skimmed the surface – but we hope we've provided the means to get under the skin of the real Kernow, to explore both its hotspots and its off-beat corners, to find the best places to stay, the finest places to eat and drink – all those special moments that will help turn your first Cornwall hit into a healthy habit.

Unmissable highlights

01 Cornish Mining World Heritage Site

Unique among the globe's designated must-dos, Cornwall's mining marvel covers 10 separate areas, scattered across the length and breadth of the peninsula, p 42.

02 The Eden Project

A world in a clay-pit biome, the south-west's best-known visitor centre, takes you on a horticultural journey from the Mediterranean to the tropics, p 149.

03 Tintagel Castle

On a crag of rock pounded by Atlantic waves, relive Arthurian legends of knights and magicians among the romantic ruins of a medieval kingdom, p 105.

04 North coast surfing beaches

Where do we start? Porthmeor, Gwithian, Porthtowan, Chapel Porth, Fistral Bay... all world-class classics, p 33.

05 St Michael's Mount

A fairy-tale castle mounted on an island of rock, this is the county's most iconic view, best seen from the shores of Marazion on Mount's Bay, p 296.

06 Camel Valley Trail

The path of a disused railway line provides 17 miles of scenic cycling from Bodmin Moor along the beautiful Camel Estuary to Padstow, p 83 and 165.

07 Cotehele House

The National Trust's perfectly preserved Elizabethan manor house overlooks the beautiful Tamar Valley, p 58.

08 Tate St Ives

A vision of white geometry, the contemporary seaside gallery celebrates the St Ives School, from a seaside landscape in the art capital of Cornwall, p 279.

09 Fifteen Cornwall

Jamie Oliver's charity-run job creation scheme mixes Cornish produce, fledgling chefs and fine dining on the beach at Watergate Bay, p 183.

10 The Minack Theatre

Speak to the sea, from this dramatic ampitheatre tucked into a cliff-top gulley above the white sands of Porthcurno beach, p 313.

Secret Cornwall

Local recommendations

01 National Maritime Museum

On Falmouth port's Discovery Quay, a 21st-century visitor centre pays homage to all things ship-shape from smugglers and seafaring heroes to salmon boats and sailing history, p 220.

02 Trebah Gardens

Not so well known as the Lost Gardens of Heligan, this little gem is a riot of colour in a sub-tropical ravine leading down to its own Helford River beach, p 266.

03 Port Eliot

Enter the charmingly eccentric stately home of the Earl and Countess of St Germans, on the Humphrey Repton estate which hosts the annual Lit Fest, p 68.

04 Lizard Point

Land's End without the tourist bling, England's most southerly point is a headland of serpentine furnished with exhilarating views from an 18th-century lighthouse, p 252.

05 Swanpool Beach

A favourite with Falmouth townies thanks to a fine blend of riviera-style seaside life, sand and seafood beach restaurant, the Indaba Fish, p 232.

06 Ferry across the Fowey River

Hop on the little foot ferry that runs back and forth between Fowey and Polruan, and enjoy the views of the estuary that captivated Daphne du Maurier, p 134.

07 St Ives Bay Line

One of Cornwall's branch-line railways, this little beauty runs from mainline St Erth to Porthminster beach and back again, p 277.

08 Rough Tor

On a windy, granite ridge on the rooftop of Cornwall, the lofty moorland summit has one of the best views in the county, p 82.

09 St Agnes

The Isles of Scilly's most westerly island, is utterly unspoilt and, according to islanders, the most authentically Scillonian, p 329.

10 Trawlers on the Quay

Locals recommended this seafoody restaurant, yards from Rick Stein's favourite fish market at Looe, p 130.

Factfile

01 Cornwall has the most westerly point in England, at Land's End, and the most southerly at Lizard Point.

02 The county has the UK's longest stretch of coastline at some 435 miles.

03 In peak season, visitor numbers reach around 275,000 at any one time, and run to 4.5 million a year.

04 The county's 1,376 square miles is home to a population of just over 500,000.

05 The National Trust owns or manages 32,200 acres of Cornwall, including 220 miles of the coast.

06 Cornwall's highest point is Brown Willy on Bodmin Moor, at 1,378ft (420m).

07 Founded in 1964, the helicopter route from Penzance to the Isles of Scilly is the world's longest running scheduled helicopter service.

08 Cornwall has 12 Areas of Outstanding Natural Beauty covering 598 sq miles (958 sq kms).

09 The ninth largest in England, Cornwall is the only county with one land border (its only neighbour being Devon).

10 The largest in the UK, Cornwall's World Heritage Site covers 20,000 hectares spread across 10 former mining regions.

THE FACTS

WHEN TO GO

Cornwall is an all-year-round destination these days. The weather helps: temperatures tend to be higher than the rest of mainland Britain and rarely fall below freezing; and thanks to the influence of the Gulf Stream, spring comes early and autumn hangs around for longer. But it's not just the climate that influences the county's go-anytime holiday calendar – for serious surfers the season's high point is in October and November – the growth of destination boutique hotels has encouraged off-season weekend breaks and high-profile visitor centres such as the Eden Project and Tate St Ives give a clear message that there is more to Cornwall than beach holidays. Off-season specials and events are often part of a deliberate strategy to entice visitors during tourism's quieter 'shoulder' periods. An example is the Atlantic coast trend for winter storm-watching breaks.

Nonetheless, there are peaks and troughs in visitor numbers. If you don't have school-age children, avoid the July–August peak season or be prepared to queue for everything from parking spaces to the Eden Project, and to pay premium prices for accommodation. Easter and the May bank holidays are also very busy, as are school half-terms and the Christmas season. Otherwise choose one of the quieter regions. The highest concentration of visitors are found around Newquay, Padstow, Penzance, Falmouth and St Ives.

Things improve markedly between school holidays, and for summer weather and fewer people, June is one of the best times to visit. Ditto September, though the first two weeks fall into high season, as the child-free and the retired grab a break before the cooler weather sets in. October and November are good months to visit, not just for surfing, but for the autumnal landscapes, particularly on Bodmin Moor and the wooded river valleys of the south coast (the Tamar, the Fowey, the Helford).

After another peak in late December, January and February are the quietest months, though many attractions are closed and even the die-hards among hoteliers and restaurateurs take the opportunity of a winter break. Where accommodation is available, however, it can cost up to half the price of a peak week. And at least the pubs stay open – so there are lots of opportunities to warm up by a cosy log fire.

Things start to warm up, in every sense, in spring. You will see gardens of camellias and daffodils in flower by February, particularly around Penzance and on the Isles of Scilly, though the tourist season doesn't get going until Easter.

GETTING THERE

By car

Follow the M5 south to Exeter, where you are presented with two choices: the **A30** via Okehampton and Bodmin Moor, or the **A38** via Plymouth and the Tamar Estuary. For the North Coast or the Far West (Newquay, St Ives, Penzance), the A30 is the best option. With dual carriageway for most of the way, certainly all the way from Exeter to Bodmin, it's the fastest route into Cornwall, though it can get congested at peak times.

The A38 crosses the **Tamar toll bridge** at Saltash (the toll is only payable on the way out). The dual carriageway peters out beyond the Tamar, and although it's slower than the A30, it's the best route into east Cornwall and the South Coast. Just west of Liskeard, join the **A390** for St Austell and Truro. You can also get to Truro, Falmouth and Helston by joining the **A39** off the A30 – but this can be a bottle-neck of traffic at rush hour and weekends.

If you are travelling to Bude or Boscastle, you will be better off using the A39's north-coast stretch, the so-called **Atlantic Highway**. For Rame Head, you can use the **Devonport–Torpoint Ferry** on the A374 (though this does mean weaving around Plymouth suburbia). And for a scenic drive into east Cornwall, cut across the Dartmoor National Park, through Tavistock and over the Tamar at Gunnislake.

In high season, try to avoid Friday afternoons and Saturdays, when traffic jams are inevitable, or leave as early or as late in the day as possible. In case of getting stuck for hours on a motorway, take drinks, snacks and entertainment for the kids. Or look for holiday cottages with mid-week changeover days.

By train

Cornwall has excellent rail links with a direct mainline route from London Paddington all the way to Penzance, and intercity connections at Exeter and Plymouth in Devon. Operated by **First Great Western** (☎ 08457 000125; www.firstgreatwestern.co.uk) and **Cross Country Trains** (☎ 0870 010 0084; www.crosscountrytrains.co.uk) all services stop at Saltash, Liskeard, Bodmin Road, Par, St Austell, Truro, Redruth, Camborne, St Erth and Penzance. The journey from Paddington takes three to four hours to Plymouth, and another two hours to Penzance, with trains running roughly every hour during the day. At the time of writing, the standard open return fare is an outrageous £249, so it's wise to capitalise on cheaper fares by travelling off peak (bringing the return fare down to around £89). Book well in advance and you can travel for as little as £40, subject to available seats.

First Great Western runs a Paddington–Penzance **Night Riviera Sleeper Service** (every night except Saturday) to all stations en route, except Saltash. Single tickets start at £49 including a cabin berth. It also runs Cornwall's useful network of branch-line services, which connect the mainline to the coast, enabling rail travellers to get much deeper into Cornwall. They are: the Tamar Valley Line, the Looe Valley Line, the Atlantic Coast Line, the Maritime Line and the St Ives Bay Line. See page 20 for more information.

By bus

National Express (☎ 08705 808080; www.nationalexpress.com) runs coach services into Cornwall from all over the UK, though you may have to change at London, Birmingham, Bristol or Plymouth on the way. There are direct services from one or other of these four cities to Newquay (via Liskeard and Bodmin), Truro, Falmouth and Penzance. Buses are cheaper than trains, but slower – up to nine hours from London Victoria to Truro – and at the mercy of traffic conditions. Expect to pay around £55 for a standard return from London Victoria to Newquay (with half-price concessions for senior citizens). Internet bookings are cheaper, and advance ticket offers are available.

By air

From a small corner of RAF St Mawgan to a busy international terminal, **Newquay Cornwall Airport** has gone from strength to strength in recent years, with passenger numbers increasing by over 40% since 2005. Deemed the fastest growing regional airport in the UK, with an eye on 1.2 million passengers by 2030, it is likely to broaden its horizons, but for the time being the international routes are limited. Most passengers arrive on domestic services from Edinburgh, Isle of Man, Belfast and Birmingham (with **Flybe**), Glasgow, Newcastle, Dublin, Cork, Leeds/Bradford, London Gatwick and Bristol (with **Air Southwest**), Manchester (with Air Southwest and **bmibaby**) the Isles of Scilly and Cardiff (with **Skybus**) and London Stansted (with **Ryanair**).

Air Southwest: ☎ 870 241 8202;
www.airsouthwest.com
Flybe: ☎ 0871 700 2000;
www.flybe.com
Ryanair: ☎ 0871 246 0000;
www.ryanair.com
Skybus: ☎ 01736 334224;
www.skybus.co.uk
bmibaby: ☎ 0871 224 0224;
www.bmibaby.com

10... places to avoid in Cornwall

1 The A30 on a Friday evening or Saturday morning in July, August or any bank holiday weekend. The traffic jams start on the M5 at Bristol and just keep going

2 Camborne Sadly, this former mining boom town is one of the most deprived urban areas, not just in Cornwall, but in the UK

3 Newquay on a Saturday night in June Party time for thousands of post-GCSE teenagers on a first break from home. Need we say more...

4 Bodmin Moor in thick fog Hard to predict but dangerous to both drivers and walkers

5 Land's End Visitor Centre With all the charm of a motorway service station, it's a waste of a beautiful space

6 St Austell A bit rough round the edges, with little to offer the visitor other than a supermarket and a suburban traffic jam

7 Jamaica Inn The theme park setting for Daphne du Maurier's novel is less coaching inn, more coach party

8 Trago Mills The vast sell-it-cheap department store on the A38. Tempting, but don't do it – you can lose a whole day in this place

9 Torpoint Arrive by ferry and keep on driving. There's nothing much to keep you here

10 Looe in winter Most of Cornwall's seaside resorts manage a bit of life in winter, but Looe is like a ghost town

A new arrivals and departures hall was opened in 2006, but with further developments and an even larger terminal in the pipe-line, an 'expansion charge' of £5 per adult passenger (under 16s exempt) is levied on all departures, on all routes. For information on flights, parking, taxis and car hire car visit the website: www.newquaycornwallairport.com. The airport is 6 miles to the north-east of Newquay.

Getting to the Isles of Scilly

There are three routes to the Isles of Scilly: by air with **Skybus**, by helicopter with **British International Helicopters** (☎ 01736 363871; www.islesofscillyhelicopter.com), or by passenger ferry, on board the *Scillonian III* (☎ 01736 334220/ 0845 710 5555; www.islesofscilly-travel.co.uk) from Penzance.

Helicopter flights are year-round subject to weather conditions and take roughly 30 minutes from Penzance Heliport to St Mary's or Tresco. Prices vary according to season. Skybus operates flights to St Mary's from Southampton, Bristol, Exeter, Newquay and Land's End. Fares can be expensive, especially in high season (up to £300 return from Bristol). The *Scillonian III* is usually the cheapest option with boats leaving Penzance Quay daily except Sundays (from March until November), taking two hours and 40 minutes, and costing from £76 for an adult saver return. The boat option is not recommended for faint-hearted sailors (the ship is built for the Scillies' shallow waters and has a tendency to roll in choppy seas). All services offer day-trips, though none operate on Sundays.

GETTING AROUND

We would like to say, leave the car at home although in truth, it's not entirely practical, particularly if staying in villages and farms off the beaten track. But look for alternatives wherever possible. With a bit of careful planning you can work walks and boat trips around bus routes or branch line railways, take advantage of park and ride schemes, go by bike, or even on horseback. Once in Cornwall, ditch the car whenever you can; you will see much more on foot or by bike, and meet more people on public transport. If using the latter, the **Ride Cornwall** scheme provides unlimited off-peak travel across the county's rail and bus service network at £10–£12 per day per adult, £7.50 per child (www.firstgreatwestern.co.uk).

Buses

The Cornish complain that their bus services are rubbish and in terms of reliable daily commuting all year round, they have a point. But tourists get the benefit of a stepped-up summer service with routes concentrated around popular destinations.

First Buses (☎ 0845 600 1420; www.firstgroup.com) runs services around Penwith, Truro, the South Coast and east Cornwall, including St Ives to St Just via Penzance (17–17B) and Mevagissey to Fowey (26B). The First Group also runs the Lizard Rambler, as well as services from St Austell (T9) or Newquay (T10) to the Eden Project and a couple of good coast-to-coast routes between Helston and north coast beaches.

The **Western Greyhound** network (☎ 01637 871871) operates services around the central, east and far west of Cornwall, including Newquay to Newquay Airport (556), Boscastle to Bude (595) and Padstow to Bodmin Parkway (555). See www.westerngreyhound.com for easy-access maps and timetables and details on **Day Explorer** tickets which allow unlimited travel for £7.50 (or £15 for a family of up to five).

Trains

Cornwall's five branch-line railways – survivors of the Beeching cuts in the 1960s – are a combination of scenic journeys and practical transport. The most scenic are the **Tamar Valley Line** (from Plymouth to Gunnislake via Calstock), the **Looe Valley Line** (from Liskeard to Looe) and the **St Ives Bay Line** (St Erth to St Ives, calling at Lelant and Carbis Bay). The **Atlantic Coast Line** (from Par to Newquay) and the coast-to-coast **Maritime Line** (Truro to Falmouth) are more practical, but all routes provide useful rail links and a car-free method of touring the county.

Devon & Cornwall Rail Partnerships: www.carfreedaysout.com. There is more information on each line in the relevant chapters of the guide, but this one-stop-shop run by the School of Geography at the University of Plymouth provides information on routes, timetables, related walks, Rail Ale trails and park and ride schemes.

Boats and ferries

Some 80% of Cornwall is on the water, either river or seafront, and travelling by boat is an essential part of life, particularly in the Isles of Scilly where more people travel by boat than by car. Wherever there's a harbour you will find boat trips, but as well as fishing and sight-seeing excursions, there are dozens of port-to-port services which can get you around the coast. Where boat trips really come into their own as essential services is in crossing Cornwall's rivers and estuaries. Among useful **seasonal foot ferries** – small floating people carriers – there are services between Falmouth and St Mawes across Carrick Roads, Padstow and Rock across the Camel Estuary, and Calstock and Cotehele Quay on the Tamar River.

Car and passenger ferries cross the Tamar between Devonport and Torpoint, the Fowey at Bodinnick and the Fal between Feock and Philleigh (the **King Harry Ferry**). You might have to queue to get on, but each ferry journey cuts miles off the more circuitous routes by road. You can download information on Cornwall's ferry services from www.visitcornwall.co.uk.

Cycling

In much of Cornwall, travelling by bike on regular roads is not an option for the novice or the unfit. This is a hilly county, with steep gradients that can get tough. The roads are winding, too, so lots of blind bends on country lanes. Indeed, competitive cyclists come to Cornwall, particularly North Cornwall, to practise before heading for the French Alps. But don't give up on pedal power.

The Cornish Way, part of the **National Cycle Network** (www.sustrans.org.uk), provides a network of routes, covering nearly 200 miles of inter-linking trails, much of them using off-road tracks, old railways and tramways and quiet country lanes. Using the National Cycle Network's Route Numbers 3 and 32, they link Bude with Land's End, and are graded from easy to challenging. They include the well-known **Camel Trail** from Bodmin to Padstow (designated as easy), the **Mineral Tramways Trails**, through the heart of Cornwall (easy/moderate) and the **St Piran Trail** from Padstow to Truro (challenging). Free copies of the Cornish Way cycling and walking guide are available from tourist information centres.

Walking

The Cornish Way routes are designed for riders and walkers, too, but walkers are already spoilt for choice. Cornwall has some of the best walking terrain in the country, with some 2,400 miles of inland footpaths and over 400 miles of coastline, all of which is served by the **South West Coast Path**, and over half of it managed by the National Trust. Again, it's tough terrain in parts, with lots of steep climbs and long descents – particularly around Bodmin Moor and along the cliff paths of the north-east coast and around Penwith. Here, you will often find yourself toiling up rock steps or teetering on the edge of sheer cliffs with nothing between you and the Atlantic but fresh air. These walks are not generally suitable for young children.

There is more gentle terrain to be found on the south coast, in the Tamar Valley, or the western end of the north coast. But always go prepared: wear proper walking shoes and take waterproofs or suncream and plenty of water. Each chapter in the guide suggests at least one good walk, but there are hundreds more. Ask at tourist information centres for suggestions, or visit the online guide to the South West Coast Path (www.southwestcoastpath.com), which not only suggests routes (everything from a stroll to a long hike) but also provides distance calculators, travel information and advice on accommodation and integrated public transport. A book with great walks in the area is *Pathfinder Cornwall* (Crimson, £11.99).

Driving

At the last count, around 87% of visitors arrived by car. At the height of the season, that's a lot of cars, with road congestion a major problem on Cornwall's roads in high season. To get the most out of motoring, invest in one of **Ordnance Survey**'s six **Landranger** or 10 **Explorer** maps (www.ordnancesurvey.co.uk) to find all those secret little coves and backwater drives, as well as the highest points, the ancient sites and the best places to park. You could also invest in National Trust membership (family membership currently costs £88.50). The Trust has a huge presence in Cornwall, and being able to park for free next to

10... great Cornwall drives

1 **St Ives to St Just on the B3306 coast road** one of the best Sunday drives in Britain according to the AA

2 **Over the Tamar suspension bridge on the A38** Cornwall's most dramatic entrance

3 **On the high cliffs coast road** between Crackington Haven and Widemouth Bay

4 **Follow the Looe River** between Liskeard and Looe, on the pretty B3254

5 **From Porth to Watergate Bay** and on to Bedruthan Steps on the B3276 (though not in high season)

6 **On the unclassified roads around the heart of Bodmin Moor** Head for Minions, Blisland, Altarnun or St Neot

7 **The B3247 from Crafthole to Kingsand,** taking a coast road detour to Freathy and Rame Head

8 **Across Goonhilly Downs on the A3083** from Helston to Lizard

9 **From Tregony to St Mawes,** down the spine of the Roseland Peninsula

10 **Wander the country lanes** that meander around Cotehele House between the A388 and the Tamar Valley

one of their many beaches and beauty spots, will save money in the long run.

When driving around, try to avoid the traffic bottlenecks, which are particularly prevalent on the link roads which head south off the A30. Be considerate of other drivers particularly in narrow lanes. Be prepared to reverse into a tight space to let other vehicles through, and say thanks to drivers who back-up to let you pass.

Irrespective of satnav guidance, avoid driving into tiny, tight-knit fishing villages like Polperro or Port Isaac, even if you can. And take care of free-range livestock in moorland areas.

ACCOMMODATION

With everything from traditional hotels and quirky B&Bs, to designer self-catering cottages and seaside campsites, Cornwall's choice of accommodation is among the best in Britain. The out-of-town boutique hotel was more or less born in Cornwall, the early model being Olga Polizzi's glamorous Hotel Tresanton in St Mawes, opened in 1997. Now hotspots such as Padstow and St Ives are awash with bijou hotels and funky little guest houses. Even some of the farmhouse B&Bs have gone all boutique. There are tired, old hotels, too, but Cornwall doesn't

The best... Cornwall hotels, B&Bs & inns

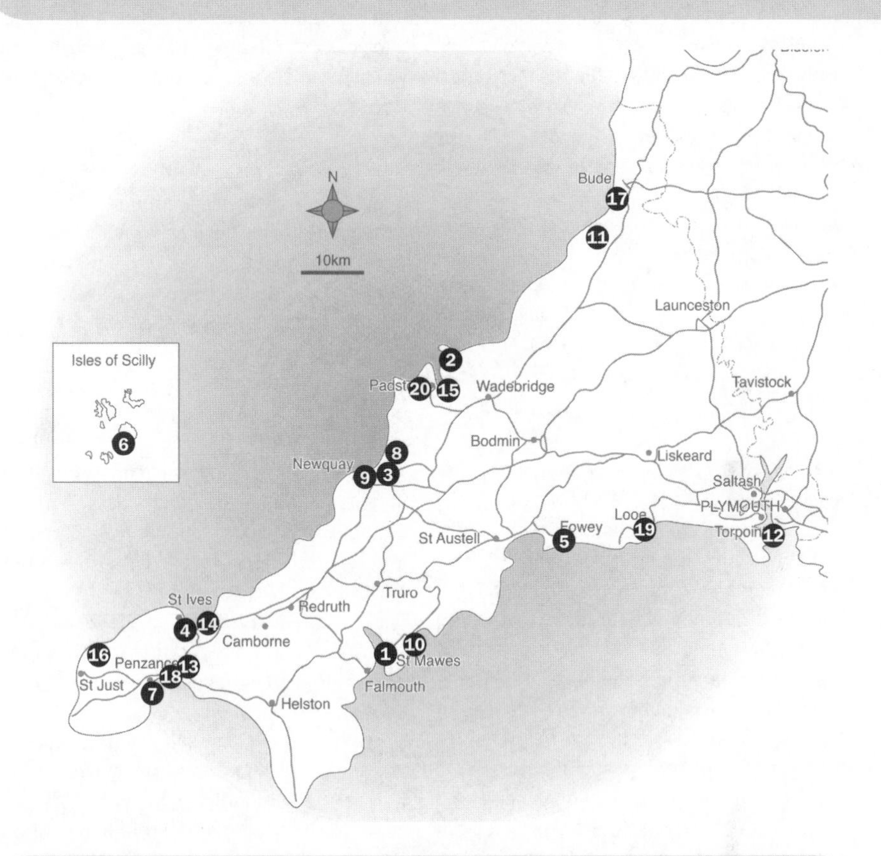

Hotels

1. Hotel Tresanton, St Mawes – a classic among boutique hotels, p. 241
2. St Moritz, near Rock – glitzy, new deco-style spa hotel, p. 113
3. Scarlet – glamorous eco-luxe beach hotel with spa, pools and fabulous rooms, p 185
4. Boskerris Hotel, Carbis Bay – cool rooms and St Ives Bay views, p. 286
5. Old Quayhouse, Fowey – slick, contemporary riverside hotel, p. 140
6. Star Castle, St Mary's – winner of 2009 Cesar award for best island hotel, p. 332
7. The Abbey, Penzance – stylishly quirky townhouse with period charm, p. 300
8. Bedruthan Steps – family friendly with fabulous location, p. 185
9. Watergate Bay Hotel – Victoriana with beach-chic décor, p. 185
10. The Rosevine, Roseland – child-friendly mini apartments, p. 240

B&Bs & Inns

11. Bangor's Organic, near Bude – Britain's first pure organic B&B, p. 99
12. Westcroft Guesthouse, Cawsand/Kingsand – modern-antique seafront townhouse, p. 74
13. Ennys, Penzance – fresh modern take on the country house idyll, p. 301
14. Headland House, Carbis Bay - elegant seaside house with crisp white décor and luxury rooms, p. 286
15. Coswarth House – Padstow's period gem with views across the Camel Estuary, p. 169
16. Gurnard's Head, Zennor – gastro pub with rooms, handy for walkers, p. 316
17. The Bay View Inn, Widemouth Bay – fun, foodie, family-friendly, p. 99
18. Ednovean Farm, Perranuthnoe – boutique barn conversion, p. 301
19. Barclay House, Looe – petite hotel-guest house in the Looe Valley, p. 128
20. Woodlands Country House – award-winning guest house overlooking Trevone Bay, p. 168

do much in the way of Travelodge or Holiday Inn.

Finding any kind of hotel room can be tough in high season, so book well in advance. Local tourist information centres can help with listings and last-minute availability, but they will only recommend paid-up members of Visit Cornwall, and, aside from official ratings, won't state a preference for one place over another. This guide includes a whole host of styles, for a variety of budgets, but it does focus on independent, family-run places dedicated to serving Cornish produce and delivering stylish décor in lovely surroundings.

B&B

Many of Cornwall's new-generation guest houses come courtesy of the many jaded professionals who have ditched the city for a new life in Cornwall, and funded the move by offering rooms in a big house they wouldn't otherwise have been able to afford. It used to be the early retired that ran guest houses by the sea, now it's forty-somethings with young families and backgrounds in the media. An urban sensibility has brought a fresh zing to interiors, and a look that could almost be said to be Cornwall's own – New England meets Rococo, with a seaside palette, beach-hut stripes and St Ives' School art. In many cases, you'd hardly know the difference between a B&B and a hotel, although up-scale rooms mean higher prices, especially if they come with sea views. For comfortable, child-friendly accommodation with hearty Cornish bacon-and-egg breakfasts at down-to-earth prices, farmstays are good value – and there are lots of good ones in Cornwall.

Pubs

With so many good places to recommend, there wasn't enough space for the old-fashioned pub with rooms in the *Places to Stay* sections. But check out the traditional inns listed under Drinking. Many offer rooms and, with a few exceptions – such as the gastro pub **Gurnard's Head** in Zennor, or the boutique-stay **Lugger** in Portloe – they tend to sit at the budget end of the price scale, offering simple, no frills family-friendly accommodation. And if you're into your Cornish ales, staying the night means you can sample them all without worrying about driving.

Self-catering

A lot of high-quality self-catering cottages and apartments have become available in recent years as a result of the burgeoning second home or buy-to-let investment market: they are often someone's real-estate toe-hold in the county they love, and thankfully there is a growing distaste for leaving holiday homes empty for months at a time. Others are the result of farm diversification schemes in which barns and out-buildings are turned into communities of holiday lets, or estate cottages. Among exceptional examples of the latter are the eco resort properties on the **Trelowarren Estate** near Helford (deemed one the greenest resorts in the world) and a collection of high-spec cottages at **Tregothnan** near Truro, one of the largest of the old-money Cornish estates.

Off-season, many self-catering properties are offered for short breaks and weekends, as well as the standard weekly rental. And there is a small but growing trend in hotels offering self-catering units by the night – the new **St Moritz hotel** near Rock is a good example. But hotel standards are the norm these days. The majority of cottage owners rent their properties through letting agencies, which insist on everything from 'kerb appeal' to sparkling décor and more kitchen kit than most people have at home.

- **Classic Cottages** – ☎ 01326 555555; www.classic.co.uk; West Country specialist with fabulous, high-spec properties all over Cornwall.
- **Helpful Holidays** – ☎ 01647 433593; www.helpfulholidays.com; friendly agency with over 600 places to stay throughout the West Country. Good on big, family-size properties.

The best... places to buy fresh local produce

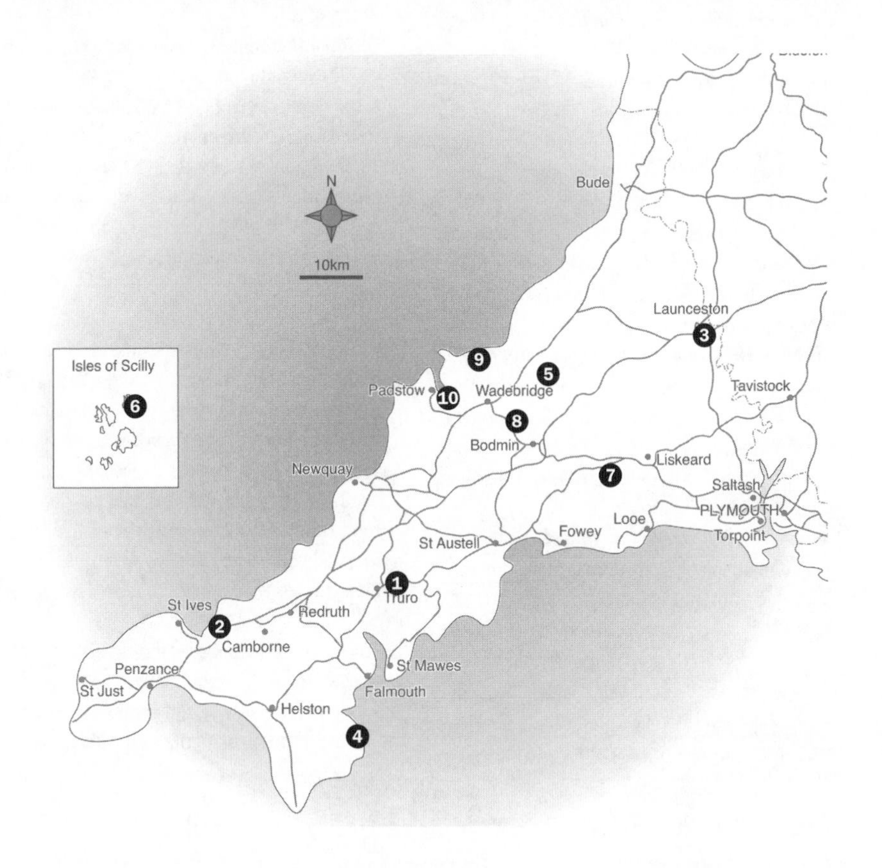

1. Lemon Quay, Truro – nearly every day is market day in this city-centre food hub, p 215.
2. Trevaskis Farm, Hayle – supermarket-style farm shop selling home-grown vegetables, home-made ready-meals and sausages, fish and meat, p 200.
3. Philip Warren & Son in Launceston – tipped to be the best butcher in the county, this is the place for true Cornish meats, p 63.
4. Roskilly's, St Keverne – organic dairy farm, producing ice creams, apple juice and preserves, p 267.
5. Cornish Kobe Beef – otherwise known as drunken beef, from a herd raised on ale, Japanese-style, on family-run Woodland Farm, near St Breward, p 90.
6. St Martin's Bakery, Isles of Scilly – sample breads, cakes, pastries and pies baked on the premises by this award-warning island baker, p 334.
7. Fran's Pantry, Lostwithiel – a local-food corner shop, close to the Cornish Guild of Smallholders fortnightly produce market, p 142
8. Camel Valley Vineyard – Cornwall's finest wines, including prize-winning fizz, p 92.
9. The Fish Cellars, Port Isaac – fresh seafood in a mini fish market on the beach, p 115.
10. Padstow Farm Shop, Trethillick – home-grown vegetables, traditionally reared meats and a local-food deli counter, p 170.

- **Rural Retreats** – ☎ 01386 701177; www.ruralretreats.co.uk; posh cottages at high-end prices, including Trinity House lighthouses cottages.
- **National Trust Cottages** – ☎ 0844 8002070; www.nationaltrustcottagesco.uk; the national collection has 95 historic properties in Cornwall, including apartments at Doyden House (Port Quin) and Cotehele.
- **Landmark Trust** – ☎ 01628 825925; www.landmarktrust.co.uk; the national conservation charity has a handful of classic properties in Cornwall.
- **Cornish Horizons** – ☎ 01841 533 331; www.cornishhorizons.co.uk; Padstow agency with large selection, particularly strong on North Coast.
- **Cornish Farm Holidays** – ☎ 0845 6028843; www.cornish-farms.co.uk; Voluntary run co-operative offering quality holiday accommodation on Cornwall's working farms.
- **Boutique Cottage Holidays** – ☎ 01872 520000; www.tregothnan.co.uk; a collection of 'six star' cottages dotted all over south-west Cornwall, with the core on the Boscawen family's Tregothnan Estate – best known for its English Estate fine teas.

Campers and camping

The world of caravanning is just too big for this series of books, but camper vans are a different story. The classic retro VW Camper sums up what Cornish holidays are all about: beetling around the coast roads, with surf boards and windswept Jamie Oliver hair, looking for waves and beach-barbecue suppers. The sight of a brightly coloured V-dub motoring into a Cornish sunset is an iconic image, and you can hire one.

- **North Coast Campers** – ☎ 01840 230232; www.northcoastcampers.co.uk; Church Town Farmhouse, Bude EX23 0NW
- **Cornwall Campers** – ☎ 01872 571988; cornwallcampers.co.uk; Carnebo Farm, Goonharven TR4 9QH
- **South Penquite Farm** – ☎ 01208 850491; www.southpenquite.co.uk; Blisland, Bodmin PL30 4LH
- **O'Connors Campers** – www.oconnorscampers.co.uk; Okehampton, Devon EX20 1UE
- **Snail Trail** – ☎ 01767 600440; www.snailtrail.co.uk; St Albans AL3 4DH
- **T@B** Holidays – ☎ 01503 250275; www.tab-holidays.co.uk; a t@b is a funky mini caravan with street cred; hire one, or have it towed to a Cornish campsite.

There are lots of good campsites in Cornwall, ranging from club-house-and-caravan 'holiday parks' to dinky little glades on smallholdings. For Cornwall's list of approved campsites see www.visitcornwall.co.uk. Many of these tend towards the former model, so look out for the more intimate, independent sites, such as **Broad Meadow House** near Charlestown (www.broadmeadowhouse.com) which has only six pitches, as well as ready-to-go tents for hire (with breakfast).

The 'glamping' trend – as in yurts, tipis and other posh tents with proper beds, bathrooms and camp kitchens – is well represented in Cornwall. And you'll find some of them listed in this book.

THE BEST... FOOD AND DRINK

Cornwall is a county of food heroes. And we are not necessarily talking about celebrity chefs. Behind the Rick Steins and the Jamie Olivers, a generation of farmers, fishermen and cottage-industry producers are not only working hard to bring quality food to the table, but they are also championing the cause for fresh, distinctive, local produce. You will, of course, see plenty of greasy chips and flabby bacon-in-a-bap sandwiches on your travels, but Cornwall's real food revolution, its rich larder of goodies, has crept into every corner of Cornish catering.

While guest houses serve up free-range eggs alongside local bacon, **Cornish apple juice** and homemade bread, pubs are chalking up fresh crab specials, **Falmouth Bay scallops**

The best... Cornish pubs

1. Blisland Inn – award-winning village local on the edge of Bodmin Moor, p. 92.
2. The Blue Anchor, Helston – try a pint of Spingo in the Old Blue, a town-centre inn with one of the oldest ale-house breweries in the country, p. 260.
3. Tinners Arms, Zennor – sup a pint of Sharp's Zennor Mermaid in the beer garden of this ancient miners' local, p. 317.
4. Driftwood Spar, Trevaunance Cove – lively, surfy bar with its own micro-brewed ales and live music, p. 202.
5. Blue Peter, Polperro – traditional harbourside fishermen's pub, with fireside snugs and views, p. 131.
6. Turks Head, Isles of Scilly – take a sunset cruise to England's most south-westerly pub, overlooking the quay on the isle of St Agnes, p. 335.
7. The Rod and Line, Tideford – this spit-and-sawdust village inn serves St Austell Ales with fresh crab sandwiches, p. 77.
8. The Rashleigh Inn at Polkerris – friendly freehouse by the sea, p. 142.
9. The Smuggler's Den, Cubert – beers from Newquay's own Atlantic Brewery, regular jazz nights and an annual Ale and Pie festival, p. 187.
10. Halzephron Inn, Gunwalloe – Halzephron Gold, made by the local Organic Brewhouse, is one of the real ales served at this seaside gastro pub, p. 259.

10... Cornish specialities

1 Pasties – the Cornish classic. A meat-and-veg meal for a miner wrapped in a shortcrust parcel (and utterly Cornish whatever they say in Devon)

2 Saffron buns – the fragrant yellow flavouring was they say, brought to Cornwall by Phoenicians in exchange for tin. The buns are lovely with butter

3 Hog's pudding – a plump variety of pork sausage – like a lightly spiced white pudding

4 Clotted cream – thick and, yes, creamy and served on a warm scone with homemade jam

5 Crab and lobster – the staple catch of the small Cornish village fishing fleet

6 Cider – proper farmhouse scrumpy, puts a bit of apple in your cheeks

7 Pilchards – traditionally salted or served heads up in a 'stargazy' fish pie

8 Cornish earlies – new potatoes, with a buttery flavour, and earlier than most spring spuds

9 Real ale – St Austell's Tribute, Sharp's Doom Bar, Skinner's Betty Stogs. Cornwall has earned a national reputation for the quality of its beers

10 Cornish Yarg – a moist, mild white cheese wrapped, like no other, in nettle leaves

and hand-cut chips. **Farmers' markets** are a Saturday-morning staple in the more traditional Cornish towns. Shopping for fresh food, eating out and eating in has become a big part of what visiting Cornwall is all about.

It wasn't always this way. Back in the mid-1990s, Cornwall's food economy looked decidedly grim. Fishing was in the doldrums, and Cornish farmers – principally running small beef and dairy farms – were hit hard by the bovine diseases that ravaged the industry. Numerous farms were sold off and broken up. For those that survived it was do or die, and the doing, for many, was to make a virtue out of small niche farming. These are our food heroes: the dairy farmer making delicious **artisan ice creams**, the local organic butcher making traditional **hog's pudding**, the craft baker, the cheese-maker, the hotelier who pops out to catch fresh lobster before breakfast.

The growing success of these ventures is a symbiotic by-product of Cornwall's growth in high-spend tourism, but **Rick Stein** deserves some of the credit, too. Bringing his love affair with Cornwall to the small screen helped kick-start cool, culinary Cornwall. Now whole schools of chefs are beating a path to Cornish shores, and nearly every other restaurateur claims a Stein kitchen on their CV. More recently, **Jamie Oliver**'s charity-run **Fifteen Cornwall** is nurturing young Cornish talent to produce a range of fresh, local home-grown chefs.

The best... restaurants and beach cafés

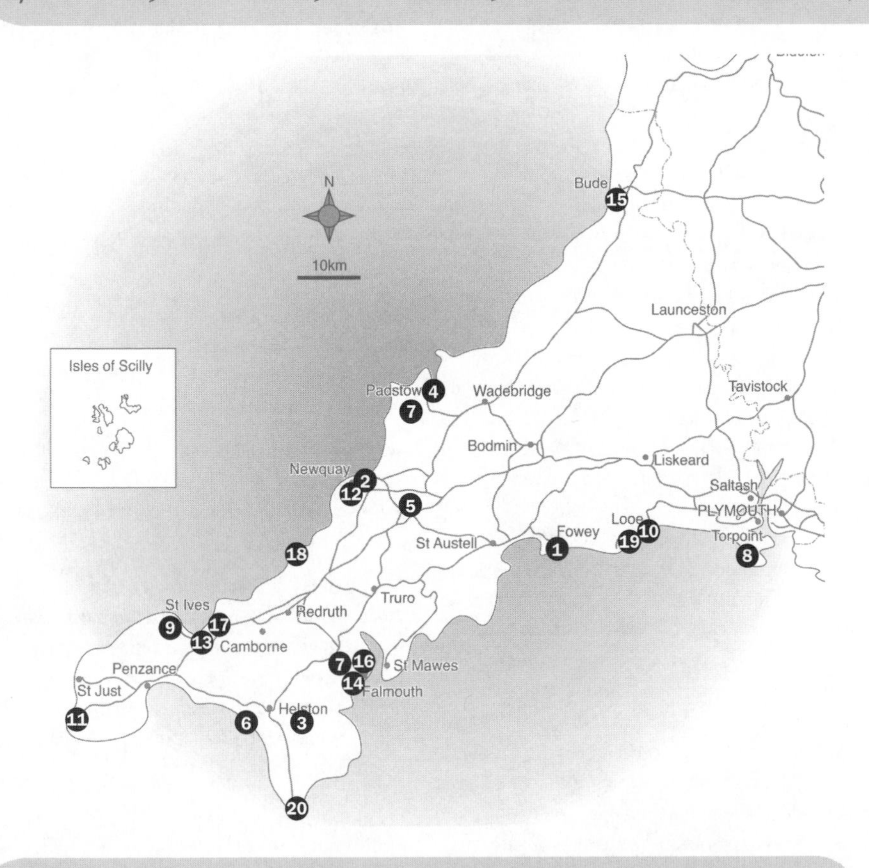

Restaurants

1. Restaurant Nathan Outlaw, Rock – two Michelin stars, it's rated Britain's best for seafood, p. 116
2. Fifteen Cornwall, Watergate Bay – part of Jamie Oliver's job-creation charity, and the food is pukkah too, p. 188
3. New Yard Restaurant, Trelowarren – all ingredients sourced within 10 miles of the estate.
4. Seafood Restaurant, Padstow – the foundation stone of Rick Stein's Cornish empire, p. 171
5. Viners Bar and Restaurant at Summercourt – an unpretentious Michelin *Bib Gourmand*, p. 188
6. Kota, Porthleven – local fish and organic farm produce with a dash of spice, p. 259.
7. The Wheel House, Falmouth - fun, friendly and big on fresh, local shellfish, page 232
8. The View, Millbrook – chef Matt Corner's surfy seafood café-restaurant, p. 76
9. Alba, St Ives – fresh, local seafood with a south-east Asian twist, p. 288
10. Trawlers on the Quay – a fishmonger's treat overlooking Looe harbour, p. 130

Beach cafés

11. The Beach Restaurant, Sennen Cove – award-winning café by the sea, p. 316
12. The Lewinnick Lodge, Newquay – seafood, tapas and Atlantic sunsets, p. 188
13. Porthminster Beach Café – laid-back Aussie attitude and great food, p. 288
14. Indaba Fish, Falmouth – scallops and sundowners on Swanpool beach, p. 232
15. Life's a Beach, Summerleaze, Bude – the name says it all, p. 102
16. Gylly Beach at Gyllyngvase beach – buckets of prawns and bags of style, p. 233
17. Godrevy Café at Gwithian – home-made crab cakes and hut cuisine, p. 201
18. Blue, Porthtowan – hip surf bar, with seafood, live music and late nights, p. 201
19. Talland Bay Beach Café – cream teas, pasties and sarnies on the beach, p. 131
20. Polpeor Café, Lizard Point – Formica, fish and chips, and the best views going, p. 259

Fishing, too, has gone from strength to strength – with shoals of cod, ling and pollack, mullet, sea bass, John Dory, and good old pilchards coming in through traditional ports. Though much depleted, Newlyn and Looe are still among the best commercial fish markets in the country, both feeding top London restaurants.

With your real food, you can enjoy real ale, produced by a growing band of microbreweries as well as long-established **St Austell Ales**, and relative newcomers **Skinner's** and **Sharp's** – all winning national awards for the quality of their beers.

And let's not forget the **humble pasty**. So proud are the Cornish of their national dish, the Cornish Pasty Association applied for EU 'Protected Geographical Indication status'. If successful, only the real thing could rightfully be called a Cornish pasty. Others meanwhile are using local ingredients to satisfy a more cosmopolitan palate: try Japanese-style beer-fed **Kobe beef**, north **Cornish salami**, fine cheeses, Loire Valley style white wines and Cornish-grown tea.

What we looked for in a restaurant was commitment to local food. And for self-caterers, each chapter provides a shopping list of specialists and real food suppliers. It's easy to grab a joint of beef from a supermarket shelf, but finding local meat in a farm shop, on a family-run farm that has survived by the skin of its teeth – that's proper Cornish.

FESTIVALS AND ANNUAL EVENTS

There are dozens of fairs, fêtes and food festivals, curious pagan rites, traditional country shows, regattas, beach parties, surf competitions and arts events scattered across the county, mainly during the summer months. We've picked out the best in each region in the relevant chapters, but these are the classics, or the crowd-pullers; the events worth travelling for:

April

Third week – North Cornwall Tor cycling event (Bodmin to Bodmin via Bude)

Fourth week – Trevithick Day (Camborne)

May

First week – The Obby Oss May Day (Padstow); Isles of Scilly World Pilot Gig Racing Championships (Isles of Scilly)

Second week – Furry Dance, or Floral Day (Helston); Daphne du Maurier Festival of Arts & Literature (Fowey)

Fourth week – Fal River Festival (Falmouth/ Truro); Run to the Sun VW Fest (Newquay)

June

Second week – Royal Cornwall Show (Wadebridge); Beach Break Live (Polzeath)

Third week – Golowan Festival (Penzance)

July

Third week – Port Eliot Festival (St Germans); Stithians Show (Stithians, near Falmouth)

Fourth week – Charlestown Regatta (Charlestown)

August

First week – Falmouth Week (Falmouth)

Third week – Camel Week Regatta (Padstow/ Rock); Fowey Royal Regatta (Fowey River)

Fourth week – Newlyn Fish Festival; August bank holiday; Cornwall Folk Festival (Wadebridge); Bude International Jazz Festival (Bude); St Endellion Music Festival (Port Isaac)

September

First week – St Ives Festival of the Arts (St Ives)

Second week – Newquay Fish Festival (Newquay); Bale Push Championships (Crantock Bay); Polo on the Beach (Watergate Bay)

Third week – Cornwall Food and Drink Festival (Truro)

October

Second week – Oyster Festival (Falmouth); Lowender Perran Festival (Perranporth)

Fourth week – British National Surf Championships (Fistral Beach, Newquay)

November

Second week – Taste South East Cornwall, Food Festival (Looe/Polperro)

December

From second week – Truro Winter Festival (Truro)

Third week – Mousehole Christmas illuminations (Mousehole)

Fourth week – Tom Bawcock's Eve (Mousehole)

The best... things to do with children

1. National Maritime Museum, Falmouth – boats, shipwrecks, seadogs, submarines and lots of buttons to press, p. 220
2. Flambards Experience, near Helson – the nearest Cornwall gets to a theme park with all-weather attractions for all ages, p. 254
3. Paradise Park, near Hayle – family-run zoo park with red pandas, free-flying birds, cockatoos and a Jungle Barn, p. 196
4. Blue Reef Aquarium, Newquay – underwater fun for all the family, p. 177
5. Lappa Valley Steam Railway, near Newquay – chuffing around the countryside in Zebedee or Muffin, p. 182
6. Crealy Great Adventure Park, near Wadebridge – heaven for the under-9s, p. 166
7. Roskilly's Organic Farm – 40 acres of farm animals, plus donkeys, ducks, a working dairy and delicious ice cream, p. 267
8. Dingles Fairground Heritage Centre, Lifton – okay, we know it's in Devon, p. 60
9. The Seal Sanctuary, Gweek - meet seals and sea lions at this veteran rescue centre, p 267
10. The Monkey Sanctuary, Looe – a happy home for once sad and lonely Woollys and Capuchins, p. 126

TRAVELLING WITH CHILDREN

When the weather's good, Cornwall's all about beaches, and with miles and miles of them, there's something to keep everyone happy. One of the things that draws families to Cornwall is the old-fashioned seaside holiday essentials: fresh air, freedom and good clean fun.

When the weather's wet, or the air a little too fresh, things get a bit trickier. Not that there aren't other things to do – Cornwall is well served with child-friendly all-weather attractions – but they aren't always nearby (the majority are clustered around Newquay). And bear in mind that on a wet day in high season, when every other family has the same idea, they can get very crowded.

SPORTS AND ACTIVITIES

Surfing

Cornwall's north coast is **Surf Central** as far as the UK is concerned with some 300,000 surfers flocking to its beaches pretty much all year round, thanks to deep Atlantic low pressure systems, wet-suit technology and the wonders of winter surf. As the industry has developed, the appeal of Cornwall has become as much about the surfing scene as it is about the quality of the waves. You see plenty of wannabe dudes hanging around, say, **Fistral beach**, dressed from head to toe in Rip Curl and Animal, who barely know one end of a board from another. Alongside surf championships, the scene has bred a host of music festivals, whole streets of surf-hire and surf fashion shops and an après surf culture of which Cornwall is the UK's epicentre. But in a place that breeds national champions, the waves are the thing.

Newquay, with its string of Atlantic beaches, is the undisputed king of surfing destinations. **Bude** comes a close second. But surfers also make a beeline for the beaches around Perranporth, St Agnes, St Ives Bay and Sennen Cove. In the right conditions, the south coast can produce some spectacular waves, too, notably at Porthleven, Praa Sands and Perranuthnoe. April to December is the best time to surf, with October being the high point. High summer (July and August) is more suited to beginners and improvers.

Proper tuition is recommended for beginners: the conditions that create great waves also present dangers, including reefs and rip-tides. Stick to beaches with a lifeguard presence and heed advice. If the red flag's flying, stay out of the sea. Safety guidelines can be accessed on the **Royal National Lifeboats Institution** (**RNLI**) website (www.rnli.org.uk). The RNLI provides the lifeguard service on the north coast. For general information, visit the **British Surfing Association** (**BSA**) website (www.britsurf.co.uk). The BSA Surf School is based in Newquay. Relevant chapters provide contact details for some of the dozens of surf schools.

On the beach

For many of Cornwall's visitors, the coastline and its multitude of beaches is the star attraction. With around 300 to choose from, you are never much more than 15 miles from the coast. And in the far west of the county, you have the unusual luxury of having two coastlines, Atlantic and English Channel, within less than 10 miles: St Ives in the north and Penzance in the south are just 9 miles apart. Two independent online beach guides, **Cornwall Beaches** (www.cornwall-beaches.co.uk) and **The Cornwall Beach Guide** (www.cornwallbeachguide.co.uk) provide maps, descriptions and practical information about facilities, access, parking, dogs and safety. On safety, take heed of the lifeguard's advice (see surfing above). Cornwall's beaches are prone to riptides, deep shelving, sudden swells that can knock you over and high tides that can cut you off. In the wrong conditions, bathing can be treacherous, especially for young children. The BBC weather website gives information on daily tides (www.bbc.co.uk/weather).

With regard to taking **dogs** to Cornish beaches, there are limited possibilities in the summer months when the majority impose a ban. Visit Cornwall (www.visitcornwall.com) provides a downloadable list of the 83 beaches

The best... Cornish beaches

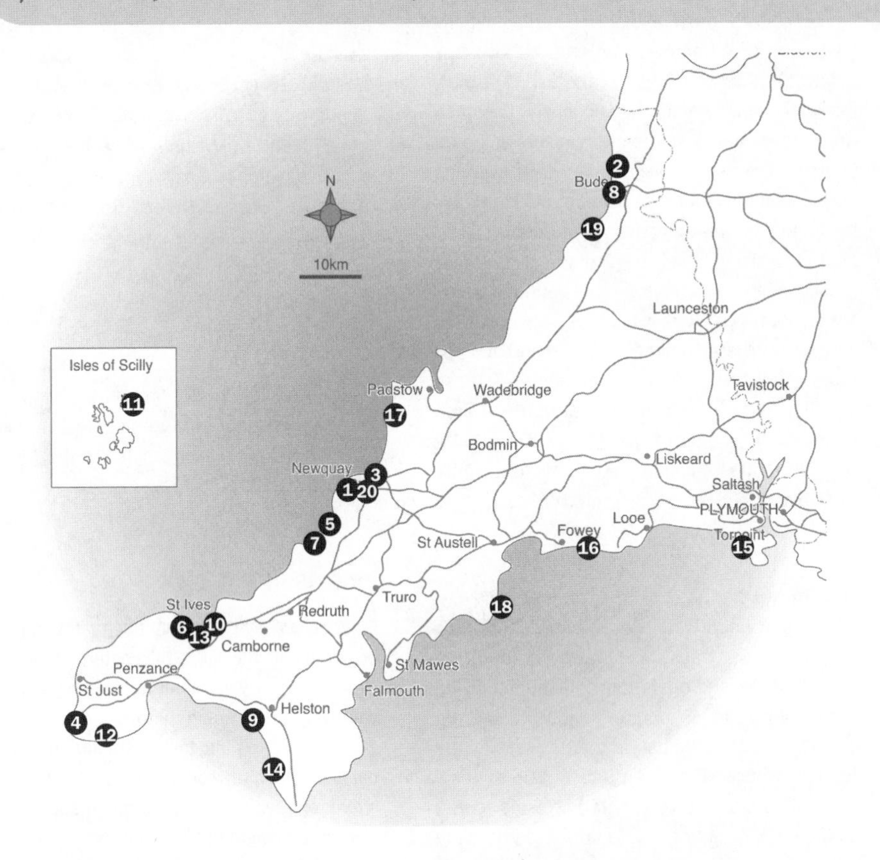

For surfing

1. Fistral Bay – Newquay's surf-champ classic, p. 177
2. Crooklets Bay, Bude – Bondi beach of the Atlantic coast, p. 95
3. Watergate Bay – beach break heaven, p. 179
4. Sennen Cove – waves to suit all levels, p. 310
5. Perranporth – pleasing swells, runway beach and rarely crowded, p. 202
6. Porthmeor, St Ives – urban surfing at its finest, p. 276
7. Chapel Porth to Porthtowan – chilled après-surf scene, p. 195
8. Widemouth Bay, Bude – lots of surf-school beginners, p. 95
9. Porthleven, Helston – one of the best reef breaks going, but not for the faint-hearted, p. 251
10. Gwithian Beach, Hayle – vast stretch of sand with fast hollow waves, p. 193

For sandcastles and sunsets

11. Great Bay, St Martin's – voted best beach in Britain, p. 328
12. Porthcurno – perfect sheltered bay of white-powder sand, p. 310
13. Carbis Bay – busy, sandy family beach two minutes by train from St Ives, p. 277
14. Kynance Cove – a rock-strewn drama queen, p. 251
15. Whitesand Bay – 4 miles of rock pools and golden sand, p. 310
16. Lantic Bay, near Polruan – one of those hidden gems the locals like to keep to themselves, p. 135
17. Constantine Bay – sit among the dunes and watch the waves crashing over rock reefs, p. 175
18. Vault Beach – an empty paradise, a rock-path walk from Gorran Haven, p. 148
19. Millook near Bude – never mind the surfers, look at that chevron folding strata, p. 95
20. Bedruthan Steps – among the footprints of giants, p. 190

which permit all-year-round use for dogs. Only six beaches impose a blanket ban, including East Looe and Pentewan on the south coast. Disability Cornwall (☎ 01736 759500) provides **Sand Chairs** (a specially designed wheelchair) on a few beaches, including Fistral Beach in Newquay, Porthminster in St Ives and Porthcressa on St Mary's (Isles of Scilly). Check the tourist information centres for details.

Cornwall's beaches, particularly on the north coast's huge stretches of wave-pounded sand, attract body-boarders, windsurfers, kite-surfers and wave-skiers among other sand-and-sea sports. A good introduction to some of these activities is to take a course at the **Extreme Academy** on Watergate Bay (☎ 01637 860543; www.watergatebay.co.uk); courses cost from £17.50 per hour, or £30 per half day.

Diving

An extraordinarily rich marine biology, spectacular underwater scenery, and hundreds of salt water wrecks put Cornwall and the Isles of Scilly among Britain's favourite diving destinations. On a submarine journey off the Cornwall coast, particularly to the west of the county, expect to see turtles, ocean sunfish, pipe fish, wrasse, dogfish, starfish, kelp forest, anemones, sponges, sea fans, seals and octopus among a myriad of species.

And if you fancy poking a torch into a wreck, classics include the ***St Chamond***, the so-called 'train wreck' sunk in St Ives Bay in 1918, the 1897 ***Syracusa*** off Newquay, and the cargo ship, ***Volnay***, wrecked off the Manacles. Off Whitsands Bay in south-east Cornwall ***HMS Scylla*** was deliberately scuppered to create an artificial diving reef (see page 72).

There is active diving all year round, though the seas are warmer between July and October when you are more likely to see pods of visiting dolphins. For basking sharks, May–June is the best time. Popular dive areas include **Falmouth Bay**, **Lamorna Cove** near Penzance, **Porthminster Reef** (or the Carracks) in St Ives Bay, the **Runnel Stone** off Land's End, and **the Manacles** – a granite reef off the east coast of the Lizard. Diving centres include **Porthkerris Divers** (www.porthkerris.com) at Porthoustock Cove (the gateway to the Manacles) and **Dive St Ives** in St Ives (☎ 01736 799229). On the Scillies, **Scilly Diving** (www.scillydiving.com) offers charters to 150 dive sites off the islands of St Mary's and St Martin's, as well as courses in scuba diving and seal snorkelling. For more information see **Diving Cornwall** (www.divingcornwall.com), or dive shop **Cornish Diving** in Falmouth (☎ 01326 313178; www.cornishdiving.co.uk).

Gig racing

Gig racing could be described as Cornwall's national sport, and on the Scilly Isles it's a passion. There are over 50 clubs in the region, 13 of them from the Scillies.

ORIGINS OF THE GIGS

Gigs or, to give the full title, **pilot gigs**, originate from the early 18th century and were designed to ferry pilots out to incoming sailing ships where they would climb aboard and help guide the vessels into tricky harbours. The six-oar gigs were hard-working little rowing boats, strong enough to withstand rough seas and were often called out to help save lives in a storm. With so many tricky harbours around the coast of Cornwall and the Isles of Scilly, there were a lot of them around, and the racing element has a precedent: the profits of piloting could be high, and where there were more than one team of oarsmen, the gigs would race to the ships to be the first to win a pilotage contract.

The practice died with the introduction of motor boats, but was revived in the form of sport in the 1940s, and has now gone international. Over 50 gig clubs form the **Cornish Pilot Gig Association**, founded in 1986. Many of the boats in use are vintage, dating from the early 19th century, and even the new models are built in elm on traditional lines.

In Cornwall, where there are boats, there are gigs: look out for races and events because it's a good spectator sport. The **World Pilot Gig Racing Championships** on the Isles of Scilly in May is a noisy, colourful event, involving over 100 gigs.

Climbing and coasteering

There is some good climbing to be had in Cornwall, and the rugged granite cliffs around Land's End are the business as far as **sea-cliff climbing** is concerned. It was here that Edwardian geographer Arthur Westlake Andrews fathered the art of sea-cliff climbing by scaling the **Bosigran Ridge** on the Penwith coast in 1902. Bosigran is still considered to be a Cornish classic and the entire coast of Penwith – the foot of the county – provides world-class sea-cliff climbs. Other serious climbs on the north coast include **Pentire Point** near Polzeath. Inland, the **Cheesewring** on Bodmin Moor and **Carn Brea Quarry** near Camborne are among favourite wall climbs. To practise, visit the **Barn Climbing Centre**, near Launceston (☎ 01822 870521; www.barnclimbingwall.co.uk). There is another indoor climbing wall at **Newquay Sports Centre** (☎ 01637 839413).

Born in the 1990s, **coasteering** is a relatively new action-adventure sport, involving a medley of climbing, swimming, caving and jumping as a high-energy means of exploring the rocky coastline.

- **EBO Adventure** (Explore Believe Overcome) – www.coasteering.org; at the Penhale Adventure Centre at Holywell Bay, provides a comprehensive website on coasteering.
- **Cornish Rock Tors** – ☎ 07791 533569; www.cornishrocktors.com; based at Polzeath this offers coasteering courses for £30 per half day.

Cycling

Aside from slow-pace off-roaders (see *Getting around*, page 20), Cornwall is attracting a growing fraternity of serious road cyclists. Since its mid-April launch in 2008, the **North Cornwall Tor** is now deemed one of the UK's toughest challenge rides. The full 100-mile circuit begins and ends in Bodmin, travelling north up the extremely hilly Atlantic coast, and back over Bodmin Moor. (See www.kilotogo.com)

For less arduous cycling, hire a bike and explore the back roads and cycle trails. A good place to start is **Bissoe Bike Hire** near Truro (☎ 01872 870341; www.cornwallcyclehire.com); not just for hired bikes, but good for maps, routes and general cycling information.

Horse-riding

Many of the **Cornish Way** walking and cycling routes (see *Getting around*, page 20) are designed for use as bridle-ways, providing miles of safe off-road riding. Riders are often seen cantering across the broad beaches of the north coast, too – particularly around **Constantine Bay**. The following riding centres are all approved by the **Association of British Riding Schools** (ww.abrs-info.org):

- **Cornish Riding Holidays** – ☎ 01209 211852; www.cornish-riding-holidays.co.uk; Wheal Buller Stables, Redruth
- **Lanjeth Riding School** – ☎ 01726 74633; Lanjeth, St Austell
- **Penhalwyn Trekking Centre** – ☎ 01736 796461; Halsetown, St Ives
- **Trenance Riding Stables** – ☎ 01637 872699; www.newquayridingstables.co.uk; Newquay
- **The Veryan Riding Centre** – ☎ 01872 501574; Veryan, Rosleand

---

ORGANISED HOLIDAYS AND COURSES

Guided tours are a good introduction to Cornwall and its many facets. There are dozens of themed options, so it's best to check out the comprehensive listings on South West England's adventure site (www.visitsouthwest.co.uk), or on the activity holidays pages of www.cornwall-online.co.uk. Here are a few suggestions to give a flavour of what's on offer:

- **Encounter Cornwall** – near Lerryn, ☎ 01208 871066; www.encountercornwall.com; self-guided, guided and tailor-made walking holidays cycling, surfing and canoeing breaks.
- **Let's Go Biking** – ☎ 01837 880075; www.letsgobiking.com; hiking and biking holidays in the West Country.
- **Classic Sailing**, Falmouth Bay – ☎ 01872 480451; www.classic-sailing.co.uk; sailing holidays around St Mawes, mainly on traditionally rigged sailing boats.
- **Elemental Tours**, Penwith – ☎ 01736 811200; www.elementaltours.co.uk; wildlife, geology and history tours on land and sea.
- **Big Friday**, Newquay – ☎ 07740 410052; www.bigfriday.com; weekend surf trips from London to Newquay. Girls' surf weekends from £245.

FURTHER INFORMATION

The county's official tourist information and marketing body is **Visit Cornwall** (www.visitcornwall.co.uk), based in Truro. For information on Cornwall's rich and diverse wildlife and landscapes, visit **Cornwall Wildlife Trust**'s excellent website (www.cornwallwildlifetrust.org.uk). For information on surfing, climbing and extreme sports take a look at **Adventure Cornwall** (www.adventure-cornwall.co.uk). For more information about the **Cornish Mining World Heritage Site** see www.cornish-mining.org.uk.

For those with an interest in the environment and sustainable travel, the **Cornwall Sustainable Tourism Project**, or CoaST (www.cstn.org.uk) is a useful social enterprise run by four women working towards 'one planet tourism', or responsible, eco-friendly tourism.

Local media

Cornwall has its own BBC radio station in **Radio Cornwall** based in Truro (broadcast on AM, FM and digital). Independent music stations include **Pirate FM** (mostly 1970s, 1980s and 1990s music), the relatively new and younger **Atlantic FM** and the community station **Radio St Austell Bay**.

- **BBC Radio Cornwall** – FM 103.9 (West), 95.2 (East), 96.0 (Isles of Scilly)
- **AM 630** – (West Cornwall), 657 (east Cornwall); www.bbc.co.uk/cornwall/local_radio
- **Pirate FM** – FM 102; www.piratefm102.co.uk
- **Atlantic FM** – FM 105.1–107; www.atlantic.fm
- **Radio St Austell Bay** – FM 105.6; www.rsab.org

For local news the *Western Morning News* is the local daily broadsheet, but although it has an office in Bodmin, its focus tends to have a Devon bias. The *West Briton* is the local tabloid daily (www.thisiscornwall.co.uk). And the Bodmin-based *Cornish Guardian* is published weekly (Wednesday). Both the latter are owned by the *Daily Mail* group. The quirky independent weekly, the *Cornish Times* (first published in January 1857), covers the east Cornwall and comes out every Friday (www.callington-today.co.uk).

Cornwall also produce some useful home-grown lifestyle magazines. *Cornwall Life* (www.cornwall-life.co.uk) is a typical glossy county magazine with an emphasis on local history, landscape and culture. *Cornwall Today* (www.cornwalltoday.co.uk) is similar but with a stronger tourism focus. The best of the bunch is *Inside Cornwall* (www.insidecornwall.co.uk) a good-looking contemporary arts, food and listings magazine put together by a small team in Newlyn. The monthly mag includes a pull-out events guide, and has a sister publication that pays lively homage to Cornish food, *Taste Cornwall*. The savvy bi-monthly *Stranger* magazine, is an eclectic mix of youth culture, music, surf, design and fashion with a sort of Cornwall-goes-global focus.

THE BACKGROUND

HISTORY

Throughout civilisation, Cornish life has been underpinned by a streak of independence that still survives. One coast short of an island, with a strong maritime culture and only one bordering county (Devon), there is a sense of identity that feels more nationalist than regional – like Wales, it has its own language, though not in common usage since the late 18th century. Its remote out-west location has protected much of its ancient history, but it's not the back-water it seems. From the mid-18th century, Cornwall was an industrial powerhouse; the richest tin and copper mining region in the world. The rise and fall of these industries has shaped almost every corner of Cornish life, a fact which has only recently been recognised by tourism.

Early history

Cornwall's early history is a little sketchy. Archaeologists believe the area may have been uninhabited until nomadic hunter-gatherers arrived from Europe in the Middle Stone Age, 10,000 years ago. Evidence of pre-historic cultures litter the countryside, particularly the more remote moorland regions, where antiquities have been preserved without interference. Relics of the Neolithic and Bronze Ages are particularly rich: Penwith Moor, to the far west of the county, claims the most concentrated collections of ancient tribal relics in Europe: among them stone circles, megalithic tombs and curious granite 'quoits', such as the Stone Age **Zennor Quoit**, and the Bronze Age holed stone, **Men an Tol**. On Bodmin Moor, **the Hurlers**, circa 1500BC, is the best example among a number of scattered standing stones.

By the Bronze Age (2100BC–750BC), western Europe was already dependent on Cornwall for supplies of tin to make bronze; the metals then produced by tin-streaming and from open-cast mines. This brought a procession of foreign traders to Cornwall. Around 600BC, the Iron Age also brought iron ploughs, axes and agriculture, and a wave of war-mongering Celts. And Cornwall became part of the Celtic kingdom of **Dumnonia**, a pre-Christian tribal community that occupied most of the West Country. Evidence of Celtic field systems and forts, such as granite-walled **Chun Castle**, can still be seen in West Penwith. The remarkable Iron Age village of **Chysauster** near Penzance dates from around the first century.

After the **Roman invasion** in 43AD, the Romans appear to have governed Cornwall and the cooperative Dumnonii with a light hand. Although the Roman road system extended beyond the Tamar, the only traces of Roman presence yet found in the county are three forts near Restormel Castle, Nanstallon and Calstock, and a villa at Magor Farm near Camborne.

The Saxons

When the Romans left Britain, the Saxons swept across the east of the country, but Cornwall, Devon and Somerset remained a stronghold of the Dumnonii. Celtic saints brought Christianity to Cornwall during this time: In the 5th century, **St Ia** floated across from Ireland to **St Ives** which now bears her name. In the 6th century, Welsh **St Petroc** founded monasteries in **Bodmin** and **Padstow**, and **St Piran**, another Irish missionary, turned up at **Perranporth** – destined to become Cornwall's patron saint. By this time, the Kingdom of Cornwall had come into being; according to legend, its most famous King, Mark, held court at **Tintagel**.

By the 8th century, when the rest of Celtic Dumnonia had fallen to the Anglo-Saxons, Cornwall still held out. But over the next 300 years, its autonomy waned, and by the reign of Edward the Confessor (1042–66) it became part of Saxon England. The Domesday Book shows that by the Norman Conquest, most Cornish lands had been seized by English landowners, with Harold taking the largest share.

The Normans

After 1066, Cornwall was carved up again, this time among the Norman ruling class. King William's half-brother Robert controlled most of the county and erected **Launceston Castle** as his headquarters. Cornwall remained under the control of the Norman and Plantagenet royal families for several centuries, and its Earls were responsible for building both the **Tintagel** and **Restormel** (**Lostwithiel**) castles we see today. Legend has it that the 15 gold bezants on the Cornish coat of arms represent the ransom raised in Cornwall to free the crusading Earl of Cornwall, captured by the Saracens in the 12th century. In 1337, Edward the Black Prince was named Duke of Cornwall, the first dukedom conferred in the Kingdom of England. The title has been awarded to the eldest son of the Sovereign, today's Prince of Wales, ever since.

During the Middle Ages, tin mining was so important to Cornwall, and to England, that organisation and regulation became necessary. By the 13th century, Cornish tin miners were grouped into four '**Stannaries**', representing Cornwall's four primary tin-producing areas. Their administrative centres were the **Stannary towns** – **Helston**, **Lostwithiel**, **Truro**, **Liskeard**, **Penzance** and briefly **Bodmin** – where the tin was weighed, stamped and taxed. The Stannaries had their own parliament and court to which Cornish miners were primarily answerable.

The Middle Ages also saw the rise of commercial fishing in Cornwall, and increased prosperity for fishing villages such as **Mousehole**, **St Ives** and **Newlyn**. In 1439, the inhabitants of Towan Blistra asked the Bishop of Exeter for permission and funds to build a new quay. **Newquay** was soon a flourishing fishing port.

Tudors and Stuarts

The Tudor dynasty's vision of England as one nation under their direct control meant a further loss of autonomy for Cornwall. In 1497, Henry VII tried to raise taxes to fund a war on Scotland, contravening a Cornish tax exemption. The Cornish also considered Scotland too remote to be their problem. Led by tin miners, 15,000 protesters marched on London. The Cornish Rebellion was put down at the **Battle of Deptford Bridge**. The ringleaders were executed, enslaved or fined, and their lands seized, further eroding Cornwall's prosperity and identity.

The Cornish rose up again in the **Prayer Book Rebellion** of 1549, opposing the Act of Uniformity. This made it illegal to use anything other than the Protestant English-language Book of Common Prayer. Cornwall was mostly Catholic, and about half the population Cornish speaking, so the act was bitterly resented. In response the King sent the army and foreign mercenaries into Cornwall, killing 4,000 men in the fighting, and 1,000 more in subsequent reprisals – an estimated 10% of Cornwall's population.

The splendour of Tudor Cornwall can be appreciated at **Cotehele** on the banks of the River Tamar, at **Prideaux Place** near Padstow, and in the spectacular stained glass windows of **St Neot Parish Church** on the western fringe of Bodmin Moor.

Civil War and its aftermath

When the Civil War began in 1642, Cornwall was a Royalist enclave. The county was the scene of several bloody battles, culminating in the official surrender of Cornwall's Royalist forces on **Tresillian Bridge**, near Truro, in 1646. **Pendennis Castle**, built in the 1540s by Henry VIII, was one of the Royalist's last strongholds.

In 1688, Jonathan Trelawny was one of seven bishops imprisoned in the Tower of London for seditious libel by James II. Son of a prominent Cornish royalist, he had immense popular support in Cornwall, and there was a public outcry. The bishops were acquitted the following year. A 19th-century poem

10... historic experiences in Cornwall

1 Chysauster – one among hundreds of ancient monuments on Penwith's moors, this Iron Age village is a remarkable collection of Celtic dwellings, p. 94

2 Tintagel Castle – romance, drama and the King Arthur legend haunt the seaside seat of Cornwall's medieval earls, p. 105

3 Cotehele House – the Edgcumbe family's perfect Tudor manor house overlooks the Tamar Valley, p. 58

4 Levant Mine – the National Trust's underground shaft houses an active steam-powered Cornish beam engine (the oldest in Cornwall), p. 309

5 Launceston Castle – the building of this motte-and-bailey stronghold established Launceston as the Cornwall's first Norman capital, p. 56

6 St Neot Parish Church – the 15th-century village church sports a fine granite tower and some of England's most glorious stained glass panels, p. 85

7 Pendennis Castle – Henry VIII's Tudor stronghold guards the entrance to the Fal Estuary, p. 223

8 The Hurlers – mysterious circle of Neolithic standing stones near the Minions Heritage Centre on Bodmin Moor, p. 84

9 Lanhydrock near Bodmin – one of Cornwall's most visited stately homes, it's a homage to the high Victorian style, p. 85

10 Chapel Street, Penzance – a legacy of mining wealth, it's of the most unaltered historic streetscapes in Britain, p. 293

commemorating Trelawny's imprisonment, *The Song of the Western Men* became the Cornish National Anthem.

The Industrial Revolution

Cornwall's first international industry was in **pilchard fishing**. Fished in their millions, salted and pressed, the pilchards were packed in wooden casks for export. Popular among fasting Catholics, **Cornish pilchards** reached Italy, France, Spain and the even the USA in vast quantities. Fishing continued to be a major source of employment until the mid-20th century, but from the early 18th century, it was overshadowed by the far more lucrative mining trade.

The pioneering days of early steam power, changed the face of **Cornish mining**. The depth of Cornwall's tin mines had always been limited by subterranean water. With steam engines pumping water out of the mines, shafts could

10... highlights of Cornwall's industrial past

1 Royal Albert Bridge – super engineer Isambard Brunel's bow-string suspension bridge provides a spectacular rail link between Devon and Cornwall, p. 66

2 Cornish Mines and Engines – the National Trust's homage to Victorian mining at Pool near Redruth, p. 194

3 The China Clay Country Park – learn all about the china clay industry at this visitor centre near St Austell, p. 151

4 The Treffry Viaduct – hidden among trees in the Luxulyan Valley, it used to carry copper ore from the mines to the sea, p. 150

5 Wheal Coates – among dozens of cliff-top engine houses, these overlook the sea at Chapel Porth, p. 195

6 Looe Valley Line – the scenic branch-line railway follows the path of the former Liskeard to Looe Union Canal, p. 122

7 The Great Flat Lode Trail – today's footpath and cycle route is named after a rich seam of tin, p. 194

8 Morwellham Quay – on the Devon side of the Tamar, once the premier copper port of the British empire, p. 59

9 Geevor Tin Mine – the Land's End tin mine, one of the last to close, is now a museum and visitor centre, p. 308

10 Poldark Mine – this mining heritage visitor centre north of Helston is run by volunteers, p. 253

be sunk deeper than before. Engine houses and foundries sprang up across the county, and a network of engineered canals, railways and tramways connected mines to ports. Barely a corner of the county was untouched by the industry, and by the 1820s there were more than 2,000 mines in operation, making Cornwall the world's leading mineral producer. The fine Georgian centres of Cornish towns, particularly Truro and Penzance, were shaped by mineral wealth. And many of the great family estates, built on mining profits, still survive. It was, however, a tough life for the average Cornish miner and his contemporaries, and mining co-existed alongside wrecking and smuggling.

THE HEYDAYS OF SMUGGLERS

Cornwall's rugged coast and rough stormy seas have seen hundreds of shipwrecks over the centuries, and poor coastal communities were quick to profit from the misfortune of others. 'Wrecking' – retrieving anything of value from wrecked ships – was a major source of income. Although legend (and Hollywood) has it that Cornish wreckers used lanterns as 'false lights' to lure ships onto the rocks, no one was ever prosecuted for it.

With taxes up to five times higher in England than in the rest of Europe, this was also the heyday of the Cornish smuggler, with the small coves and inlets of the south coast, at the heart of this illicit trade. The revenue men became more effective during the 19th century, when penalties such as transportation or public hanging were meted out. Smugglers upped their game, sinking contraband for later retrieval, and using caves and tunnels to move merchandise inland. The **Polperro Heritage Museum of Smuggling and Fishing** brings this period to life.

In 1746, Quaker apothecary William Cookworthy discovered **china clay** at Tregonning Hill. Until then most porcelain clay had been imported from China but here, and in the hills around St Austell Bay, lay the world's largest china clay deposits. By the early 19th century, the Cornish china clay industry was a global success. It still is, but tin mining has not fared so well. A world copper crash in 1866 left the entire industry reeling and a slow decline of tin mining followed. Many Cornishmen left for mines in the Americas, Australia, New Zealand and South Africa.

Fishing continued to flourish, reaching its zenith in the 1870s, but this too suffered decline and by the 1950s was virtually wiped out by over-fishing.

There was a kind of saviour in the **Cornwall Railway**. Completed in 1859, the last stage of the rail connection between Paddington and Penzance, it had boosted farming and fishing by providing a fast, reliable way of transporting goods to the lucrative national market. Soon, however, the railway led to a surge in tourism. In 1889 the Great Western Railway took over the route, and in 1904 introduced the **Cornish Riviera Express**, taking just seven hours to get from Paddington to Penzance. This was the first stage in Cornwall's gradual transition from industrial heartland to tourism hotspot.

Modern history

Tourism saw further expansion with the opening of the **Tamar Bridge** between Plymouth and Saltash in 1961, greatly improving access to eastern Cornwall. When the bridge opened, 4,000 vehicles used it daily. By the 1990s this had risen to 40,000. Consequently it was widened and strengthened between 1999 and 2001 – the only bridge in the world to undergo this process while remaining open.

The Cornish china clay industry's success continues. In 1919, three producers formed **English China Clays Limited**, the world's foremost clay producer. Despite recent redundancies, it is still Cornwall's largest private employer with 80% of the three million tonnes of china clay produced going into paper making. There are sufficient reserves to sustain the Cornish industry for another century.

The last working tin mine, South Crofty, closed in 1998, but there is talk of reviving production in 2010 thanks to a meteoric rise in world metal prices. In 2006, the Cornwall and West Devon Mining Landscape was given UNESCO World Heritage status. The **Cornish Mining World Heritage Site**, covering 10 separate areas of the county, will help boost tourism in relatively undiscovered corners of the county.

For all this, Cornwall and the Isles of Scilly are among the poorest areas of Western Europe. With the decline in tin mining, agriculture and fishing, they depend primarily on tourism. In recognition of its low levels of prosperity, the region was awarded Objective One status in 1999 thereby qualifying for £350 million in European Union (EU) aid.

As for Cornwall's independence, the political party **Mebyon Kernow** – Sons of Cornwall – was formed in 1951 to encourage Cornish nationalism and is still going strong. In 2001, Cornish inhabitants could record their ethnicity as Cornish on the national census for the first time. In 2009 the District, Borough and County Councils of Cornwall amalgamate under the control of one administrative body, **One Cornwall**, to provide a single, strong voice for the county.

GEOGRAPHY AND GEOLOGY

Cornwall is a finger of sedimentary rock with a granite backbone. Where the granite reaches the Earth's surface the landscape is dominated by granite moorlands – **Bodmin**, the **St Austell highlands** and **Penwith**. The headwaters of most of Cornwall's rivers are found in these elevated moors, particularly Bodmin, where the Fowey, Lynher, Camel and Ottery all begin their journeys. Away from the moorland, where the soils are deeper, pasture and arable land have replaced ancient woodland, which now only covers 5% of Cornwall's surface. All this is hemmed in by a coastline dominated by sheer cliffs, occasionally relieved by sandy or rocky beaches, and wide estuaries.

Cornwall's complicated geology began to take shape 400–350 million years ago, when the muddy sea floor was compressed, heated, folded and sheared by tectonic movements, to form dense layers of slate, called 'killas' by Cornish miners. Over time, layers of slate became interleaved with coarser sedimentary rocks such as sandstone and siltstone. This is shown to great effect by the zigzag folds of strata in the cliffs at **Millook Haven** near Bude. Then 300–270 million years ago molten magma bubbled beneath this spur of sedimentary rock. In places it punched right through to the surface in lumps called plutons,

CORNISH MINING – A WORLD HERITAGE SITE

When Cornwall's mining legacy was granted World Heritage status in 2006, it joined an A-list of historic global wonders including the Taj Mahal, the Pyramids and the Great Wall of China. And it's rather unusual, not only because it celebrates the grime and grind of industry, but also because its unlikely gems are scattered across 20,000 hectares, divided into 10 areas, shared between Cornwall and west Devon.

Each area represents a part of what was once the richest tin and copper mining region on the planet. The industries which thrived here between 1700 and 1914, had a profound effect on Cornwall's landscapes, turning a backwater of farming-and-fishing into a key player in the global economy of the British Empire. And it wasn't just about digging out minerals from holes in the ground. Cornish mining was a breeding ground of the technological ingenuity that shaped the Industrial Revolution; it was also the driving force behind most of the county's finer architecture, its transport routes and its social life and communities. Few corners of Cornwall were left untouched by mining.

The idea behind the World Heritage bid was to give the legacy 'brand value', enabling the public to recognise and understand the distinctive landmarks of Cornwall's industrial past. The visitor centres and attractions which take part in the dispersed collection of treasures include the magnificent houses of the mining elite, but in general we are not talking glittering palaces, but ports, pits, railways, tramways and some 200 ruined engine houses. Relics which until now have simply been part of the landscape, are now forming part of a world-class discovery trail. If you like your history unmarked and still covered in ivy, then discover them for yourself before everyone else does.

before cooling to form granite. One pluton became the **Isles of Scilly** – the other four are Cornwall's granite moorlands. You can see the exposed face of one of these plutons at the dramatic cliffs at **Land's End.** Cornish granite is rich in naturally radioactive elements, particularly uranium. The decaying uranium emits heat, and over millions of years this heat has pumped water through cracks in the cooling rock, depositing veins of tin, copper, arsenic and other valuable minerals throughout the granite. In some places, particularly around **St Austell**, the flow of heated water also broke feldspar down into kaolinite – china clay.

Lizard Peninsula's geology is completely different from the rest of Cornwall. It was made from rocks from deep in the Earth's crust, subjected to extreme alteration. **Serpentine**, the most common rock on the Lizard, is mottled with red, green and white like a serpent's skin, and isn't found anywhere else on mainland Britain.

It has taken millions of years for the element to mould and shape these ancient rock layers into the Cornish landscape we see today. On some areas of the coast, wave erosion has created towering cliffs and headlands: **High Cliff**, to the east of the Atlantic coast is the highest sheer-drop cliff in southern Britain at 735ft. In others, tonnes of sand have been deposited to make long white beaches, sculpted by the Atlantic winds into billowing dunes, such as those at **Gwithian Towans** beaches near Hayle. Rivers and streams have cut into the bedrock, creating river valleys and wide estuaries (such as the **Fowey** and the **Fal**). Because Cornwall is a narrow peninsula, the rivers in the county tend to be shorter than elsewhere in the UK – the **Tamar** is the longest at 94km (54 miles).

The county's mineral deposits have been exploited for thousands of years, leaving a landscape pocked with deep mine workings. The countryside around **St Austell** has been dramatically altered by china clay extraction and 'mountains' of waste material have the appearance of lunar Alps, while settling pits filled with water provide Cornwall's own artificial lake district.

WILDLIFE AND HABITATS

Cornwall's wildlife habitats have been shaped by the warm waters of the Gulf Stream, the fierce south-westerly winds that blow in from the Atlantic, and 10,000 years of human occupation. The Gulf Stream gives Cornwall a warmer and wetter climate than many other parts of the UK; indeed, the south-west of the peninsula and the Isles of Scilly are categorized as sub-tropical. A visit to the **Abbey Gardens** at **Tresco** or the botanical gardens at **Trebah** bears this out.

Marine life

The seas around Cornwall are among the richest and most diverse marine habitats in the UK. **Grey seals** can be seen all year round, particularly around the breeding colonies of the Isles of Scilly. While **Orcas**, **Minke** and **Pilot whales** are occasionally sighted, you're more likely to see groups of **Bottlenose dolphins**. If you want to try to spot them from the shore, checkout the Cornwall Wildlife Trust website (www.cornwallwildlifetrust.org.uk), which has up-to-date records of Bottlenose sightings. Between July and October, the bizarre **ocean sunfish** can sometimes be spotted lying on the surface of the water. If you're lucky you might see another summer visitor, the **leatherback turtle** which, like the sunfish, lives almost entirely on jellyfish.

In 2007 a Great White Shark was reputedly spotted off Porthmeor Beach near St Ives, but it's the **basking sharks** that pull the crowds. These harmless plankton eaters, the second largest fish in the world, appear from April to August to feed and mate. Spectacular marine life isn't restricted to the summer – in December and January, **fin whales**, the second largest, pass Land's End on their annual migration.

Coast

The 435-mile long Cornish coastline, its golden beaches, sand dunes, granite cliff and broad estuaries and marshes, support a wide range of flora and fauna. The more exposed north coast is characterised by rare and highly specialised heathland, maritime grassland and stunted woodland. Colourful banks of sea pinks thrive in early summer. Between April and August, puffins can be seen nesting in their cliff burrows on the uninhabited Scilly Isle of **Annet**, a bird sanctuary and an Area of Outstanding Natural Beauty.

The Lizard Peninsula is home to one of England's rarest breeding birds, the **Chough**. This red-beaked member of the crow family appears on the Cornish crest, grasping the ducal coronet in its talons. Nesting in cliffs, it hunts for insect prey on well-grazed coastal pastures. As this habitat disappeared from Cornwall, so did the Chough, last nesting in 1952. Local groups worked with farmers to restore suitable areas of pasture, and a single pair of choughs returned and bred in 2002. Numbers have risen slowly but surely since. The Lizard's flora is highly specialised, with the pink-flowering **Cornish heath**, the county flower of Cornwall, found nowhere else in the UK.

Cornwall's estuaries are internationally important havens for huge number of waterfowl and wading birds. **Hayle Estuary** is the most south-westerly estuary in the UK and never freezes. In cold winters up to 18,000 birds can be seen here – but the bird life here is spectacular throughout the year, with **curlew**, **teal**, **egrets**, **plover**, and **oystercatchers** all putting in an appearance. The **Tamar Estuary**, on the border of Devon and Cornwall is one of the largest mudflats in the south-west, with a resident population of **Shelduck**, and **Kingfishers** patrolling the inlets. The **Fal Estuary** between St Mawes and Pendennis is regularly visited by dolphins. The sand dunes at **Gwithian Towans** on St Ives Bay are a Site of Special Scientific Interest (SSSI), and home to a fifth of Cornwall's plant species. **Adders** can be spotted here, and it's also good place to see rare **orchids**, **butterflies** and **glow worms**. Careful management of the dunes of **Perran Sands**, the largest in Britain, has seen the rare **skylark** double its numbers here in recent years.

Inland

Cornwall's countryside is a refuge for many quintessentially English plant and animal species, with the highest otter population in England. **Otters** are found in all Cornish river catchments. Although most of Cornwall's ancient woodland was cleared for agriculture in the Iron and Bronze Ages, there are still pockets such as **Devichoys Wood** between Truro and Falmouth, and **Cabilla and Redrice Nature Reserve** near Bodmin. The dormouse, 13 bat species, badgers, woodland birds and red, fallow and roe deer all inhabit these ancient stands of oak and hazel. Luckily, many woodland animal species exploit the 30,000 miles of hedges in Cornwall which criss-cross the farmland. The hedges are also important wildflower sites – in spring they bloom with primrose, bluebell, campion and cow parsley, replaced in summer by the orchids, foxgloves and wild honeysuckle. Consequently many of the 42 species of butterfly found in Cornwall can be seen around hedgerows.

Bodmin Moor is an 80sq mile expanse of dramatic, undulating, wind-blown moorland, punctuated by gigantic granite tors. Most of the moor is an SSSI and an Area of Natural Beauty. Ten thousand years ago it was covered in forest, but prehistoric man cleared it for farming. Today cattle, ponies and sheep graze the moors. Bogs and marshes in low lying areas are home to internationally rare species such as **Bog Moss** and the **Marsh Fritillary**, as well as **frogs**, **newts** and **grass snakes.** In the summer, **stonechats**, **wheatears** and **skylarks** breed on the moor. Thousands of **golden plover** overwinter here too. The valleys and tors are good places to see **buzzards**, **kestrels** and **sparrowhawks**.

A checklist of the 400 birds species living in the region can be found on www.erccis.co.uk, the website for the **Environmental Records Centre for Cornwall and the Isles of Scilly** (ERCCIS). Run by the Cornwall Wildlife Trust, ERCCIS is interested in details of any animal sightings (dead or alive), and supplies beautifully illustrated identification guides and recording forms. The **Cornwall Wildlife Trust** manages more than 50 nature reserves, all

The best... Cornish wildlife sites

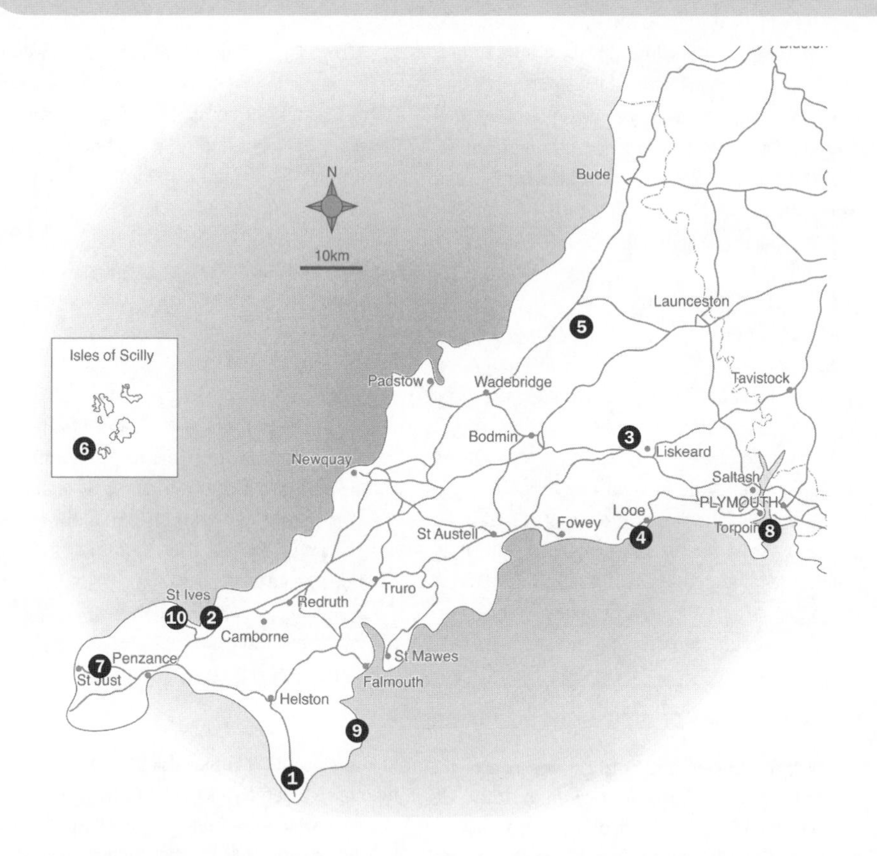

1. The Lizard – Cornwall's first nature reserve is noted for its rich variety of rare flora, including hairy buttercup and, a world exclusive, Cornish heath, p. 247
2. Upton Towans – early summer brings butterflies and rare Pyramidal Orchids to the rolling desert sand dunes of this seaside nature reserve near Hayle, p. 193
3. Golitha Falls – at the head of the verdant Fowey River, see wildflowers, nuthatch, buzzard and bluebells, against a backdrop of ancient oaks, lichens and cascading water, p. 84
4. St George's Island (better known as Looe Island) – discover a colony of great black backed gulls on this off-shore Marine Nature Reserve, p. 124
5. Davidstow Moor – see a million starlings swoop over the edge of Bodmin Moor at dusk between October and March, p. 83
6. The Isle of Annet – a boat tour from St Mary's to this tiny Scilly islet may be rewarded by the sight of nesting puffins between April and August, p. 324
7. Chun Downs – part of the West Penwith Moors, inhabited since the Stone Age, it's criss-crossed with ancient Cornish hedges and home to 25% of Cornwall's heathland, p. 307
8. Tamar Estuary – on one of the largest areas of mudflats in the south-west, see shelduck, kingfishers and a large wintering population of avocet, p. 66
9. The Manacles – a granite reef off the east coast of the Lizard peninsula, it's one of Cornwall's most popular dive sites, p. 266
10. Seal Island – 3 miles west of St Ives, a hunk of rock supporting Atlantic greys, p. 277

with free access (see www.cornwallwildlifetrust.org.uk).

While 50 species of mammal are recorded in Cornwall, the Isles of Scilly are a different matter. Of the 11 species of small mammal found in Cornwall, only four are found in Scilly – the **woodmouse**, **house mouse**, **brown rat** and **Scilly Shrew**.

CULTURE

Cornwall's seascapes, its untamed natural beauty, have long been a place of inspiration for writers and artists. The lure of West Cornwall in particular, helped nurture the Newlyn and St Ives' schools of artists – both groups inspired by Cornwall and the special quality of its light. In the 1990s, the foundation of **Tate St Ives** boosted a renaissance of Cornish art. But while galleries proliferate, the artists themselves can no longer afford St Ives, and have moved on to form artistic colonies in Penzance, St Just and Penryn among dozens of other, cheaper places.

Cornwall's Celtic heritage is powerfully represented by a thriving traditional music scene, celebrated every August at the **Cornwall Folk Festival** in Wadebridge. Writers, meanwhile, have found inspiration not just in the Cornish landscape, but in its people – their maritime culture and eventful history, and the intrigues of smuggling and wrecking have proved rich pickings for some of the UK's best-known authors.

Art

Among the first tourists to Cornwall, after the opening of the railways, was the swarm of artists who flocked to Newlyn and St Ives, looking for cheap studios and beautiful light. Many of them were so impoverished they paid their landlords in kind, one reason, perhaps, why so many of the St Ives and Newlyn Schools' works are still in private Cornish collections.

NEWLYN AND ST IVES' SCHOOLS OF ART

Walter Langley (1852–1922) was one of the first painters to arrive in Newlyn in 1882. His sentimental watercolours depicted the daily life of the Cornish working class, particularly coastal communities. **Stanhope Forbes** (1857–1947), known as the father of the Newlyn School, arrived in Newlyn two years later and stayed for the rest of his life. He wanted to paint in *en plein air* – a term and practice borrowed from the French impressionists – and found the mild Cornish climate allowed him to work outside almost all year round. Like Langley, he was fascinated by the grass roots of maritime life and painted, among other things, fishermen at work. Forbes and Langley were soon joined by a flurry of like-minded artists keen to pursue *plein air* painting: Edwin Harris, Norman Garstin, Frank Bramely, Ralph Todd, Fred Millard, and Henry Scott all settled in Newlyn. The work of the Newlyn School is now displayed at the **Penlee House Museum** in Penzance. Artists have hung around the port of St Ives, since **JMW Turner** visited in 1811. But its reputation is largely founded on the generation of artists who arrived after the First World War. In 1929 abstract painter **Ben Nicholson** visited St Ives with opium-addled artist **Christopher Wood**. There they encountered **Alfred Wallis** (1855–1942) a fisherman who had taken up painting in 1922, at the age of 67, to console himself after his wife died. Completely untrained, he produced naïve images of St Ives street scenes, or seascapes remembered from his seafaring days. Wallis's work inspired Nicholson to pursue abstract modernism, and in 1939, he and his wife, the sculptor **Barbara Hepworth** (1903–75) moved to St Ives to work. After the war, the couple formed the core of a group of radical young 'moderns' with whom the tag St Ives' School is associated. In the 1970s, the St Ives tradition continued with a new generation of abstract artists, among them Terry Frost, Peter Lanyon, Patrick Heron and Bryan Winter.

Today's creative scene is fed by Falmouth University's art degree courses which are turning out a new wave of world-class Cornish artists. Alumni include visual artist **Tacita Dean** who uses 16mm film to explore eerie or abandoned spaces, and sculptor **Hew Lock** famous for using throwaway materials such as cardboard and plastic in huge flamboyant sculptures. **Tim Shaw** who graduated in 1989 sculpts disturbing pagan figures that seem to come straight out of *Pan's Labyrinth* or the murals at Knossos. You can get a good look at some of them in the Mediterranean biome of the Eden Project. There, in an installation called Dionysus, a group of copper figures live it up among the greenery. Like many of Cornwall's artists, Tim returned within two years of graduating, and has lived in Falmouth ever since.

Literature

In 1870, before he hit the big time, novelist and poet **Thomas Hardy** visited Boscastle to supervise renovations at St Juliot's Church, and in the process fell in love with the rector's sister-in-law, Emma Gifford. They married in 1874. The area inspired the location for his early novel *A Pair of Blue Eyes* – a fictionalised account of his courtship of Emma. After his wife died in 1912, Hardy returned to North Cornwall, a trip which inspired 21 heartfelt (some might say downright miserable) poems, published under the imaginative title *The Poems of 1912–1913*. Today, St Juliot's Church has a stained glass window commemorating Hardy's link to Cornwall. **Kenneth Grahame**, of *Wind in the Willows* fame, married and honeymooned in Cornwall and took family holidays in Fowey. In 1907, when staying at the Greenbank Hotel in Falmouth, he began writing a series of letters to his son that became the basis for *Wind in the Willows*. Some people believe that the first chapter was inspired by a cruise on the River Fowey near Lerryn; others say the Helford River gave birth to Toad and Ratty.

Born in Bodmin, and resident in Fowey for most of his adult life, **Arthur Quiller-Couch** was one of Britain's most popular novelists at the turn of the 20th century. He first used the pen name 'Q' writing for the *Oxford Magazine*, and continued to do so throughout his career. He was best known for the epic *Oxford Book of English Verse 1250–1900*, but also wrote adventures, mysteries and humorous bestsellers including *The Delectable Duchy*, and *Troy Town*, the latter modelled on Fowey. A Quiller-Couch protégée was young Alfred Leslie Rowse, the son of a china clay miner from Tregonissey near St Austell – now better know as the poet, historian and Shakespearean scholar, **AL Rowse**. In a classic example of bad timing, **DH Lawrence**, and his German wife Frieda moved to a rented seaside cottage near Zennor in 1916, half way through the First World War. While he was pottering around writing *Women in Love* and having violent arguments with Frieda, the locals became convinced that the pair were German spies. The rumour was that the couple were signalling to U-boats at night by showing a light in their window. The paranoia reached such a pitch that the police finally made them leave the area in October 1917.

Growing up in London, writer, broadcaster and former Poet Laureate, **John Betjeman** spent many happy childhood holidays in Trebetherick near Polzeath, where his father owned property. He wrote the *Shell County Guide* to Cornwall in 1934, and several beautiful poems including *Sunday Afternoon Service at St Enodoc* and *Cornish Cliffs* which capture his enduring love of Cornwall. After the Second World War, he spent more time in Trebetherick, and is buried at nearby St Enodoc Church. Writer **Daphne du Maurier** is probably more closely associated with Cornwall in the public mind than any other author. She not only spent most of her life in and around Fowey, but Cornwall's landscape and history featured in her most famous works such as *Rebecca*, *My Cousin Rachel*, *Frenchman's Creek* and *Jamaica Inn*. The 12 *Poldark* novels, set in and around Perranporth in the 18th and 19th centuries, were just a fraction of the work of prolific author **Winston Graham**. Perranporth was Graham's home from the age of 17 to 51. In the 1970s, the Poldark books were made into a BBC television series.

Nobel and Booker Prize winner, **William Golding** was born at his grandmother's house St Columb Minor, near Newquay, returning there

The best... book, TV and film locations

1. Charlestown Harbour – the south coast's Georgian port starred in 1970s maritime drama the *Onedin Line*, *Moll Flanders*, *Hornblower* and *A Respectable Trade* among numerous costume drama roles, p. 147
2. Port Isaac – after several minor film roles, the village rocketed to fame when cast as Port Wenn, the home of TV's *Doc Martin*, played by Martin Clunes, p. 107
3. The Gribben Peninsula and Polridmouth Cove were among the settings for Daphne du Maurier's classic *Rebecca*; the 1940s film adaptation starred Laurence Olivier, p. 135
4. Zennor – DH Lawrence wrote *Women in Love* while staying in the Land's End village in 1916. The Tinners Arms was his local, p. 313
5. Cadgwith Cove – this tiny Lizard village hosted the two great dames, Maggie Smith and Judi Dench on location in *Ladies in Lavender*, p. 253
6. Boscastle – while visiting in 1870, Thomas Hardy fell in love with Emma Grifford while renovating St Juliot's church. The courtship is fictionalised in his early novel *A Pair of Blue Eyes*, p. 95
7. St Austell Clay Pits – the lunar landscape was a favourite 1970s sci-fi setting having appeared in *Dr Who* and *Blake's Seven*, p. 149
8. Towan Beach – used as a setting for the Beatles loony 1967 road movie *Magical Mystery Tour*, p. 177
9. Watergate Bay – otherwise known as Echo Beach in the TV surf-soap of the same name, p. 177
10. Penwith – a place of pilgrimage for fans of Lelant-born Rosamund Pilcher, whose autobiographical novel, *The Shell Seekers*, was set in Cornwall's far west, p. 313

10... cultural sites in Cornwall

1 Tate St Ives – in the capital of Cornish art, the country's best known gallery overlooks Porthmeor beach, p. 279

2 Minack Theatre – sculpted from a Penwith cliff, the iconic open-air ampitheatre is a drama in itself, p. 313

3 The Royal Cornwall Museum – a former savings bank in Truro houses an impressive collection of art and antiquities, p. 211

4 Newlyn Art Gallery – with an architect-designed extension, the Newlyn School classic has teamed up with younger sibling the Exchange in Penzance, p. 295

5 Truro Cathedral – a neo-Gothic marvel, and one of Cornwall's most visited buildings, p. 208

6 Falmouth Art Gallery – award-winning family favourite, with works ranging from Alfred Munnings to Peter Markey automatons, p. 228

7 Sterts Theatre – charity-run theatre, gallery and arts centre on the rim of Bodmin Moor, p. 88

8 Barbara Hepworth Museum and Sculpture Garden – in the former home she shared with fellow St Ives School artist, Ben Nicholson, p. 280

9 The John Betjeman Centre – the former Wadebridge station celebrates the life of the Cornwall-loving Poet Laureate, p. 174

10 Hall for Cornwall – Cornwall's answer to the Albert Hall, is the county's premier venue for live performance, p. 212

on holiday throughout his youth. One can only hope that it wasn't his childhood experiences in Cornwall that inspired his first, and most famous novel, *Lord of the Flies*, published in 1953. He moved to Perranarworthal, near Truro, with his wife in 1985, and died there eight years later. **WJ Burley** (William John) the creator of Detective Superintendent Charles Wycliffe was born in Falmouth and lived in Cornwall most of his life. His first Wycliffe novel was published when he was in his 50s and he produced 21 more in the next 25 years, all set in a fictional, crime-ridden Cornwall. In the 1990s, Wycliffe was adapted for television by ITV.

Launceston was the birthplace and lifelong home of **Charles Causley**, Cornwall's foremost poet. He wrote for adults and children and made little distinction between the two forms. Novelist and former Mills & Boon writer **Rosamund Pilcher** was born and grew up in Lelant near St Ives. Her best-selling 1987 family saga *The Shell Seekers* was set in west Cornwall and London, and she later admitted it was largely autobiographical. Many subsequent books including *Another View* and *Coming Home* are also set in the county, leading to a surge in tourists from Germany, where her work is particularly popular. **John Le Carré** is the pen name of David Cornwell, who has found refuge in St Buryan for more than 40 years. He writes on his website: '*I live on a Cornish cliff and hate cities.*'

Music

In a region where mining and fishing forced large groups of men together in harsh conditions for long periods of time, the temperance movement was keen to find something to occupy their leisure hours and keep them away from the demon drink. This led to the formation of brass bands and male voice choirs in 19th century Cornwall, and many are still going strong today. The **Camborne Town Band**, based near the famous School of Mines plays all over Cornwall.

Folk music is alive and well in Cornwall, too – thanks in part to Cornish folk singer **Brenda Wooten** known as 'the Voice of Cornwall', who opened her own folk club in St Buryan. Celtic dance bands such as **Dalla** and **Sowena** have spearheaded Cornish Celtic dance events called **Noze looan** (Cornish for 'happy night') which encourage audience participation, without complicated steps. **Troyls**, the Cornish equivalent of a ceilidh, are also popular across the county. The band **Skywarda** performs Cornish language pop and rock, while **Krena** plays anything from funk to punk.

Cornwall has produced very few A-list musicians, though **Richard D James**, better known as **Aphex Twin** – one of the most influential figures in modern electronic music – grew up in Lanner; as a teenager he did a bit of DJ-ing at the Shire Horse in St Ives. Almost two decades after his first record release in 1991, he's changed the face of electronic music, while staying close to his Cornish roots, using Cornish words as track titles. The home-grown folk-rock band **Thistletown**, based on a boat in Penryn, have also made inroads into the national music scene. **Roger Taylor**, the drummer from Queen, grew up in Truro. Among incomers, singer **Tori Amos** has lived near Bude since 1998.

LOCAL HEROES

The past

Many of its most revered sons come from the world of engineering. The most revered, and the only one to have a day devoted to his memory is **Richard Trevithick**. Born in near Camborne in 1771, Trevithick not only grew up with the industry but helped pioneer its boom. While working as an engineer for the Ding Dong mine near Penzance he developed a high-pressure steam engine which revolutionised tin extraction by enabling deeper, richer mining. He is also credited with the first pre-Stephenson, self-powered steam locomotive 'the Puffing Devil'. His inventions, and his development of the steam engine helped power the Industrial Revolution. Buried in an ummarked grave at Dartford in Kent, where he died in poverty in 1833, he never really earned the recognition he was due during his own lifetime. Now, his memory and achievements are celebrated by the Trevithick Society, the mining conservation group behind the annual Trevithick Day in Camborne.

Gifted chemist **Sir Humphry Davy** was born in Penzance in 1778 and is credited with inventing the miners' safety lamp, as well as discovering gasses and working on the properties of acids and alkali earth elements. One of his most famous discoveries, he was to say, was his laboratory assistant **Michael Faraday**. From 1820 to 1827 he was President of the Royal Society; his statue stands proudly at the head of Penzance's Market Jew Street. A younger contemporary, **Joseph Treffry** was a significant industrialist and civil engineer. Born in Plymouth in 1782, he moved to Fowey when he inherited the Place estate through his mother's line. He is responsible for creating Par Harbour, but his best-known legacy is the Treffry Viaduct that crosses the Luxulyan Valley. Also worth a mention is **William Bickford**, inventor of a safety fuse for igniting gunpowder, a device which saved many lives in mining. A Devonian by birth, Bickford moved to Cornwall in the late 18th century, founding the Trevarno Estate, north of Helston.

At a tangent to mining, the steady growth of Cornwall's still prevalent Methodist faith was largely down to evangelical zeal of brothers **Charles** and, in particular, **John Wesley** who travelled the county preaching temperance and the non-conformist faith to remote mining and fishing communities in the mid-18th century. The Quakers, too, were a driving force in 18th century Cornwall though unlike the humble Wesleyians they were wealthy, land-owning entrepreneurs. Noted among them was geologist and philosopher, **Robert Were Fox**, born in Falmouth in 1789, and known for inventing the dipping needle compass. He could, no doubt, afford to philosophise, being married to Maria Barclay, whose family founded Barclay's Bank. Their son **Charles Fox** created the wonderful Trebah Gardens at the family home at Mawnan Smith. In 1746, fellow Quaker, the Devonian pharmacist **William Cookworthy** discovered china clay at Tregonning Hill, to the north of Helston, thereby providing the means to create English porcelain.

Among Cornish inventors, **Sir Goldsworthy Gurney**, born near Padstow in 1793, was responsible for the so-called Bude Light, a bright pre-electric light, that was used in lighthouses, theatres and the Houses of Parliament. Gurney's former home, Bude Castle in Bude, was built to prove that a house could be built on sand. It is now open to the public as a heritage centre.

A non-Cornish engineer who deserves a place among the heroes is the railway pioneer **Isambard Kingdom Brunel**, who not only drove the railway west from Paddington all the way to Penzance - kick-starting the first inklings of Cornish tourism - but designed and built the magnificent Royal Albert Bridge across the Tamar in 1859, providing a rail link between Devon and Cornwall. Among other famous Cornishmen is *The Cornishman*, the legendary express train, the last to use Brunel's broad gauge railway between London and Cornwall in 1892.

The present

John Nettles, the actor who personified *Bergerac*, was born in St Austell in 1943. Otherwise, most modern Cornish heroes are pioneers in the world of food, tourism and adventure.

The music-bizz entrepreneur **Tim Smit** pioneered the rediscovery of the Lost Gardens of Heligan, before securing £58m of Millenium Commission Lottery funding to create the Eden Project in a disused clay pit, thereby generating some £800m for the local economy. Some

FAMOUS AND INFAMOUS

Mary Bryant was a fisherman's daughter from Fowey, who was transported to Australia with the First Fleet in 1787. As a convicted thief, her reputation is hardly illustrious, but Mary was among a band of escapees - among them her convict husband and two children - who stole a boat and sailed through uncharted waters, all the way to Timor, a journey that took 66 days. Claiming to be shipwreck survivors they were taken in, but when their true identity was revealed Mary and her crew were sent on a voyage back to England, during which her family perished. A wave of public sympathy accompanied her trial in London and with the help of famous lawyer James Boswell, Mary was granted a pardon. Her story is told in the book *To Brave Every Journey* by Judith Cook.

Another colourful story is that of **Reverend Robert Stephen Hawker**, the eccentric vicar of Morwenstow, known not only for his unusual lifestyle (he is said to have dressed up as a mermaid, probably after a session on the opium pipe), but for his poem, *The Song of Western Men*, later adopted as Cornwall's county anthem. The rousing chorus, '*And shall Trelawny die*!', refers to the Cornish-born **Bishop Trelawny**, one of seven bishops accused of seditious libel by James II in the 17th century. Later appointed Bishop of Exeter, Trelawny is buried in his native Pelynt.

10... great figures of Cornish history

1 St Piran – the Irish missionary sailed over on a millstone to be anointed Cornwall's patron saint, p. 203

2 Richard Trevithick – unsung hero of the Industrial Revolution, credited with inventing the first steam locomotive, p. 193

3 Daphne du Maurier – the novelist's love affair with Cornwall fuelled her writing and coloured her stories, p. 135

4 Reverend Stephen Hawker – the eccentric Morwenstow cleric penned the Cornish anthem *The Sons of Western Men*, p 103

5 Thomas Treffry – his pioneering network of horse-worked tramways are still in use as part of the Par-to-Newquay Maritime Line, p. 150

6 William Cookworthy – he wasn't strictly Cornish, but where would Cornwall be without the discovery of china clay? p. 51

7 Humphry Davy – born in Penzance, the gifted chemist and gas man, invented the miner's safety lamp, p. 293

8 Arthur Quiller-Couch – under the pen-name Q, the Bodmin-born author wrote *Troy Town*, the town of the title modelled on Fowey, p. 47

9 Alfred Wallis – the St Ives fisherman turned inspirational primitive artist, took to painting aged 67, p. 46

10 William Bickford – founder of the Trevarno Estate near Helston, he saved countless lives with the invention of a safety fuse for igniting explosives, p. 50

years earlier, **Rick Stein**, who opened his first Padstow fish restaurant opened in the 1974, can be credited with putting Cornwall on the map through his series of food programmes, *Taste of the Sea* in 1995 and *Rick Stein's Seafood Odyssey* in 1999. Even Stein's Jack Russell terrier **Chalky**, who died aged 17 in 2007, has since had a Sharp's ale named after him. **Jamie Oliver** added to the county's culinary credentials when he opened charity-run job-creation scheme, **Fifteen Cornwall** in Watergate Bay in 2006.

The adventurers include intrepid explorer and travel writer **Robin Hanbury-Tennison**, the president and co-founder of Survival International, who lives in Cardinham. And **Dame Ellen MacArthur** crowned a long tradition of Cornish seafaring triumphs when she finished her record-beating round-the-world trip in Falmouth in 2005.

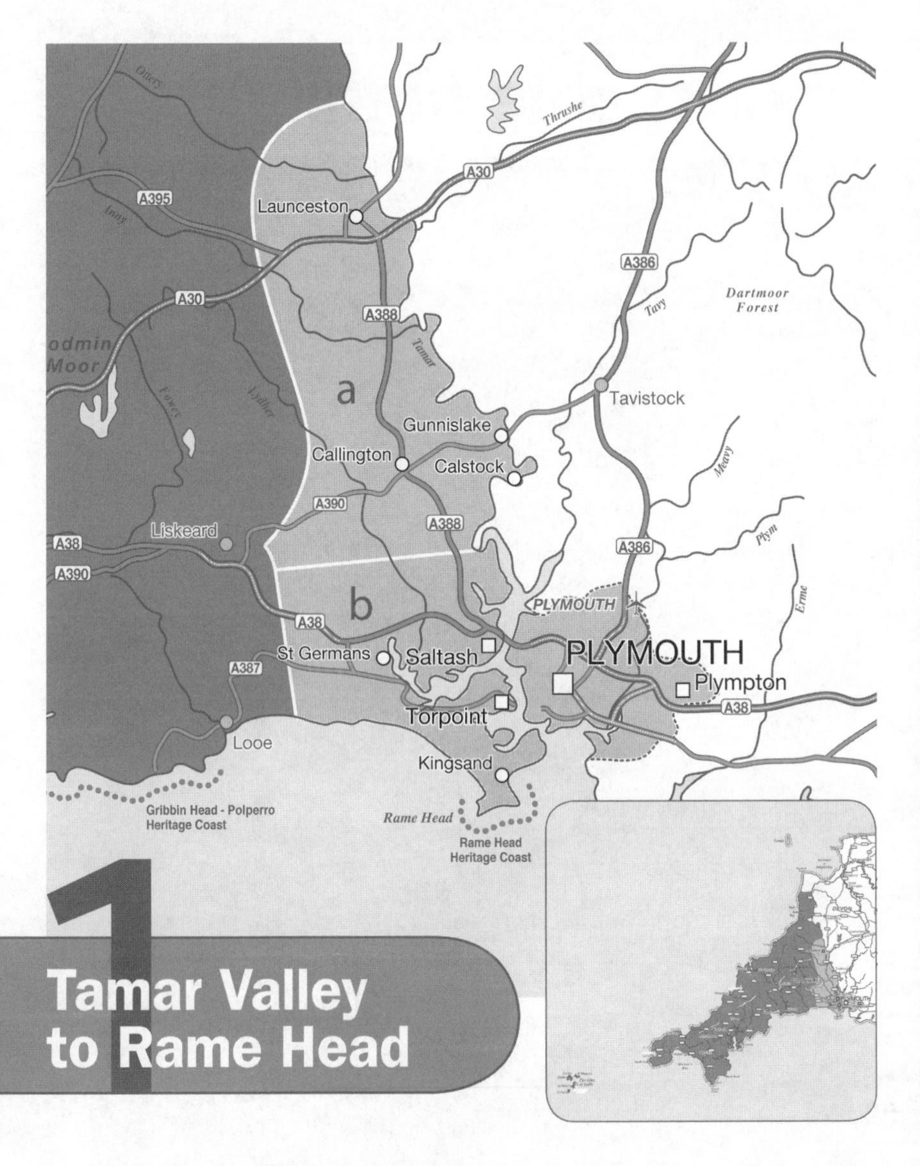

1 Tamar Valley to Rame Head

a. Upper Tamar Valley

b. Tamar Estuary to Rame Head

Unmissable highlights

01 Visit Cotehele House, a time-warped Tudor mansion with Tamar Valley views and enchanting gardens, p. 58

02 Take a boat trip from Calstock to Morwellham Quay, a journey upriver, a step back in time, p. 59

03 Nose around the Grade I listed state rooms and the Repton parkland of the Earl and Countess of St Germans' magical Port Eliot home, p. 67

04 Climb down to the yellow sands of the Whitsand Bay beach below Tregonhawke Cliff, p. 72

05 Marvel at what the locals call the 'Saltash bridges', road and railway side by side straddling the Tamar, between Devon and Cornwall, p. 72

06 Explore 865 acres of seaside parkland on the Mount Edgcumbe estate, p. 70

07 Grab a crab sandwich in the Rod and Line at Tideford, a traditional pub just off the A38, p. 76

08 See the rooftops of Cornwall's medieval capital from the shell-keep of Launceston Castle, p. 56

09 Walk to the top of Kit Hill for mining history, wild heathland and amazing views, p. 60

10 Enjoy tea and homemade cakes at The Old Boat Store in Cawsand, home to the curious Museum of Celebrity Leftovers, p. 76

TAMAR VALLEY TO RAME HEAD

The River Tamar has been recognised as Cornwall's county boundary since Saxon times. From its source, only 4 miles short of the Atlantic coast, it travels south, through steep gorged valleys all the way to Plymouth Sound, forming a neat, natural line between two counties. You want to beep the horn, as you motor over the river: Welcome to Cornwall, goodbye Devon.

Creep in by the back door, across the tiny medieval bridge at Gunnislake, or 20 miles downriver, sail across the estuary on one of the iconic Tamar bridges; rail, road or ferry, here lies Cornwall's most dramatic entrances.

At the river's upper reaches, the legacy of Tamar Valley's Victorian industry – the abandoned mines and mineral quays, the lime kilns, boatyards and over-grown engine-house chimneys – is now a key part of the Cornish Mining World Heritage Site. Some development of tourist centres is expected but hopefully not enough to disturb the tranquillity of this otherwise unspoiled corner of inner Cornwall.

Industry still thrives downriver, where the Tamar widens into a mighty urban estuary, lined with warships and naval dockyards. Beyond, on the Cornish side of Plymouth Sound, lies Rame Head's fist of headlands, the Forgotten Corner, the very tip of south-east Cornwall.

UPPER TAMAR VALLEY

Launceston, a mile from the Devon border, has guarded the entrance to Cornwall's Tamar Valley since the Normans built the castle just after 1066. The former medieval capital, *Dunheved*, is now a bustle of shops on a market square, and according to John Betjeman, has one of *'the most perfect collections of 18th century townhouses in Cornwall'*.

A few miles south, pick up the Tamar as it wanders south through an Area of Outstanding Natural Beauty, which spreads east and west from its green river banks up to Callington on the Cornish side, and to Tavistock in Devon. Follow the valley through dense forests of oak, hazel and willow to Gunnislake and the quays at Morwellham, Calstock and Cotehele. Hard to imagine now, but until the late 19th century, these were crowded, noisy mineral ports, sending out boat-loads of granite, copper and arsenic, sliding down-river to the sea.

West of the river, you can look down on it all, from the ghosts of old mines on the lofty Kit Hill. Like a chip of Dartmoor granite that's strayed into Cornwall, it stands at the Tamar Valley's highest point with views to die for. Explore the area below, on foot, by boat, by branch-line train, or all three in one day. As you will discover, the valley's once-poisonous industries are barely even a memory. Tranquil tidal waters, mud-flats and reed beds provide habitats for herons, waterfowl and kingfishers among an abundance of wildlife.

WHAT TO SEE AND DO

Launceston

From the A30, your route into the region is via **Launceston** (pronounced 'Lanson' by the locals), a proper Cornish town, confined within the remnants of medieval walls, and overlooked by an ancient motte-and-bailey castle perched atop a pudding-basin hillock. The original **Launceston Castle** was begun soon after the Norman Conquest in the 11th century, and was remodelled nearly 200 years later by Richard Earl of Cornwall, a sibling of Henry III. After Richard's death in 1272, his son Edmund shifted the Duchy's capital to Lostwithiel (see page 133) and the castle began a slow process of decay, although it was still in use as courts and jail until well into the 17th century. George Fox, founder of the Quakers was incarcerated in the north gatehouse in 1656.

All that remains today is the ruined keep set in a public garden, but it still has immense gravitas, and is worth the climb, up worn stone steps, for the views of the countryside beyond Launceston's slate rooftops, its red-brick Georgian buildings, and the granite tower of the ornate 16th-century **Church of St Mary Magdalene**. The sound of the Town Hall clock chiming every quarter of an hour, is one of the few things about Launceston that gives a sense of time moving on.

Around Launceston

Launceston is the beginning of the long-distance footpath, **the Tamar Valley Discovery Trail**, which picks up the river at the isolated Greystone Bridge, and follows it south all the

The ruins of Launceston Castle

way to the suburban edge of **Plymouth**, some 30 miles away. There are, however, less strenuous ways of seeing the Valley. Driving from Devon on the A390, you will cross the river at New Bridge at **Gunnislake**, in reality a very old packhorse bridge, built of moorland granite by Sir Piers Edgcumbe, Lord of Cotehele until 1539. Amazingly, no other road crossed the river between here and Plymouth until the Tamar Bridge was built in 1961 (see page 41).

LAUNCESTON CASTLE: Castle Lodge, Launceston PL15 7DR; ☎ 01566 772365; www.english-heritage.org.uk. Entry: adults £3.40, child £2.00; open daily mid-Mar to Nov, 10am–4/5/6pm depending on season.

Within deep valleys of dense broad-leaf woodland, Gunnislake and neighbouring **Calstock** are two sleepy villages. Calstock, on a no-through road to the river, is the prettier of the two, with a huddle of white-washed riverbank cottages, set one on top of the other, vaguely reminiscent of a Greek island village. Until the 1900s, its quays were the hub of intense industry; first in trading and shipping copper and, after the mining slump of the 1880s, papermills, boat-building and brick-making. There is still a boatyard here and, among the trees that surround the village, you can see the chimney stacks of well-preserved engine houses and the ruins of Danescombe paper mill.

Church of St Mary Magdalene at Launceston

Tamar Valley Line at Calstock Viaduct

The thing to see in Calstock, though, is the magnificent **Calstock Viaduct**. The 12-arch viaduct, which towers 120ft over the river, was built in 1907 to serve a short stretch of railway that extended an existing line from Plymouth to Bere Alston in Devon, over the Tamar to Calstock and on to Gunnislake.

TAMAR VALLEY LINE: Devon and Cornwall Rail Partnership; ☎ 01752 233094; www.trailsfromthetrack.com. Cheap day return: adults £4.80, children £2.40 (subject to change); trains approx. every two hours, in both directions.

The still-thriving **Tamar Valley Line** provides a great introduction to the area. The 14-mile journey, taking roughly 45 minutes, edges out of Plymouth via Devonport Docks, before crossing the River Tavy to the Bere Peninsular, and finally rattling over the viaduct into Cornwall. The scenery alone is worth the ride.

Trails from the Track (www.trailsfromthetrack.com) suggests a number of footpaths that can be covered in conjunction with the railway. A favourite is the walk through woodland from Calstock up to the National Trust's **Cotehele House**. If you don't have much time, then Cotehele is the thing to do around here. One of the most complete Tudor manor houses in the country, it was built by the powerful Edgcumbe family, *c.* 1500, on the site of a much older property, and is set in an enchanting valley garden, rolling down to the Tamar. The house was barely used beyond the 17th century, when the Edgcumbes moved to Rame Head, which explains its largely unaltered state.

Beyond the Great Hall, where lime-washed walls are hung with weaponry and armour, there are dark, unlit chambers furnished with tapestries, pewter, oak and brass; there is a remarkably original Tudor kitchen and, in the 15th century chapel, the *'oldest domestic pre-pendulum clock still in working order'*. Take warm clothing, the hall is unheated apart from an open fire, in fact the house has no electricity. Outside, beyond formal gardens and a medieval dovecote (with doves), you can see the distant Calstock Viaduct framed by a jungle of rich foliage. The views are even better from the three-sided Prospect Tower, an 18th-century folly, just behind the house.

COTEHELE HOUSE: St Dominick PL12 6TA; ☎ 01579 351346; www.nationaltrust.org.uk. Entry: adults £10, children £5; open daily, 10am to dusk for the gardens; from Mar to Nov, 11am–4.30pm for the house.

Horse and carriage at Morwellham Quay

A short walk downhill from the manor, **Cotehele Quay** (also National Trust), is an untouched relic of Tamar Valley industry, complete with restored sailing barge, the *Shamrock*. The 57ft vessel, *c.* 1899, is typical of the ketch-rigged barges that used to run minerals up and down the river. Alongside, the small **Quay Museum** (☎ 01579 350830, closed in winter) gives the full story and there's a tea room in one of the quay's stone and slate buildings. The *Shamrock* occasionally sets off on river voyages, and in the summer the **Calstock Ferry** (www.calstockferry.co.uk, 01822 833331) runs a regular boat service between Cotehele Quay and Calstock.

A few miles up-river, on the Devon side, **Morwellham Quay** presents a theatrical re-enacment of life in the Tamar Valley. What was once the busiest port in England, has been rescued from dereliction and reborn as a themed museum and visitor centre with a Victorian tea room, designed to whisk you back to the 1800s. Actors in costume wander Morwellham's 200 acres, where you can see overcrowded miners cottages and horse and carriages clattering over quays, where there's a water wheel and a restored ship. There are costumes available if you fancy dressing up, but there is a serious side to the pageantry: an underground rail tour of a copper mine gives some idea of the harsh conditions of Morwellham's 19th-century workers.

MORWELLHAM QUAY: Near Tavistock PL19 8JL; ☎ 01822 832766; www.morwellham-quay.co.uk. Adults £7.95, children £4.95; open daily 10am–4/5.30pm (depending on season).

On the river

In summer there are numerous opportunities to get out on the river including regular ferries between Calstock and Cotehele. From Plymouth's Barbican Quay, **Sound Cruising** does regular trips upriver to Calstock and Morwellham Quay (☎ 01752 408590, www.soundcruising.com). For a more peaceful riverboat experience, paddle your own canoe through **Canoe Tamar**. Trips are timed to travel with the tide, and the price includes transport to the starting point, safety briefings and buoyancy aides. Paddling the route between

CANOE TAMAR: Dartmoor Outdoor Company, Gulworthy PL19 8JE; ☎ 01822 833409/ 0845 4301208; www.canoetamar.co.uk. Entry: Adults £25, under-18s £21 (under-5s, free); boats available from July to Sept, subject to tides and conditions.

Morwellham and Cotehele quays, this is a wonderful way to explore the woods and wildlife of this peaceful 3-mile stretch of the water.

Callington and Kit Hill

To the east of the river, **Callington** is a little town, made less ordinary by its colourful **Mural Trail** (☎ 01579 384039; www.callington.uk.net). Around 14 of the town's buildings have been embellished with murals by a mix of local, amateur and professional artists, all celebrating the area's heritage, landscape and industry.

To the north of the town, about 1,000ft above sea level, **Kit Hill** offers some of the best views in Cornwall – on a clear day stretching all the way to Plymouth Sound and Eddystone lighthouse, 37 miles away. In 1985, Kit Hill was given to the people by the Duchy of Cornwall to celebrate the birth of Prince William, and offers 400 acres of walks on wild heath, among heathers, grasses and bilberry, riddled with ancient burial mounds. At its summit, the 80ft chimney stack of **South Kit Hill mine**, built in 1858, is a prominent local landmark. There's a campsite and café at Compton Park on the southern side of the hill.

Wet weather

Just over the Devon border, the **Dingles Fairground Heritage Centre** is home to the National Fairground Collection, all vintage rides and vivid colour, housed undercover in a warehouse-style building 7 miles east of Launceston. Highlights include a late 19th-century steam-driven 'gallopers' (better known as a merry-go-round), and the huge Victorian 'Rodeo Switchback', thought to be the oldest surviving fairground ride in the country. You can also try out a 1930s Noah's Ark, an original 1940s dodgem track furnished with 1970s cars and an arcade of 1950s penny-slot machines, adapted for modern use.

DINGLES FAIRGROUND HERITAGE CENTRE: Milford, Lifton PL16 0AT; ☎ 01566 783 425; www.fairground-heritage.org.uk. Entry: adults £7, child/senior £5; open mid-Mar to end Oct, Thurs-Mon 10am-5pm (all week during school holidays).

Dingles Fairground Heritage Centre

LAWRENCE HOUSE MUSEUM: 9 Castle Street, Launceston PL15 8BA; ☎ 01566 773277; www.lawrencehousemuseum.org.uk. Admission free; open Easter to end Oct, Mon–Fri, 10.30am–4.30 pm.

In Launceston, the **Lawrence House Museum** has exhibits presented in a series of elegant rooms in a handsome Georgian townhouse built in 1753, including a Victorian kitchen and the Launceston Room. The latter is packed with local history artefacts – including a model of the town during its castle years, *c.* 1530. Children can play in the Toy Room with antique teddies and vintage Sindy.

What to do with children

Tamar Valley Donkey Park, near Gunnislake, is home to some 30 retired and rescued donkeys, including former Clovelly veteran, Copper, Grizelda and son Beamish (both found running wild on Bodmin Moor) and young Treacle. Kids can meet the donkeys, take a ride on Happy or Snubs and romp around in an indoor playbarn on wet days.

TAMAR VALLEY DONKEY PARK: St Anne's Chapel, Gunnislake PL18 9HW; ☎ 01822 834072; www.donkeypark.com. Entry £6.95 (under-2s, free); Easter to Sept, daily, 10am-5pm; Oct, Thurs - Sun; winter, weekends and holidays, 10.30-4pm.

For more animal magic, head for the **Tamar Otter and Wildlife Centre**. Originally founded as a breeding centre for otters, at the time endangered, the centre is now home to a variety of creatures - mainly British short-claw otters, as well as fallow deer, owls, peacocks and, strangely, wallabies. There are nature trails through the wildlife park and a waterfall. Get there for 12pm or 3pm to see the otters at feeding time.

TAMAR OTTER WILDLIFE CENTRE: North Petherwin, Near Launceston PL15 8GW; ☎ 01566 785646; www.tamarotters.co.uk. Entry: adults £7.00, children £4.00; open daily from Good Friday to end of Oct, 10.30am–6.00pm.

From Launceston to Newmills, trundle through the Kensey Valley on the narrow-gauge **Launceston Steam Railway**. Trains hauled by Victorian 'Quarry Hunslet' steam engines on 2.5 miles of privately owned track first opened in 1983. The 5-mile round trip takes about 40 minutes, or you can make a day of it (unlimited travel on one all-day ticket), stopping in the valley en route for picnics or walks. Trains run roughly every 50 minutes. At Launceston there's a café and booking office built for the first Ideal Home exhibition in 1919.

LAUNCESTON STEAM RAILWAY: St Thomas Road, Launceston PL15 8DA; ☎ 01566 775665; www.launcestonsr.co.uk; Adult rtrn £8.75, child rtrn £5.75 (under-3s free), dogs 50p; open Easter, and then from mid-May to mid-Sept, daily from 10.30am, except Sat.

At Gulworthy, on the Devon side of the Tamar, older, braver kids (and adults) can try a bit of **Tree Surfing** (www.treesurfers.co.uk, 01822 833409). A trail of rope courses, ladders, bridges and zip wires, takes woodland surfers on high-adrenaline tours through the treetops above the river. Each course takes around 2-3 hours and cost £21 per child (the minimum age is 8). Compulsory safety harnesses are included.

Entertainment

Special events

The bi-annual **Cornwall and Devon Countryman's Fair** (www.countrymansfair.co.uk; August 2012) at Werrington Park near Launceston is one the biggest events in the West Country. The fund-raising charity fair includes equestrian ring events, lurcher racing, clay pigeon shooting and thousands of people in waxed jackets and green wellies. On Midsummer's Eve, the **Old Cornwall Society** continues a tradition (begun in 1929) of lighting a bonfire on top of Kit Hill. **Morwellham Quay** (☎ 01822 832766; www.morwellham-quay.co.uk) hosts a number of annual events including a vintage car rally in May and a popular Folk Festival in August.

The best... PLACES TO STAY

FARMSTAY

Trevadlock Farm

Trevadlock, Congdon Shop, Launceston PL15 7PW
☎ 01566 782239
www.trevadlock.co.uk

One of 11 farms on the Trebartha Estate on the western edge of Bodmin Moor, Trevadlock has 450 acres of sheep and dairy. Guests get simple, country-style rooms with a rural views, Cornish cream teas and a hearty farmhouse breakfast.

Price: from £70–£75 for a double per night.

Cadson Manor Farm

Callington PL17 7HW
☎ 01579 383969
www.cadsonmanor.co.uk

A granite-pillared country house with views over a fishing lake to the iron-age fort at Cadson Bury. There are gardens, walks through the farm's 200 acres to nearby River Lynher, three lovely rooms with five-star comforts, Wi-Fi and free-range farm eggs for breakfast. Self-catering also available.

Price: B&B £98 per double per night.

Old Solomon's Farm

Latchley, Gunnislake PL18 9AX
☎ 01822 833242
www.oldsolomonsfarm.co.uk

A proper Cornish farmhouse with low beams, blue china on the dresser and a penchant for big breakfasts. There are three double rooms, but only one set of guests at a time (ideal for families or groups). Self-catering is offered in a barn-like converted Apple Loft.

Price: from £64 per double per night.

B&B

Hornacott B&B

South Petherwin, Launceston PL15 7LH
☎ 01566 782461
www.hornacott.co.uk

Tucked into a wooded corner of the River Inny Valley, this 18th-century slate-hung home, offers one lovely self-contained guest suite, with its own sitting room. There's an extra single room available if needed.

Price: £80 per double per night.

Lower House

Callington PL17 7AN
☎ 01579 383491
www.lower-house.com

With names like 'Untitled' and 'Work in Progress', there is one double, two family and one single room in this handsomely restored Georgian townhouse in Callington. You get king-size oak beds and pale but interesting décor.

Price: from £70 per double per night.

SELF-CATERING

Danescombe Mine

Calstock
☎ 01628 825920
www.landmarktrust.org.uk

The former engine house of the 1820s Cotehele Consols' copper and arsenic mine, repaired and converted by the Landmark Trust. Closed since 1900, it used to contain a rotary beam engine, now it sleeps four in two bedrooms, one right at the top of the stone tower.

Price: from £170 (midweek break) to £1,287 (high-season week).

The best... FOOD AND DRINK

One of the most traditional farming communities in Cornwall, market gardens and orchards remain part of the Tamar landscape, the steep south-facing slopes of the valley being perfect for growing soft fruit. Local cooperative, Tamar Grow Local, based in Calstock (www.tamargrowlocal.org), promotes opportunities to grow and market local produce, and runs the occasional event. Launceston, Callington and Tavistock remain true to their roots as traditional market towns with good local food shops.

Staying in

Launceston's **Butter Market** (basically a farmers' market) takes place on the first Saturday of the month in the town square. Also in Launceston, **Philip Warren & Son** on Westgate Street (☎ 01566 772089; www.philipwarrenbutchers.co.uk) is widely thought to be the best butcher in Cornwall, selling only 'true Cornish' and farm-direct meats, naturally raised on Bodmin Moor, and traditionally hung on the bone. From Warrens, you can also buy rare-breed pork, and its own white pudding and farmhouse sausages, made to an 18th-century recipe. Warrens work closely with **Edwards Fishmongers** (☎ 01566 777297; www.edwardsfishmongers.co.uk).

There's a farmers' market in Callington's Town Hall on the second and fourth Friday of each month (9am–1pm). For farm shops, look for **Dupath Farm**, near Callington (☎ 01579 382197; www.dupathfarm.co.uk) for lamb and beef; **Sleepy Hollow Farm Shop and Café** at Harrowbarrow, Callington (☎ 01579 351010; www.sleepyhollowfarm.co.uk), open daily 8am-5pm (opens 9am on Sunday). **Tavistock Farmers' Market** (www.tavistockfarmersmarket.com), the best in the south-west, is held in Bedford Square on the fourth Saturday of the month.

Drinking

For Tamar Valley views it's hard to beat the quaintly named **Who'd Have Thought It Inn** at St Dominick (☎ 01579 350214; www.whodhavethoughtitinn.co.uk), an atmospheric St Austell Brewery pub, known for good food. In Launceston, you can get a pint of St Austell's at **The White Horse Inn** on Newport Square (☎ 01566 772084), a 17th-century town-centre pub which has live music at the weekends.

The Tamar Valley Line Rail Trail (see www.railaletrail.com) suggests the **Boot Inn** at Calstock (☎ 01822 834866) which serves Bass, Fullers and London Pride, or the nearby **Tamar Inn** on the Quay (☎ 01822 832487; www.tamarinn.co.uk) which offers a selection of real ales, occasional live bands and outdoor tables right by the Tamar.

For peaceful Tamar views, head for Gunnislake's 17th century inn the **Rising Sun** (01822 832201, www.rising-sun-inn.co.uk), or slip down to the middle-of-nowhere freehouse, the **Royal Inn** at Horsebridge (01822 870214, www.royalinn.co.uk).

EATING OUT

RESTAURANT

Langmans

3 Church Street, Callington Pl17 7RE
☎ 01579 384933
www.langmansrestaurant.co.uk

A consistent winner in the Cornish Tourism Awards, chef Anton Buttery's restaurant has two AA rosettes. Modern British dishes using fresh local produce are the benchmarks of his beautifully presented food, which includes a six-course tasting menu (£35 per person). Open Thurs to Sat.

The Horn of Plenty

Gulworthy, Tavistock PL19 8JD
☎ 01822 832528
www.thehornofplenty.co.uk

On the Devon side of the Tamar, just a few minutes drive from Gunnislake, this up-market hotel restaurant has dreamy views of the valley, two AA rosettes and a deserved reputation for excellent food and service. Three-course dinner costs £49.50; two-course lunch costs £19.50.

GASTRO PUB

The Springer Spaniel

Treburley, Launceston PL15 9NS
☎ 01579 370424
www.thespringerspaniel.org.uk

Just off the A30, this hospitable eating house combines Cornish ales, fine wines and delicious food cooked by a Stein-trained chef. The menu includes organic lamb reared on the owner's own farm (which also offers B&B in a 17th-century farmhouse nearby). Great for winter comfort food and Sunday lunch. Main courses from £8.75.

Who'd Have Thought It Inn

St Dominic, Saltash PL12 6TG
☎ 01579 350214
www.whodhavethoughtitinn.co.uk

A great pub with great views and award-winning food. The meaty menu includes Honeycurl sausages, rack of lamb, steaks and fish dishes, with most ingredients sourced from within 10 miles. The inn also grows its own salads, greens and herbs and raises its own pigs. Main courses from £11.50.

CAFÉ

Food@cowslip

Newlands Farm, St Stephens, Launceston PL15 8JX; ☎ 01566 772654
www.cowslipworkshops.co.uk

Farmhouse food cooked on an Aga and served in the cafe of a family-run organic farm. Open daily until 5pm, plus three-course Sunday lunches (£21.50).

TEA ROOM

Louis Tea Rooms

Kit Hill, Callington, Cornwall PL17 8AX
☎ 01579 389223
www.comptonpark.co.uk

At the entrance to Kit Hill, 800ft up with far-reaching views of the Tamar Valley. All the usual tea room fare, plus hot dishes and snacks (from £3.00). Open daily during the summer.

Visitor Information

Tourist information centre: Launceston Tourist Information Centre, Market House Arcade, Market Street, Launceston PL15 8EP. ☎ 01566 772321.

Hospitals with A&E: Launceston General Hospital, Link Road, Launceston PL15 9JD, ☎ 01566 765650 (for minor injuries); Derriford Hospital, Brest Road, Derriford, Plymouth PL6 5AA, ☎ 0845 1558155 for A&E.

Doctors: Gunnislake Health Centre, The Orchard, Gunnislake PL18 9JZ, ☎ 01822 832641; Callington Health Centre, Haye Road, Callington PL17 7AW, 01579 382666.

Pharmacies: Boots, 28, Broad Street, Launceston PL15 8AE, ☎ 01566 772085; Lloyds Pharmacy, 17–18, Fore Street, Callington PL17 7AE, ☎ 01579 383106.

Police station: Launceston Police Station, Moorland Road, Launceston PL15 7HY.

Supermarkets: Tesco, Tailstocks Road, Launceston PL15 9HG, ☎ 845 6779403; Somerfield Stores, 12–14, Broad Street, Launceston PL15 8ER, ☎ 01566 773139.

Parking: Callington: Back Lane, New Road North, New Road South, Pollard Road; Calstock: Calstock Quay, Calstock Railway Yard; Launceston: Pannier Market shopper car park, Race Hill.

Internet access: Fowey Library, Passage Lane (Tues, Thurs, Fri and Sat morning).

Boat hire: Calstock Boatyard, Lower Kelly Calstock PL18 9RY, ☎ 01822 835968, www.imecalstockboatyard.co.uk.

ATMs: Lloyds TSB (Callington) 13, Fore Street PL17 7AF; HSBC (Launceston) 18 Broad Street. PL15 8AQ.

Local taxis: Callington Cars ☎ 01579 383624; Pridham's private hire, Gunnislake, ☎ 01822 832454; Launceston Taxis ☎ 01566 785364.

TAMAR ESTUARY TO RAME HEAD

This is the first point of entry for A38 travellers - and what an entrance. The view of the two bridges that span the estuary between Plymouth and Saltash is Britain's answer to San Francisco's Golden Gate - especially when photographed, as they often are, shrouded in an early morning river mist. To the south, you can cross the Tamar on the chain ferries that chug back and forth between Devonport and Torpoint, where fleets of Royal Navy ships slip in and out of Plymouth Sound.

Bridges and battle ships aside, neither Torpoint nor Saltash make the most auspicious of first impressions; both are drive-through kind of places with little to keep you hanging around. But beyond the urban fringes of these two gateway towns, the countryside is instantly captivating, all rounded hills and wooded slopes wrapped around the creeks and waterways where the Lynher and Tiddy rivers meet the Tamar. Between the English Channel and Plymouth Sound, the tiny Rame Peninsula, the so-called 'Forgotten Corner', is trimmed with beaches, studded with Napoleonic forts and seaside smuggling haunts.

Among the highlights of the area are the legacies of three families: the Carews of Antony House, the Edgcumbes of Mount Edgcumbe, and the Eliots, the Earls of Port Eliot in historic St Germans. The influence of these medieval families, two of them still in residence, has had a profound impact on the landscapes and villages of the region.

WHAT TO SEE AND DO

Crossing the Tamar

Before the **Tamar toll bridge** was opened in 1961, the only way across the estuary was by train or car ferry, thus its opening was a massive fillip for Cornish tourism. These days most drivers use the faster A30, but the Saltash route is worth a detour, or a daytrip, just for the sheer spectacle. There's a free pedestrian walkway on the suspension bridge, affording side-on views of trains rattling across Brunel's famous **Royal Albert Bridge**. For overhead views of the bridges' undercarriages, walk along the quays of Saltash waterside below or grab a pint at the eye-catching **Union Inn**, painted all-over with a Union Jack. The £1.50 standard toll to cross the road bridge is only payable on the way out of Cornwall.

Union Jack mural at the Union Inn beneath Royal Albert Bridge

Tamar Crossings, Torpoint chain ferries from Devonport cross the part of the river they call Hamoaze, sailing just shy of Devonport Docks, the largest Naval base in Europe. The route's three recently upgraded 73-car ferries, mean it is deemed the busiest 'estuarial' car ferry crossing in the UK, carrying nearly two million vehicles a year. Expect queues at peak times and high season.

TAMAR CROSSINGS: ☎ 01752 361577 (bridge), ☎ 01752 812233 (ferry); www.tamarcrossings.org.uk. Toll/ticket, £1..50 (payable one way only); ferries run every 10 minutes (at peak times), 24 hours a day every day of the year.

Railing across the Royal Albert

Isambard Kingdom Brunel's tour de force, the majestic Royal Albert Bridge, is unique in bridges, being the only one of its type to carry main line trains. A bow-string suspension bridge, opened in 1859 - and celebrated its 150th anniversary in 2009 - it's characterised by two wrought iron tubular arches, with a railway track slung between them. Supported on hefty granite piers, the bridge stands 100ft above the river, allowing ships to pass underneath, and is testament to the genius of Brunel who pioneered the Great Western or, as it was then known, the Cornish Railway. As the bridge approaches Saltash station on the western bank of the Tamar, it sweeps into a dramatic curve - the most photographed view of this iconic Victorian crossing. All mainline trains, travelling between Paddington to Penzance cross the 1,100ft long Albert Bridge.

Historic estates

Just off the A38, west of Saltash, lies **St Germans**, a pretty village of stone cottages clustered around the 1,000-acre **Port Eliot Estate**, at the point where the Lynher and Tiddy meet. Dominating the village are the walls of Port Eliot itself; the castellated Grade I listed mansion, built on the site of a former monastery, sits just behind the 12th-century church - Cornwall's former cathedral. Port Eliot is well known for its annual Lit Fest, and prior to that a series of Elephant Fair festivals, but in March 2008, the house opened to the public for the first time in 450 years. For three months, from spring to early summer, you can wander around the state rooms, as well 100 acres of Humphrey Repton parkland (also Grade I listed) rolling down to the banks of the Lynher. In a courtyard of converted Georgian stables designed by Sir John Soane, there is a tea room (12.30 - 5pm) serving home-made cakes and lunches.

PORT ELIOT; St Germans, Saltash PL12 5ND; ☎ 01503 230211; www.porteliot.co.uk. Entry: adults £7, children free (for house and grounds); open 2-6pm daily (except Fridays) from approx 10 Mar to mid-Jun, and again in late Jun to early Jul.

Port Eliot

Loved, lived-in and deliciously eccentric, it's not your usual stately home, and visiting Port Eliot feels a little like a personal invitation to peek into the lives of Peregrine Eliot, the rock-and-roll Earl of St Germans and his wife Catherine.

Port Eliot is shabby chic at its finest: a glory of gilt, damask and grandeur, but dimly lit and furnished with threadbare silks, exhausted sofas and a patina of damp. The roof, which covers half an acre, has never been watertight in living memory. But that's partly what makes the house so enchanting. In what other stately home would you find a Harley Davidson propped up against an unfinished panoramic mural by the late artist, Robert Lenkiewicz, on a rug made for a Brighton Pavilion dome in a circular room designed in 1805 by Sir John Soane? In the centre of this round room, a disco glitter ball dangles from a 19th-century French crystal chandelier. At its entrance, original Joshua Reynolds portraits – 14 of them in all – hang on 16th-century walls embellished with faded Georgian wallpaper.

Visitors are confined to the principal areas of this great house which, the guide will tell you, has 120 rooms, 11 staircases, 15 back doors and 82 chimneys; the latter are still very much in use, as there are only nine radiators.

Grand interior of Port Eliot

LOCAL KNOWLEDGE

Catherine St Germans is the chatelaine of Port Eliot, an ancient stately home in St Germans. She and her husband, Peregrine, the 10th Earl, opened their magnificently shabby home to the public for the first time in 2008. Catherine also runs the Port Eliot Lit Fest which takes place on the estate in July.

Favourite restaurant: Trawlers on the Quay in East Looe, where you can eat great seafood sitting right on the quayside, yards away from Rick Stein's favourite fish market. As you eat, you can watch the boats come in. Proprietors Nick and Mark will personally wrap you in a rug if the evening turns nippy.

Favourite beach: The cliff road along Whitsand Bay to Rame Head is spectacular and there are beautiful sandy beaches all the way along. One of the best is immediately beneath Tregantle Fort – don't be alarmed by the firing range, it's only in use when the red flag's flying. The next beach at Sharrow Cliff is excellent and has steps down to it.

Favourite café: The View near Rame Head. Set high on the cliffs, it was once a café but is now a stylish restaurant. Chef Matt is also a keen surfer, and his seafood is superb. On a clear day you can see as far as the Lizard. Not to be missed.

Favourite pub: The Rod and Line in Tideford has got everything you want in a good pub: roaring fire, cosy bar, fabulous landlord, fresh local seafood and the world's best crab sandwiches.

Favourite shop: Watts Trading in Lostwithiel is a fabulously quirky little shop. An 'organic emporium', they sell finely crafted everyday goods. You will find the most beautifully made household brushes of every size, as well as feather dusters and wicker baskets.

Secret tip for lunch: Get a takeaway picnic and drive up onto Bodmin Moor and eat by the side of Golitha Falls. The falls are reached by a footpath through a beautiful wood on the Fowey River – all dappled light, rare moss and the constant sound of rushing water.

Favourite visitor attraction: The Monkey Sanctuary near Looe. It's home to Woolly monkeys and rescued ex-pet Capuchins. This is a world class sanctuary tucked away in an unlikely setting.

One imagines there might have been some rivalry between the Eliots and the Carews, residents of neighbouring **Antony House**, on the River Lynher just west of Torpoint. This house too has parkland designed by Humphrey Repton, and Reynolds on the walls. One of the few National Trust properties still inhabited by the owners, Antony has been in the same family for 600 years. The current house, built between 1711 and 1721 for William Carew, is a magnificent Palladian mansion, clad in Pentewan stone, and straight out of a Jane Austen novel (at the time of writing, the house was in use as a film set for *Alice in Wonderland*). The interior features Dutch oak panelling and original 18th-century furniture. The gardens, still under the ownership of the resident Carew-Pole family, feature a knot garden and a national collection of lilies.

ANTONY HOUSE: Torpoint PL11 2QA; ☎ 01752 812 191; www.nationaltrust.org.uk. Entry: adults £7.90, children, £5; house and garden open Mar to Oct, Tues-Thurs and Sun from end of May, 1pm-5pm.

MOUNT EDGCUMBE COUNTRY PARK: Cremyll, Torpoint PL10 1HZ; ☎ 01752 822236; www.mountedgcumbe.gov.uk. Entry: adults £7.50, children £3.75 (under-5s free; Earls Garden only, £2.50; open 1 Apr to 30 Sept; free entry to park: (open all year).

If one-upmanship truly existed between the Tamar estuary's rival families, then the Edgcumbes would have won hands down on location. On its own Rame Head peninsular, at the mouth of the Tamar, **Mount Edgcumbe**'s fabulous parkland is surrounded by water.

The original 16th-century mansion was gutted by fire during the Second World War bombing raids that destroyed much of Plymouth. It was restored when the Earls of Mount Edgcumbe sold the house and its 865 acres to Cornwall County and Plymouth City councils in 1971; but though it's open to the public in the summer, the parkland and gardens are the star of the show. There is a fee to see the 18th-century Grade I listed Earl's gardens, but it's free to wander around the formal gardens (complete with Orangery tea room) and the vast seaside estate, the earliest landscaped park in Cornwall, stretching all the way to **Rame Head**. Miles of footpaths meander through woodland, over cliff-top meadows, often with spectacular views of Drake's Island and Plymouth Sound.

Open all year round, the park is dotted with romantic ruins, forts, follies and deer. In 1515 Sir Piers Edgcumbe was given permission by King Henry VIII to keep them, and they still roam the peninsula.

You can reach Mount Edgcumbe by road (on the B3427) but more fun is the **Cremyll Ferry**, operated by **Tamar Cruising**, the little foot ferry – believed to have been in continuous operation since 1204 – which crosses the estuary between Stonehouse in Plymouth and Mount Edgcumbe Quay.

TAMAR CRUISING (AND THE CREMYLL FERRY): Cremyll Quay, Cremyll, Near Torpoint PL10 1HX; ☎ 01752 822 105; www.tamarcruising.com. Tickets: adults £1.20, children 60p; runs daily,1 Apr - 30 Sept, 6.45am-8.45pm/9.45pm (Mon-Fri), 8am-9.45pm (Sat), 9am-9.15pm (Sun).

An alternative is to approach the estate on foot, taking the South West Coast Path which loops around Cawsand Bay from

Tamar Cruising boat trip

Rame Head, via **Kingsand and Cawsand**. This is what they call 'the Forgotten Corner', not exactly forgotten, but out on a limb, right at the end of Rame's mis-shaped peninsular, lying between **Whitsand Bay** and the Tamar Estuary. The peninsula is lined with Napoleonic forts, built to protect Plymouth Sound from the French and Spanish. One of the most prominent, **Polhawn Fort**, is an up-market wedding venue. You will pass it on the way to Rame Head, the very tip of south-east Cornwall. Where the road meets the footpath, there is a little 11th-century church, with no electricity and one of the last remaining hand-pumped organs.

Tucked into a bay, beyond **Penlee Point**, Kingsand and Cawsand is actually one place; the twin names being a leftover from the days when the county border ran through the village: Kingsand, on the Devon side and Cawsand on the other. It's a cute, little fishing-cum-sailing village with a history of smuggling, colour-washed houses overlooking a baby beach and splendid views of Plymouth Sound.

CELEBRITY CONNECTIONS

It all started with **David Bailey's** sandwich. After lunching at the Old Boat Store café in Cawsand, the famous photographer left a bit of crust on his plate – and café owners Michael and Francesca Bennett decided to keep it as a souvenir. Thus, the **Museum of Celebrity Leftovers** was born. And if nothing else this gallery of scraps, each leftover displayed under a tiny glass dome, shows just how many celebs find their way to Cornwall's Forgotten Corner.

Comedian **Hugh Dennis**'s contribution is a piece of egg shell; TV newsreader **Jan Leaming** left a single blackcurrant. The smallest exhibit, is actor **John Woodvine's** croissant crumb. The prize exhibit? A morsel of cheese and tomato pesto toastie left by singer **Pete Doherty**. *'It's just a bit of fun really,'* says Francesa. *'Only one in 100 people don't get the joke.'*

SOUND CRUISING: Plymouth PL9 9WX; ☎ 01752 408590; www.soundcruising.com. Tickets: adults from £6.25 return, children £3 (depending on trip); various cruises available from Apr to Oct.

On the river

Explore this spectacular marine and river landscape, on the many harbour cruise vessels that operate around the Tamar Estuary. **Sound Cruising** does a Dockyards and Warships cruise, taking in Plymouth Hoe, Mount Edgcumbe, the ships of Devonport's Naval Dockyard and the Saltash bridges.

Beaches

By a mile (or four to be precise), the finest are on **Whitsand Bay,** the best bits being the continuous line of sand at **Freathy** and **Tregonhawke**. Here you'll find a bit of everything: fine sand, rock-pools, safe bathing (as long as you don't venture too far out) and two cafés, the Cliff Top café up top and the Eddystone Café on the beach. The downsides are the danger area at the Tregantle Fort end (often closed off due to a military firing range), and the steep path that drops down to the beach from a high clifftop road (where there is very little parking). But as a result, Whitsands rarely gets as crowded as it might.

There are more steep paths down to **Portwrinkle** at **Crafthole** at the neck of the peninsula, where there are two sand-and-shale beaches, often with decent surf (particularly at **Finnygook** to the east of the bay). For easier access, head for **Downderry** and **Seaton**. The nicer of the two is Downderry, but both have parking and facilities.

All ship-shape on the Scylla Reef

The sunken ship, *HMS Scylla*, lying half a mile off Whitsand Bay, is no ordinary wreck. The former Royal Navy frigate was deliberately scuttled in 2004 to create Europe's first artificial reef. Naturalist David Bellamy set the charges that sent *HMS Scylla* to her final resting place on the seabed.

Launched in 1968, *HMS Scylla* was the last warship built in Devonport; she made news in 1975 when she collided with the Torpoint ferry. Decommissioned, aged 25, the 2,500-tonne ship had been idling in Portsmouth for a decade when she was bought by the National Marine Aquarium to serve a new life as an ocean reef.

The idea behind the £1m project was to encourage sea life and provide a destination for divers. The project also serves as a scientific study of the sub-marine structure's metamorphosis into a living reef. According to David Bellamy, hundreds of species would have moved in within a week. Now one of the UK's most popular dives, the ships lies virtually upright, listing slightly to starboard. Divers report seeing mussels, anemones, sponges, spiny starfish, sea scorpions and spider crabs in the rusting hulk.

Wet weather

The best bet is to head into Plymouth. Find your way to the **National Marine Aquarium** in the Coxside area, close to the city's Elizabethan harbour, the Barbican.

If you are passing through Saltash on the way, take a look at **Elliott's Store** on Lower Fore Street. The time-warped corner shop, run by the Elliott family since 1902, was turned into a curious little museum when the last Mr Elliott died in 1972, leaving the property and its contents to the Tamar Protection Society on condition that the shop and its contents would be preserved. Stocked with shelves of bygone groceries and period packaging, the shop evokes a nostalgic sense of post-war domestic life.

NATIONAL MARINE AQUARIUM: Rope Walk, Coxside, Plymouth PL4 0LF; ☎ 01752 600 301; www.national-aquarium.co.uk. Entry: adults £11.50, children £7 (under-4s free); open daily 10am–5pm/6pm depending on season, all year round.

ELLIOTT'S STORE: 27 Lower Fore Street, Saltash PL12 6JQ; ☎ 01752 843388/ 07767 444816; www.tamarprotectionsociety.org.uk. Entry: adults £1, children 50p. Open Easter to end of Oct, Wed (2pm-4pm) and Sat (10am-12pm).

What to do with children

During the summer holidays, get lost in the **Amazing Cornish Maize Maze** on Smeaton Farm near Saltash. Created by amazing maze designer Adrian Fisher, it's different each year, and always themed (2008 was the year of the Maze Raiders, ancient civilisation maze; 2011 was the Bee a Hero maze - all about bees, pollination and searching for flowers and nectar). The farm also offers tractor and trailer rides, bouncy castle, sandpit, bale tower, café, shop and picnic area.). And you can stay the night in the farmhouse B&B.

AMAZING CORNISH MAIZE MAZE: Smeaton Farm, Pillaton, Saltash PL12 6RZ; ☎ 01579 351833; www.amazingcornishmaizemaze.co.uk. Entry: adults £5.50, children £4 (under 3s, free), family of 4, £16. Open daily, mid-July to early Sept, 10.30am–5pm.

Aerial view of the Amazing Cornish Maize Maze

The best... PLACES TO STAY

BOUTIQUE

Westcroft Guest House

Market Street., Kingsand PL10 1NE
☎ 01752 823216
www.westcroftguesthouse.co.uk

This modernised 18th-century coaching inn, on the seafront at Kingsand, offers three gorgeous rooms, including a four-poster suite and an entire attic floor with antique French bed and a star-gazing bathtub. Great bathrooms, and thoughtful extras such as i-pod docks, goose-down duvets and flexible breakfast times. Evening meals by arrangement.

Price: from £90 for a double.

FARMSTAY

Lantallack Farm

Landrake, Saltash PL12 5AE
☎ 01752 851281
www.lantallack.co.uk

A Georgian farmhouse with two comfortable rooms furnished with big beds, pretty rural views and a solar-heated pool. A country breakfast, served in or out, includes local organic sausages and the farms' own eggs. Painting courses also available.

Price: from £100 for a double.

Buttervilla Farm

Polbathic, St Germans PL11 3EY
☎ 01503 230315
www.buttervilla.com

In 15 acres of countryside, this is an eco-friendly, organic farm B&B with knobs on. The luxury rooms have solar-heated power showers and free Wi-Fi, and the food features homemade bread and home-grown produce.

Price: B&B from £85 for a double (Apr-Oct).

B&B

Bulland House

Antony, Torpoint, Cornwall PL11 2PE
☎ 01752 813823

This whitewashed farmhouse on the Anthony estate lies at the end of a long private drive, just off the A38. The rooms are plain but super-comfortable, and breakfast comes with free-range eggs and homemade marmalade.

Price: from £65 for a double.

SELF-CATERING

Whitsand Bay Holiday Chalets

Tregonhawke, Whitsands
☎ 01647 433593
www.helpfulholidays.co.uk

The views from Tregonhawke Cliff are among the best in south Cornwall, and this place has a got a ringside seat. Among a community of timber chalets (several offered by Helpful Holidays) overlooking Whitsand Bay, this one has two bedrooms, a garden and simple beach-style décor.

Price: from £275 for a week.

UNUSUAL

The Old Luggage Van

Happaranda Station, Nut Tree Hill,
St Germans PL12 5LU
☎ 01503 230783; www.railholiday.co.uk

One of three converted railway carriages, parked on the railway siding at the station at St Germans (on the Paddington to Penzance route). Built in 1896, it has a lounge-diner, bunk room, bathroom, kitchenette and small garden.

Price: from £295–£595 for week (sleeps 4)

Entertainment

Special events

The annual **St Germans May Festival** is a weekend of Bach, Handel, Vivaldi and other classical and choral music set in the medieval St Germans Paris Church. June is the **Saltash Regatta** (www.saltashregatta.co.uk) a community affair, but in a spectacular location right underneath the Tamar bridges. In July, the **Port Eliot Festival** at St Germans is a three-day arts event on the Port Eliot Estate (☎ 01503 230211; www.porteliotlitfest.com). Described as a "festival of ideas" (by Jarvis Cocker) and a "downright decadent garden party" (by an enthusiastic punter) the festival offers a wonderfully eclectic programme of events from poetry, comedy and cabaret to fashion, film and an alternative flower show. There's a campsite for overnighters, but day tickets are available, too.

The best... FOOD AND DRINK

With one or two exceptions, most of the best food around here is served in pubs or cafés. The Forgotten Corner is, indeed, a bit of a backwater as far as fine dining is concerned. But don't knock it, because it's certainly rich in good old-fashioned homemade food, and so local, the village fisherman is quite likely to deliver the day's catch wearing oilskins.

Staying in

Saltash Farmers' Market, on Reagle Street takes place on the fourth Saturday of the month (9am–1pm). Just outside Saltash, Smeaton Farm at Pillaton (☎ 01579 351833; www.smeatonfarm.co.uk) sells joints of home-reared lamb, beef and pork, the latter from rare breed Saddleback pigs. The shop also sells farm-produced dry-cured bacon and sausages.

Moran's, in a former bakery in Cawsand, has a good deli counter, and in Plymouth, the **Pannier Market** in New George Street (☎ 01752 304378) features a monthly produce market on the second Saturday in the month (9.30am–2pm).

EATING OUT

RESTAURANT

The View

Trenninow, Cliff Road, Millbrook PL10 1JY
☎ 01752 822345
www.theview-restaurant.co.uk

And what a view – on the cliffs at Whitsands, The View looks out over the sea towards Rame Head. The décor is fresh and modern, as is the food. Chef-owner Matt Corner's ever-changing menu is big on fish and local goodies (try tiger crab and prawn risotto). By day, it's more beach-hut bistro; in the evening, it's more posh, and perfect for sunset dinners (main courses from £12.50). The best place to eat around here by far. Open 1 Apr - 31 Oct.

GASTRO PUB

Rod and Line

Church Road, Tideford PL12 5HW
☎ 01752 85132

A few yards off the A38, this unpretentious spit-and-sawdust village pub is popular with the Port Eliot festival set, often has a big log fire, and serves blackboard specials, including Cornish crab, scallops and steaks (main courses from £10). There's a terrace with a few outdoor tables. Open daily, 11am–1am.

The Eliot Arms

Fore Street, St Germans PL12 5NR
☎ 01503 232733
www.eliotarms.co.uk

In the centre of the village, a traditional coaching inn, about 1850, recently bought by St Austell Brewery, but maintaining a reputation for good food of the 'pie-of-the-day' variety. The menu features local sausages, curry of the day (£7.95), local fish, Sunday roasts and meals for kids and vegetarians.

CAFÉ

The Old Boat Store

The Cleave, Kingsand PL10 1NF
☎ 01752 829011
www.theoldboatstore.co.uk

On the seafront at Kingsand, this fun-loving friendly café serves vegetarian dishes with a Mediterranean flavour, fresh fish when available, salads, cakes and puddings, mostly homemade with locally sourced ingredients. It's also home to the mini Museum of Celebrity Leftovers, and there's a holiday apartment available upstairs. Open daily, July to Sept, 10am–4pm (and in winter if they feel like it).

Drinking

There are some great little pubs tucked away in the nooks and creeks of the Tamar Estuary. One of the best is the easiest to find: The **Rod and Line** (☎ 01752 85132) is just off the A38 at Tideford, and offers a cosy fireside bar serving St Austell's beers, wines by the glass, a play area for kids across the road, and some quality live music by the likes of John Martyn. **The Edgcumbe Arms** at Cremyll (☎ 01752 822294; www.edgcumbearms.co.uk) is where you grab a pie and a pint of Cornish ale after walking around the Edgcumbe estate. The place gets packed on Sunday lunchtimes.

Around Rame, **The Halfway Inn** (☎ 01752 822279; www.halfwayinn.biz) sits roughly on the point where Kingsand meets Cawsand, and is an old-fashioned real ale bar serving Betty Stogs and Doom Bar, a good range of pub grub, and a weekly rendering of the Cornish Male Voice Choir.

Kingsand-Cawsand is well served with pubs. On the Square, **The Crosskeys Inn** (☎ 01752 822 706; www.crosskeyscawsand.co.uk) serves a variety of guest ales which include Skinners, Abbot Ale and SS Great Britain. For more real ale there's the nearby **Rising Sun** (☎ 01752 822840). **The Devonport** (☎ 01752 822869) right on the beach, has tables outside and the occasional Saturday night disco, and in Crafthole, the 15th-century **Finnygook Inn** (☎ 01503 2303388; www.finnygook.co.uk), has a low-beamed bar serving ale from three Cornish breweries.

Visitor Information

Tourist information centre: Tamar Valley Tourism Association, ☎ 0845 058 0621; Plymouth, ☎ 01752 306330.

Hospitals with A&E: Derriford Hospital, Derriford, Plymouth, ☎ 01752 777111.

Doctors: Quay Lane Surgery. Old Quay Lane, St Germans ☎ 01503 230088; The Surgery, 16 Antony Road, Torpoint ☎ 01752 813277.

Police station: Torpoint Police Station, 4 Ferry Road, Torpoint, Caradon PL11 2AX, ☎ 01752 812420.

Pharmacies: Alliance Pharmacy, 16 Fore Street, Torpoint PL11 2AD, ☎ 01752 812591; Lloyds Pharmacy, 19 Fore Street, Saltash PL12 6AF, ☎ 01752 842606.

Supermarkets: Waitrose, Tamar View, Saltash PL12 6LD, ☎ 01752 848874; Co-op, 53 Fore Street, Torpoint PL11 2AD, ☎ 01752 812429.

ATMs: NatWest Bank, 40 Fore Street, Saltash, Cornwall PL12 6JL; Lloyds TSB Bank, 57 Fore Street, Torpoint, Cornwall PL11 2AB.

Car hire: Plymouth Car Hire ☎ 01752 668899, www.plymouthcarhire.co.uk.

Local taxis: Callington Cars ☎ 01579 383624; Cottons Cars, Saltash ☎ 01752 848484.

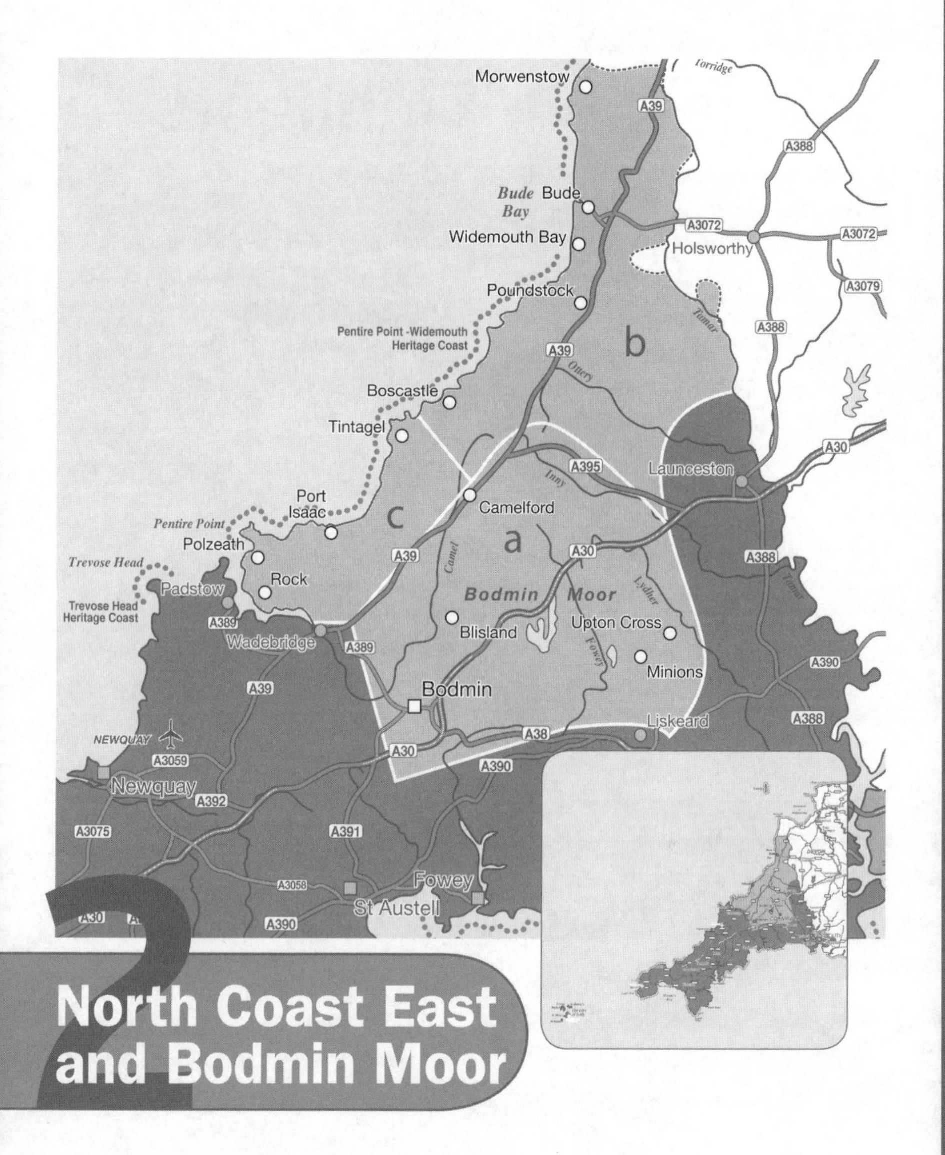

2 North Coast East and Bodmin Moor

a. Bodmin and the moor
b. Boscastle, Bude and beyond
c. Rock to Tintagel

Unmissable highlights

01 Relive the Arthur legend among the romantic ruins of Tintagel Castle, a place of myths, Celtic kings and medieval earls, p. 105

02 Climb Rough Tor, on the roof of Cornwall, overlooking Brown Willy, its highest point, p. 82

03 Stroll along the rebuilt harbour at Boscastle, to the rocky headland at Penally Point, p. 96

04 Listen to the rush and tumble of ice-cool water, at the woodland nature reserve of Golitha Falls, p. 84

05 Down a pint of real ale at the Blisland Inn, a proper beer drinkers' pub overlooking a peaceful village green, p. 92

06 Check out the Reverend Hawker's Hut, where the eccentric cleric wrote Cornwall's stirring anthem, p. 103

07 Clamber up to the Cheesewring, a curious Bodmin Moor rock formation, p. 84

08 Make a pilgrimage across the dunes to poetic St Enedoc's Church, were Sir John Betjeman is buried under a crooked tower overlooking Daymer Bay, p. 108

09 Catch the famous Fishermen's Friends choir on a summer evening on Port Isaac harbour, p. 107

10 Try Cornish yeast splits, at Bangor's Organic near Bude, p. 102

NORTH COAST EAST AND BODMIN MOOR

Between the Camel Estuary and the Devon border, the north-east coast and its moorland inner core is a place of extremes, of stark contrasts.

There are sunny, surfy resorts at either end, Rock and Polzeath to the west and Widemouth and Bude to the east. But in the hinterlands that meld them together you'll find the tallest cliffs in Cornwall, the steepest hills, the highest points, and some of the wildest places. Rock can even boast the most expensive real estate.

It's a place of pilgrimage, too: this is King Arthur and John Betjeman country (the former Poet Laureate is buried at St Enedoc's Church on Daymer Bay). It's the home of granite quarries, old copper mines and the oldest slate quarry in England. Beyond Bodmin Moor, green fields and wind farms drop down to the Atlantic. You can party in Polzeath, surf the waves at Crooklets, get lost in your thoughts on Cambeak Cliff. All this, and you're barely halfway into Cornwall.

BODMIN AND THE MOOR

What most people know of Bodmin Moor is glimpsed through the windows of a car whizzing past on the A30. A shame, because the moor is a treasure chest for nature lovers, historians and escapists. Among craggy tors and rolling granite uplands, the place is awash with ancient standing stones, barrows, hut circles and ruined medieval villages. There are thousands of miles of footpaths, old copper mining tramways, farm tracks and bridleways. Although it lacks National Park status, the moor is largely protected by its remote nature – at its epicentre there are few proper roads.

The moor can be bleak, boggy and forbidding; treeless in parts and prone to low glowering skies. But on a good day, its true colours shine through: a subtle palette of bracken, heath, heather, gorse and pine forest traced with the silvery granite which has been quarried here for centuries.

Cut in two by a ribbon of dual carriageway, there is a town at each corner: Bodmin to the west, Camelford to the north; to the east, Launceston (see page 56), and to the south Liskeard (see page 122). The northern half is higher, bleaker and less accessible. To the south, it's greener, more wooded, with small villages clustered around the dome-like Caradon Hill. There is a handful of tourism hotspots: Jamaica Inn, the Cheesewring and Golitha Falls attracts busloads of visitors in the summer. But elsewhere Bodmin Moor is the perfect place to escape the crowded coast in the heat of summer. And at Cornwall's highest point, it's worth a day trip just for the views.

WHAT TO SEE AND DO

West of the A30

One of Bodmin Moor's best-known landmarks is **Rough Tor** (pronounced *row*, as in argument), but even so, on a weekday, off-season, you can still climb to the twin summits of Cornwall's second highest point without seeing a soul. There is a car park off the A39 at **Camelford** (heading north, turn right down Roughtor Road, just as you are leaving the town). From there you simply follow the rough, often boggy, footpath up to a ridge of stones and boulders, 1,313ft up. At the top, a sombre plaque set in a granite, explains that the tor was given to the nation *'in memory of those who lost their lives ...in the North-West European Campaign 1944/45'*.

The easy climb takes about 45 minutes and the views are stupendous: to the west, the Atlantic Coast and Tintagel; to the east, the brooding hills of the empty **High Moor**, in the foreground, **Brown Willy**, Cornwall's highest point, but only just at 1,378ft. More intrepid walkers can continue on to this higher point, but it's further than it looks (taking two or three hours to do the round trip from the car park to Brown Willy and back again). As is the case with any Bodmin Moor walk, don't attempt it without drinking water, proper walking shoes and windproof or rainproof clothing – the weather up here can be wild and unpredictable. If you plan to explore the moor further, invest in an OS map (number 109) and stick to the way-marked routes.

Three miles north of Rough Tor, the less well known **Davidstow Moor** is home to the eerie remnants of a Second World War airfield; a Coastal Command base from 1942 to 1945, it was known to the RAF as DD (hence the nick-name 'Double Diamond'). When it closed, the runways provided 2.6 miles of motor racing track, the last race being a Formula One held in 1955. Now you can see sheep and Bodmin ponies roaming the pot-holed runways and the derelict shell of the control tower set in a filmic landscape, particularly atmospheric on a misty day. In winter, you can see clouds of roosting starlings – around a million birds – swoop over the moor at dusk (between October and March).

At the entrance to the airfield, close to the industrial Dairy Crest factory, there are two museums. The larger of the two, the **Cornwall at War Museum**, is devoted entirely to the history of this and other North Cornwall airfields.

Davidstow Moor RAF Memorial Museum has broader appeal, being less concerned with hardware, more with the minutiae of wartime life. The charming, privately run museum is housed in the sergeants' shower block (some of the plumbing is still in place) and presents a colourful exhibition of airfield memorabilia (stories, photographs, letters, the odd propeller), enhanced by a background of war-time songs with a suitably crackly gramophone sound.

CORNWALL AT WAR MUSEUM: Davidstow Airfield, Camelford Pl32 9YF; ☎ 01208 816311, cornwallatwarmuseum.mysite.orange.co.uk. Entry: adults £4, children £3; open Wed-Sun from Apr to Jun, daily from Jul to Sept and half terms.

DAVIDSTOW MOOR RAF MEMORIAL MUSEUM: 19 Trefrew Road, Camelford PL32 9TL; ☎ 01840 213266. Free entry; open daily Easter to Oct, 10.30am–4pm.

A mile or so south, a delightful place for a picnic is on the grassy banks of **Penpont Water** at **Bowithick Bridge**. You can swim here, too, or just dangle your legs in clear, ice-cold water. There is pleasant easy-ish walk from here to the top of **Bray Down**. Nearby **Altarnun**, nudging the A30, is one of the prettiest of Bodmin Moor's northern villages, with its 15th-century packhorse bridge and the 'cathedral of the Moors', the Church of St Nonna.

Other villages worth a nose are **Blisland** (with its square of Georgian houses, village green and Blisland Inn) and **St Breward.** The Church of St Breward, the highest in Cornwall at 700ft, is built of silvery granite from the nearby **De Lank Quarry**. Still in use, the quarry provided the raw material for Eddystone Lighthouse, Tower Bridge in London and, much later, parts of the Tamar Road Bridge.

On the south-west fringe of Bodmin Moor **The Camel Trail**, Cornwall's best-known cycle route, begins and ends (depending on which way you are heading) at **Wenfordbridge**, and travels south for 6.2 miles before hitting **Bodmin**. From Bodmin, the track follows a green and densely wooded stretch of the Camel Valley, past Dunmere Station halt (where there's a car park). The full 17-mile route continues on to Wadebridge and Padstow.

East of the A30

The southern half of the moor is greener, more populated, more accessible, with patches of high moor broken up by valleys of farmland and forestry plantations. **Cardinham Woods**, the largest Forestry Commission site in the south-west, lies to the east of Bodmin (between the A30 and A38), offering way-marked footpaths, gravel cycle tracks and picnic and barbecue

The beast of Bodmin: fact or fiction?

The Beast, or possibly beasts, of Bodmin Moor is Cornwall's answer to the Loch Ness monster. Rumours that a puma, or panther-like creature, has been stalking the moor mutilating farm animals have been doing the rounds since the 1980s. There have been numerous alleged sightings and even paw prints, but no proof, no convincing pictures. Indeed, after an official investigation was carried out in 1995, it was concluded that there was 'no verifiable evidence' of alien cats on the moor; but neither could it prove that the beast was a fiction. Within days of the denial, a young boy walking alongside the Fowey River, found the skull of what looked uncannily like a big cat complete with a pair of large fangs. The Natural History Museum confirmed that it was indeed a young male leopard, but the creature had not met its end on Bodmin Moor. The exotic trophy, possibly a hoax, was the head of an imported leopard skin rug. The case continues...

areas in 650 acres of mixed woodland on the Cardinham River. You can download a map, with details of walks, from the commission's website (www.forestry.gov.uk).

Around the bowl-like **Caradon Hill** to the east of the area is **Minions**, Cornwall's highest village, and also the best starting point for walks up to the **Cheesewring** - a curious stack of boulder-like granite plates, perched on the side of **Stowe's Hill**. It looks like one stone is precariously balanced on another, but it's a solid, natural rock formation. En route to the Cheesewring, you will pass **The Hurlers**, three circles of Bronze Age standing stones which, according to legend, are a group of Cornishmen turned to pillars of stone for daring to play hurlers (a bit like rounders) on a Sunday. All is explained at the nearby **Minions Heritage Centre**, housed in a former engine house at what was the South Phoenix Mine.

Bronze Age standing stones, The Hurlers

MINIONS HERITAGE CENTRE: Liskeard PL14 5LE; ☎ 01579 362350. Admission free; open daily, 10am–dusk.

One of Cornwall's key mining heritage sites, the moor is littered with the legacies of copper mining which thrived around Caradon Hill, from boom to bust (*c.*1840 to 1890). **South Caradon Mine** featured on BBC2's *Restoration* series in 2004, and there are plans to consolidate its crumbling stacks, shafts and railway arches and create a visitor centre. For the time being, it remains an untouched relic of industrial archaeology. Below, in the Fowey River valley, which meanders down from the high moor to the south coast, **Golitha Falls** at Draynes, is a delightful place for a walk or a picnic. The English Nature reserve provides narrow, rocky paths through ancient woodland to the cascading falls, where water tumbles down a steep gorge. Kingfishers and otters are occasionally spotted.

Local legends: the still waters of Dozmary Pool

The romance of Dozmary Pool has been eroded over the years by encroaching artificial neighbours - such as Colliford Lake Reservoir and the widened A30. But the water of this natural tarn, they say, can rise and fall like the tide, treasure lies beneath the surface, and the rogue Jan Tregeagle (whose Bodmin Moor ghost is hunted by the devil), was sentenced to empty it with a sea shell. It was here, too, that King Arthur's sword Excalibur was cast into the waters, where it was grasped by the mysterious Lady of the Lake. They also say it's bottomless, but the pool is so shallow that it completely dried out during the droughts of 1859 and 1976. There was no sign of treasure, or the gilded Excalibur.

The 15th-century **St Neot Church** in the village of St Neot is famed for its exquisite stained glass and **Jamaica Inn** at Bolventor was the inspiration for Daphne du Maurier's novel *Jamaica Inn*. The latter, an atmospheric old coaching inn until it was given a theme-park makeover, is now a big roadside pub with a gift shop and mini du Maurier museum.

JAMAICA INN: Bolventor, Launceston PL15 7TS; ☎ 01566 86250; www.jamaicainn.co.uk.

Just south of Bodmin, the National Trust's popular **Lanhydrock House** provides an insight into upstairs–downstairs Victorian life in a handy location off the A30. Originally built in the 17th-century by tin-trade toffs, the Robartes, the house was remodelled in the 1850s by George Gilbert Scott (of St Pancras Station fame). In 1881, a devastating fire destroyed everything bar the north wing of the Long Gallery. The house you see today was designed for Thomas Robartes by Scott's protégée Richard Coad in the high Victorian style. The public have access to 49 meticulously furnished rooms, from the state rooms to the tiny servant bedrooms in the

LANHYDROCK HOUSE: Bodmin PL30 5AD; ☎ 01208 265950; www.nationaltrust.org.uk. Entry: adults £11.50, children £5.70; open Mar to Oct, Tues–Sun, 11am–5pm; garden open all year, daily 10am–6pm.

Lanhydrock House

attic and the larders and sculleries below. One of the main attractions is the surviving Long Gallery, thanks to the delicate plasterwork on its barrel-shaped ceiling. Beyond a crenellated gate house, which also survived the fire, you can walk through part of the estate's 450 acres to the River Fowey at Respryn Bridge.

Wet weather

The **Bodmin Jail** offers a chilling journey into the belly of the British penal system from 1779 to until the jail closed in 1927. The semi-derelict Georgian jail was originally built by prisoners from solid hunks of granite brought from Bodmin Moor's Cuckoo Quarry. The smells, the dank air, the half light, are all too real, and it's impossible not to be moved by the poignant stories of wretched lives, and the terrible injustices that far outweigh the heinous crimes. Elizabeth Osborne, aged 20, we learn, was hanged in 1813, simply for setting light to a hay rick.

Bodmin's **Courtroom Experience** invites visitors to assume the role of jurors in the re-enacted trial of the Matthew Weeks, accused of murdering young Charlotte Dymond on the slopes of Rough Tor in 1844. In former County Court, you will hear the evidence and deliver your verdict. The 45-minute court session, conducted by mannequins with recorded voices, includes a visit to the holding cells where Weeks would have awaited his fate. He was found guilty, and hung by the neck at Bodmin Jail. Was he innocent? You decide.

BODMIN JAIL: Berrycoombe Road, Bodmin PL31 2NR; ☎ 01208 76292; www.bodminjail.org. Entry: adults £6.50, children £3.95 (under-5s free), seniors £4.75; open daily 10am–dusk; free parking.

THE COURTROOM EXPERIENCE: The Shire Hall, Mount Folly, Bodmin PL31 2DQ; ☎ 01208 76616. Entry: adults £3.95; children (up to 12) £2.25; family £10.95; Easter to Oct, Mon–Sat, court sessions on the hour, 11am–4pm; Nov to Easter, Mon–Fri.

What to do with children...

Cornwall's only standard gauge steam railway, **Bodmin and Wenford Railway** makes use of 6.5 miles of discontinued branch line, closed since 1967. All trains depart from the railway's own Bodmin General, and takes one of two routes: north to Boscarne (change for the Camel Trail), or south to Colesloggett Halt (for Cardinham Woods) and Bodmin Parkway. The latter connects to the Paddington to Penzance mainline, as well as a footpath to Lanhydrock. During the summer, the railway runs up to three return trips a day in each direction, and though it virtually closes between November

BODMIN AND WENFORD RAILWAY: Bodmin General Station; Bodmin PL31 1AQ; ☎ 01208 73666; www.bodminandwenfordrailway.co.uk. Entry: adults £7.50–£10, children £4–£6; Mar to Oct; see website timetables.

Steam locomotive on the Bodmin and Wenford Railway

and February, it puts on several events throughout the year, including grotto-on-the-train Santa Specials in December.

Bodmin Moor has miles of waterfront on the two neighbouring reservoirs, **Colliford Lake** at Bolventor and **Siblyback Lake** at St Cleer. On the larger of the two, there was a farm-based, woodland attraction with play areas and rides. At the time of writing, it was closed for refurbishment, re-opening in 2012 as **Bodmin Wildlife Park** – a multi-media expedition into the moor's wild past; from prehistoric beasties and woolly mammoths to native flora and fauna. The message is conservation told through a series of "interactive play environments".

Nearby **Siblyback Lake Watersports Centre** provides a range of courses for adults and children, including Junior Club windsurfing and sailing lessons. You can also hire rowing boats or kayaks and, on dry land, there's a children's play area and a tea room.

BODMIN MOOR WILDLIFE PARK: Colliford Lake Park (just off the A30), St Neot, PL14 6PZ; ☎ 01208 821469; www.bodminmoorwildlifepark.co.uk. Opening in 2012. For times, prices and details, check website.

SIBLYBACK LAKE WATERSPORTS CENTRE: Common Moor, Near Liskeard PL14 6ER; ☎ 01579 346522; www.swlakestrust.org.uk. Rowing boats from £14 an hour; kayaks from £10 an hour. Junior Club sailing/windsurfing sessions (Sat mornings) from £15; open Apr to Oct.

 ... and how to avoid children

Step out into the wilds of **Twelve Men's Moor**, and scale remote Kilmar Tor, described by Joss Merlyn, a character in Daphne du Maurier's *Jamaica Inn*, as '*a great crag of granite like a devil's hand*'. The highest point on the East Moor, this is demanding unpopulated terrain, and some of the walks around here are more like scrambling than rambling. The nearest villages are Henwood and Sharptor or, for a longer walk, start at Minions.

Entertainment

Theatre and cinema

Sterts Theatre at Upton Cross on the south-east edge of the moor (☎ 01579 362382 www.sterts.co.uk) is a superb arts venue, with an outdoor amphitheatre – roofed with a unique floating structure – and a gallery. Sterts is an educational charity, offering a rolling programme of music, dance and theatre performances, art exhibitions and other events.

Special events

The annual **North Cornwall Tor** (Cornwall's answer to the *Tour de France*) was deemed the toughest cycle ride in the UK when the two-day event was launched in April 2008. The full 100-mile route begins and ends at the Dragon Centre in Bodmin, wiggling around Bodmin Moor and the north-east coast, and up and down some tortuous hills. For information, see www.kilotogo.com (reference the Wiggle Cornwall Tor). In July, **Bodmin Riding** is a community festival that celebrates events leading up to the hanging of the town mayor in the 15th century (www.bodminridingandheritage.org.uk). Revived in the 1970s, it now takes the form of a medieval street fair.

The best... PLACES TO STAY

HOTEL

Trehellas House

Washaway, Bodmin PL30 3AD
☎ 01208 72700
www.trehellashouse.co.uk

In a Grade II listed Cornish courthouse, on the A389 just a few miles north of Bodmin, this small country hotel has pleasant rooms, furnished with brass beds, chandeliers and patchwork quilts, cosy sitting rooms, and an award-winning restaurant.

Price: B&B from £90–£160 for a double.

FARMSTAY

Higher Lank Farm

St Breward, Bodmin PL30 4NB
☎ 01208 850716
www.higherlankfarm.co.uk

Designed for families with young children, the accommodation is in nursery rhyme barns or Bo-Beep cottage (with play rooms, stair gates, mini beds, baby listeners and the like), or 'Toddler Dream' farmhouse B&B. And the kids get to collect eggs or feed the lambs.

Price: B&B from £790 for a week.

The best... PLACES TO STAY

B&B

Te Chy

Post Office House, Minions PL14 5LE
☎ 01579 363386
www.minionsbandb.co.uk

They say it's the highest Post Office in Cornwall, in the highest village, and there are fabulous moorland views from the self-contained flatlet (lounge, bedroom, bathroom). The full Cornish breakfast is served in Te Chy's own tea room next door.

Price: B&B £70 for a double.

Bedknobs

Polgwyn, Castle Street, Bodmin PL31 2DX
☎ 01208 77553
www.bedknobs.co.uk

In a detached Victorian villa in the centre of Bodmin, there are three 4-star guest rooms, all with generous en suite bathrooms with spa baths and/or power showers, and use of a large wooded garden. No children under 12.

Price: B&B from £80 to £105 per room.

CAMPSITE

Belle Tents

Owls Gate, Davidstow, Camelford PL32 9XY
☎ 01840 261556
www.belletentscamping.co.uk

Each of the three Belle Tent camps provide two canvas sleeping tents (one double, one twin) and a fully-equipped kitchen tent. The mini big tops, furnished with carpet, proper beds and solar lights, are set in a pretty rural garden, plus there is a bar tent (bring your own booze) and hot showers. Open from end May to September.

Price: from £215 (two nights) to £610 (per week), from Apr to Oct.

South Penquite Farm

Blisland, Bodmin PL30 4LH
☎ 01208 850491
www.southpenquite.co.uk

Stay in a yurt on this 200-acre organic farm. They are available in three sizes, from Baby Bear to Daddy Bear (sleeping 2–6), each providing futon beds, woodburner and gas stove, plus walks, wildlife, livestock and solar-heated showers. There is also a VW camper van available for hire.

Price: from £190–£320 for a week (May to Oct).

SELF-CATERING

Camel Valley Cottages

Nanstallon, Bodmin PL30 5LG
☎ 01208 77959
www.camelvalley.com

Part of the Camel Valley Vineyard's estate, there are two barn conversions, Lions Barn and Cowel Gwenyn (Cornish for beehive), both sleeping 4. There is access to a private stretch of the Camel River, and price includes complimentary salmon fishing licence and a bottle of house wine.

Price: from £290 to £880 for a week.

Dozmary Pool and Littleworth Barns

Dozmary Estate, Near Colliford Lake
☎ 01962 779598
www.dozmary.co.uk

In walled gardens, just yards from the banks of Dozmary Pool, this converted granite barn has slate floors, light, bright open-plan space and three bedrooms. Nearby Littleworth, is set in 8 acres and has two bedrooms and a vast upper floor lounge.

Price: from £365–£1,020. Dogs £20.

The best... FOOD AND DRINK

This is farming and small-holding country, where niche-market agriculture and local village shops are part of the fabric of life. Try to take the time to seek out the many small producers which, thanks to a variety of supportive initiatives, are meeting the challenges of '*low-income agriculture in an Area of Outstanding Natural Beauty*'.

Staying in

The Allertons of Pensilva had never farmed before when they bought the 32-acre Caradon Farm in 1996. Now their **Happy Hen Farm Shop** (www.happyhenfarmshop.co.uk) sells fresh local produce, bread, cakes and preserves, free-range eggs and home-reared chickens, Cornish pork, beef and sausages (including gluten-free, to order). A similar array of produce is available at **Taste of the West Country** (☎ 01579 345985; www.tasteofthewestcountry.co.uk), a farm shop at St Cleer, though this one has a greater emphasis on fruit and vegetables, as well as unusual not-so local meat cuts (kangaroo or wild boar).

One of the most unusual food enterprises in the region is **Cornish Kobe Beef**, or 'Drunken Beef', supplied by Darren and Kate Pluess of Woodland Farm near St Breward (☎ 01208 850503; www.cornishkobe.com). The farm is the first in Cornwall to use the Japanese kobe method, in which cows are fed on beer and given massages, to help promote a tender, succulent meat. **South Penquite Farm** (☎ 01208 850491; www.southpenquite.co.uk), a 200-acre family-run organic farm between Blisland and St Breward, doesn't have a shop but you can buy joints of lamb or moorland mutton (order in advance, and you can collect from the farm every other Wednesday). Their meats are also sold through **Button Meats** (☎ 01208 851116; www.buttonmeats.co.uk), a butcher in St Tudy, near Camelford.

Small **farmers' markets** are held in the Sports Hall in Pensilva (second Saturday of the month, 9.30am–12.30pm), at Rilla Mill village hall (third Saturday on the month, 9am–12pm), and St Neot's village hall (first Saturday of the month, 9am–12pm).

In Camelford, **A1 Fruiterers**, Market Place (☎ 01840 212414; www.a1fruiterers.co.uk) mixes farm-fresh vegetables with deli/health foods and fair trade and organic produce.

EATING OUT

RESTAURANT

Trehellas House Restaurant

Washaway, Bodmin PL30 3AD
☎ 01208 72700
www.trehellashouse.co.uk

Small country hotel with decent restaurant serving à la carte and table d'hôte menus, featuring local seafood and Cornish meat (smoked wild venison, rib-eye steak, fish pie), cocktails and Camel Valley Wines. Three courses costs around £24. Open daily for lunch and dinner (except Saturday lunch).

GASTRO PUB

The Rising Sun

St Clether, near Altarnun PL15 7SN
☎ 01566 86636

Old-fashioned village inn, on the northern rim of the moor, serving real ale and really good food. A broad range of dishes, includes daily specials and fresh seafood (chowder, mussels, oysters and more). Around £15 per head.

Manor House Country Inn

Rilla Mill PL17 7NT
☎ 01579 362354

A modern restaurant in a village local, the emphasis is on good quality traditional pub food, prepared with fresh Cornish ingredients. Thai chicken salad and tortellini may be offered, but the staples are British classics such as sausage and mash and Sunday roasts. Dishes from £4 to £16.

The Old Inn and Restaurant

Churchtown, St Breward PL30 4PP
☎ 01208 850711
www.theoldinnandrestaurant.co.uk

Billed as the highest public house in Cornwall, this medieval village inn, does a nice line in traditional home-cooked pies, platters and grills, fresh fish and seasonal local produce as well as bar meals, cream teas, Cornish ales (and wines) and a Sunday carvery. In summer, take a seat on the deck outside and enjoy views across Bodmin Moor.

TEA ROOM

Woods Café

Cardinham Woods, Bodmin PL30 4AL;
www.woodscafecornwall.co.uk
☎ 01208 78111

A refurbished woodsman's cottage on Forestry Commission land, it has a fireside tea room, offering homemade cakes, cream teas, soups, sandwiches, lunches and daily specials (such as butternut squash and chickpea tagine or savoury quiche with salad). Light lunches from around £6. Open daily all year round though prices vary.

Drinking

There are some great little village pubs tucked away on the moors. One of the best being the **Blisland Inn** at Blisland (www.bodminmoor.co.uk/blislandinn). The affable landlord Gary Marshall insists that his award-winning establishment (national CAMRA pub of the year in 2001) is a pub with food, not a restaurant with a bar – and asks that you eat outside or in back room in the evening, so as not to get in the way of the beer drinkers. Regulars included King Buddha's Blisland Special and Sharps Blisland Bulldog, and there are always half a dozen guest ales.

Other good moorland pubs include: the **Crow's Nest Inn** at Crow's Nest (☎ 01579 345930), an atmospheric 17th-century St Austell Brewery local; **The Rising Sun** at St Clether, near Alturnun (☎ 01566 86636); **The London Inn**, in St Neot (☎ 01579 320263); and the freehouse **Old Inn** at St Breward (☎ 01208 850711). They all do good pub food.

The Camel Valley Vineyard at Nanstallon, between Bodmin and Wadebridge, is not only Cornwall's finest vineyard but the best in the UK, judging by consistent triumphs in national awards. Founded in 1989, on the sunny slopes of the mid-Cornwall valley, the vineyard produces crisp zesty white, fruity rosé and classy sparkling wines. '*Loved the place, loved the wine*', was wine pundit Jilly Goolden's conclusion when she visited the vineyard in 2005. In the same year, the sparkling Camel Valley Brut beat 250 international competitors at the International Wine Challenge and was the only fizz outside of the Champagne region to come away with a gold medal.

THE CAMEL VALLEY VINEYARD: Nanstallon, Bodmin PL30 5LG; ☎ 01208 77959; www.camelvalley.com; Tours: Apr to Sept, Mon–Fri at 2.30pm, £5. Easter to Oct, Wed at 5pm, £7.50; all tours include wine. Wine sales: Easter to 30 Sept, Mon–Fri, 10am–5pm; Sat, closed Sun (except bank holidays).

Visitor Information

Tourist information centres: Bodmin Tourist Information Centre, Shire Hall, Mount Folly, Bodmin PL31 2DQ, ☎ 01208 76616; North Cornwall Museum (and Tourist Information Centre), The Clease, Camelford, ☎ 01840 212954.

Hospitals with A&E: Bodmin Hospital, Boundary Road, Bodmin PL31 2QT, ☎ 01208 251300.

Doctors: The Surgery, Still Moor House, Bell Lane, Bodmin PL31 2JJ, ☎ 01208 72488; St Breward Surgery, Row, St Breward PL30 4LN, ☎ 01208 851194; The Medical Centre, Church Field, Camelford PL32 9YT, ☎ 01840 213893.

Pharmacies: Day Lewis, 7 Fore Street, Bodmin PL31 2HT, ☎ 01208 72579; Alliance, 25 Market Square, Camelford PL32 9PD, ☎ 01840 532327.

Police stations: Devon & Cornwall Constabulary, Priory Road, Bodmin PL31 2AA, ☎ 0845 2777444; Devon & Cornwall Constabulary, 18 High Street, Camelford PL32 9PQ, ☎ 0845 2777444.

Supermarkets: Morrisons, Priory Road, Bodmin PL31 2ST, ☎ 01208 78763; ASDA, Launceston Road, Bodmin PL31 2AR, ☎ 01208 261800; Sainsbury's, Dennison Road, Bodmin PL31 2SS, ☎ 01208 269743.

Car hire: Enterprise Rent-A-Car, Church Square, Priory Road, Bodmin PL31 2DP, ☎ 01208 265860; Bluebird Car Hire, Longstone, St Mabyn, Bodmin PL30 3BZ, ☎ 01208 77790.

ATMs: HSBC, 3 Fore Street, Bodmin PL31 2HU; Lloyds TSB, Fore Street, Bodmin PL31 2HP; Barclays, 7 Mount Folly Square, Bodmin PL31 2DE.

Bike hire: East Rose Farm Cycle Hire, ☎ 01208 850674; Bodmin Bikes and Cycle Hire, Denison Road, Bodmin PL31 2LL, 01208 73192.

Local taxis: Parnell's Taxis, Bodmin, ☎ 01208 75000; Parkway Taxis, Bodmin, ☎ 01208 77340, North Cornwall Taxis, St Teath, ☎ 01208 850071; Camel Taxis, Camelford, ☎ 01840 212963.

BOSCASTLE, BUDE AND BEYOND

People tend to say that Bude isn't very Cornish. That's partly down to the location – it's only 4 miles short of the Devon border – but it is a little out of character. Unlike the hugger-mugger harbour villages further west, the town is wide and open; a broad smile of terraced townhouses and Riviera-style hotels overlooking its two beaches from the gentle, grassy cliffs that roll down to the River Neet and the parallel Bude Canal. By contrast Boscastle, 15 miles to the south-west, is as Cornish as they come; its cottages tumbling down the steep hills of the Valency and Jordan Valleys to a narrow cliff-hung harbour inlet, guarded at one end by a pair of dark, rocky headlands. Having recovered from devastating floods in 2004, Boscastle is back on its feet, revitalised as one of the region's most popular walking centres.

In between the two lies one of the loneliest, loveliest coastlines on the Atlantic coast.Every inch of it National Trust, an Area of Outstanding Natural Beauty or both; much of it empty other than a few isolated farms. Even mining didn't stretch this far. On cliffs that rise and fall like a roller coaster, fulmars and housemartins nest on ledges and rock-faces. The aptly named High Cliff south of Crackington Haven is Cornwall's highest.

WHAT TO SEE AND DO

Bude

Rather like Newquay in spirit, but less rugged, less with it, more bucket and spade, **Bude** is all about beaches; among Britain's best, they say, and stretching for miles from **Crackington Haven** to **Crooklets** and up to the Devon border. The town's main beach is **Summerleaze**, the big bay of yellow sand at the mouth of the River Neet. The tides here can be dangerous, but the beach is popular with families and has the benefit of seawater pools and a car park right by the lock where the river meets the picturesque **Bude Canal**.

Close by is **Bude Castle**, a Victorian castellated mansion built on sand for inventor Sir Goldsworthy Gurney, responsible for, among other things, the pre-electricity 'Bude Light', a means of introducing oxygen gas into a flame. His invention helped improve the beams in lighthouses, the 'limelight' in theatres, and the lighting in the House of Commons. The Castle is now a heritage centre with gallery and a restaurant.

THE CASTLE HERITAGE CENTRE: The Castle Bude, EX23 8LG; ☎ 01288 357301. Entry: adults, £3.50, children £2.50 (under-5s free); open Easter to Oct, 10am–5pm; Nov to Easter, 11am–4pm.

Outside, the **Bude Light** and its creator are commemorated in a tall, needle-like millennium sculpture. The 30ft sculpture hardly merits a second look in the daylight, but comes into its own at night.

The heritage centre at Bude Castle

From Summerleaze, Bude's busy surf-shop high street slopes up to the undulating golf greens of Summerleaze Down, which overlooks **Crooklets** beach to the north of the town. Cornwall's answer to Bondi beach, Crooklets was home to Britain's first life-saving club, back in 1953, and is a favourite with surfers and body-boarders.

Further north **Sandymouth** is a National Trust beach. Further north still, tucked away down a wooded path, the small cove at **Duckpool** has serious surf (not for beginners) and sand at low tide, overlooked by the high cliff of Steeple Point. Just south of Bude, the vast beach at **Widemouth Bay** (pronounced 'Widmouth') is the area's best, or at least the most popular; sandy, surfy and well served with beach-holiday facilities. But the most beautiful is **Millook Haven.** In the V of a steep-sided valley, accessed by narrow Cornish lanes, its pebble beach is backed by high cliffs demonstrating an example of zig-zagging, or 'recumbent folding' strata. With one of the nation's best left-hand reef breaks, it attracts expert surfers, and occasionally plays host to championship surf events. The rest of the time, it's just a wonderful place to hang out - no facilities, barely any parking and few people.

At **Crackington Haven**, 5 miles south, mighty cliffs plunge down to a more typical north Cornwall beach; pebbly and marred by caravans, but with all the makings of a family day-out. Between Crackington Haven and Boscastle there are some cracking coastal walks, some of the best in the county, for those with plenty of puff and stamina. Toiling up the footpath to say, **Cambeak Cliff**, is not for the unfit. **High Cliff**, to the south is not only the highest in Cornwall at 735ft, but it's the highest sheer-drop cliff in southern Britain. **The Strangles**, one of Cornwall's wildest beaches is a long climb down brittle slate cliffs, but so beautiful you could weep. The challenge is to find it in the first place (invest in an OS map).

Boscastle

After four years of reconstruction, **Boscastle** is back to its old self, its cottages and harbour walls rebuilt after the destructive floods of 2004. And it has lost none of its magic, nor its brooding atmosphere, redolent of smugglers and seadogs. Boscastle is a village of two halves: the upper half, the heart of the community, was the site of the 12th-century Bottreaux Castle (now no more), and consists of a few sleepy streets of stone houses and a village shop. At the bottom of a steep hill that descends to the sea, you'll find the more touristy side of Boscastle with shops and tea rooms clustered around the little stone bridge that crosses the once

CELEBRITY CONNECTIONS

On the edge of ravishing Millook Haven, the Shack is a lone spectator, the only building on the beach. Built in 1929, the former Tea House, looks a bit like a colonial bungalow washed up on the Atlantic coast. But this modest timber dwelling has star quality; and since its owners started hiring out their hut as a film-and-fashion location, it's welcomed a procession of A-list guests.

American celebrity photographer, **Annie Leibovitz** was there doing a photo-shoot for *Vanity Fair*. It was used as a location for 2006 movie *Half Light*, starring **Demi Moore**. **Kate Winslet** rented the Shack for a holiday, as did **Samantha Morton**, and **Boris Johnson**. American singer, **Tori Amos**, who has a home in nearby Whitstone, shot a music video there, followed by a photo shoot for *Marie Claire*. But it's not all Hollywood and hair-and-make-up. For a few weeks a year, the one-bedroom Shack is available as a holiday rental (www.millook.com) – yours for £850 for a three-night stay out of season.

torrid Valency River. The rebuilt visitor centre and National Trust shop on the north side of the harbour introduces walks and local wildlife.

There is a footpath either side of the ravine-like harbour, and both routes provide a short and reasonably easy walk to the cliffs. The quickest is on the north, or left, side past the visitor centre, with rows of cottages and converted former pilchard stores and on up to **Penally Point**, where you can admire the view, or look down on the little stone harbour wall.

The harbour is notoriously difficult to enter, and in the 19th century, ships had to be towed through the entrance by rowing boats and horses on towpaths. The footpath to the south of the harbour climbs up to **Willapark Point** and its distinctive white lookout, built as a summerhouse for a Victorian merchant. You can return by way of **Forrabury Common**, where you can see evidence of the Celtic strip-farm system, known locally as 'the stitches'. An inland walk up the Valency Valley will take you to **St Juliot's Church**. While overseeing its restoration in 1870, a young Thomas Hardy, met and married the rector's sister-in-law, Emma Gifford.

 Wet weather

BOSCASTLE MUSEUM OF WITCHCRAFT: The Harbour; Boscastle PL35 0HD; ☎ 01840 250111; www.witchcraft.co.uk/boscastle.htm. Entry: adults £4, children £3; open Easter to 31 Oct, Mon–Sat, 10.30am–6pm, Sun 11.30am–6pm.

As one of the many victims of the Boscastle floods, and the man who called the emergency services, Graham King still feels a little nervous during a heavy downpour. Butt he will gladly talk you through the rescue operation that saved his **Museum of Witchcraft**. The genuine relics of witchcraft's history, include a remarkable collection of magic dolls, puppets, potions,

Remembering the Boscastle flood

In Boscastle, 16 August 2004 will always be remembered as 'flood day', the day the village was washed away by a wall of water that tore through its heart like a tsunami. The day started with heavy thundery showers; they got heavier, with some 8 inches of rain falling within a few hours. The River Valency broke its banks and a 10ft wave roared through Boscastle.

Dozens of Boscastle residents found themselves trapped in upstairs rooms, as their worldly goods floated on the surface of the rising waters below. By 5pm, rescuers were winching people into helicopters. In all, over 150 people were airlifted to safety – making this the largest peace-time rescue operation in the history of mainland Britain. Some 440 million gallons of water rampaged through the village that day. Miraculously, there were no fatalities, but even when the water had receded, Boscastle's troubles were far from over. Peter Templar of the Riverside Hotel recalls the agony of returning to the wreckage of his home and business. Trees hung out of bedroom windows, there was a car in the dining room and, like all 58 of the village's flooded properties, every room was thick with what they call the 'black mud'.

It took four years to restore the harbour, repair the bridge, and to engineer a £4.5m flood defence scheme. Inevitably, the flood has become something of a tourist attraction. News footage of the rescue operation is still on show in the newly built visitor centre. And the nearby Witchcraft Museum keeps a thin line of disaster-scene images placed like a dado rail along the level of the flood water. The fact that almost every item in the museum's collection, every curse and charm, was rescued from the black mud, cleaned and disinfected, is as fascinating to today's visitors as the exhibits themselves.

charms, cures and curses. You will meet Cornwall's little people (piskies, goblins, pixies and spriggans) and hear the voice of Aleister Crowley. Just as chilling is the persecution of supposed witches: neck shackles and a ducking chair are testament to their suffering.

The **Bude-Stratton Museum** is worth a nose, particularly if you are interested in the history of the **Bude Canal** on which it sits. The 35-mile waterway, started in 1823, was designed to take sand and seaweed inland to improve the acid soil, and slate and grain down to the sea for export. The broad plan was to link north and south coasts (a sort of Suez for Cornwall), but the arrival of the railway stopped it in its tracks and the canal came to an abrupt halt just short of Launceston. It was in operation until 1891. Only 2 miles of abandoned canal remain navigable, from Bude to Helebridge, though there are moves to raise the necessary funds to restore and preserve it.

BUDE-STRATTON MUSEUM: Lower Wharf Bude EX23 8LG; ☎ 01288 353576. Entry: adults adults 50p, children free (if accompanied); open Easter to Oct 31, daily 12pm-5pm.

What to do with children

The **Bude Sea Pool** on Summerleaze beach offers safe bathing in seawater. It can be a bit seaweedy and quite deep in parts but it's free of strong currents and big waves, and patrolled by lifeguards for much of the summer. For more information contact North Cornwall District Council on 01208 262822. During high season, the pool is open from 10am to 6pm, weather and tides permitting.

Entertainment

Theatre and cinema

The only cinema, the family-run **Rebel Cinema** (☎ 01288 361442; www.rebelcinema.co.uk), closed down in 2009, but at the time of writing there were plans to reopen after complete refurbishment. In an oddly rural location at Treskinnisk Cross in the village of Poundstock, the Rebel is 5 miles south of Bude.

Special events

Bude International Jazz Festival (☎ 01288 356360; www.budejazzfestival.co.uk) is a week-long celebration of music, covering all schools of jazz from ragtime and blues to New Orleans and classic. A packed programme of over 150 live music events, held in various venues around central Bude, usually takes place during the last week of August.

In early October, Boscastle's **Festival of Food, Arts & Crafts** (www.visitboscastle.co.uk) showcases North Cornwall's culinary and cultural landscape, with cookery demonstrations and local produce stalls. In 2008, the festival was supported by Rick Stein, Jamie Oliver's Fifteen Cornwall and chef Kevin Viner, who made a personal appearance.

Nightlife

Despite the lively local surf scene, Bude's nightlife is limited – with just one decent nightclub, the youthful **Kazbar** on The Strand (☎ 01288 350712). For pre-club drinks head for J J's Bar on Crooklets Road (☎ 01288 352555). The Inn on the Green at Crooklets Beach (☎ 01288 356013; www.innonthegreen.co.uk) has regular live music nights and a lively **Legends Bar**.

Bedroom at Bangor's Organic

The best... PLACES TO STAY

BOUTIQUE

Boscastle House

Tintagel Road, Boscastle PL35 0AS
☎ 01840 250654
www.boscastlehouse.com

On the upper edge of the village, this was the Tolcarne House Hotel until new owners Sean and Morwenna Gee gave it a complete makeover in 2008, delivering a package of cool design, Cornish produce, gorgeous gardens and green principles (solar panels, wool insulation and recycled everything).

Price: B&B from £120 for a double per night.

Bottreaux Hotel

Boscastle PL35 0BG ☎ 01840 250231
www.boscastlecornwall.co.uk

Looking down on Boscastle, from the B3266 access road, this little hotel has eight small but nicely furnished bedrooms, with distant seaviews from some of them, and a decent restaurant (the latter, closed Wed and Sun).

Price: B&B from £80-£110 per room per night.

HOTEL

Elements Hotel

Marine Drive, Bude EX23 0LZ
☎ 01288 352386
www.elements-life.co.uk

On the coast road between Widemouth and Bude, this is one of an emerging brand of surf hotels, springing up the North Cornwall coast: offering smart bedrooms, gym, sauna, surf school and contemporary seaview restaurant.

Price: B&B from £105 for a double per night; kids/extra beds £15 per night.

INN

The Bay View Inn

Widemouth Bay, Bude EX23 0AW
☎ 01288 361145
www.bayviewinn.co.uk

Breathtaking views of the Atlantic, great location (right on the sea at Widemouth Bay), good food, lively real ale bar with cliff-top terrace and bright contemporary rooms – all crisp, white linen, nautical stripes and luxury bathrooms (some have balconies). Two family rooms sleep up to five.

Price: from £40-£60 per adult per night; children 1–14 yrs £15 per night.

B&B

The Old Rectory

St Juliot, near Boscastle
☎ 01840 250225

Thomas Hardy fell in love with his first wife, Emma, while staying in this charming former rectory. The rooms are all rustic Victoriana (one has an en suite thunderbox), you can roam the rectory's three acres and breakfast on fresh fruit and free-range eggs from its own walled garden.

Price: B&B from £70–£98 for a double per night.

Bangor's Organic

Bangors House, Poundstock EX23 0DP
☎ 01288 361297
www.bangorsorganic.co.uk

Britain's first 100% organic B&B, is just off the A39, in a Victorian house on a five-acre smallholding. Gorgeous rooms, plus home-baked, home-grown produce, delicious breakfasts and evening meals.

Price: from £110–£120 for a double per night.

The best... PLACES TO STAY

The Old Parsonage 

Boscastle PL35 0JD
☎ 01840 250339; www.old-parsonage.com

Just what you'd expect of a Georgian parsonage, except the rooms are sleek and contemporary, with roll-top tubs and king-size beds. There are a lot of thoughtful extras (such as Wi-Fi, organic produce, bathrobes and drying space for wet walkers) – and a 10% discount if you come without a car.

Price: B&B from £90–£104 per night.

The Old Vicarage 

Morwenstow, Bude EX23 9SR
☎ 01288 331369
www.rshawker.co.uk

Not just any vicarage, but the former home of iconic Victorian eccentric, the Rev RS Hawker – now a family-run guest house. The bedrooms are comfortably old-fashioned with frills, fireplaces and private bathrooms, and there is a lounge, library and snooker room.

Price: B&B £40 per person per night; dogs, by arrangement, £10 extra; no credit cards.

SELF-CATERING

Coombe Hamlet

Morwenstow, Near Bude
☎ 01628 825925
www.landmarktrust.org.uk

A chocolate-box hamlet of eight dwellings (including four thatched cob cottages and a former Bible Christian meeting room) run by the Landmark Trust and on National Trust land close to the beach at Duckpool. Sleeping three to six people, each has a solid fuel stove and a small garden.

Price: from £267–£1,892 for a week (short breaks available).

Penally Cottage

Penally Terrace, The Harbour, Boscastle
☎ 01326 55555; www.classic.co.uk

With a fabulous location right above the water, on the elevated footpath leading to the cliffs, this lovely old end-of-terrace cottage has flagstone floors, fireplaces and low beams, plus snazzy bathroom, modern kitchen and attractive décor. Sleeps six in two double and two single rooms.

Price: from £447–£1149 for a week.

Beach Modern

Bude
☎ 01288 275006
www.beachmodern.com

Two roomy, ultra-modern seaside holiday houses: Number 28 (sleeps up to 20, in a large villa, close to the links golf course near Crooklets Bay) and Bude House (sleeps eight, in a stylish five-bedroom house in central Bude – all white walls, gloss and red leather).

Price: Number 28 from £1,250–£5,000 a week; Bude House from £500–£2,500 for a week.

HOSTEL

Boscastle Youth Hostel

Palace Stables, Boscastle PL35 0HD
☎ 0845 371 9006
www.yha.org.uk

Rebuilt after the floods, this is one of the new generation youth hostels, and with rooms sleeping three to six, it's great for families and groups of friends. There's a lounge and self-catering kitchen, and it's so close to the harbour you can hear the ebb and flow of the tide.

Price: from £10.00 per single per night.

The best... FOOD AND DRINK

Cornwall's north-east corner is one of the county's most unspoilt agricultural landscapes: a patchwork of small farms, mainly fields of grazing dairy herds. Cheeses and dairy ice creams are among the produce that has sprung from the region, but local restaurants also capitalise on the rich store of farm produce that creeps across the Tamar from Devon. Some of the best places to eat around here are part of some of the best places to stay, and among them, there's a higher-than-average dedication to home-grown and organic foods.

Staying in

Sarah Talbot-Ponsonby of Helsett Farm started making ice cream back in 1985 as a means to survive the EU milk-quota crisis which limited the amount of milk each farm could produce. The result was **Helsett Farm Organic Dairy Ice Cream** made on the farm at Lesnewth near Boscastle, available in dozens of delicious flavours, and made with natural ingredients. You can try it at Harbour Light tea room in Boscastle, or call the farm for stockists (☎ 01840 261207; www.helsettfarm.com).

Another local dairy producer is **Whalesborough Farm** at Marhamchurch, near Bude (☎ 01288 361317). The farm's small artisan cheesemaking enterprise, using organic milk from a herd of Ayrshire cows, has created four award-winning cheeses: hunt local delis for Miss Muffet (a washed curd cheese), Keltic Gold (semi-soft and cider washed) and Cornish Crumbly.

For bread, the small **Boscastle Bakery** in Boscastle (☎ 01840 250205) sells fresh bread, pastries, hand-raised pork pies and traditional pasties.

EATING OUT

FINE DINING

The Castle

The Castle Heritage Centre, The Wharf, Bude EX23 8LG
☎ 01288 350543
www.thecastlerestaurantbude.co.uk

This modern bistro-style eatery, run by chef Kit Davis, is part of the castellated Victorian heritage centre (former home of Sir Goldsworthy Gurney) and, aside from a great position overlooking Summerleaze beach, offers delicious food. Lunch (beer-battered fish and chips) from £8.50; two-course dinner (pan-fried scallops and langoustines) around £24, and posh Sunday lunch (from £8.95). Closed Sunday evenings.

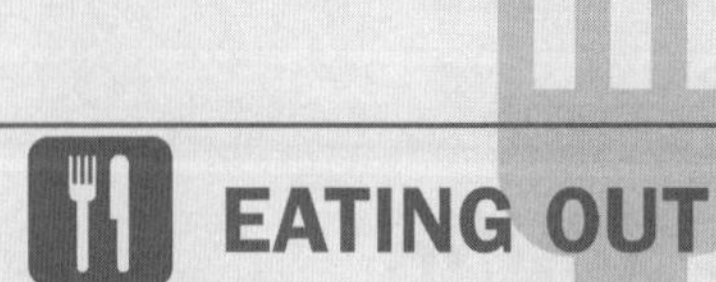

EATING OUT

RESTAURANT

Bangor's Organic

Bangors House, Poundstock EX23 0DP
☎ 01288 361297
www.bangorsorganic.co.uk

This is proper homemade food, some of it made from home-grown herbs and vegetables fresh-picked from the kitchen garden, and more or less everything is organic (including the wine). You can drop in for tea (try the cream tea with Cornish yeast splits), or a light lunch, or book a table for a three-course dinner (£26 per head).

Trevigue Farm

Crackington Haven EX23 0LQ
☎ 01840 230418
www.trevigue.co.uk

On the B3263 near High Cliff, this out-of-the-way restaurant, is dedicated to fresh farm produce, including its own Gloucester Old Spot pork and organic vegetables. Dine on Cornish blue soup and south Devon beef (two courses £21.50) in a 16th-century barn. Farmhouse B&B is also available.

GASTRO PUB

The Beach Hut

The Bay View Inn, Widemouth Bay, Bude EX23 0AW
☎ 01288 361145
www.bayviewinn.co.uk

Buzzy, busy bar-restaurant using fresh, local ingredients to make simple but beautifully presented dishes and classics with a Cornish twist. The evening menu includes fish pie, ling fillet in a Betty Stogs beer batter, local mussels and crab, steaks, burgers and daily specials. Two courses cost £15–£22 per person.

The Bush Inn

Morwenstow EX23 9SR
☎ 01288 331242
www.bushinn-morwenstow.co.uk

In a 13th-century freehouse between Bude and Hartland, the emphasis here is on fresh, seasonal produce – like Morwenstow meat and game and Bude Bay seafood. Lunch (including Sunday roasts) and dinners are served in a cosy modern-meets-rustic dining room, or in the garden in summer, and washed down with real ales. Two courses from £15 per head.

CAFÉ

Life's a Beach

Summerleaze Beach, Bude
☎ 01288 355222; www.lifesabeach.info

By day, it's a beach-bum hang-out and ice cream parlour, but at night it transforms into a sunset restaurant. The menu majors on seafood (Cornish mackerel, seared Fowey scallops, Bude Bay lobster), but also features local beef, vegetarian dishes, kids' portions and ocean views. Two courses cost around £23 per person. Open all year round.

TEA ROOM

Rectory Tea Rooms

Rectory Farm, Crosstown, Morwenstow EX23 9SR; ☎ 01288 331251
www.rectory-tearooms.co.uk

This traditional farmhouse tea room has been going since the 1950s but hasn't lost its touch – it has a string of awards for excellence. The rooms themselves are all shipwreck salvage, antiques and open fires. And the tea? An in-house Smugglers' blend or Tregothnan teas grown in Cornwall, plus homemade scones, cakes, soups, pasties, fresh local fish and the farm's own beef and lamb. Open daily, 11am–5pm, Easter to end of October.

Drinking

With its brooding harbour and tales of smuggling, Boscastle is the place for atmospheric old pubs, our favourite being the **Cobweb Inn** (☎ 01840 250278; www.cobwebinn.co.uk), a big stone building, tucked under a cliff, just opposite the village's riverside car park. Full of dusty antiques, dark beams, creepy spider-theme nicks-nacks and a motley crew of drinkers, it's not a place you'd go on a sunny day, but on a wet or wintry evening, with the lights low, the fires aglow, it's perfect. As well as Cornish ales, the Cobweb does reasonable food, and live music every Saturday night.

At the upper end of Boscastle, the **Napoleon** on High Street (☎ 01840 250204) is a white-washed 16th-century pub (a long steep climb from the harbour), serving St Austell Brewery ales, bar meals, live-music evenings and quiz nights. Another excellent village local is **The Bullers Arms**, a freehouse at Marhamchurch, near Bude (☎ 01288 361277; www.bullersarms.co.uk). And by the sea, try the **Coombe Barton Inn** at Crackington Haven (☎ 01840 230345; www.thecoombebartoninn.co.uk).

FURTHER AFIELD

Morwenstow

This little place, right on the Devon border is noteworthy for one reason: the legendary **Reverend Robert Stephen Hawker**. The eccentric cleric was vicar of Morwenstow for 40 years, joining the parish of **St John the Baptist Church** in 1834. He is best-known for having penned the *Song of the Western Men*, which became Cornwall's national anthem, and he is also credited with having started the tradition of the Harvest Festival, the first in 1843. But it's the man himself that fascinates. Parson Hawker, as was known, was a colourful dresser, usually seen walking his pet pig wearing a fisherman's jersey and wellingtons. Married twice, the first time to money, he was an opium-smoking poet, and pious, too. He is said to have excommunicated his cat for mousing on a Sunday. Rev Hawker is quite a celebrity in Morwenstow, and his legacy is worthy of a pilgrimage.

First, visit the churchyard where around 40 sailors are buried; all of them drowned in shipwrecks and dragged from the beaches, often by Hawker himself, to save them the indignity of an un-Christian burial. You can also visit the driftwood **Hawker's Hut** (free access, owned by the National Trust), tucked into a cliff, down some steep steps. A 19th-century version of a shed, this is where Hawker wrote many of his poems. His former rectory is now the B&B, the Old Vicarage.

The coastline here is spectacular, with gentle pasture finishing abruptly on the edge of high cliffs of layered shale. Just inland you can see the incongruous dishes of **Cleave Camp Satellite Station**. And north of the village, **Henna Cliff**, at 450ft, one of the highest in the UK, marks the point at which Cornwall becomes Devon.

Visitor Information

Tourist information centres: Bude Tourist Information Centre, The Crescent, Bude EX23 8LE, ☎ 01288 354240; Boscastle Visitor Centre, The Harbour, Boscastle PL35 0HD, ☎ 01840 250010.

Hospitals with A&E: Stratton Hospital, Hospital Road, Stratton, Bude EX23 9BP, ☎ 01288 287700.

Doctors: Neetside Surgery, Methodist Church Halls, Leven Road, Bude EX23 8LA, ☎ 0844 8151358; The Stratton Medical Centre, Hospital Road, Stratton, Bude EX23 9BP, ☎ 01288 352133; The Bottreaux Surgery, Boscastle PL35 0BG, ☎ 01840 250209.

Pharmacies: Boots, 20 Belle Vue, Bude EX23 8JL, ☎ 01288 352906; Lloyds Pharmacy, 9 Belle Vue, Bude EX23 8JL, ☎ 01288 352000.

Police station: Devon & Cornwall Constabulary, Lansdown Close, Bude EX23 8BP, ☎ 0845 2777444.

Supermarkets: Somerfield Stores, The Headland, Bude EX23 0LY, ☎ 01288 355521; Morrisons Supermarkets, Stucley Road, Bude EX23 8UA, ☎ 01288 355546; Tintagel Londis, Bossiney Road, Tintagel PL34 0AJ, ☎ 01840 770323.

Internet access: The Coffee Pot, 6 Morwenna Terrace; Bude EX23 8BU, ☎ 01288 356142. Bude Library, the Wharf, Bude EX23 8LG, ☎ 01288 352527.

Surf schools: Big Blue Surf School, Bude ☎ 01288 331764; Bude Surf Centre ☎ 07533 034499; Shoreline Outdoor Pursuits, Crooklets Beach ☎ 01288 354039; Outdoor Adventure Centre, Widemouth Bay, ☎ 01288 361 312. For more surf schools, see www.visitnorthcornwall.com.

ATMs: Barclays Bank, 2 The Strand, Bude EX23 8QX; Lloyds TSB Bank, 1 Belle Vue, Bude EX23 8JJ.

Bike hire: North Coast Cycles, 2 Summerleaze Avenue, ☎ 01288 352974.

Local taxis: Bea-line, Bude, ☎ 07747 196090; Curtis Cars of Cornwall, Bude, ☎ 07791 192021; Camelot Taxis, Boscastle, ☎ 01840 770172.

ROCK TO TINTAGEL

Summing up a region as diverse as this one isn't easy. But how about Champagne Coast meets Knights of the Round Table? At one end, salubrious Rock is all rich kids and millionaire real estate; at the other romantic Tintagel is about ruins and Arthurian fables – although beyond the money and the myths, both places can seem rather ordinary.

Princes William and Harry may hang out in Rock, alongside rafts of celebrities (Hugh Grant, Harry Enfield, Jay Kay and others) but unless you are learning to water ski on the Camel Estuary, it doesn't have a great deal to offer other than a handful of waterside restaurants, and a water-taxi exit to Padstow.

Tintagel is more user-friendly, more folksy, but its village centre is marred by touristy bling: Goth gift shops, Merlin memorabilia, plastic Excaliburs and, indeed, excaliburgers. You may dine in Rock, you will almost certainly visit Tintagel Castle, but it's the bits in between that will captivate. Take in the splendid estuary views from the rolling sands of Daymer Bay, party in Polzeath with its surf and seafood cafés, explore Port Isaac's fishing harbour, follow dizzy cliff-top footpaths to seaside Trebarwith, Treknow, Trebetherick (the Tre prefix simply means farm), and on to Rocky Valley – pure escapism.

WHAT TO SEE AND DO

If you only have time for one thing, head for **Tintagel Castle**. King Arthur's legendary birthplace, this iconic medieval monument sits atop the cliffs of an island-like outcrop linked to the mainland by a narrow bridge. The castle is a ruin – a majestic ruin, but rubble nonetheless – though you can still smell the history in this inspirational place. The location alone makes it worth the effort, but it does require stamina. Access to the castle's inner sanctum involves several flights of vertiginous metal steps.

The supposed birthplace of the Celtic King Arthur – born to King Uther and Igraine Pendragon in the 6th century – was a 13th-century stronghold of the Earls of Cornwall. You can see the remains of their Great Hall, but the earls rarely stayed there, and the place was derelict within 200 years. Much of the site's earlier history is unclear, though excavations in 1998, unearthed pieces of 5th-century pottery and, more significant, the so-called 'Arthnou stone', a slate slab, inscribed with the words: '*Artognou, father of a descendant of Coll, has had [this] made*'. Enough, it seems, to get the cult of King Arthur in a ferment of speculation about the real identity of Artognou.

The island's cliffs are a Site of Special Scientific Interest, a breeding ground for sea birds and butterflies. A good vantage point for those not visiting the castle is from the footpath below **Camelot Castle Hotel** (a clumsy Victorian fake, occasionally mistaken

TINTAGEL CASTLE: Tintagel PL34 0HE; ☎ 01840 770328; www.english-heritage.org.uk. Entry: adults £5.50, children £3.50 (EH members/under-5s free); open daily 10am–4/5/6pm depending on season, year round (closed Christmas/New Year); parking 600m away.

for the real thing). And on pebbly **Castle Beach** below you can see seawater sloshing in and out of Merlin's Cave.

On the same theme, but from quite a different era, **King Arthur's Great Halls** in the centre of Tintagel is a 1930s fantasy (see box) on a vast scale. It claims to be '*the only building in the world dedicated to the Arthurian legend*', but there's not a lot to see except impressive carved stonemasonry, stained glass and a low-key laser light show, part of a recorded Knights of the Round Table story narrated by actor Robert Powell.

KING ARTHUR'S GREAT HALL: Tintagel PL34 0DA; ☎ 01840 770526. Entry: adults £3.50, children £2.50, family tickets £10; open daily (except Christmas); winter 11am–3pm, summer 10am–5pm.

The court of the custard king

The story of **King Arthur's Great Halls** in Tintagel is almost as colourful as Camelot's. It began with Trevena House, built in the 1860s by newspaper editor John Douglas Cook, and bought in the 1920s by a London pudding millionaire Frederick Glasscock. Glasscock had sold his firm to Birds custard and retired to Tintagel, where he developed a passion for the King Arthur legend. Trevena provided him with the raw material for a Disney-like expression of Arthurian fantasy. Remodelling the house, at huge expense he converted it into the church-like 'Hall of Chivalry', open to the public since 1933. Gothic kitsch at its finest maybe, but the hall is a Cornish granite marvel: nine hefty pillars, an 8ft Round Table, a 6-ton throne and 125 shields. The 72 stained glass windows, designed by William Morris protégée, Veronica Whall, are also worth a look. And if the King Arthur moment strikes a chord, you can join the cultish Fellowship of the Knights of the Round Table, founded by Glasscock and still going strong.

On foot

Tintagel is a favourite starting or finishing point for walkers, with spectacular clifftop footpaths in either direction. Head south to the beach at **Tebarwith Strand**, an hour's walk (about 1.5 miles) past tall rock stacks and old mine and quarry workings. For a more challenging hike, head north for **Bossiney Cove**. The little beach completely disappears at high tide, but the footpath takes you over a wooden bridge and on to the beautiful **Rocky Valley** – where you can sit on cliff ledges and watch a foaming stream tumble over rocks into the sea. If you follow the stream inland, you will reach the head of **St Nectan's Glen** where a 60ft waterfall cascades through a rock arch into natural 'kieve', or bowl. The site is said to be a spiritual haven, though it's privately owned, and was recently offered for sale.

ST NECTAN'S GLEN AND WATERFALL: Near Bossiney ☎ 01840 770760. Entry: adults £3.50, children £1.75; open daily Easter to end of Oct, 10.30am–6.30pm.

Fishing boat on the beach at Port Isaac

Walking is a prerequisite of visiting **Port Isaac** in summer, as the little fishing village is closed to traffic. Park on the clifftop pay-and-display, and follow the cliff path that winds down to the harbour, where there's an indoor fish market, boats on the beach (which doubles as local car park) and a slipway crowded with nets, ropes and lobster pots. There's not a lot to do here, but it's charming with white-washed granite cottages on narrow alleys, or 'opes', that hairpin around tight corners (look out for Squeeze-ee-Belly Lane). A starring role in BBC drama series, *Doc Martin*, has put the place on the map in recent years, and it's turning into a mini Padstow with galleries and boutique gift shops. For a taste of grassroots Port Isaac, catch the now famous local choir, the **Fishermen's Friends**, singing sea shanties on the beach on Friday evenings.

Neighbouring **Port Gaverne**, to the east, has a small safe beach, ideal for children. To the west, at **Port Quin**, there's a tiny tranquil harbour inlet with rock pools, and handful of stone cottages and little else. From Fort Quin, there's a lovely half-mile cliff walk, carpeted in sea pinks in early summer, to the remote and rocky beach at **Lundy Bay.**

CELEBRITY CONNECTIONS

Port Isaac can boast more celebrities than Padstow, thanks to its popularity with film crews on location. Recent roles include *Nightmare Man*, a dubious horror in which Port Isaac was portrayed as a Hebridian village. In 1997, the Joseph Conrad novel *Amy Foster* was translated into film as *Swept from the Sea*, the Cornish coast shipwreck drama starring **Rachel Weisz**, **Ian Mckellen** and **Kathy Bates**. And in *Saving Grace*, filmed in 2000, the village appeared alongside **Brenda Blethyn**.

But it was ITV's drama soap series *Doc Martin*, that put the place on the map. In *Doc Martin*, **Martin Clunes** plays a hapless doctor living in the fictional Port Wenn, a picture-perfect fishing community – and most of the action was filmed on location in Port Isaac.

On the beach

Polzeath, the most popular beach on this stretch of coast, has changed somewhat since Sir John Betjeman wrote odes to its beauty in the 1930s. It's still lovely, but this one-time family favourite – featured in Enid Blyton's *Famous Five* stories – now has a reputation as a playground for public-school teenagers, guzzling lashings of vodka and Cornish Knocker ale. There was a crackdown in 2007 when the 17-year-old son of a merchant banker was found dead on the beach, but the party rolls on. Polzeath is also popular with surfers (particularly beginners), and you'll find surf hire shops and a surf school alongside cool seafood cafés on the seafront.

From **New Polzeath**, to the east of the beach, you can walk across National Trust coastland to **Pentire Head**, passing the cove at **Pentire Glaze**, and on to **Rumps Point**, for fabulous ocean views towards Tintagel Castle. To the west, the coast path takes you past the sands of little-known **Greenaway beach**, and on to **Daymer Bay** – a vast stretch of fine yellow sand on the mouth of the Camel River. There's a large, rather expensive car park, or it's an easy half-hour walk from Polzeath. Many people come here, not for the surf, but to visit **St Enedoc's Church**, where John Betjeman was buried after he died, aged 92, at nearby **Trebetherick** in 1984. The delightful 15th-century church is something of a curiosity, having a crooked spire and unusual location among the sand dunes of St Enodoc Golf Course which completely surrounds the little building. Before restoration in the 19th century, the church was almost buried in sand.

At low tide, Daymer Bay's sand bar continues along the estuary to **Rock**. Here, you can learn to waterski with the **Camel Ski School** (where Prince William had lessons).

The main reason to visit Rock, however, is to take the daytime foot ferry (see page 163) or

CAMEL SKI SCHOOL: The Pontoon, Rock PL27 6PD; 01208 862727; www.camelskischool.com. Lessons cost £25 per person per 15 minutes; from Easter to Oct.

Rock Water Taxi evening service

LOCAL KNOWLEDGE

Cornish-born **Mike Parnell** and wife **Clare** have farmed Carruan Farm since 1993. The Parnells sell beef and lamb, and even supply Waitrose, as far afield as Oxford Street. Opening Carruan to the public, says Mike, helps people to understand what goes on behind the scenes.

Best thing about living here: The combination of people and place – and such an incredible mix of people, from all over the world and all walks of life. I think Cornwall is unique in that respect.

Favourite restaurant: The Waterfront at Polzeath – with spectacular views across Polzeath Bay, great food and an excellent host.

Favourite beach: Lundy Bay between New Polzeath and Port Quin. It's a bit of a trek to get there, but well worth the effort. There is sand at low tide, caves to swim in and out of and, best of all, not a lot of people know about it.

Favourite café: The one by the weekly Hallworthy Livestock Market, near Camelford. It's part of the Wilsey Down Hotel, and does proper food for farmers and hungry passers by.

Favourite pub: The Fourways at St Minver. It's good to see a few traditional locals surviving in an era of gastro pubs – plus this one serves the best steaks going.

Best walk: The climb from Rough Tor from Rough Tor Ford on Bodmin Moor just outside Camelford. Spectacular.

Best view: From our own fields at Carruan Farm, near Polzeath you can look down across Lundy Bay in one direction, turn around slightly to view Pentire Head and then right round to look across Polzeath Bay – what a place to work.

Favourite visitor attraction: For kids, the Maritime Museum in Falmouth – well worth the journey.

Secret tip for lunch: Take a picnic up to the river at Delphi Bridge on Bodmin Moor. The water is freezing cold – but it's beautiful and more or less undiscovered.

Gull Rock at Trebarwith Strand

ROCK WATER TAXI: ☎ 01208 863090; www.rock-watertaxi.co.uk. Entry: adults £6 return, children £3; Easter–31 Oct continuous service 7pm–12am.

the evening **Rock Water Taxi** service across the Camel Estuary to Padstow. Leaving the ferry point on Rock beach from 7pm, the boat (a 10m, twin-jet catamaran), runs until midnight, so plenty of time for a seafood supper in Padstein.

Trewbarwith Strand, just north of Tintagel, is a peach of a beach, approached via a narrow valley which opens out into a wide bay, furnished with the enigmatic islet, Gull Rock. It gets very busy in summer, though access is via a causeway of slippery rock, and there's a real danger of being cut off at high tide.

Wet weather

THE OLD POST OFFICE: Fore Street, Tintagel PL34 0DB; ☎ 01840 770024; www.nationaltrust.org.uk. Entry: adults £3.80, children, £1.90; open daily mid-Mar to Sept, 11am–5.30pm, Oct to early Nov, 11am–4pm.

In Tintagel, get inside the National Trust's **Old Post Office**, a gnarled and tipsy-roofed but gloriously intact example of a medieval Cornish longhouse. The low-beamed rooms are furnished with 16th-century oak and you can wander upstairs to the dolls' house bedrooms. The 600-year-old building was the village post office, before the trust acquired it in 1903.

What to do with children...

Meet the animals at **Carruan Farm**, only a mile inland from Polzeath. According to farmers Mike and Clare Parnell, this is where 'fun meets farming', and throughout the year their gates are open to visitors, allowing kids to meet the livestock (sheep, cows, pigs and sheep dogs) as well as learning about life on the farm, from lambing and hay-baling to ploughing fields. The lambing seasons in spring and late autumn are particularly popular. Carruan also offer tours around the farm by tractor and trailer and a play area. Oh, yes, and the joys of sheep racing... place your bets please.

CARRUAN FARM CENTRE: Polzeath PL27 6QU; 01208 869 584; www.carruan.co.uk. Free entry; open Wed–Sat, 10am–6pm; daily from 8am to 8.30pm during summer holidays.

... and how to avoid children

Book a treatment at the **Cowshed Spa** at the glamorous new St Moritz Hotel in Trebetherick (☎ 01208 862242; www.stmoritzhotel.co.uk). The luxury spa offers relaxing massages, scrubs, 'cowgrooms' and facials (from £30), using an exclusive range of natural botanical products made from plants grown at Babington House in Somerset.

Entertainment

Theatre and cinema

The nearest cinemas are in Wadebridge (see page 167) and Padstow (see page 167). However, in August, **Carruan Farm** (☎ 01208 869 584; www.carruan.co.uk) offers a summer programme of theatre and music events.

Special events

In the Collegiate Church of Endelienta, near Port Isaac, the annual **St Endellion Music Festival**, celebrated its 50th year in July 2008 (www.endellion.org.uk; ☎ 01208 880298). Under the direction of conductor, Richard Hickox, the 10-day festival featured performances of Britten's Peter Grimes, Elgar's Piano Quartet and Vaughan Williams' Blake Settings.

A complete contrast is Polzeath's beach-party music event **Beachbreak Live** (www.beachbreaklive.com) in July – an all-night, youth-fest of indie, electro and break beat, featuring the likes of the Wombats, the Enemy and Boy Kill Boy.

Nightlife

Rock is the only place that rocks around here, and even then it's fairly low key. The place to find the rich and the beautiful people in Rock is **Mariners Rock**. Other cool hangouts include **The Blue Tomato** on the cliffs overlooking Polzeath (late bar until 12am), and **The Mill House** at Trewbarwith (see Restaurants), which often presents live music on Saturday nights. In Tintagel,

Luxurious Cowshed Spa at the St Moritz Hotel

the **Tintagel Arms** also does Saturday music nights, covering blues to Goth, with a bar until midnight.

Shopping

Among the many gift shops in Tintagel and Port Isaac, **Charmed** (44 Fore Street, Port Isaac, ☎ 01208 881101), run by Laurence Llewelyn-Bowen and his wife, Jackie, is all hearts, lace, flowers, crystal jewellery and scented candles (see www.charmedincornwall.co.uk).

You will find the dark slate floors common to north Cornish buildings at the **Delabole Slate** quarry. Slate has been quarried here for centuries; it's part of the vernacular of the region, and the Delabole quarry is still going strong – producing slate block from a mile-wide quarry, said to be the largest manmade hole in Britain. Aside from floor tiles, specialities include custom-made house signs and pet memorials.

DELABOLE SLATE COMPANY: Pengelly, Delabole PL33 9AZ; ☎ 01840 212242; www.delaboleslate.co.uk. Walkabout tours, adults £7; children (over 11), £5; May to Aug, Mon–Fri, except bank holidays, at 2pm.

The best... PLACES TO STAY

BOUTIQUE

St Enodoc Hotel

Rock PL27 6LA
☎ 01208 863394
www.enodoc-hotel.co.uk

Set back from the waterfront, this is one of Cornwall's most polished hotels, a country house by the sea, with ultra-tasteful rooms furnished with original paintings and Cornish slate, modish cuisine and the odd celebrity guest. It's child-friendly in a grown-up sort of way, and celebrated chef Nathan Outlaw runs the restaurant.

Price: B&B from £130–£235 for a double per night; two-bed family suites from £155.

The Longcross

Trelights, Port Isaac PL29 3TF
☎ 01208 880560
www.longcrosshotel.co.uk

In the sticks but close to Port Isaac and Polzeath, it's classic Victorian with a contemporary up-grade. Next door is the hotel's own 4-acre Long Cross garden, the only public garden on the North Coast.

Price: B&B from £110–£210 for a double per night; dogs £5 a night.

HOTEL

St Moritz Hotel

Trebetherick, near Polzeath PL27 6SD
☎ 01208 862242
www.stmoritzhotel.co.uk

The first purpose-built hotel to emerge on Cornish soil for years, this glamorous deco-style spa-retreat has fabulous seaview suites, ocean-liner decks, two pools and a tropical garden. There's also a hip bistro-style restaurant and the Cowshed Spa (both open to non-residents) and a gym. Accommodation includes penthouse apartments, and suites – hotel rooms with self-catering facilities.

Price: B&B £105–£315 for a double per night.

Slipway Hotel

The Harbour Front, Port Isaac PL29 3RH
☎ 01208 880264
www.portisaachotel.com

A 16th-century building, a former ships chandlery, it's right in the heart of the village and, as the name suggests, within spitting distance of the harbour slipway. Some of the rooms are on the small side and parking is tricky but the place has style, atmosphere and good food.

Price: B&B from £90–£180 for a double per night.

Camelot Castle Hotel

Tintagel PL34 0DQ
☎ 01840 770202
www.camelotcastle.com

Tintagel's other 'castle' is so vast you can see its bulky outline from the top of Rough Tor. Close up it's an awesome Victorian look-alike with impressive mock baronial interiors; beloved of coach tourists and eccentric, to the point of barmy, but fantastic clifftop views from its own headland.

Price: B&B from £78–£270 per night.

The best... PLACES TO STAY

B&B

The Gallery

44 Fore Street, Port Isaac PL29 3RD
☎ 01208 881032
www.bed-and-breakfast-port-isaac.co.uk

The boutique guest house run by local artist Martyn Dempsey, is perched on the hillside overlooking Port Isaac harbour. The rooms are light and fresh; there are art classes (or surfing lessons) and a gallery next door.

Price: B&B from £70–£100 per night.

SELF-CATERING

Trevathan Farm

St Endellion, Delabole
☎ 01208 880248
www.trevathanfarm.com

A collection of charming four and five-star cottages (a former pigsty, a wagon house, a converted stables) on a working farm 3 miles from the coast. There's a farm shop, tea room and an array of animals (cows and bunnies among others).

Price: from £210–£1,360 for a week (cottages sleep two to eight).

Mayrose Farm Cottages

Helstone PL32 9RN
☎ 01840 213509
www.mayrosefarmcottages.co.uk

Six stylish farm cottages and a 'glamppod' (an all-singing safari tent) on 17 acres overlooking the Allen Valley south of Delabole. The high-spec cottages have wood-burners and pretty gardens, plus there's a communal pool and duckpond.

Price: from £360–£1,250 for a week (cottages sleep four to six).

UNUSUAL

Cornish Tipi Holidays

Tregeare, Pendoggett, St Kew PL30 3LW
☎ 01208 880781
www.cornishtipiholidays.co.uk

A back-to-nature holiday, offering a choice of 40 tipi tents scattered around a spring-fed lake on 16 wooded acres. The tipis (available in three sizes) are furnished with camping basics: no bedding (bring your own) and no electricity, but campfire cooking and communal flush toilets.

Price: from £340–£880 for a week. Short breaks (minimum two nights) available off season.

Shepherd's Hut

Moyles Farm, St Minver PL27 6QT
☎ 01208 862331
www.moylesfarm.co.uk

For holidays a deux there's nowhere quite like this compact rustic hut, once used to shelter duty shepherds during lambing. There is room inside for a king-size double, woodburner, small stove and not much else, but there's a camp-fire pit outside, and a private bathroom a few yards away.

Price: from £50 per night.

Tregosse House

Treknoaw, Tintagel PL34 0EP
☎ 01840 779230
www.tregossehouse.co.uk

A good choice for walkers, this family-run guest house is a short hop across fields to the coast path, 10 minutes from Trebarwith Strand. All three rooms are double aspect with Atlantic views and ensuite bathrooms.

Price: from £35 per person per night.

The best... FOOD AND DRINK

The combination of traditional farming country and well-heeled holiday hotspot has given rise to a wealth of real-food enterprises. There are some excellent restaurants around here, too, specially around the waterfront at Rock. But it's not all delis and dairies. The seaside fish market at Port Isaac couldn't be more 'real', there are some down-to-earth farm shops, and even the posh do pasties.

Staying in

Salami is not quite what you'd expect of the north Cornish countryside, but Jean Cole and Martin Edwards of the **Deli Farm Charcuterie** at Delabole make convincing Italian-style charcuterie meats from Cornish produce. You can buy their air-dried salamis and hams online (☎ 01840 214106; www.delifarmcharcuterie.co.uk) or through various outlets including the nearby farm shop at **Trevathan Farm** (☎ 01208 880248; www.trevathanfarm.com). Trevethan also stocks Cornish cheeses, clotted cream, ales and home-produced beef (the latter, to order). Trevethan's shop and tea room is open daily from 10am.

The shop at **Carruan Farm**, near Polzeath (☎ 01208 869 584 www.carruan.co.uk) sells a range of home-reared beef and lamb (matured on the bone), homemade ready meals, Cornish free-range chickens, breads, chutneys and jams.

Nearby **Moyles Farm** (☎ 01208 862331; www.moylesfarm.co.uk) specialises in home-cooked freezer meals, available for collection or for delivery. A two-person meal (Thai green curry or fish pie, for example) costs £10.

For fresh fish and lobster, head for the unpretentious salt-and-sawdust **Fish Cellars**, home to **Just Shellfish** (☎ 01208 880449) and **Dennis Knight Fish Merchant** (☎ 01208 880498), right on the slip way in Port Isaac. In Tintagel, the **Good Food Deli** (and café) sells lots of local and Mediterranean goodies (☎ 01840 770880; www.thegoodfoodcompany.co.uk) and, for pasties try, **Pengenna Pasties** (☎ 01288 355169): eat in, takeaway or mail order (delivered to your doorstep within 24 hours). In Rock, **Di's Dairy and Pantry** (Rock Road, Rock, www.disdairyandpantry.co.uk) sells its own freshly made pasta, pies, cakes and soups, plus loads of Cornish-made produce and they will deliver (at least in Rock).

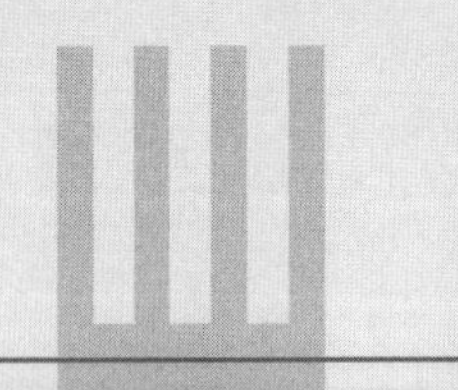

EATING OUT

FINE DINING

Restaurant Nathan Outlaw

St Enedoc Hotel, Rock PL29 6LA
☎ 01208 862737
www.enodoc-hotel.co.uk

Under Cornwall's most celebrated chefs, the contemporary restaurant at the St Enedoc hotel, won two Michelin stars in 2011 and was rated the UK's best seafood restaurant. The food of course is excellent, though expensive – a tasting menu costs £75 per head. For a more informal dining experience visit the hotel's Nathan Outlaw Seafood and Grill (main courses from £13). Open Tues-Sat, 7pm-9pm.

RESTAURANT

The Dining Room

Rock Road, Rock PL27 6JS
☎ 01208 862622
www.thediningroomrock.co.uk

In place of Burridges, a long-standing favourite, this new-ish restaurant, serves up-scale (foie gras terrine, brioche crusted Pollock, roasted megrim sole and the like). Dinner costs around £30 per head. On a fine day, it's great place for lunch on the terrace, admiring the estuary views. Open Wed-Sun.

The Mote

9 Fore Street, Port Isaac PL29 3RB
☎ 01208 880226
www.the-mote.co.uk

In a white-washed smugglers' den, dating from about 1540, this cosy little restaurant and bar champions Cornish produce, from Port Isaac seafood (straight off the boats) to vegetables grown on a local allotment. A two-course dinner costs around £16–£25.

Sea Side

St Moritz Hotel, Trebetherick PL27 6SD
☎ 01208 862242
www. stmoritzhotel.co.uk

In 2011, St Moritz added a laid-back pool-side restaurant to the hotel's gardens offering a fresh summery menu of antipasta, seafood lunches (Porthilly mussels with lemon grass and ginger, for example) and dishes to share. In a light open-plan pavilion, under a wave-shaped roof, it has a terrace and great views of Daymer Bay. Lunches cost around £10-£12. Open daily, 12pm-6pm.

GASTRO PUB

The Millhouse Inn

Trebarwith PL34 OHD
☎ 01840 770200
www.themillhouseinn.co.uk

Between Treknow and Trebarwith, this former corn mill is hidden away in the shade of a wooded valley, but its bar is hip and happening, and the restaurant is a local favourite – serving high quality mid-priced bistro food in a modern-rustic restaurant. There are rooms upstairs, so you can stay the night, too.

The Slipway

The Harbour Front, Port Isaac PL29 3RH
☎ 01208 880264
www.portisaachotel.com

Right on the sea front at Port Isaac, the pub-like but atmospheric eatery capitalises on the local catch. Whole gilt head bream, Cornish squid, local plaice and Port Isaac crab are typical of the menu. Two courses cost around £25.

EATING OUT

Mariners Rock

Slipway, Rock PL27 6LD.
☎ 01208 863679
www.marinersrock.com

In an 1970s-style waterfront pub, this Rock institution serves ketchup food to a caviar clientele – Princes Harry and Wills and chums, for example; and if not them, an army of identikit Sloanes. For a more sophisticated dining experience, neighbouring Tides Restaurant, under the same management, features upscale dishes by head-chef Tom Scade, and a collection of vintage railway posters.

Wyldes Café

Bossiney Road, Tintagel PL34 0AH
☎ 01840 770007
www.wyldestogo.co.uk

This fresh-food temple offers breakfasts, lunches, frothy cappuccino and afternoon teas with vegetarian and gluten-free options in a varied menu. Light lunches from £3.65. Open Apr to end Oct.

TEA ROOM

Lewis's Tea Rooms

Bossiney Road, Tintagel PL34 0AH
☎ 01840 770427

In the sub-tropical gardens of a creeper-clad Georgian house in downtown Tintagel, this has cream teas written all over it. Watch the world go by from behind the garden walls or cosy up inside.

Drinking

The *Good Pub Guide*'s Brewery of the Year 2008 was the **Sharps Brewery** (☎ 01208 862121; www.sharpsbrewery.co.uk) based in Rock. Founded in 1994, it's now the largest brewer of cask-conditioned beers in the south-west, and needless to say it's a favourite among Cornish ales. Sadly, they don't do tours but you can visit the brewery shop (open Mon–Fri, 9am–5pm) to stock up on Doom Bar, IPA, Eden (after the Eden Project) and Chalky Bites (after Rick Stein's dog) among other brews. Or you can sup a pint of Sharps in the **Crow's Nest** at Port Isaac (☎ 01208 880305) and the **Cornishman Inn** at Tintagel (☎ 01840 770238).

For seaside watering holes, head for the **Golden Lion** at Port Isaac (☎ 01208 880336), **The Rock Inn** at Rock (classic pub food and Cornish ales, ☎ 01208 863498), the bar at the **Port Gaverne Hotel** in Port Gaverne (☎ 01208 880244), or **The Port William**, right on the sea at Trebarwith Strand (reasonable food, dog-friendly and St Austell ales, ☎ 01840 77023). The 15th-century village local, the **St Kew Inn** at St Kew (☎ 01208 841259) has a flag-stoned bar, large garden, plus St Austell's Hicks, Tinners and Tribute ales.

Visitor Information

Tourist information centres: Tintagel Tourist Information Centre, Bossiney Road Tintagel PL34 0AJ, ☎ 01840 779084/250010.

Doctors: Tintagel Medical Centre, Bossiney Road, Tintagel, Cornwall PL34 0AE, ☎ 01840 770214.

Pharmacies: Alliance Pharmacy, 8–10 Fore Street, Tintagel PL34 0DA, ☎ 01840 770219.

Police station: Wadebridge Police Station, Whiterock Road, Wadebridge, North Cornwall PL27 7DR, ☎ 0845 2777444.

Supermarkets: The nearest is in Wadebridge (see page 165), though Tintagel has a convenience store:
Tintagel Stores, Bossiney Road PL34 0AJ, ☎ 01840 770323; there is also a Spar shop on Rock Road in Rock (☎ 01208 863328).

Internet access: Available at the Visitor Centre in Tintagel (see above) for a small fee.

Surf schools: Surfs Up Surf School ☎ 01208 862003; www.surfs upsurfschool.com at Polzeath.

Watersports centres: Sailing at Rock ☎ 01208 841 246; Camel Ski School, Rock ☎ 01208 862 727; Cornish Rock Tors, Polzeath ☎ 07791 534 884; www.cornishrocktors.com.

ATMs: Tintagel Post Office, Bossiney Road, Tintagel PL34 0AA; the Rock Post Office, Pavilion Building, Rock Road, Rock PL27 6JU.

Local taxis: Camelot Taxis, Tintagel, ☎ 01840 770172; Valency Taxis, Tintagel, ☎ 01840 311702; Rock Taxis, Rock, ☎ 01208 815775.

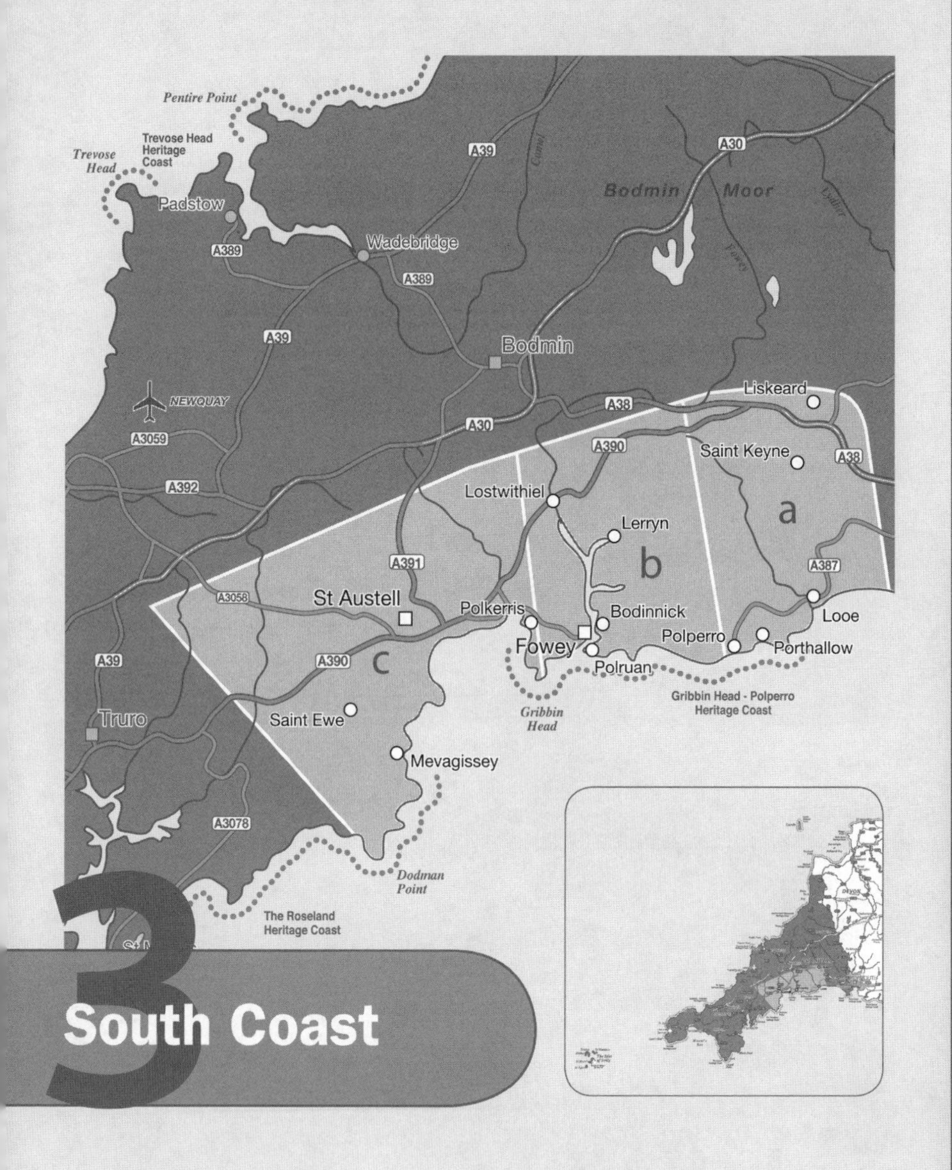

3 South Coast

a. The Looe Valley
b. Fowey River and surrounds
c. St Austell Bay

Unmissable highlights

01 Discover a world of plant life at Eden Project's amazing biomes – a journey from tropical rainforest to a Cornish garden, p. 149

02 Take the Looe Valley train on the scenic branch-line railway from Liskeard to the seaside – getting there is half the fun, p. 122

03 Lose yourself in glorious greenery, in the rediscovered Lost Gardens of Heligan, p. 149

04 Cross the Fowey River estuary on the foot ferry to Polruan and back again – just because you can, p. 134

05 Find your own half-mile of empty sand at Vault Beach, just across the rocks from pretty Gorran Haven, p. 148

06 Dine on fresh seafood at Trawlers on the Quay – right next to Looe's famous fish market, p. 130

07 Catch the movie-star tall ships on historic Charlestown Harbour – like stepping into the film set of a costume drama, p. 146

08 A ramble across fields, a scramble down cliffs, the beach at Lantic Bay is worth the effort, p. 135

09 Sup a pint of Polperro Pride at the Blue Peter Inn, overlooking the village's perfect little harbour, p. 131

10 Dance to the tune of a Belgian café organ among Paul Corin's eccentric display of Magnificent Music Machines, p. 122

SOUTH COAST

The sunny south coast doesn't have the rugged drama of the north, nor the runway beaches, but it's softer, greener and less exposed. This is proper Cornish countryside, scattered with cream tea dairy farms, rolling down-river to the south-facing English Channel.

Between cliffs and headlands, you'll find secretive little coves and the occasional wide stretch of sand, but very little surf. Tourism around here is all about picture-postcard harbour villages, market towns and medieval history, all co-existing with traditional local industry – an odd mix of farming, shark-fishing, pilchards and china clay.

To the east, the Looe River makes a gentle descent through the prettiest of valleys to the fish quays of Looe harbour. Right in the centre, the River Fowey (pronounced Foy), rises on Bodmin Moor, flows down through the Glyn Valley, past Restormel Castle to Lostwithiel where it widens into a lush green estuary, and continues on to maritime Fowey. Urban St Austell, the china clay capital, offers a slice of Cornish history at Charlestown at the gateway to the Cornish Riviera. Mevagissey is the beach-tourist hotspot. But inland is just as busy. The Eden Project's futuristic biomes now attract a million visitors a year.

THE LOOE VALLEY

At the head of the East Looe River, Liskeard is the main centre. A former mining town, with a weekly livestock market, its position on the A38 and the mainline railway makes it a good base. But the majority of visitors head for the seaside. Take the branch-line Looe Valley railway down to Looe, where the East and West Looe rivers meet at this salty medieval port, its two riverbank quays linked by a 15th-century bridge. Looe's tourist industry goes back to the days of bathing machines, but today it's best known for its shark boats and fish market – the latter, one of the best in Cornwall.

Nearby, Polperro dates from the 13th century, and looks its age, with crooked stone buildings and terraces of cottages packed in like sardines or clinging to the sides of a deep green valley. The Pol River, which rushes through narrow channels between houses, flows under a Saxon bridge and into the inner harbour. Climb the steep cliffs either side of the rocky outer harbour and you can walk for miles across National Trust land.

WHAT TO SEE AND DO

A great introduction to the area is the single-track **Looe Valley Line**. One of the most scenic rail journeys in Cornwall, it connects to the mainline at **Liskeard** station and meanders south through the beautiful Looe Valley to **East Looe**. For most of the route, it travels alongside the East Looe River, calling at Coombe Junction, St Keyne, Causeland and Sandplace. Trains leave Liskeard every hour or so and return at similar intervals, but try and time a trip at high tide when the river almost touches the track. On the final approach, the train appears to be floating on water (or would do, if not for the clatter of wheels on metal).

LOOE VALLEY LINE: First Great Western; ☎ 08457 000 125; www.firstgreat western.co.uk. Tickets, single/return: £3.40/ £3.60; cheap day return: £2.90/ £3; services run 6am–9pm year round; check timetable for seasonal changes.

Following the towpath of the former Liskeard to Looe Union Canal, the route plunges through tunnels of riverbank greenery, through achingly pretty countryside that seems almost unchanged since the railway was built in 1860. From Liskeard, the track takes a steep horse-shoe loop sweeping down to Coombe, where the driver operates points to enable the train to change direction.

For walks and trails you can do in conjunction with the railway, see www.trailsfromthetrack.com. For details of a Looe Valley Line pub crawl, see www.railaletrail.com.

St Keyne

A good non-pub stopover en route is **St Keyne**, a tiny village with two attractions: the **Holy Well** (dedicated to the Celtic St Keyne herself), and **Paul Corin's Magnificent Music Machines**, an eccentric museum of mechanical organs and player pianos housed in a rather fusty old mill right by the station.

Wurlitzer organ at Paul Corin's Magnificent Music Machines

There is nothing Paul Corin doesn't know about these music machines, each churning out an automated repertoire of old-fashioned tunes programmed on perforated paper rolls, punched cards or metal discs. Ranging in age from Victorian to the 1930s, they include Belgian 'café organs' and a 'mighty' Wurlitzer Theatre Pipe Organ, originally made in America in 1929 and shipped to the Regent Cinema in Brighton where it once rose from the orchestra pit during intervals.

PAUL CORIN'S MAGNIFICENT MUSIC MACHINES, St Keyne Station, Liskeard PL14 4SH; ☎ 01579 343108; www.paulcorinmusic.co.uk. Entry: adults £6, children £3; open daily Good Friday to 31 Oct, 10.30am–5pm.

Looe

After the beauty of the river, Looe proper is a bit of a disappointment; there are narrow car-free streets of half-timbered medieval buildings, a jostle of coloured boats on riverside fishing quays, but a veneer of tacky shops undermines its potential charm (a factor which is being addressed by a Heritage Economic Regeneration scheme). The little museum at the **Old Guildhall and Gaol** (☎ 01503 263709) in Higher Market Street, gives an insight into the town's history.

East Looe beach is safe and sandy, but it's marred by concrete terraces and, in summer, too many people – though you can escape some of them by walking east to what the locals call **Second Beach**. To the west of the main beach, lies the so-called **Banjo Pier**: a long stone promenade with a round banjo-like head, designed by engineer Joseph Thomas to prevent sand silting up the river. There is a longer, rockier but often quieter beach at **Hannafore**, accessed via the cliff-top **Marine Drive** on the **West Looe** side of the river. It's good for rock-pools and dog-walking and has views out to **Looe Island**, a marine nature reserve run by the Cornwall Wildlife Trust (www.cornwallwildlifetrust.org.uk) a mile out to sea.

They bought an island: the mistresses of St George's

Sisters Babs and Evelyn Atkins were already middle-aged when they decided to fulfil a dream and spend the rest of their days on an island. In 1965, they borrowed £22,000 and bought one: Looe Island (also known as St George's Island). A mile off Hannafore Point, on the coast of Looe, it wasn't exactly remote, but for two single women from Epsom it was a huge undertaking: a 22.5-acre hump of green and partly wooded rock, more or less wild, often wet, frequently cut off from the mainland by rough seas, and, in the early years, without a telephone.

Still, their island idyll was no desert: Island House, built by HM Custom in 1876 to ward off smugglers, provided the Atkins sisters with a comfortable home. They also had two guest cottages, Jetty and Smugglers, two beaches and the scant remains of a 12th-century Benedictine chapel – all set in a maritime climate so mild that daffodils are known to bloom at Christmas. From the outset, the sisters welcomed a procession of tenants, volunteers and day-trip visitors.

Evelyn, who died in 1997, wrote two books about their life on the island: *We Bought an Island* (1976) and *Tales from our Cornish Island* (1986). Sister Babs remained there alone until she died in 2004, aged 86. Left to Cornwall Wildlife Trust, the island is run as a low-key visitor centre during the summer months; a warden lives in Smugglers Cottage, and Island House is now a small museum of bits and bobs, mostly belonging to the sisters. You can walk around the island, listen to the birds, admire the views. It is, they say, one of the few places left in Britain where you can simply be at one with nature. We can thank Babs and Evelyn for keeping it that way.

On the water

Looe Island excursions are among a number of **boat trips** on offer, most of them leaving from **The Quay**, between the Banjo Pier and the East Looe fish market. Shark fishing is big in Looe, and with the help of **the Shark Angling Club of Great Britain** (SACGB), founded here in 1953, you can join shark-boat day trips to the gulf-stream fishing grounds, 10–15 miles off the coast. Anglers need to land a 7ft blue shark, or a 4ft 6in, porbeagle, mako or thresher shark, before they are eligible for full membership of the SACGB.

You can also book trips through the **Looe Chandlery** in West Looe. A good start for novices is a two-hour mackerel trip; the more adventurous can do full-day, deep-sea trips, fishing for conger, pollack, cod and other fish, in the rocks and reefs between Eddystone Lighthouse and Dodman Point.

THE SHARK ANGLING CLUB OF GREAT BRITAIN, The Quay, East Looe PL13 1DX; ☎ 01503 262 642; www.sharkanglingclubofgreatbritain.com. Shark trips from £45 per person; open all year round; acts as a booking agency for fishing boat charters.

LOOE CHANDLERY: Millpool Boatyard, West Looe PL13 2AE; ☎ 01503 264355; www.looechandlery.co.uk. Fishing trips from £10 (2-hour mackerel) to £40 (full-day deep sea).

Local hero: Nelson the seal

On Pennyland Rocks at the mouth of the Looe River is a bronze statue of Nelson the seal. The one-eyed grey bull seal made Looe his home for over 25 years, and was well known in the area (he also made regular day trips to Polperro). The rocks of Looe Island were his lounge, the harbour his dining room. And when he died in 2003, the town mourned.

Statue of Nelson the Seal on Pennyland Rocks

The bronze statue, made by sculptor Suzie Marsh, was unveiled in May 2008 by sailing legend Robin Knox-Johnston – and it's not just a bit of sentimental whimsy. Nelson has since given his name to a campaign to raise awareness about Cornwall's colonies of grey seals, their habitats and environmental issues. Conservation charity the Cornwall Seal Group helped raise funds for Nelson's statue. He was, says the commemorative plaque, *'a grand old man of the sea... a splendid ambassador for his species'.*

The less adventurous can just cross the river to **West Looe** on the little foot ferry (tickets 40p) which runs backwards and forwards in tune with the tide – though getting there is the thing: West Looe has a few quayside pubs, restaurants and hotels, but it's largely residential. On the West Looe side of the bridge, the Millpool car park provides access to way-marked footpaths through the nature reserve of **Kilminorth Woods**, an ancient oak woodland on the pristine banks of the West Looe River. It's open to the public all year round and is particularly lovely in autumn or when the bluebells are out in April/May.

A good coastal walk is to head for **Talland Bay**, via Hannafore Point, along the South West Coast path, 3 miles west and taking roughly 1.5 hours. Talland Bay's sheltered cove is ideal for children, with clear waters and a beach café (open in the summer). For those wanting a longer walk, you can continue on to Polperro, a further 1.25 miles, taking 45 minutes. The footpath on both sections of the walk involves fairly stiff climbs in parts.

Polperro

If you drive to **Polperro** you will have to park the car at the **Crumplehorn car park** and walk. The village is closed to all traffic in summer and if you need to know why, look at the local community website's 'jammed' page, dedicated to all the scrapes and scraps caused by unwitting motorists following satnav directions through streets designed for donkeys. In the summer, you can travel from Crumplehorn to the village in a horse-drawn carriage or electric omnibus (like a glorified milk float) for a small fee, though the harbour is an easy 15-minute walk through charming streets of terraced cottages and shops.

Look out for the **Shell House** on the aptly named Warren. An example of exuberant fisher art, the house is a kitsch mosaic of sea shells, each shell pressed into cement by a handy fisherman, from nobody knows quite where or when. On the inner harbour, at the mouth of the

Harbour at Polperro

River Pol, old warehouses with jettied upper storeys over-hang the water. There is a tiny fish market, and around the corner, the picturesque outer harbour, where shoals of fishing boats lie on one side of a granite breakwater and a sandy little beach on the other. Climb the steps to the rear of the **Blue Peter pub**, to join the footpath, which takes you up over **Chapel Cliff** and, if you have the energy, along miles of National Trust coast, all the way to **Polruan-by-Fowey**.

Wet weather

POLPERRO HERITAGE MUSEUM OF SMUGGLING AND FISHING, The Warren, Polperro PL13 2RB; ☎ 01503 273005; www.polperro.org. Entry: adults, £1.60, children, 50p (under-5s, free); open daily Mar to Oct 10.30am–5.30pm.

In a former fish-processing factory on the harbour, the folksy **Polperro Heritage Museum** celebrates its traditional 18th and 19th-century industries: fishing and smuggling. You will learn about Polperro's 'gaffers' (or gaff-rigged boats), drift nets and salted pilchards; or revisit the mid-18th century when contraband goods were smuggled across the channel from Guernsey on a vast scale. The illustrated stories of Zephaniah Job, the smugglers' banker, the privateering Quiller family, and the crew of the *Lottery*, hunted for the murder of a customs officer, give quite a different perspective on Polperro life.

What to do with children

THE MONKEY SANCTUARY TRUST, St Martin's, Looe PL13 1NZ; ☎ 01503 262 532; www.monkeysanctuary.org. Entry: adults £8, children £5 (under-5s free), family £25; Easter to Sept, Sun–Thurs, 11am–5pm (closed Fri/Sat except Easter).

Meet Max, Maya and Pablo, members of the colony of Amazonian woolly monkeys that inhabit the **Monkey Sanctuary**. Founded in 1964 by musician Leonard Williams, it was set up as a charitable rescue centre for ex-zoo or inappropriately kept pet monkeys, and provides a home for gangs of woolly

Two rescued capuchins at The Monkey Sanctuary

and capuchin primates, set in the grounds of a Victorian house just outside Looe. Housed in grassed enclosures the monkeys are semi-free range and you can watch them forage for food or play around in the trees. For the humans, there is also a kids' play area and activity room and a Tree Top café.

Entertainment

Theatre and cinema

The **Cinema by the Sea** run by the Looe Film Society (☎ 0845 8681021; www.looefilmsociety.org.uk) shows movies around 14 times a year (mainly in the summer months) at Looe Primary School. Non-members, or guest tickets, cost £5 per film.

Special events

In June, the **Polperro Festival** (www.polperrofestivalsandlights.co.uk) celebrates the arts with a week of music and exhibitions. Looe's **Festival of the Sea** (also in June) is a community celebration of 'all things Cornish' from local history and legends to food and drink and, in particular, fishing and boating. A popular element is the Grazing on the Quay food tastings organised by local producers and restaurants. For information see www.looefestivalbythesea.org.

In July (second Saturday), the **Liskeard Agricultural Show** (☎ 01579 342955; www.liskeardshow.org) is a good old fashioned produce show (from cows to sponge cakes), all very local, very Liskeard. Looe's **Carnival Week** (☎ 01208 872 213) usually runs from the end of July to the beginning of August. And in winter, the town is well known for its lively street party on **New Year's Eve** (fancy dress and fireworks).

The best... PLACES TO STAY

BOUTIQUE

Barclay House & Cottages

Barclay House, St Martins Road, East Looe PL13 1LP; ☎ 01503 262 929
www.barclayhouse.co.uk

This handsome Victorian villa set in 6 acres overlooking the East Looe River, is more home than hotel, but the rooms are Looe's finest with fresh colourful décor, comfy beds, and modern bath/showers. There is a heated outdoor pool and an award-winning restaurant.

Price: B&B from £115 for a room per night.

HOTEL

Talland Bay Hotel

Porthallow PL13 2JB
☎ 01503 272667
www.tallandbayhotel.co.uk

Fabulous location overlooking Talland Bay, this smart hotel has seaside gardens, bistro, bar and a plush lounge. Rooms range from cute to glam (go for a balcony suite if you can). The excellent Terrace Restaurant has two AA rosettes.

Price: B&B from £100–£225 for a double.

B&B

House on the Props

Talland Street, Polperro, Looe PL13 2RE
☎ 01503 272 310
www.houseontheprops.co.uk

With sloping walls, timbers and masts, the 'props' is one of Polperro's oldest, quaintest buildings, right on the inner harbour and overhanging the stream that rushes past. The antique rooms are cosy (as in small) with great views.

Price: B&B from £80 for a double.

SELF-CATERING

Trefanny Hill

Trefanny Hill, Duloe, Near Liskeard PL14 4QF
☎ 01503 220622
www.trefanny.co.uk

In the village of Duloe, near Looe, a collection of big-hearted, family-friendly Cornish cottages. The style is traditional English, with fireplaces or woodburners, brass or four-poster beds and country views. Self-cater or eat in the nearby Trefanny Inn.

Price: One, two or three-bedroom cottages from £279–£1,400 for a week.

Meadowside Barn

Horningtops, Near Looe
☎ 01647 433593
www.helpfulholidays.co.uk

A dinky converted barn in the grounds of a small-holding between Liskeard and Looe (4 miles from each), there is one double and one single room, a lawned garden, perfect for small children (they also enjoy the owners' chickens, Shetland ponies and cute pygmy goats).

Price: from £198–£418 for a week.

The best... FOOD AND DRINK

The countryside around here is a patchwork of small farms, mainly dairy farms at its heart. Liskeard, a centre for agriculture since the 13th century, one of the few Cornish towns to still hold a weekly market and livestock auction (every Thursday). Down in Looe, there are daily auctions at the quayside fish market; with catches coming in from Polperro and Mevagissey as well as Looe, it's one of the best in the West Country (both Rick Stein's and Jamie Oliver's restaurants source fish from here). In terms of eating out, however, the area has always been a bit fish-and-chip, but a modern generation of seafood restaurant is waking up to the riches on its doorstep; a fact reflected in Looe's Taste of South East Cornwall foodie festival in November.

Staying in

Looe's fish market is mainly for wholesale buyers, but you can buy from quayside fishmongers such as the **Blue Sail Fish Company** on Buller Quay (☎ 01503 264 069). There's a good one in nearby Liskeard too: **Pengelly's Fishmongers** in the granite arcade under the clock tower on Fore Street (☎ 01579 340777).

For farm-fresh produce check out **Soupa Doupa**, a farm-gate shop at Lower Killigorrick Farm in St Keyne (☎ 01579 320268; www.lowerkilligorrickfarm.co.uk). Produce includes home-grown vegetables (salad, greens, soft fruit, beetroot and butternut squash among others), and fresh meat (pork, lamb, chicken and meaty sausages), milk, butter and a homemade range of vegetable soups.

An alternative is to order your produce from **Food4myholiday.com** (☎ 01579 324176; www.food4myholiday.com) which supplies 'chef selected' Cornish food, pre-ordered and delivered to your holiday cottage. Based in Liskeard, the company delivers to most of south-east Cornwall, charging £7.99 for each order (minimum £40). **Purely Cornish Deli**, based at Herodsfoot, 6 miles inland from Looe (☎ 01503 262680; www.purelycornissh.co.uk), supplies a large range of Cornish goodies and goodie-packed hampers.

In Polperro check out the **Polperro Bakery** on Little Green (☎ 01503 272000); and look out for **Treleavens** hand-made Cornish ice creams and sorbets, made in East Looe in a variety of yummy flavours (Cornish Gingerbread, Coconut Kisses or Chocolate Peanut Butter Crunch). Treleavens has its own shop in Fore Street, Looe, and Lansallos Street in Polperro as well as cafés and restaurants all over Cornwall (☎ 01503 220969; www.treleavens.co.uk).

For the best pasties in the region – indeed, among the best in Cornwall – make your way to **Sarah's Pasties** (01503 263973) and join the queue. This family bakery, tucked away in Buller Street, in the back streets of East Looe, makes their own oven-fresh pasties from good quality local produce (including tender chunks of beef) wrapped in rich pastry. As well as a traditional Cornish, they also do a Full English breakfast pasty, at least one vegetarian option (spiced chick pea and lentil) and a very good gluten-free.

EATING OUT

FINE DINING

Couch's

Saxon Bridge, Polperro PL13 2QT
☎ 01503 272 554
www.couchspolperro.com

In down-town Polperro, head chef Richard McGeown (ex-Gordon Ramsay and Raymond Blanc), serves up haute cuisine with a Cornish twist. Try Trenant Farm beef, Looe scallops or Lostwithiel dairy cream, in a space that mixes Macintosh-style chairs with rustic stonework. Four courses cost £32. Open for dinner seven days a week.

Barclay House

St Martins Road, Looe PL13 1LP
☎ 01503 262929
www.barclayhouse.co.uk

Modern British 'coastal cuisine', impeccable service, fish straight off the day boats, two AA rosettes and a Taste of the West Gold award. From the restaurant's French windows step out onto the terrace and drink in the views. Four-course dinner costs £29. Open Mon–Sat, Sunday lunch in summer.

Trawlers

The Quay, East Looe PL13 1AH
☎ 01503 263593
www.trawlersrestaurant.co.uk

Another Taste of the West Gold goes to this popular harbourside restaurant run by Mark Napper and Nick Love. The food is fresh and imaginative: seafood from the fish market (just yards away), home-baked breads, Cornish cheeses, delicious puddings and tables on the quay. One of the best fish restaurants in the county, it's worth a special trip. Dishes from £6.50–£15.95. Open Tues–Sat and Sun lunch.

RESTAURANT

Old Sail Loft

Quay Street, East Looe
☎ 01503 262131
www.theoldsailloftrestaurant.com

The building is 16th century, one of Looe's oldest, furnished with oak beams, wreck salvage, and situated right on the quay. Dishes include warm mackerel salad, Fowey mussels, poached monkfish, lobster, steak and homemade linguini. Three courses cost around £25. Open daily; closed for lunch Tues/Wed off-season.

Tapenades

14 Dean Street, Liskeard PL14 4AA
☎ 01579 344844

Lively little restaurant close to the town's cattle market, serves traditional English food with a modern take; majoring on fresh local produce (scallops, crab, sea bass, lots of veggie dishes) and all prepared on the premises. Three-course dinner around £25. Closed on Tuesday. Booking essential at weekends.

EATING OUT

CAFÉ

Talland Bay Beach Café
Talland Street, Looe PL13 2RE
☎ 01503 272088
www.tallandbaybeachcafe.co.uk

An old-fashioned beach-hut café, spruced up by young owners Neil and Jo Robinson, and right on the sea at Talland Bay. Best for cream teas, Cornish crab sarnies, pasties, homemade cakes and children's lunch boxes. Open Easter to October. Light lunches from £3.25.

TEA ROOM

Lansallos Barton Farm
Lansallos, Looe, PL13 2PU
☎ 01503 272 293

This National Trust farm serves organic Cornish cream teas in the garden or in the rustic farmhouse tea room. Open from Easter and through the summer holidays.

Drinking

One of south Cornwall's finest pubs, **The Blue Peter** is a traditional fishermen's inn right on the quay in Polperro (☎ 01503 272743, www.bluepeter.co.uk). A great mix of low beams, real ale and old salts, 'the Blue', serves Polperro Pride, as well as variety of guest ales and live music. Grab a snug with views of the harbour and read the wit on the walls: *'I wouldn't have married Mr Right, if I'd known his first name was Always'.* Deep in the heart of the village the nearby **Old Mill House** (☎ 01503 272362; www.oldmillhouseinn.co.uk) is another old-fashioned inn, with a riverside beer garden. And at top of the village by the car park, the **Crumplehorn Inn** (☎ 01503 272348; www.crumplehorn-inn.co.uk) serves good selection of Cornish beers (St Austell's, Sharps, Skinners) in a bar that used to be a cow shed.

In East Looe, try **Ye Olde Salutation Inn** on Fore Street (☎ 01503 262784); it's authentic but often crowded. In West Looe, the 16th-century **Jolly Sailor** (otherwise known as 'the Jolly') is one of the oldest pubs in Britain (☎ 01503 263387). Inland, the 17th-century **Punch Bowl Inn** (☎ 01503 220778) at Lanreath, serves it own brew alongside a variety of guest ales. What was Ye Olde Plough House Inn at Duloe has been rebranded by new owners, the Barclay House Hotel in Looe (see page 128). Now simply the **Plough Inn** (01503 262556), www.ploughduloe.co.uk), it's more restaurant than pub, but still serves a pint and a decent glass of wine. And in Liskeard, the **Barley Sheaf** on Church Street (☎ 01579 342055; www.thebarley.com), offers St Austell ales, a rain-proofed garden, live-music nights and a digital juke box, featuring every top-40 hit single since 1952.

Visitor Information

Tourist information centres: Looe Tourist Information Centre, The Guildhall, Fore Street, PL13 1AA, ☎ 01503 262072; www.looecornwall.com; Liskeard Tourist Information Centre, The Foresters Hall, Pike Street Liskeard PL14 3JE, ☎ 01579 349148.

Hospitals with A&E: Liskeard Community Hospital, Clemo Road, Liskeard, PL14 3XD, ☎ 01579 335 600 (nurse-run minor injury unit operating from 8pm to 10pm ☎ 01579 335278).

Doctors: Pelynt Surgery, Looe PL13 2LB, ☎ 01503 220443; Lanreath Doctor's Surgery, New Village Hall, Lanreath, Looe PL13 2NX, ☎ 01503 220923; Dr A D Smalley, 8 Dean Street, Liskeard PL14 4AQ, ☎ 01579 343133.

Pharmacies: Looe Pharmacy, 65 Fore Street, Looe, Cornwall, PL13 1DT, ☎ 01503 262243; Boots the Chemist, 21–22, Bay Tree Hill, Liskeard PL14 4BG, ☎ 01579 343183; Roberts Pharmacy, The Coombes, Polperro, Looe PL13 2RG, ☎ 01503 272250.

Police station: Looe Police Station, Station Road, East Looe, Caradon PL13 1HN. ☎ 08452 777444 (closed at weekends); Liskeard Police Station, Luxstowe Road, Liskeard, Caradon PL14 3HP.

Supermarkets: Somerfield, Fore Street, East Looe, Looe PL13 1AD ☎ 01503 262015; Morrisons, Horningtops, Liskeard PL14 3PR, ☎ 01579 340873.

Internet access: Looe Library Millpool, Looe PL13 2AF, ☎ 01872 322005. Free Wi-Fi at Barley Sheaf pub on Church Street in Liskeard, ☎ 01579 342055.

Car hire: Andrews Garage, Pound Street, Liskeard PL14 3JT, ☎ 01579 342122; www.CarHireLiskeard.co.uk; East Taphouse Trade Centre, Doublebois Ind Est, Liskeard PL14 6LE, ☎ 01579 320822.

Boat trips: Looe Bluewater Seafaris, from Looe, ☎ 07748 505 871; Polperro Boat Trips, ☎ 01503 272 476.

Websites: www.polperro.org

ATMs: Barclays Bank, Fore Street, East Looe PL13 1DL; HSBC Bank, Higher Market Street, East Looe PL13 1BL; NatWest Bank, Trehawke House, Liskeard PL14 4AG; Lloyds TSB Bank, The Parade, Liskeard PL14 6AW.

Cycle hire: Liskeard Cycles, Peg Meadow Lane, Liskeard PL14 6AF, ☎ 01579 347696.

Local taxis: Crystal Cars, Looe ☎ 01503 263636; Kells Kabs, Looe, ☎ 01503 263532; Anytime Taxis (Liskeard) ☎ 01579 346007.

FOWEY RIVER AND SURROUNDS

Thanks to the deep-water harbour that lies at the river's mouth, Fowey has been an important English Channel port since the Middle Ages, more recently as a servant of the china clay industry. When the delights of the valley first enraptured Daphne du Maurier in the late 1920s, it was still a dirty fisher town, its waters milky with clay. It continued thus well into the 1960s, but centuries of industry have failed to tarnish the natural beauty of the setting: a wide stretch of blue water, dotted with sailing boats; Fowey's fine houses tumbling down one steep riverbank, little Polruan, perched on the other. On the coast on either side of the estuary, a line of ravishing beaches awaits.

Fowey is still a working port, with big ships slipping up-river to the industrial wharves at Golant, hidden in the trees to the north of the town. But its livelihood these days is in tourism. Sailing, strong literary ties and the annual Daphne du Maurier Festival have helped turn this colourful little town into the St Ives of the south coast – its quayside lanes of merchants' houses packed with chic boutiques and seafood restaurants.

Fowey is the crowd-puller around here – it was recently voted one of the UK's most desirable places – but in terms of history, Lostwithiel rocks. As John Betjeman said: *'There is history in every stone in Lostwithiel'*.

WHAT TO SEE AND DO

Lostwithiel, meaning 'tail of the forest', occupies one of the prettiest stretches of the Fowey River, crossed by a Tudor bridge at its tidal reach. Right on the A390, it tends to be a bit of a drive-through, but the town merits a closer look – for this former Norman stronghold was an important medieval trading centre. By the 13th century it was the Duchy of Cornwall's seat of power, its capital city, with a busy river port, despatching wool, leather and, in particular, tin. The Stannary Parliament, which controlled Cornwall's ancient tin trade, was based here and, ironically, it was the spoils of tin mining, carried downriver from the moors, that eventually ended Lostwithiel's glory days by clogging its passage to the sea.

A few remnants of its early history remain: you can see part of the former Duchy Palace, or **Great Hall** (Grade I listed and Cornwall's oldest non-ecclesiastical building), the soaring tower of **St Bartholomew's** medieval church, and **Restormel Castle**. The elevated Norman Castle, a mile to the north of the town, was rebuilt by Edmund the Earl of Cornwall in the 13th century, and still belongs to the Duchy. Managed by English Heritage, it is open to the public. Though largely a ruin, you can walk

RESTORMEL CASTLE, Lostwithiel PL22 0BD; ☎ 01208 872687; www.english-heritage.org.uk. Entry: adults £3.40, children, £2 (under-5s free); open daily Mar to Oct, 10am–5pm (closes 6pm Jul/Aug, 4pm in Oct).

around the cobbled battlements of the circular shell-keep, imagine the grand mansion it once was, and enjoy fantastic views over the Fowey Valley.

You can learn more about Lostwithiel and its buildings on a guided walk run by **Lostwithiel Museum** every Thursday morning during the summer. Tickets (£2.50, children go free) are available from the Tourist Information Centre (☎ 01208 872207).

En route to Fowey, the peaceful little village of **Lerryn** sits among banks of trees on Lerryn Creek (a branch of the Fowey). Said to be the setting for Kenneth Grahame's *Wind in the Willows*, it has a village green, a waterside pub, and access to some wonderful riverside nature walks. At low tide, you can cross the river on stepping stones. From the west side of the river, access to Fowey is via the **Bodinnick Car Ferry**, a noisy truck of a boat, carrying only six cars at a time (hence long queues in the summer). There is a large car park on the Fowey side, but note, there is no vehicle access into the town on this approach.

In general, park and walk is the golden rule. Park at the village car park at **Polruan** (a baby Fowey, about 3 miles south of Bodinnick), and it's a short walk to the little **foot ferry** which runs between Fowey and Polruan Quay. The five-minute journey across the estuary is worth doing – especially at dusk on a warm night: Fowey seen from the river, all twinkling lights, is truly magical.

Indeed, there is no better way to explore the Fowey estuary than by boat. In the summer, small-boat operator **Fowey River Cruises** runs a series of daily trips. The basic is a 45-minute whizz around the harbour entrance, pointing out the places of interest (Fowey's **St Finbarrus Church**, Golant docks, Bodinnick village). Longer trips cruise up-river to Lostwithiel and Lerryn Creek, into densely wooded stretches of water with an Amazonian quality. Sea cruises include daytrips to Polperro (see page 125).

BODINNICK CAR FERRY: Car and 2–4 passengers, £1.75/£1.80; foot passengers: adults 50p, children 35p; daily, 7am–20.45pm (Sat/Sun from 8am/9am) all year round (subject to weather).

POLRUAN PEDESTRIAN FERRY, From Polruan Quay to Whitehouse Slip or Town Quay, 70p each way (under-13s 50p); May–Sept, daily, 7.15am–11pm (Sun from 10am).

FOWEY RIVER AND SEA CRUISES, ☎ 07891 516635; www.foweycruise.com. 45-minute Fowey river cruise, adults £6, children £3; Lerryn/Lostwithiel cruise, £10/£5; sea cruises (Polperro or Charlestown) from £15/£10; daily Apr to Oct.

By the sea

Most of the local beaches are best approached on foot. **Ready Money Cove**, for example, is an easy 15–20 minute walk from Fowey Quay. Pleasantly sandy, this little suburban beach is overlooked by the remnants of **St Catherine's Castle**, built by Henry VIII in 1536 to guard the mouth of the estuary. You can drive to **Polridmouth** (pronounced Pridmouth) but it's a 20-minute walk from the car park to this unspoilt beach on the **Menabilly estate** – where Daphne du Maurier's former home overlooks St Austell Bay (the house is not open to the public).

Flowers in Fowey

For keen walkers, a good route is to follow the coast path from Fowey to Polridmouth and on to **Polkerris**, via the National Trust's **Gribben Head** (or 'the Gribben'), a 250-foot shoulder of rock, topped by a curious 84ft, red-and-white striped day marker – erected in 1832 to enable ships to tell the Gribben apart from St Anthony Head on the other side of Falmouth Bay (see page 237). Look out for a flag atop the day marker, indicating that the tower is open for visits. Returning to Fowey, follow the clearly marked inland route known as the **Saints Way**. The whole route, there and back, takes about five hours. There is parking at Polkerris if you prefer to drive.

On the National Trust coastline to the east of the estuary, between Polruan and Polperro (see page 125), lies a pocket of secretive little bays: **Lansallos**, **Lantivet** and, the beautiful **Lantic Bay**. From the car park on the road, follow the waymarked path, cutting across fields, before take a steep descent down to the beach (remember, it's quite a walk). In a horseshoe bay, sheltered by high cliffs, Lantic is a gem of a beach, with clean, clear waters, but there are no facilities, and it can get busy with boat traffic at weekends in high summer.

On the trail of Daphne du Maurier

From Bodmin Moor's Jamaica Inn, to the Helford River's Frenchman's Creek, Daphne du Maurier drew her inspiration from all over Cornwall. But though other regions lay claim to a corner of 'Daphne du Maurier Country', the Fowey River is the real thing. Du Maurier not only set many of her novels here, she ended her days in the town she called home for 60 years. Her love affair with Fowey began in childhood, when in 1926 her parents bought Ferryside, a holiday house on the east bank of the Fowey River close to Bodinnick Ferry. As a budding writer, in her early 20s she persuaded them to let her use the house as a retreat. Her first novel *Loving Spirit*, published in 1931, was written there. Set in fictitious Plyn, about a community of Cornish boat-builders, the book was so admired by Major Tommy 'Boy' Browning, he sought to meet the author. The couple were married in 1932, at nearby Lanteglos Church (Lanoc Church in *Loving Spirit*).

In 1943, the Brownings moved into Menabilly, a sleeping mansion in a decaying estate, set back from the cliffs between Fowey and Gribben Head. *'The place called to me,'* du Maurier said of the rented house, and the call had come years earlier. Manderlay, the infamous house in *Rebecca*, published in 1938, was partly inspired by Menabilly. Nearby Polridmouth Cove, was the setting for the novel's shipwreck scene. When Browning died in 1965, Daphne moved to nearby Kilmarth, where she wrote *House on the Strand*. When she died in 1989 her ashes, according to her wishes, were scattered on the cliffs near the home she had loved.

Wet weather

Dive into the **Fowey Literary Centre** on South Street (☎ 01726 833619). A glorified book shop cum museum, it's devoted to authors with local connections, not just Daphne du Maurier, but also Kenneth Grahame and his contemporary, writer and literary critic, Sir Arthur Quiller-Couch. The latter, a Bodmin boy, who published his work under the enigmatic pseudonym, Q, moved to Fowey in 1892; the town provided the setting for his best-known novel, *The Astonishing History of Troy Town*.

A literary history is one is one of the many aspects of the town's past life explored in the **Fowey Museum**, housed in a stone-built former council chamber. Here you will meet the Fowey Gallants – the 15th-century pirate seamen whose legendary name is now taken by a Fowey River sailing club.

FOWEY MUSEUM, Trafalgar Square, Fowey PL27 1AY; ☎ 01726 833513. Entry: adults £1, students 50p; Easter to Oct, weekdays only, 10.30am–5pm.

CELEBRITY CONNECTIONS

When **Dawn French** and her estranged husband **Lenny Henry** bought a house just outside Fowey, they joined an A-list of stars who have fallen for the area's charms. **Gloria Hunniford** has a house in Fowey. Husband-and-wife presenters **Richard and Judy** live nearby. **Cliff Richard** has been spotted there on occasions. **Prunella Scales, Charles Dance** and **Edwina Currie** have stayed at the Fowey Hotel.

For Dawn French, however, the move to Fowey was about coming home. The *Vicar of Dibley* star spent part of her childhood in Saltash. She went to school in Plymouth. Her mother lives in nearby Looe. And she doesn't do things by halves. In 2007, she and Lenny bought a 40-room Gothic mansion on the coast by Readymoney Cove. Dawn announced plans to do a Daphne du Maurier, and write her memoirs there, thereby adding to the area's literary connections. Fowey, she told the *Telegraph*, would allow her to *'die slowly and nicely, in great surroundings, with my family'*.

 What to do with children...

Most of the activities around here involve the outdoor life: crabbing off Fowey quay, playing Pooh sticks off the bridge at Lerryn, or pootling around the peaceful upper reaches of the river in a borrowed boat. You can hire traditional wooden rowing boats by the week, or 16ft fibre-glass 'Orkney Longliner' motorboats by the day, from **Fowey River Boat Hire**. The hire price includes maps, itineraries and local information.

FOWEY RIVER BOAT HIRE, ☎ 01726 832874 / 832001; www.fowey-river-boat-hire.co.uk. Rowing boats, from £100 per week; motor boats, from £65 per day, £165 per week.

LOCAL KNOWLEDGE

With a background in museum development, **Deborah Boden** moved to Cornwall in 2003 to lead the team preparing the bid to UNESCO for Cornwall's World Heritage Site. Since the Cornish Mining site was finally granted World Heritage status in 2006, Deborah took up the post as its coordinator. She lives in Polruan, on the Fowey estuary.

Favourite restaurant: Trawlers on the Quay in East Looe – among a number of good new restaurants that take advantage of access to Looe's fishmarket. Webbs in Liskeard is also a favourite.

Favourite beaches: Lantic Bay is a jewel – completely undeveloped with plenty of space for a game of beach cricket and lots of sand and fascinating rock pools. Its natural charms make it worth the steep climb back. In the care of the National Trust, it is accessible via the South West Coast path, or go by boat.

Favourite café: Muffins in Fore Street, Lostwithiel, has won several awards for its food. It's right in the heart of this lovely ancient town and has a lovely sheltered garden at the back for sunny days.

Best walk: The Hall Walk, a 4-mile circular route along the Fowey estuary from Polruan via Bodinnick car ferry to Fowey, and then back to Polruan on the passenger ferry. It skirts Pont Pill, a sublimely beautiful creek where you might spot herons and kingfishers. And you pass through Fowey, if you fancy a bit of posh retail therapy.

Favourite pub: I'm very happy to stick to my home pubs, the Russell and the Lugger Inn in Polruan. Another authentic local gem is the Old Ferry Inn at Bodinnick, which is a welcome sight when you are two-thirds of the way along the Hall Walk...

Best view: The panoramic sweep of Fowey harbour, from the Quiller-Couch memorial on the Hall Walk, takes some beating.

Favourite shop: If I'm planning a special meal, I always visit both Fowey Fish, to check out the best of the catch and their small but well chosen wine selection, and Tiffins deli, also in Fowey.

 ... and how to avoid children

Become a 'wild food gourmet' at Lostwithiel's **Wild Food School**, a lesson in the art of collecting and cooking the goodies that grow freely in the fields and hedgerows around us. Founder Marcus Harrison reckons there are some 100 edible species of plant life, ripe for the picking (depending on season) if you know where to look.

Foraging around the countryside, you will first learn how to identify wild foods then learn to rustle up, say, an acorn and nettle flan, a bowl of pignut noodles, sweet violet and ground ivy greens, and a dandelion coffee, among dozens of recipes.

WILD FOOD SCHOOL, Lostwithiel; ☎ 01208 873788; www.wildfoodschool.co.uk. Half-day or full-day starter courses: £30–£90; weekend courses, £140.

Bocconic Steam Fair at Boconnoc House

Entertainment

Special events

Fowey's **Daphne du Maurier Festival** in May (☎ 01726 833847; www.dumaurierfestival.co.uk) is now one of Britain's best known literature fests, celebrating the arts with 10 days of drama, talks, reading, concerts, guided walks and community events, some of them staged in a marquee-style 'festival village'. In 2008 a typically eclectic programme featured Ric Wakeman, Marc Almond, novelist Stella Duffy, writer Justine Picardie (author of *Daphne*) and Pam Ayres. Running concurrently with the lit fest, **Fowey Fringe Festival** (www.foweyfringe.co.uk) puts on a mixed bag of live music, mostly in the town's pubs.

Much busier and certainly noisier than either is the annual **Fowey Royal Regatta** in mid-August (☎ 01726 832133; www.foweyroyalregatta.co.uk), a week-long sailing jamboree, with hundreds of boats racing up and down the estuary, music, carnival, fireworks and the Red Arrows. In early December, the **Fowey Christmas Market** (☎ 01726 67719; www.foweymarket.co.uk) offers a mix of local food, arts and crafts. In mid-July, Boconnoc House near Lostwithiel hosts the **Bocconic Steam Fair** (www.boconnocenterprises.co.uk).

Shopping

Lostwithiel is Cornwall's so-called 'antiques capital': in essence, a colony of collectors' shops and an **antiques and bygones fair** every second Sunday of the month (at the town's community centre on Liddicoat Road, 10am–4.30pm, ☎ 01736 793213 for details).

Retro shop Nanadobbie

Among the best of the shops, **Nanadobbie** on Fore Street (☎ 01208 873063; www.nanadobbie.com) specialises in retro classics from the 1950s to the 1970s, mainly furniture of the Eames and Jacobsen ilk. **Deja-Vu** across the road (☎ 01208 873912; www.deja-vu-antiques-lostwithiel.com) sells rustic painted furniture, linens and French flea-market kitchenalia. **Mark Royle Antiques**, also on Fore Street (☎ 01208 873990; www.antiqueoakandcountryfurniture.co.uk) is more high-end: oak and mahogany, silverware, paintings and early English glass.

The best... PLACES TO STAY

BOUTIQUE

The Old Quay House

28 Fore Street, Fowey PL23 1AQ
☎ 01726 833302
www.theoldquayhouse.com

The best hotel in town by a mile, this is the sophisticated redesign of an 1850s seamen's mission in the heart of Fowey. The stylish rooms are simply but luxuriously furnished, and a few have river views. There's no parking, but that's Fowey for you.

Price: from £130–£390 for a double.

HOTEL

Fowey Hall

Hanson Drive, Fowey PL23 1ET
☎ 01726 833866
www.luxuryfamilyhotels.co.uk

Said to be the inspiration for Toad Hall in Kenneth Grahame's Wind in the Willows, this splendid Italianate mansion looks down on the town from on high. It's big on families with children and offers a Bears' Den crèche and lots of activities, plus spa facilities, 12-metre swimming pool and Hanson's restaurant (which boasts 2 AA rosettes).

Price: B&B from £170–£265 for a standard double. Quality of service can be patchy.

FARMSTAY

Botelet Farm

Herodsfoot PL14 4RD
☎ 01503 220225
www.botelet.com

This rustic farmhouse's two boho guest rooms are all junk-shop antiques and rustic colours (there is only one bathroom). In *Elle Deco* in 2000, it featured in artful pictures of fashion and chickens, a still life of wellies and coal scuttle by a latched back door. In 250 acres of farmland, you can also stay in Manor or Cowslip Cottage (both sleep five), a yurt in a field, or a campsite in a meadow.

Price: B&B from £70 for a double Easter to Nov. Cottages from £300 per week.

Tredithick Farm Cottages

Lostwithiel PL22 0LE
☎ 01208 873618
www.tredethick.co.uk

A past winner in the all-England tourism awards, this is gold-star self-catering with child-friendly facilities – like an indoor pool, outdoor play area and Toby the pony. A series of nicely furnished converted farm buildings (wagonhouse, dairy, hayloft) the nine cottages, sleeping two to six, feature woodburners and all mod cons.

Price: from £485–£2,195 for a week.

B&B

The Dwelling House

6 Fore Street, Fowey PL23 1AQ
☎ 01726 833662
www.thedwellinghouse.co.uk

A Grade II listed Georgian merchant's house in central Fowey, provides one spacious guest room with a roll-top tub, period furniture and an appropriate antique look. It can be a little noisy on Fore Street, but the house backs onto the river.

Price: from £70 for a double.

The best... PLACES TO STAY

UNUSUAL

The Old Exchange

12 Lostwithiel Street, Fowey PL23 1B
☎ 01726 833252
www.foye-old-exchange.co.uk

It is, indeed, an old telephone exchang… a homage to its roots is furnished wit… collection of vintage phones. The gu… are simply furnished and quite ordin… from one four-poster bed), but the re… all black Bakelite and rotary dials.

Price: B&B from £60–£75 for a dou…

SELF-CATERING/B&B

Coriander Cottages

…ventinue Lane, Fowey
…98
…fowey.co.uk

… edge of Fowey, this offers …een' cottages, created from the … old watermill and cider barn, … the night. More traditional B&B …with courtyard terraces are also

Price: …s from £90–£140 per night (off season, sev… nights for the price of five). B&B from £90 per room.

The best... FOOD AND DRINK

With its smart waterfront restaurants, fresh seafood from the river (bass, sea trout, mullet, mussels and oysters), Fowey is the eating-out capital of the south coast, but the heart of the local food industry is Lostwithiel. It has a growing community of foodie outlets and is home to one of the best farmers' markets in Cornwall. In the world of 'slow food', Lostwithiel is tops.

Staying in

Run by the **Cornish Guild of Smallholders** (☎ 01579 324125; www.cgos.co.uk). Lostwithiel's local produce market takes place on the first and third Friday of the month at the community centre, from 10am to 2pm; in this case local means within a 35-mile catchment area. Most of the goodies on offer at **Fran's Pantry** on Quay Street (☎ 01208 872407; www.franspantry.com) come from within an even smaller area and include clotted cream, butter and yoghurt from nearby Trewithen Dairy, south Cornish cheeses and home-baked pasties and pies (like the 'Full Monty' – breakfast served in pastry).

Neighbouring **Lostwithiel Bakery** (☎ 01208 873233) makes its own rustic breads and delicious cakes. Both are also available at **The Lerryn River Stores** (☎ 01208 872375), on the village green in Lerryn; a small sell-everything general village shop with an emphasis on local produce. In Fowey, there's an excellent butcher, **Kittow & Sons** in South Street (☎ 01726 832639; www.kittowsbutchers.co.uk) which has been in the same family for five generations and is accredited by the Rare Breeds Survival Trust. Organic meat is supplemented by an interesting range of pies (mixed game and plum, for example). **Fowey Fish** on Fore Street (☎ 01726 832422; www.foweyfish.com), sells everything for the fishy kitchen from cod fillets and crabmeat to cookware and Cloudy Bay wines.

Drinking

One of the best pubs around here is the **Rashleigh Inn**, a friendly freehouse by the sea at Polkerris beach (☎ 01726 813991), serving Doom Bar, Taylor Landlord and guest ales – a good place to round off a walk across Gribben Head. In Fowey, **The Ship Inn** on Trafalgar Square (☎ 01726 832230) is one of the town's oldest buildings built *c.* 1570, and you get Elizabethan panelling and 'ye olde' stained glass with your pint of St Austell's.

Around the corner, **The Lugger** on Fore Street (☎ 01726 833435), is a lively high-street pub with a good selection of real ales. Or on the Quay, **The King of Prussia** (☎ 01726 833694) is an unpretentious local with seaviews and occasional evening entertainment. Across the river at Polruan, the **Lugger Inn** (☎ 01726 870007) is a St Austell's Ales inn on the quay. At **The Ship Inn** at Lerryn, Betty Stogs, Sharps Doom Bar, Atlantic IPA, Lerryn Ale and St Pirans feature among other Cornish beers. A similar choice of ales are on offer at Lostwithiel's **Globe Inn** on North Street (☎ 01208 872501; www.globeinn.com).

EATING OUT

FINE DINING

Q @ The Old Quay House

28 Fore Street, Fowey PL23 1AQ
☎ 01726 833302
www.theoldquayhouse.com

What people tend to say about this cool restaurant is that the portions are a wee bit small, but nobody quibbles about the food, the presentation, the service or the superb location. And chef Ben Bass has earned the place 2 AA rosettes. Dining on the waterfront terrace in fine weather is sublime. Lunch (every day except Tues) from £15; dinner £35 per person for three courses.

RESTAURANT

Trewithen

3 Fore Street, Lostwithiel
☎ 01208 872373
www.trewithenrestaurant.com

Cosy little restaurant, run by husband and wife, Paul and Claire Murray. Lunch and dinner menus raid the Cornish larder and include salads, risotto, local duck, beef and veal, as well as vegetarian dishes (like St Endellion brie tortellini). Two-course lunch costs from £11.95; dinner main courses from £14.50.

Food for Thought

Town Quay, Fowey PL23 1AT
☎ 01726 832221
www.foodforthought.fowey.com

As close to the water as you can get in Fowey, with tables spilling out onto the quay, this long-established restaurant is housed in a medieval 'havering hall' with shale walls and low beams. Local fish, Cornish meat and Mediterranean dishes, from £6.95. A three-course fixed menu costs £19.95. Open from Easter to October.

The Other Place

41 Fore Street, Fowey PL23 1AQ
☎ 01726 833636
www.otherplacefowey.co.uk

Rick Stein reckons it's one the best seafood diners in Cornwall, and it takes a leaf out of his book: classy fish-and-chip takeaway on the ground floor, and relaxed bistro-style restaurant upstairs. The house speciality is sustainable, locally sourced fish (mackerel, pollock, John Dory, skate) most of it fresh off the day boats in nearby Looe. Fish dishes, from £8.95 (plus burgers, steaks and views of the Fowey River). Open evenings in the summer from 5.30pm; off-season, Thurs to Sat.

EATING OUT

CAFÉ

Sam's

20 Fore Street, Fowey PL23 1AQ
☎ 01726 832273
www.samsfowey.co.uk.

Fun, funky little café-bar with a lively Latino vibe. Lunch and dinner dishes include specials (bouillabaisse, perhaps, or tempura fried mullet) and freshly made classics (salads, fish, chips and Samburgers). Main courses from £7.50. No bookings taken so get there early. Also check out Sam's On the Beach at Polkerris.

The Toll Bar

1 Lostwithiel Street, Fowey PL23 1BD
☎ 01726 833001
www.thetollbarfowey.co.uk

This cosy bar-bistro-restaurant serves fresh fishy dishes on a waterfront terrace with great views. A café-style lunch menu includes fish and chips and sandwiches. In the afternoon, it's all cream teas and cakes. And in the evening (open Thurs–Sat, from 6pm), a bistro-style menu includes mussels, prawns and specials (crab and crayfish bake) with main courses around £12.95.

TEA ROOM

Muffins

32 Fore Street, Lostwithiel PL22 0BN
☎ 01208 872278
www.muffinsdeli.co.uk

In a Georgian townhouse, built for Lieutenant George Lawrence in 1815, Muffins is the classic town-centre cream tea shop, dedicated to the finest Cornish produce (homemade scone with local jam and Trewithen clotted cream, £1.75). Lunches include Cornish sausages, or a Yarg cheese ploughmans. Fresh food, low prices and a little walled garden, too. Open Tues–Sat, 10am–5pm, and also Mondays during August.

Visitor Information

Tourist information centres: Fowey Tourist Information Centre, ☎ 01726 833616; www.fowey.co.uk; Lostwithiel Tourist Information Centre, Lostwithiel Community Centre, Liddicoat Road, Lostwithiel PL22 0HE, ☎ 01208 872207.

Hospitals with A&E: Fowey Community Hospital (minor injuries unit), Green Lane, Fowey PL23 1DU, ☎ 01726 832241.

Doctors: Fowey River Practice, Rawlings Lane, Fowey, Cornwall PL23 1DT, ☎ 0844 4992767.

Pharmacies: Boots, 16–18, Fore Street, Fowey PL23 1AQ, ☎ 01726 833332. Mountchase Pharmacy, 13, Fore Street, Lostwithiel PL22 0BW, ☎ 01208 872368.

Supermarkets: Nearest convenience store is Fowey Mini Market, 39 Fore Street, Fowey, PL23 1AH; Co-op, Fore Street, Lostwithiel PL22.

Parking: Two long-stay car parks, one short-stay, all just outside the centre of town. The main car park is on Hanson Drive.

Internet access: Fowey Library, Passage Lane (Tues, Thurs, Fri and Sat morning).

ATMs: Barclays Bank, 2 Trafalgar Square, Fowey PL23 1BA; HSBC Bank, 2 Fore Street, Fowey PL23 1AD; Barclays Bank, 17 Queen Street, Lostwithiel PL22 0AD; Lloyds TSB, 17, Fore Street, Lostwithiel PL22 0BW.

Boat hire: Town Quay Boat Hire, Town Quay, Fowey, ☎ 0798 999 1115, www.fowey-boat-hire.co.uk.

Local taxis: Coastal Cars, Fowey, ☎ 01726 832 372; Fowey Taxi Service, ☎ 01726 832676; Lerryn Cars, Lostwithiel, ☎ 01208 872322.

ST AUSTELL BAY

Some call it the Cornish Riviera, others 'China Clay Country', and both serve the area well. As in much of Cornwall, industry and tourism sit by side, often in harmony. An exhausted china clay pit provided the raw material for the Eden Project, one of the county's biggest tourist attractions. And those white-capped 'mountains' you see in the distance? Those are the Cornish Alps; vast conical spoil heaps, made from china clay waste, they add a lunar quality to an otherwise English landscape. Tourism and china clay history meet again at Charlestown, St Austell's Grade II listed Georgian port, where an authentic 18th-century aura is enhanced by the masts of the movie-star tall ships, property of the famous Square Sail.

St Austell itself doesn't have much to offer the visitor besides the £75m White River Place shopping complex. But sub-tropical palms and tree ferns thrive at the nearby Lost Gardens of Heligan – rediscovered beneath a jungle of weeds to revive the lush colours of its 19th-century heyday. Nearby Mevagissey is the busiest fishing village on the south coast, but cute Gorran Haven wins the beauty contest. And on the Riviera, between Gribben Head and Dodman Point, there are beaches, as white as clay, that wouldn't look out of place on the Mediterranean.

WHAT TO SEE AND DO

Charlestown

The best thing about St Austell is **Charlestown**, an atmospheric period piece to the south of the town; it's like stepping back in time. The rectangular harbour was built between 1790 and 1810 to support copper and china clay mining, and developed as an industrial village with its own tin smelter and foundry. Local mine owner Charles Rashleigh paid for the entire enterprise (hence the name, Charles' town). The best-preserved port of its kind in the world, today's harbour, with its original Georgian buildings, is a popular film location; its also the

Charlestown Harbour

shipyard of **Square Sail**: a company that run a small fleet of square riggers – the only one left in the world, they say, *'that earns its keep by trade alone'*.

During the summer season, Square Sail's vessels are open to the public, allowing you to wander around the poop decks on your own, or take part in guided tours – but only if one of the ships is docked at Charlestown. Check first to make sure when and if they're at home – though the best time to see them is leaving the harbour. Square Sail also offers hands-on sailing cruises for novices with a taste for life on the ocean wave.

SQUARE SAIL SHIPYARD LTD, Charlestown Harbour, St Austell PL25 3NJ; ☎ 01726 70241; www.square-sail.com. Ships in the harbour are open Easter to Oct.

I saw three ships...

Square Sail's fleet of three square riggers may well look familiar when you spot them docked at Charlestown Harbour. And the chances are you have seen them before – sailing across the big screen. These fine ships are hard working dream boats, with a speciality in maritime costume dramas.

The flagship of the fleet is the 153ft *Kaskelot*. One of the largest wooden ships still sailing, the one-time fisheries support vessel built in 1948, has been re-rigged as a 19th-century three-masted Barque. Film roles include *Shackleton* and *The Three Musketeers*. The good ship *Earl of Pembroke* was built in Sweden in 1948. After trading timber in the Baltic, she was bought by Square Sail in 1979, and transformed into a three-masted 18th-century Barque. Movie credits include *Frenchman's Creek*, *Moll Flanders* and *Hornblower*, in which she co-starred with Square Sail sister ship, *The Phoenix*. The 1929 former missionary schooner, remodelled as a two-masted Brig, also starred in *The Scarlet Pimpernel*. Square Sail's shipwrights can adapt and re-rig these ships to replicate any period or ship the role demands. They are replicas, but nonetheless, what a history.

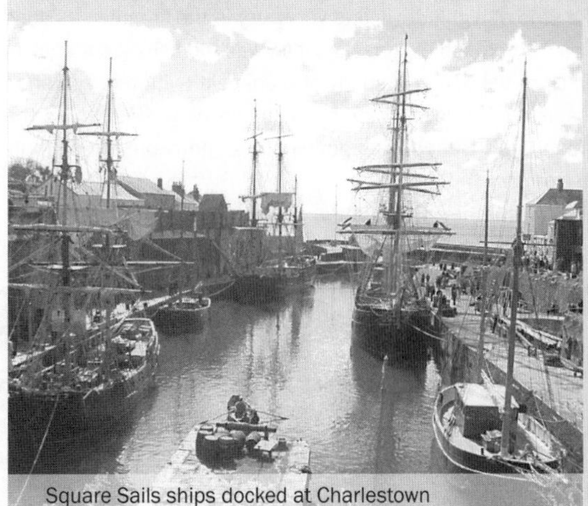
Square Sails ships docked at Charlestown

CHARLESTOWN SHIPWRECK AND HERITAGE CENTRE, Quay Road, Charlestown, St Austell PL25 3NJ; ☎ 01726 69897; www.ship wreckcharlestown.com. Entry: adults £5.95, children £2.95, under-10s free with adult; open Mar to Oct, 10am–5pm.

Also on the harbour, the **Charlestown Shipwreck and Heritage Centre** provides an engaging insight into Cornwall's maritime history. The building was originally a clay dry, and you can walk along the original tunnel linking the building to the dock. A series of animated scenes depict life in Charlestown through the ages. The museum also has artefacts from more than 150 shipwrecks in the area, exhibits on sea rescue, the history of diving, Second World War medical supplies, the Royal Yacht Britannia... the list is endless.

To the south of the bay, 5 miles from Charlestown, **Mevagissey** is a typical south Cornish fishing village, more touristy than most, thanks to the Lost Gardens effect (Heligan is just up the road). There's not a lot to do here other than poke around in back-street gift shops, and wander around the harbour, but there a several boat trips from here, including daily day trips to Fowey.

By the sea

Of the white beaches that fringe St Austell Bay, **Pentewan Sands** is one of the most popular. Just off the road between St Austell and Mevagissey, it has a big wide stretch of sand, and even manages the occasional ruffle of surf. But if you don't like caravans (Pentewan is owned by the Pentewan Sands Holiday Park) head for somewhere less commercial.

Nearer St Austell, **Par Sands** is too big to be crowded, and the shallow waters are perfect for children (though another holiday park lurks behind the dunes). Nearby **Porthpean** is a favourite with families, but a bit of a strip at high tide, it gets very busy in the summer, as does **Gorran Haven**, to the west of the bay. Embraced by a row of white-washed fishing cottages in the crook of a fishing-harbour pier, Gorran's beach is sandy and unspoilt (with a beach shop offering deck chairs for hire). Escapists (and, indeed, nudists) should head west along the rocky stretch of cliff path that leads to **Vault Beach**, a gorgeous mile of gritty but often empty white sand, 20 minutes' walk from Gorran.

To the south-west of St Austell Bay, **Dodman Point** is the highest headland on the south coast. On a clear day you can see as far as the Lizard. Fortified since ancient times, this bold,

The Eden Project's futuristic biomes

spectacular promontory has been the site of many a shipwreck, and is still a danger to shipping. It can be reached via a small National Trust car park at Penare. A 3-mile walk takes in the headland's secluded **Hemmick Beach**, Iron Age earthworks and Bronze Age barrows.

The Eden Project

Cornwall's most famous attraction is run by an educational charity, the Eden Trust, and is designed to illustrate how much we owe our existence to plant life. Eden has three biomes, each representing a different climate type, and collectively creating a global garden in the crater of a disused clay pit. The lush **Humid Tropics** Biome, complete with rainforest and waterfall, is deemed the largest greenhouse in the world – a jungle of banana trees, mango, rubber and giant lily pads. The smaller **Warm Temperate Biome** contains Mediterranean species such as olives and grapes. The third is the **Outdoor Biome**, where landscape gardens burst with plants that thrive in the Cornish climate – in spring, tulips and daffodils, in summer lavender, agapanthus and sunflowers. A summer highlight is a zip wire, allowing you to see Eden from the air. At the Mechanical Theatre, botany is brought to life by robots and puppets. High season and school holidays brings mega crowds and long queues.

THE EDEN PROJECT, Bodelva, St Austell PL24 2SG; ☎ 01726 811 911; www.edenproject.com. Entry: adults £20, children £7.50, under-5s free; open daily mid-Mar to late Oct, 9.30am–6pm; winter 10am–3.00pm. Some late night openings. Last entry 90 minutes before closing.

The Lost Gardens

The Eden Project's founder, Tim Smit, was also a driving force behind the restoration of the magnificent **Lost Gardens of Heligan**, 9 miles south of St Austell. For 400 years they were part of the Temayne family's 1,000-acre Heligan estate. The gardens reached their peak at the end of the 19th century. But when 16 of the 22 gardeners were killed on the Western Front during the First World War, the decline began and as the 20th century progressed, the gardens disappeared under a tangle of ivy and brambles. In 1990 they were rediscovered, and work began to clear the undergrowth and restore them, a process documented by a 1996 Channel 4 series. Today, the 100-acre site is a pleasure ground of summerhouses, sunken gardens and grottos, four walled kitchen gardens, the Jungle, home to Britain's

THE LOST GARDENS OF HELIGAN, PENTEWAN, St Austell PL26 6EN; ☎ 01726 845100; www.heligan.com. Entry: adults £10, children £6, under-5s free; open daily Apr to Oct, 10am–6pm, last entry 4.30pm; winter 10am–5pm, last entry 3.30pm.

largest collection of palms and tree ferns, and the Lost Valley, where native Cornish woodland thrives. The gardens also contain Europe's only working pineapple pit, in which fermenting compost keeps the plants warm enough to bear fruit.

Tim Smit: a man with a mission

Tim Smit is the man behind two of Cornwall's most popular visitor attractions – the Eden Project and the Lost Gardens of Heligan. Born in Holland in 1954, he was educated in England before reading archaeology and anthropology at Durham. He worked in the music industry for 10 years, and in 1987, on a whim, moved to Fowey. In 1990 he was one of the team who unearthed the overgrown formal gardens at Heligan, and helped bring them back to life – writing a best selling-book in the process, snappily entitled *The Lost Gardens of Heligan*.

With Heligan established as the most visited private gardens in the UK, Smit moved on to his next challenge. He wanted to create a place that would showcase mankind's place in nature – a new and sustainable Eden. Smit and his team raised an estimated £130m to transform an abandoned clay pit. The dream that began in 1995 became reality in 2001 when the Eden Project opened to the public. Now Britain's fourth largest tourist attraction, it has generated £800m for the local economy. Awarded a CBE in 2002, Smit has since become a Social Enterprise Ambassador, championing his belief in modern business as a force for positive change.

Mining trails

Part of the Cornish Mining World Heritage Site, the **Luxulyan Valley** is a hidden gem, its steep slopes of mature woodland running down to the banks of the River Par. This is where entrepreneur Thomas Treffry engineered a series of leats, tramways and watermills, all oiling the progress of mid-19th-century mining. Highlights include the water wheel pit, and gushing waterfall, at **Carmears Rocks**, and the spectacular **Treffry Viaduct**. Almost hidden in greenery, the latter was built to carry copper ore from the mines to the port at Par. To explore the valley, its woodland and wildlife, park at the Treffry Viaduct car park, roughly a mile from Luxulyan, and then follow the waymarked paths and trails through the valley. For more information visit the conservation website of the Friends of Luxulyan Valley (www.luxulyanvalley.co.uk).

Cyclists can explore the region on the designated **Clay Trails** that surround St Austell. A series of traffic-free routes include the **Pentewan Trail**, which travels between Pentewan Beach, along the bed of an old narrow gauge railway, to the bizarrely named hamlet of London Apprentice. The two-mile long **St Austell Trail** (also known as the Green Corridor) runs from Tremana Gardens, through woods and past abandoned clay dries to the **China Clay Country Park**. For full details see www.claytrails.co.uk. The China Clay Country Park **Mining Museum**

and Heritage Centre sits in 26 acres of the Ruddle Valley, outside St Austell. Yet another part of the Cornish Mining World Heritage Site, it provides an encyclopaedic insight into the history of the Cornish china clay industry, from its discovery in 1774 to modern extraction methods.

CHINA CLAY COUNTRY PARK, Wheal Martyn, Carthew, St Austell PL26 8XG; ☎ 01726 850362; www.wheal-martyn.com. Entry: adults £8.50, children £4.75, under-6s free; open Feb to Sept, 10am–4/5/6pm depending on season.

 Wet weather

Mevagissey's **World of Model Railways** is a hobbyist's Hornby fest, with 40 trains running through miniature towns, fields, a Cornish tin mine and China clay works and, curiously, an Alpine ski resort. There is also an indoor reconstruction of a large-scale garden railway, featuring a rockery and water feature, which children of all ages can operate.

THE WORLD OF MODEL RAILWAYS, Meadow Street, Mevagissey, PL26 6UL; ☎ 01726 842 457; www.model-railway.co.uk. Entry: adults £4.50, children £3, infants 2–5 £2; open daily Easter to Oct, 10am–5pm; winter, Sat–Sun, school holidays, 10am–4pm.

 What to do with children...

Mevagissey's model railways are good, but an alternative is the newly refurbished **KidzWorld**, which closed for nine months after the damaging Mevagissey floods of November 2010. Outdoors there's mini golf, rides and a picnic area. Indoors, there is a scary ghost house, a ballpool, a soft play area and various slides and rides.

KIDZWORLD, Stadium Retail Park, St Austell PL25 3RP; ☎ 01726 815553; www.kidzworldcornwall.co.uk. Open daily throughout the year. For prices and opening times, see website or phone for details.

 ... and how to avoid children

The **St Austell Brewery** – founded by maltster Walter Hicks in 1851 – is a Cornish institution owning over 160 pubs and hotels across Devon and Cornwall, and selling more than 40,000 barrels of beer a year. The St Austell story unfolds in an interactive museum in the visitor centre and brings to life a family history of brewing. The hour-long

ST AUSTELL BREWERY, 63 Trevarthian Road, St Austell, PL25 4BY; ☎ 01726 66022; www.staustellbrewery.co.uk. Entry: adults £8, children (over-8s only) £5; open daily in the summer; Nov to Mar, closed on Sun.

The St Austell Brewery

Victorian brewery tour takes you through all stages of the process and ends at Hicks Bar, where you can sample some of the brewery's award winning products – a pint of ale is included in the cost of the ticket.

Entertainment

Theatre and cinema

Cornwall's newest venue is the 250-seat performing arts space called **The Keay** (☎ 01726 226777 www.thekeay.co.uk). Set in the grounds of Cornwall College, it hosts a variety of live music, theatre and dance performances. In June and July, the **Eden Project** provides an alternative venue with the staging of the **Eden Sessions**, a series of live performances from the likes of Bill Bailey, KT Tunstall, The Verve and Vampire Weekend. Tickets sell out fast (www.edenproject.com).

Special events

On summer evenings plays are staged on **Flora's Green** at the Lost Gardens of Heligan. The **Mevagissey Feast Week** (www.mevagisseyfeastweek.org.uk) at the end of June offers an overwhelming programme of events on land and sea, accompanied by live music. The **Charlestown Regatta** celebrates maritime Cornwall on a grand scale during the last week of July. The **St Ewe Country Fair** in mid-August, is all things rural from cake-making to Cornish wrestling. In late October the **Heligan Harvest Display** celebrates the amazing array of produce grown in the gardens.

Nightlife

Puls8 on High Cross is the nightclub in St Austell (☎ 01726 624 620 www.puls-8.co.uk). Otherwise it's live music venues such as **Carlyon Arms** (☎ 01726 721129) or Mevagissey's **Ship Inn** (☎ 01726 843324). For live music on Friday nights in winter try the **Welcome Home** (☎ 01726 816894) in Par or the **Britannia Inn** at Tregrehan (☎ 01726 812 889). Away from the coast, the **Bugle Inn** (☎ 01726 850307 www.bugleinn.co.uk) puts on live bands most Sunday evenings.

The best... PLACES TO STAY

BOUTIQUE

Trevalsa Court

School Hill, Mevagissey PL26 6TH
☎ 01726 842468
www.trevalsa-hotel.co.uk

A welcoming cliff-top haven overlooking Mevagissey beyond elegant gardens. The period house, with its dark panelling and stone mullioned windows, is furnished with big squashy sofas and sunny colours. The rooms are generous. And the coast path, and a private beach, is a few steps away.

Price: B&B from £110–£225 per night.

Boscundle Manor

Boscundle, St Austell PL25 3RL
☎ 01726 813557
www.boscundlemanor.co.uk

A mile from the Eden Project, a rustic Georgian manor in five acres of peaceful grounds. The rooms are all pretty wallpapers, king-size beds, Roberston radios, and luxury bathrooms. Self-contained cottage rooms and a garden suite are available. And there's a spa, pool and award-winning restaurant.

Price: B&B from £100–£315.

HOTEL

The Carlyon Bay Hotel

Sea Road, St Austell PL25 3RD
☎ 01726 812304
www.carlyonbay.com

This huge and recently refurbished four-star hotel is set in 250 acres high above St Austell Bay. There is a cliff-top golf course, indoor and outdoor pools, a spa and the Bay View restaurant.

Price: B&B from £140–£310 per room per night.

Porth Avallen Hotel

Sea Road, St Austell, PL25 3SG
☎ 01726 812802
www.porthavallen.co.uk

A traditional, family hotel, Porth Avallen has magnificent views over St Austell Bay, a pretty garden terrace for sitting out on, a restaurant and comfortable rooms.

Price: B&B from £84–£155 per room per night.

The Pier House Hotel

Harbour Front, Charlestown PL25 3NJ
☎ 01726 67955
www.pierhousehotel.com

On Charlestown Harbour, this Georgian hotel combines historic charm with sea views. The rooms are okay (some nicer than others) but not as good as the restaurant, where lobster is a feature of the seafood menu. The hotel incorporates the Harbourside Inn – and live music on a Saturday.

Price: B&B from £72–£138 per room per night.

B&B

Lower Barn

Bosue, St Ewe PL26 6EU
☎ 01726 844881
www.bosue.co.uk

In a rural setting, there are four spacious boutique-style guest rooms, nicely quirky with big beds and bright colours. One, the Hayloft, is designed for disabled access. There's a gym and hot-tub and you can have dinner, by arrangement, in 'the Shack' next to a roaring fire.

Price: B&B from £100–£130 per night.

The best... PLACES TO STAY

CAMPSITE

Court Farm Camping

Court Farm, St Stephen, St Austell PL26 7LE
☎ 01726 823684
www.courtfarmcornwall.co.uk

In countryside with so little light pollution, a campsite with an 'astronomy facility' is a neat idea. This 30-acre working farm, 4 miles west of St Austell, has four acres of beautiful pastureland for tents, a modern shower block, and a 9ft Newtonian reflector telescope. Open 1 April to 30 September.

Price: from £9.50–£12.50 for a two-berth tent per night

Higher Kestle Farm

St Ewe, Mevagissey, St Austell PL26 6EP
☎ 01726 842001
www.higherkestle.co.uk

A rustic campsite, set in a 300-acre working farm with dreamy views of rolling countryside. A mile from Heligan, two miles from Mevagissey, the site has grass pitches, hook-ups, picnic tables and a shower block with freezer.

Price: From £8 per pitch per night.

SELF-CATERING

The Apple Store

Charlestown
☎ 07967 104131
www.antoniaspearls.co.uk

In a one-bedroom wing of a large Georgian house on the quay at historic Charlestown, this is stylish little place has modern-rustic décor with nautical touches, and a big solid-oak bed with a romantic view of the sea.

Price: from £595–£795 for a week (sleeps two plus cot).

The Retreat

Mevagissey
☎ 01244 500524
www.sykescottages.co.uk

On the edge of town, this smart, roomy house overlooks the fields and woodlands which lead up to Heligan Gardens. It sleeps 8 in four bedrooms, and has a big kitchen (with Aga), Gothic-style conservatory, luxurious sauna and hot-tub and a thatched summer house in the garden.

Price: From £570-£1,835 for a week.

The best... FOOD AND DRINK

Fishing on the south coast is not what it was, but Mevagissey and Charlestown still bring in fresh fish, lobster and crab. For the beer drinker, this is home ground for the well-known St Austell Brewery and its award-winning beers, including Tribute – CAMRA's champion Cornish ale. And the soil is proved ideal for wine-growing, Cornish vineyards Polmassick and Bosue (www.cornwallwines.co.uk), both near St Ewe, produce palatable red, white and sparkling wines.

Staying in

At Heligan, near St Ewe **Lobbs Farm Shop** (☎ 01726 844411; www.lobbsfarmshop.com) sells beef and lamb born and reared on the 850-acre Kestle Farm, and stocks a wide range of other products sourced from Cornish farms. The **Cornish Smoked Fish Company** (☎ 01726 72356) on Charlestown Quay sells hot and cold smoked fish including mackerel, salmon, kippers and trout. **The Little Cornish Curry Company** uses local meat and seasonal Cornish vegetables in their handmade curries. These ready-meals can be bought in Spars across Cornwall, or direct from their stall at Truro market each Saturday (☎ 01208 832 268; www.thecornishcurryco.com).

The Mevagissey Farmers' Market takes place every Sunday between 10am and 2pm at the Courtyard Indoor Market on Mevagissey's west wharf. **Boddington's Berries** (☎ 01726 842346; www.boddingtonsberries.co.uk) just outside Mevagissey sell pick-your-own strawberries and raspberries between May and August, and also makes its own conserves.

Drinking

The **Rashleigh Arms** (☎ 01726 73635) in historic Charlestown is popular with the locals, and has two bars and a walled beer garden with sea views. Also on Charlestown harbour, the **Harbourside Inn** (part of the Pier Hotel) serves Sharps, Skinners and guest ales, in a converted warehouse with a nautical flavour.

Inland, the **Hewas Inn** (☎ 01726 73497) in Sticker is a traditional country pub in the centre of a quiet village south-west of St Austell. The Grade II listed building is crowded with vintage relics of tin mining and farming. The **Kings Arms** in Luxulyan is another good pub. Less traditional **Sharksfin** (☎ 01726 842969) is a stylish new bar/restaurant overlooking Mevagissey harbour, offering modern leather sofas, mood lighting and St Austell beers.

EATING OUT

FINE DINING

Austells Restaurant

10 Beach Road, Carlyon Bay, St Austell PL25 3PH
☎ 01726 813888
www.austells.net

With two AA rosettes under the belt this is a restaurant on a mission for a Michelin star. Chef proprietor Brett Camborne-Paynter (late of the Ivy, the Waldorf and The Four Seasons) uses local produce to create impressive modern British dishes, prepared in a theatre kitchen and served in a fresh open dining room. Open for dinner, Wed–Sun. Main courses cost from £14.50.

Trevalsa Court

School Hill, Mevagissey PL26 6TH
☎ 01726 842468
www.trevalsa-hotel.co.uk

Part of the seaside hotel on the cliffs above Pentewan, dinner is served in an atmospheric panelled dining room, all white linen and candlelight. The menu majors on Mevagissey seafood and local meat, fresh vegetables and herbs. Three courses from £30.

RESTAURANT

Salamander Restaurant

4–6 Tregoney Hill, Mevagissey PL26 6RD
☎ 01726 842254
www.salamander-restaurant.co.uk

Freshly caught Mevagissey fish, Cornish dairy produce, game from St Ives, Kestle farm beef and Roskilly's ice cream are among an impressive list of local foods served up by this intimate family-run restaurant. Main courses from £14.50. Open every evening between Apr and Sept, from 6pm – booking advisable.

GASTRO PUB

The Hop and Vine Steak and Ale House

3 Market Street, St Austell, PL25 4BB
☎ 01726 72758

As the name suggests, this St Austell Brewery pub specialises in good old fashioned meat and ales, though with a former Rick Stein chef at the helm, it has a little more finesse than the usual steak house. The menu includes Cornish steaks, Moroccan tajines, pasta dishes and salads. Food served 11am–10pm.

CAFÉ

Wreckers

Charlestown Harbour, St Austell PL25 3NJ
☎ 01726 879053
www.wheelhouse.me.uk.

Wreckers moved from Mevagissey to Charlestown in 2008, turning an old boat shed and harbour terrace into a bistro-bar-café serving everything from tapas, light lunches and afternoon teas to a full à la carte dinner. The emphasis is on informal dining; mussels and a glass of wine, Cornish seafood, local meat or tasty vegetarian dishes. Main courses cost from £9.95.

Visitor Information

Tourist information centres: St Austell Tourist Information Centre, Southbourne Road PL25 4RS, ☎ 01726 879 500; Mevagissey Tourist Information Centre, St Georges Square, PL26 6UB, ☎ 01726 844 857.

Hospitals with A&E: Penrice Hospital, Porthpean Road, St Austell PL26 6AA, ☎ 01726 291100.

Doctors: The Park Medical Centre, 19 Bridge Road, St Austell PL25 5HE, ☎ 01726 73083; Mevagissey Surgery, River Street, Mevagissey PL26 6UE, ☎ 01726 843701; Middleway Surgery, Middleway, Street. Blazey, Par PL24 2JL, ☎ 01726 812019.

Pharmacies: Alliance Pharmacy, 1–3 Victoria Place, St Austell PL25 5PE, ☎ 01726 72478; Alliance Pharmacy, 3 Fore Street, Mevagissey PL26 6UQ, ☎ 01726 842349.

Police station: St Austell Police Station, 1 Palace Road PL25 4AL.

Supermarkets: ASDA, Cromwell Road, St Austell, PL25 4PR, ☎ 01726 223800; Tesco, Daniel Lane, St Austell PL25 3HR, ☎ 0845 677597.

ATMs: Barclays Bank plc, 10 Church Street, St Austell PL25 4AS; Lloyds TSB Bank plc, Fore Street, Mevagissey, St Austell PL26 6UQ.

Car hire: BYPASS Garage Ltd, Southbourne Road PL25 4RS, ☎ 01726 77737, www.eurodrive-staustell.co.uk; The Garage, 26 Beech Road PL25 4TS, ☎ 01726 72 969.

Bike hire: Pentewan Valley Cycle Hire, ☎ 01726 844 242, www.pentewanvalleycyclehire.co.uk.

Local taxis: Mike's Taxis, Mevagissey, ☎ 01726 843 001.

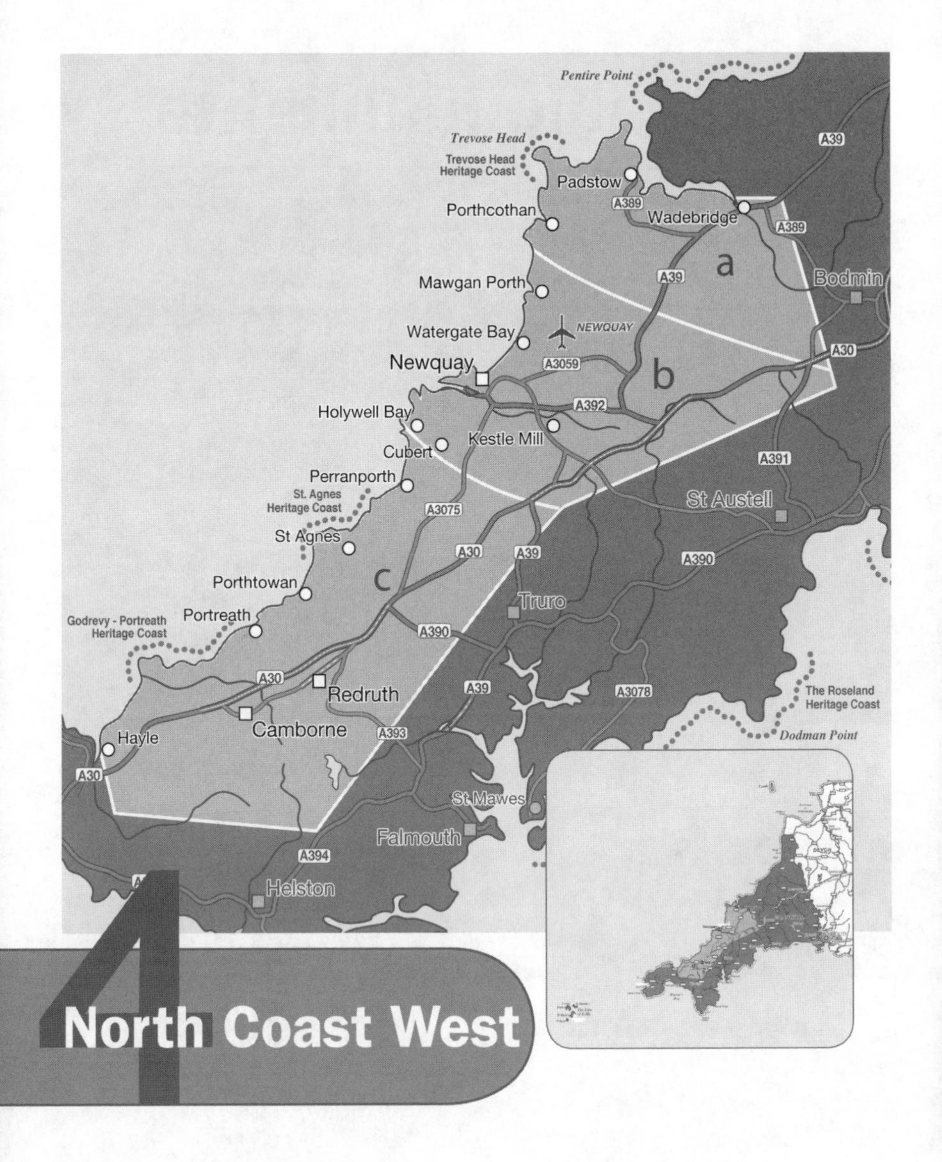

4 North Coast West

a. Padstow and the Camel Estuary

b. Newquay and surrounds

c. Hayle to St Agnes

Unmissable highlights

01 Enjoy the views of Godrevy lighthouse and St Ives Bay on a sunset stroll to Godrevy Point, p. 193

02 Book a table at Fifteen Cornwall, Jamie Oliver's stonking restaurant on the dream beach at Watergate Bay, p. 188

03 Walk among giant rocks, under gigantic cliffs at the foot of Bedruthan Steps, p. 190

04 Get steamed up over the giants of Victorian engineering at the National Trust's Cornish Mines and Engines Centre at Pool, p. 193

05 Surf the waves at Fistral Bay, or neighbouring Crantock, to name just a few of those world-class Atlantic beaches, p. 177

06 Sit down to a fish supper on Padstow harbour: lobster at Rick Stein's Seafood restaurant or cod and chips on the quay, p. 171

07 Meet the Tudors at Prideaux Place, a lived-in Elizabethan mansion complete with deer park, p. 163

08 Hire a bike in Wadebridge, and follow the Camel Valley Trail to the sea at Padstow Harbour, p. 165

09 Down a pint of Blue Hills Bitter while you boogey with the bikers in the bar at Driftwood Spars, p. 202

10 Wander around St Agnes, the prettified former mining village meanders down a wooded valley to Trevaunance Cove, p. 195

NORTH COAST WEST

This is Surf Central. Some of the best, or at least the best-known, beaches in Britain, lie on this rugged stretch of Atlantic coast. Newquay alone has 10 glorious beaches, each one a runway of golden sand, sheltered by dunes and high granite cliffs and pummelled by foaming waves. Indeed, the north-west coastline, between Hayle harbour to the Camel Estuary, is just one big, yellow beach after another.

While seaside life attracts hordes of tourists to mass-market Newquay, up-market Padstow has a reputation as the county's culinary capital; these two neighbouring towns are the most visited in Cornwall. Just a few miles away, Camborne, Redruth and Hayle are among the poorest, but dig deep and you will find rich seams of history and culture that have yet to be exploited. At the heart of the Cornish Mining World Heritage Site, they harbour the highest concentration of historic mineral sites on earth.

Despite its popularity, the region has quieter moments: follow the path of medieval pilgrims to the site of St Piran's 'lost church' on Penhale Sands; check out the lesser known beaches around Harlyn and Treyarnon Bays; walk from pretty St Agnes to Porthtowan along soaring cliffs with views that take your breath away...

PADSTOW AND THE CAMEL ESTUARY

With a superb position on the mouth of the Camel Estuary, a busy fishing quay and the annual Obby Oss festival, Padstow was always one of Cornwall's most popular harbour towns. And under Rick Stein's influence, Padstow has been reinvented as Seafood Central.

The transition from pilchard port to 'Padstein' didn't happen overnight, but it's certainly stepped up in the past few years. The celebrity chef's culinary empire now includes a harbourside cookery school, two restaurants, a fish and chip shop, patisserie, wine shop, two hotels and three guest houses. Stein has an uneasy relationship with grassroots Padstow, which has seen ordinary shops disappear and colonies of humble cottages turned into Kensington-on-Sea. These days you're just as likely to see yachts in the harbour as fishing boats. But Padstow has other fish to fry and other heroes.

The name is actually a derivation of Petroc-stow, after St Petroc, the Welsh missionary who turned up in the 6th century to found a monastery. The town has flourished as a port since the 15th century; Sir Walter Raleigh, once Warden of Cornwall, lived here (his Court House, on South Quay, is now a private home). Nearby, Prideaux Place is one of the finest Elizabethan mansions in the West Country.

Padstow is the beginning and the end of the excellent Camel Trail which follows the route of a disused railway line from Wadebridge to the sea. It has access to some of Cornwall's most beautiful beaches and thanks to the Padstein effect, a burgeoning community of boutique hotels and guests houses makeing it an excellent base for exploring the area.

Rick Stein's Seafood Restaurant

Prideaux Place

WHAT TO SEE AND DO

What most people 'do' in Padstow is just wander around the harbour eating pasties and ice cream or snapping pictures of the golden sandbars that sweep away from the Camel Estuary. In high season, a typical day-trip starts in a queue for a car parking space and ends in a queue for Stein – fresh fish and chips (if you want to eat at one of the finer restaurants, book well in advance). The place is way too busy in high season but, however crowded, the true character of old Padstow shines through: the narrow lanes of white-washed fishing cottages, the granite harbour quays, the smell of history.

Prideaux place

Soak up some of the history at **Prideaux Place**, a lived-in Elizabethan mansion, quaintly described by its owners Peter and Elisabeth Prideaux-Brune as a 'well-known secret'. On a hill overlooking Padstow harbour, the house is filled with treasures from fine furniture, porcelain, and paintings to family memorabilia and an exquisite embossed plaster ceiling in the Great Chamber. Continuously remodelled over 400 years, the house is a conglomerate of styles, mixing Georgian panelling with Regency Gothic plasterwork (and the odd Art Nouveau light switch). A crowd of alleged ghosts includes a phantom dog who hangs around in one of the bedrooms. There are 40 acres of landscaped grounds and, beyond, one of the oldest deer parks in the country.

PRIDEAUX PLACE, Padstow PL28 8RP; ☎ 01841 532411; www.prideauxplace.co.uk. Entry: £7.50 (house and garden), £2 (garden only); open early May to early Oct (and Easter holidays), Sun–Thurs; house tours 1.30–4pm.

Activities

Aside from the restaurants, the harbour and the low-tide beach at **Harbour Cove**, some of the best things to do in Padstow involve leaving (or, indeed, arriving) on foot, ferry or bicycle. You can take the Port of Padstow's **Black Tor pedestrian ferry** across to Rock and Daymer Bay

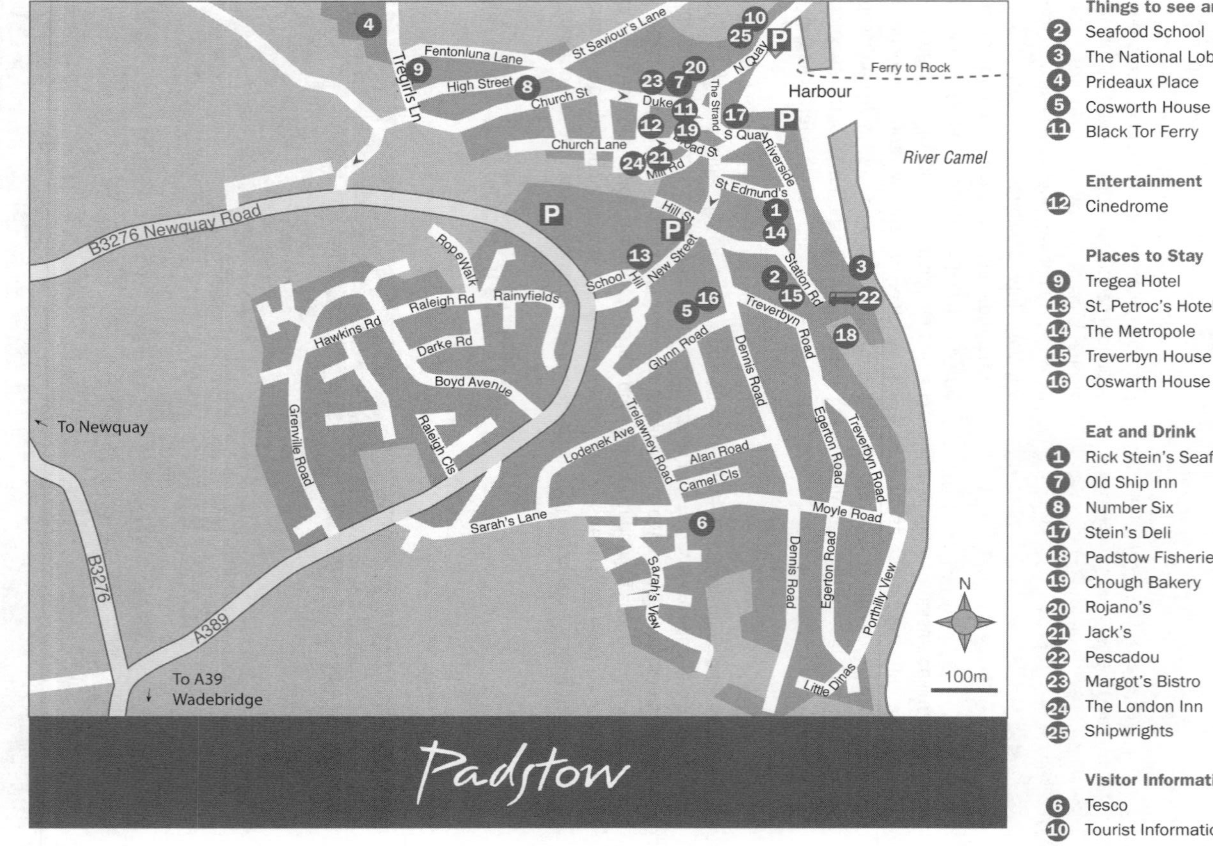

Things to see and do

2 Seafood School
3 The National Lobster Hatchery
4 Prideaux Place
5 Cosworth House
11 Black Tor Ferry

Entertainment

12 Cinedrome

Places to Stay

9 Tregea Hotel
13 St. Petroc's Hotel
14 The Metropole
15 Treverbyn House
16 Coswarth House

Eat and Drink

1 Rick Stein's Seafood Restaurant
7 Old Ship Inn
8 Number Six
17 Stein's Deli
18 Padstow Fisheries
19 Chough Bakery
20 Rojano's
21 Jack's
22 Pescadou
23 Margot's Bistro
24 The London Inn
25 Shipwrights

Visitor Information

6 Tesco
10 Tourist Information Centre

(see page 108). The ferry leaves from the North Quay slipway or Lower Beach depending on the tides, and is a pleasantly breezy 10-minute sail across the mile-wide estuary.

BLACK TOR FERRY, The Harbour Office, Padstow PL28 8AQ; ☎ 01841 532239; www.padstow-harbour.co.uk; Tickets: Adults/bikes £3 rtn, children £2; ferries run daily (except Sun in winter) on demand from 7.50am until 7.30pm (July/Aug), until 5.50pm (Apr to May, Sept/Oct) or 4.50pm (Nov to Mar); water taxis available on summer evenings.

Padstow Boat Trips also offers a noisy 15-minute trip around the estuary on a speedboats or a mackerel trip aboard the Boy Darren. The popular **Jubilee Queen** (☎ 01841 521093; www.padstowboattrips.com) runs regular trips to **Puffin Island** in summer. A little hump of Atlantic rock the island does, indeed, support the odd pair of puffins; you might also see seals, dolphins or basking sharks. On high evening tides, the Jubilee Queen also runs up-river trips to **Wadebridge**.

The **Camel Trail** is the 10.5-mile walking and cycling route that follows the beautiful Camel River along the former Atlantic Coast Express railway line. The Wadebridge to Bodmin stretch is possibly the prettier section (see page 92), but Padstow to Wadebridge is the more popular, and is often used by walkers and cyclists as a traffic-beating way to do a Padstow day-trip. Starting at Wadebridge, the 5-mile route hugs the south bank of the river, following its curves, creeks and ponds, as it widens into a spectacular estuary. Look out for kingfishers, egrets, herons, goldfinches or the occasional otter. Northern lapwing and golden plover are among the rich birdlife that attracts armies of twitchers to the estuary.

The Saints Way is a 28-mile coast-to-coast, port-to-port trail, beginning at Padstow and finishing at Fowey (see page 133). Said to have been used by traders, missionaries and pilgrims during the Middle Ages, the trail travels through wooded valleys, across moorland and farmland, passing ancient relics, rustic churches and quiet little villages. Closer to home, in the opposite direction, you can take the footpath north along the estuary to the sandy beaches at **St George's Cove**, **Harbour Cove** and **Hawkers Cove**. It takes about 20 minutes to get to St George's, and it's a great place to watch the boats sliding in and out of the Camel.

Local legends: wrecked at the bar

Padstow has one of the most secure shipping harbours on the north coast, with nothing to rival it this side of Avonmouth, but entry can be tricky, thanks to the Camel Estuary's notorious **Doom Bar**, at its most dangerous between low and high tide. The word 'doom', in this instance, is actually a derivation of *dun* or *dunne*, simply meaning sand, but it has proved apt given the number of ships that have been wrecked on the bar – at least 300 in the two centuries since records began. According to legend, the Doom Bar is the curse of a Padstow mermaid who is said to have guided ships into the harbour. After she was shot by a visiting sailor (who mistook her for a seal), a violent storm brewed, sweeping sand and silt into the estuary, and throwing up the sandbank. Talking of brewing, the sand bar has since given its name to a Sharp's Brewery ale. A pint of Doom Bar, please landlord...

Wet weather

The **National Lobster Hatchery** on Padstow quay is a non-profit-making, marine-laboratory visitor centre; it's more interesting than it sounds and it's a fitting a complement to Padstow's modern seafood culture. The principal function of the place is to maintain the species, by giving pregnant females a chance to lay and hatch their delicate young in a predator-free environment (in the wild, less than 1% survive more than two weeks). At three months old, the little lobsters are released into the sea, but you can see their development from tiddler to fully-fledged lobster.

THE NATIONAL LOBSTER HATCHERY, South Quay, Padstow PL28 8BL; ☎ 01841 533877; www.nationallobsterhatchery.co.uk. Entry: adults £3.50, seniors, £2, children £1.50 (under-5s free); open daily all year, from 10am.

Hatchling lobster at the National Lobster Hatchery

What to do with children...

Divided into various activity zones, **Crealy Great Adventure Park** between Padstow and Wadebridge has more than a day's worth of fun, ranging from a water chute ride in the Wild Realm to miniature ponies in the Animal Realm. There are play zones for small children, a soft-toy Fun Fort for toddlers, a few thrill rides, some wet-weather indoor activities and a sunflower maze.

CREALY GREAT ADVENTURE PARK, St Issey, Wadebridge PL27 7RA; ☎ 01841 540276; www.crealy.co.uk. Tickets from £13.45 (off-season/online tickets, £12.45), infants free; open Mar to Nov (season varies), daily 10am–6pm.

 ... and how to avoid children

Sign up to a cookery class at Rick Stein's **Seafood School**. Right on the harbour, within sight of the local fishing fleet, the school offers one- or two-day non-residential courses. A typical one-day course might include a morning's shopping in Newlyn fish

PADSTOW SEAFOOD SCHOOL, Riverside, Padstow PL28 8BY; ☎ 01841 532700; www.rickstein.com. Day courses from £195 per person.

Voyage of the Obby Osses

'Unite and unite let us all unite, For summer is acome unto day, And whither we are going we will all unite, In the merry morning of May.'

So goes the song which accompanies the legendary Obby Oss on its journey around Padstow, during one of the oldest and best-known of Cornwall's pagan rituals. The celebration is thought to have originated as a spring fertility rite, and is centred around the passage of two Osses, the Old Oss and the Blue Ribbon Oss, each taking a different route as they prance around the town to a hypnotic drum-and-accordion beat, followed by a troop of white-clad teasers, or mayers. The strange dancing changes tempo from furious to melancholy and continues thus until the two Osses meet up at the end of the day when they are restored to their 'stables' – the Old Oss to the Golden Lion Inn, the Blue to the Harbour Inn.

There is an Obby Oss choir, spring-flower decorations, a maypole and a group of baby 'colt' osses but the defining element of the proceedings is the Osses' curious costumes: an oilskin drape, hanging from a circular frame, some six foot in diameter, worn at shoulder height and topped by a comic but grotesque mask with fearsome teeth. If a maid is captured beneath the skirts of the Old Oss, she will be pregnant within the year, or so they say, though it's very unlikely to happen to a non-Padstonian. This is a very much a community festival, and the visitor can never really be more than a mere spectator.

market, making a hollandaise sauce, preparing a lobster or mixing spices. They all include demonstrations, practical sessions and eating the results.

Entertainment

Theatre and cinema

Padstow's **Cinedrome** (Landwell Street, ☎ 01841 532344) is one those little old picture houses that's worth a visit with or without a film show. It was a music hall and theatre when it first opened in 1919, but was converted for the silent screen in 1924. The former Capitol Cinema was renamed the Cinedrome when it was renovated in 1997. It now has Dolby Digital stereo sound and luxury seats, but it's only open during school holidays and summer season. In Wadebridge, the **Regal** (The Platt, ☎ 01208 812791) is open all year round. For information on the both cinemas see www.wtwcinemas.co.uk.

Special events

The big crowd-puller is the May Day **Obby Oss** festival (see box). The celebrations take place on 1 May (or a day later, if it falls on a Sunday). In June, **the Royal Cornwall Show** (www.royalcornwallshow.org) takes place on the county show ground near Wadebridge. In August, **Camel Week Regatta** sees a series of boating events on both sides of the river. The **Wadebridge Folk Festival** (☎ 01208 814638; www.wadebridgefolk.co.uk) usually takes place over the August Bank Holiday and features live music, ceilidhs, workshops and other folk events in various venues around Wadebridge.

The best... PLACES TO STAY

BOUTIQUE

St Petroc's Hotel

New Street, Padstow PL28 8EA
☎ 01841 532700
www.rickstein.com

One of six options on Rick Stein's accommodation menu, the mid-priced St Petroc's is a smart but informal Georgian house with a pretty courtyard garden. Some of the colonial-style rooms are small-ish and not all have estuary views, but they all live up to the Stein standards.

Price: B&B for two from £145–£220 per night. Children over 4, £30. Dogs £20.

Tregea Hotel

16–18 High Street, Padstow PL28 8BB
☎ 0800 005 3903/01841 532486
www.tregea.co.uk

In one of Padstow's oldest buildings, the rooms are on the cosy side, though nicely furnished in a vaguely nautical style and very good value. The owners also run the Cross House Hotel and the Estuary Restaurant, and there is an annex of further rooms at the Ruskin House.

Price: B&B from £128 for a double per night.

HOTEL

The Metropole

Station Road, Padstow PL28 8DB
☎ 0800 005 3903/01841 532486
www.the-metropole.co.uk

The grand old lady of Padstow's railway heyday, the Met is a big Victorian 58-roomer with great views across the estuary. The rooms look a bit corporate but they are high-spec, comfortable, and there's a pool (in the summer), a café-bar terrace, free Wi-Fi and private parking.

Price: B&B from £152–£186 per room per night. Dogs £10 per night.

B&B

Treverbyn House

Egerton Road, Padstow PL28 8DA
☎ 01841 532855
www.treverbynhouse.com

Minutes from the harbour, this handsome period villa is old-fashioned (antique beds, roll-top tubs, real fires) without being stuffy. There is a romantic turret room, a garden terrace (where you can breakfast on fresh croissants and homemade jams) and lovely estuary views.

Price: B&B from £85–£120 per room per night.

Woodlands Country House

Treator, Padstow PL28 8RU
☎ 01841 532426
www.woodlands-padstow.co.uk

A handsome red-brick Victorian house, this award-winning family-run guest house sits on a hillside overlooking Trevone Bay. One room has a four-poster; all have lovely views and lots of home comforts (fridge, DVD, robes). The breakfasts are generous and good enough to warrant a recipe book.

Price: B&B from £108–£148 for a double per night. Closed Christmas and January.

The best... PLACES TO STAY

Coswarth House

12 Dennis Road, Padstow PL28 8DD
☎ 01841 534755
www.coswarthhouse.com

Voted best 'hidden gem' by Tripadvisor, this lovely slate-hung house (once part of the Prideaux estate) has a pretty veranda and views of the Camel Estuary. The five-star rooms are French style and romantic, with painted floors, antique beds and roll-top baths. The gourmet breakfast is all about local produce.

Price: B&B from £118–£125 per room per night.

SELF-CATERING

Trevorrick Farm

St Issey, Padstow PL27 7QH
☎ 01841 540574
www.trevorrick.co.uk

There are seven self-catering cottages, six on the farm and one in St Issey. The 11-acre smallholding is geared up for family holidays, and Padstow is a 2.5 mile walk along the Camel Trail. Bed and breakfast is also available in the farmhouse.

Price: Self-catering from £340–£1045 for a week. Dogs allowed in some of the cottages.

Gull Cottage

Porthcothan
☎ 01841 532555
www.gullcottage.co.uk

A family-size seaside retreat overlooking the beach at Porthcothan Bay, it sits at the end of a cliff road. A gateway leads from the garden onto the coast path, 100 yards from Golden Burn beach. There are four bedrooms (for up to nine people) and amazing views from picture windows.

Price: Self-catering £575–£1,690 for a week.

Ocean Blue

Treyarnon Bay
☎ 01872 572602
www.oceanbluecornwall.co.uk/

A block of contemporary apartments, including suites, cottages, and a duplex penthouse, all 50 metres from the sea. Typically, they have two bedrooms, two bathrooms, a private garden, all mod cons and fabulous sea views.

Price: from £375 - £1625 per week (plus off-peak three-day breaks).

UNUSUAL

Trevose Lighthouse

Trevose Head, Padstow
☎ 01386 701177
www.ruralretreats.co.uk

Reached by a mile-long private drive, there are four beautifully furnished, former keepers' cottages, each sleeping four. The Victorian lighthouse is still operational, so beams of light and fog horns are part of the experience. So, of course, is a fabulous position on the cliffs at Trevose Head.

Price: from £251 (2 nights) to £967 (for a week).

The best... FOOD AND DRINK

The fish, the shellfish and the lobster are not necessarily any better than any other Cornish-harbour catch, but Padstow's reputation as seafood capital is assured. Rick Stein may have started it all, but having crowds of hungry foodies on the doorstep has inspired other culinary enterprises – including Ripley's, run by one of Stein's former head chefs (the only restaurant in the area with a Michelin star). Fresh fish is not the only good local ingredient: Cornish Earlies (spuds) grow in the fields that border the Camel Estuary, and up-river there is the acclaimed Camel Valley vineyard. When dining out in high season, be sure to book ahead – and in some cases (eg Stein's Seafood Restaurant) we are talking weeks ahead.

Staying in

Stein's Deli on South Quay (in the town's main car park), does some good ready-meals and has a wet-fish counter, though nearby, **Padstow Fisheries** (next to Rig Marine) is cheaper. On the edge of the Prideaux-Brune estate, north-west of the town, **Padstow Farm Shop** at Trethillick (☎ 01841 533060; www.padstowfarmshop.co.uk) is pretty much a one-stop shop, selling everything from home-grown vegetables, salad leaves and herbs, Cornish cheeses, beers, preserves, fresh bread and home-reared lamb and beef. Local butcher Norman Brooks (who used to run a butcher's shop in town) runs the meat counter.

Nearby Wadebridge is the best local centre for food shopping, and the café-deli at **Relish Food and Drink** at Foundry Court (☎ 01208 814214; www.relishwadebridge.co.uk), has a great selection of posh foods; much of it Mediterranean, but laced with local goodies, such as Bodmin Moor Blue cheese or organic Brie from Watergate Bay. For wines, head for **Bin Two Wine Bar** on South Quay (01841 532022; www.bintwo.com) in Padstow or the **Camel Valley Vineyard** near Wadebridge (see page 92).

Takeaway

Padstow's best pasties, in our opinion, are made by the **Chough Bakery** (3, The Strand; ☎ 01841 532835). **Stein's Fish and Chips** on South Quay, is a good, fresh and rather pricey chippy (expect long queues at weekends and during the summer), although **Fryer Tucks** at St Merryn (☎ 01841 520724) or **Barney's Fish and Chip Shop** in Molesnorth Street, Wadebridge (☎ 01208 812389) are just as good. The best local pizzeria is **Rojano's** on Mill Square, Padstow (☎ 01841 532796; www.rojanos.co.uk); the pizzas are freshly made to order and include free delivery within Padstow (or as far as Treyarnon Bay on orders over £15).

EATING OUT

FINE DINING

Rick Stein's Seafood Restaurant

Riverside, Padstow PL28 8BY
☎ 01841 532700
www.rickstein.com

This is Stein's original Padstow fish restaurant, the classic that started it all; the idea being that the day's catch comes straight off the boats and onto the table. The place had a revamp in 2008, adding a theatre-style seafood bar, enabling diners to watch the chefs preparing platters of Cornish oysters, langoustines or Japanese sushi. From £30 to £50 per head (for two courses). Cod and chips is £18.

Number Six

6 Middle Street, Padstow PL28 8BG
☎ 01841 532093
www.number6inpadstow.co.uk

Chef Paul Ainsworth's sharp, chic restaurant and private dining rooms combine exciting gastronomy, fresh local produce, Georgian architecture and contemporary design. Indeed, Number 6 was only two years old, when the *Which? Good Food Guide* (2007) reckoned it was Cornwall's number one. Three courses cost around £38. Express lunch, from £13.

RESTAURANT

Trehallas House Hotel

Washaway, near Wadebridge PL30 3AD
☎ 01208 72700
www.trehellashouse.co.uk

In a Grade II listed courthouse, on the Bodmin side of Wadebridge, the hotel's restaurant offers classical cooking using local ingredients: Fowey mussels, Padstow crab, Roskilly's ices, Cornish meat cheeses and Camel Valley wines. Open for lunch, Tues–Sun (£10.95 for two courses) and every night for dinner (£15–£30 for two courses).

CAFÉ

Jack's

Parnell Court, Lanadwell Street, Padstow PL28 8BH
☎ 01841 533238
www.padstowjacks.co.uk

Tucked away in a little sun-trap courtyard behind Rick Stein's patisserie, this easy-going eaterie offers a reasonably-priced menu of Mediterranean dishes for lunch or dinner: charcuterie plates to share, Cornish seafood dishes, tapas (from £3.50) and home-made bread and olives, plus great coffee and cream teas. Closed on Sundays.

GASTROPUB

Pescadou

The Old Custom House Inn, South Quay Padstow PL28 8BL
☎ 01841 532359
www.smallandfriendly.co.uk

On the quayside, in a former customs and excise building, built around 1800, this Mediterranean-style bistro is part of the St Austell's Ales inn (which also has rooms upstairs). As the name suggests, fish is the main dish, though steaks other meat dishes are available. Three courses dinner costs around £25 per person.

EATING OUT

Margot's Bistro
11 Duke Street, Padstow PL28 8AB
☎ 01841 533441
www.margotspadstow.blogspot.com

Adrian Oliver's unpretentious little restaurant, serves imaginative, seasonal dishes, with homemade everything including the bread. Fish soup, grilled mackerel, scallops, Cornish lamb, Padstow new potatoes and classic puds all feature. Three-course lunch/dinner costs from £25–£30 per head. Closed Sundays and Mondays.

Drinking

Even the local brewery, **Sharps** (based in Rock), has been Rick Stein-ed – by naming a beer after the chef's much-loved dog Chalky who died, aged 17, in 2007. The Belgian-style English beer, **Chalky's Bite**, won gold at the Quality Drinks Award in 2008. Most of the area's best pubs are found around Padstow's harbour, among them:

- **The Olde Ship Inn** – Mill Square; ☎ 01841 532357; www.oldshiphotel-padstow.co.uk; Chardonnay and Sharp's Doom Bar in a gastro pub setting.
- **The London Inn** – Llanadwell Street; ☎ 01841 532554; Tinners and Tribute in a flower-decked fishermen's local.
- **Shipwrights**, North Quay; ☎ 01841 532451; St Austell ales, lobsters pots, flagstone floors and a sunny rear garden.

In and around Wadebridge, try the **Earl of St Vincent Inn**, at Egloshayle (furnished with over 400 antique clocks). The **Pickwick Inn** at Burgois, St Issey (☎ 01841 540361) does good food as well as real ale. Surfer hang-outs include **The Dog House** (Dining Room and Wine Bar) and the **Cornish Arms**, both in St Merryn.

Visitor Information

Tourist information centres: Padstow Tourist Information Centre, Red Brick Building, North Quay, ☎ 01841 533449; Wadebridge Tourist Information Centre, Rotunda Building, Eddystone Road, ☎ 0870 122 3337.

Hospitals with A&E: The nearest is Bodmin Hospital, Boundary Road, Bodmin PL31 2QT, ☎ 01208 251300.

Pharmacies: Alliance, 8 The Market, Padstow PL28 8AL, ☎ 01841 532327; Day Lewis, Regency Arcade, Molesworth Street, Wadebridge PL27 7DH, ☎ 01208 812760.

Police station: Wadebridge Police Station, Whiterock Road, Wadebridge PL27 7DR.

Supermarkets: Tesco, Sarahs Lane, Padstow PL28 8EL, ☎ 0845 6779529; Tesco, West Hill Wadebridge, ☎ 01208 254400; Co-op, Jubilee Road, Wadebridge, ☎ 01208 254400.

Village stores: Constantine Bay Stores, (☎ 01841 520967) in Constantine Bay, sells just about everything, and if they don't they'll order it for you.

Car hire: Ayres Garage, Brooklyn Garage, Wadebridge PL27 7AT, ☎ 01208 812758; Tregoning Rent-a-Car, West Hill, Tollgate, St Breock, Wadebridge PL27 7HT, ☎ 01208 893006.

ATMs: Lloyds, 6 Duke Street, Padstow PL28 8AB; Barclays, Molesworth Street, Wadebridge PL27 7DN.

Cycle hire: Padstow Cycle Hire, South Quay, Padstow, ☎ 01841 533533; Trail Bike Hire, Unit 6, South Quay, Padstow, ☎ 01841 532594; Bridge Bike Hire, Eddystone Road, Wadebridge, ☎ 01208 813050; Bridge Cycle Hire, 4 Bridge View, ☎ 01208 814545; Camel Trail Cycle Hire, Eddystone Road, Wadebridge, ☎ 01208 814104.

Local taxis: A2B Padstow & Harbour Taxis, ☎ 01841 533333; Padstow Cabs, ☎ 01841 532384; Wadebridge Taxi Service, ☎ 01208 812725; Call-a-Cab, Trevone, ☎ 01841 521184.

FURTHER AFIELD

Wadebridge

At the head of the estuary, roughly 8 miles from the sea, Wadebridge straddles the River Camel, its two banks linked by a 17-arch bridge built, as they say, 'on wool' in about 1460 (there is controversy as to whether it was actually built on wool sacks, or whether its construction was simply financed by the proceeds of the medieval wool industry). The town's long-held prosperity took a hit when the cattle market closed in 2001, but it's still the heart of the local farming community, home to the annual county-set agrifest, the Royal Cornwall Show in June. And thanks to the rise of nearby Rock and Padstow, Wadebridge is one of the most desirable inland towns in Cornwall. From a visitor's point of view, one of the main reasons to go there is to make use of the everyday shops and amenities that Padstow lacks, but it does have other attractions.

The John Betjeman Centre in Wadebridge

THE JOHN BETJEMAN CENTRE, Southern Way, Wadebridge PL27 7BX; ☎ 01208 812392; www.johnbetjeman.org.uk. Admission free; open weekdays 2pm–4pm.

TRISTAN'S GALLERY, 49 Molesworth Street, Wadebridge PL27 7DR; ☎ 01208 815767; www.tristansgallery.com. Admission free; open daily 10am–4pm.

Wadebridge is one of the main access points for the popular **Camel Trail**. The two entrances to the trail are clearly marked. Between the two, you will find **The John Betjeman Centre**, housed in a disused Victorian railway station. A homage to the late Poet Laureate, who loved this part of Cornwall, the centre displays a range of Betjeman memorabilia, reflecting on his life and works. Poignantly, the former station was Betjeman's point of arrival when, as a boy, he came for the first of many holidays in Trebetherick on the northern side of the Camel Estuary: '*On Wadebridge station what a breath of sea/Scented the Camel valley Cornish air...*'.

Among a range of art and antique shops, Wadebridge is also home to **Tristan's Gallery**, a prestigious photographic gallery, showing both vintage and contemporary images by many of the big names in international photography: Martin Parr, Helmut Newton, Bill Brandt, Man Ray and others.

Trevose Head beaches

Three miles west of Padstow, the cliff-walled cove at **Trevone Bay** begins a string of beautiful sandy beaches set either side of **Trevose Head**, a rugged, storm-battered granite headland, 2.5 miles long and tipped by **Trevose Head Lighthouse** (not open to the public). The beaches are long stretches of clean, yellow sand, edged with dunes or craggy cliffs and pounded by Atlantic waves.

Novice surfers should head for sheltered **Harlyn Bay** – one of the safest places in Cornwall to learn to surf, thanks to the protective headland and the well-respected **Harlyn Surf School** (☎ 01841 533076; www.harlynsurfschool.co.uk). At **Constantine Bay**, a combination of dangerous rips and a rocky off-shore reef can provide exhilarating, often challenging, surfing conditions, but it's not recommended for the inexperienced. Swimmers too, should be very careful here. But you don't have to get wet: many come here just to sit among the marram grasses in the soft sandy dunes and enjoy the scenery, collect the many-hued pebbles and fish for tiny crabs in the rock pools.

There are some lovely walks around Trevose. You could, for example, park at **Treyarnon** and take the coast path to Constantine (around 10–15 minutes walk), and continue west across the headland to **Mother Ivey's Bay**, another attractive beach (best reached on foot, as there's no parking). Treyarnon is one of North Cornwall's cleanest beaches, but it's somewhat marred by caravanning crowds unleashed on the sands in high season. A mile or so west, the sandy, surfy beach at **Porthcothan** is a little quieter.

Constantine Bay

NEWQUAY AND SURROUNDS

At its roots, Newquay is a good old-fashioned family resort. The location is superb, with all of Cornwall within a 45-minute drive (give or take the odd hour of high-season holiday traffic). It's not everyone's cup of tea. In high summer, the streets are a youth fest of young surfheads in skimpy clothing; all hip hop, flip flops and alcopops, the air laced with burgers and fries, an undertone of suntan lotion. The surf population is swelled by the thousands of 16-tear-olds who descend on Newquay for a post-GCSE beach-party, the crowds of stag weekenders, and the coach parties of pensioners, for whom Newquay is an old favourite. But let's not forget why people come here in the first place: 7 miles of golden beaches will do for starters. Add world-class surf and an international airport on the doorstep, and it's easy to see why this is Europe's favourite surfing destination.

The name Newquay refers to the New Quay which expanded the town's pilchard industry in the 15th century. It jogged along quite happily until the railway arrived; by the 19th century, it was a thriving resort, with hotels spreading along the clifftops from the town centre to seaside suburbia. An air of post-1970s neglect still lingers in back-street rows of tired guest houses, but Newquay is slowly being driven up-market. A multi-million shopping quarter is in the pipeline. Rick Stein is investing in a Fistral beach venture. Jamie Oliver is already cooking up a storm in Watergate Bay. Even some of the doss-house surf lodges have gone all boutique. Or you can escape the mayhem at nearby Bedruthan Steps or Holywell Bay.

Bedruthan Steps

The best of... THE CORNISH COAST

FROM THE GLITTERING BAYS OF THE ISLES OF SCILLY TO THE RUGGED CLIFFS AND ROLLING DUNES OF CORNWALL'S WILD ATLANTIC BEACHES, THE REGION HAS ONE OF THE MOST VARIED AND THE MOST EXCITING, COASTLINES IN BRITAIN. ALL SURF, SEAFOOD, SAILING AND SPECTACULAR SUNSETS, IT'S A SHELLSEEKER'S DREAM, A MARINER'S PARADISE.

Sub-tropical landscape of St Martins on the Isles of Scilly

Top: Kite surfing at Watergate Bay; Middle: Visitors spot a dolphin at St Mawes;
Bottom: Porthtowan beach

Top: Towan Beach, Newquay; Middle: View from the Hell Bay Hotel on Bryher;
Bottom: Aerial view of Tresco in the Isles of Scilly

Top: Gwithian Towans at Hayle; Middle: Sunset at St Michael's Mount; Bottom: Dusk on the Fowey Estuary

The best of... CORNWALL'S CULTURE & HERITAGE

FISHING AND FARMING HAVE BEEN THE CORNERSTONES OF CORNISH LIFE SINCE PRE-HISTORY, BUT MINING MADE THE GREATER IMPACT ON THE PENINSULA'S LANDSCAPES. FROM RAILWAYS TO FINE HOUSES, THE COUNTY IS SCATTERED WITH RELICS OF ITS RICH INDUSTRIAL PAST. EVEN THE EDEN PROJECT ROSE FROM THE WASTELAND OF A FORMER CLAY PIT.

Boats at St Ives

Top: The Wheel Pit in the Luxulyan Valley; Middle: Working boat house at the Trevarno Estate; Bottom: St Germans Viaduct over the River Tiddy, seen from the Port Eliot estate

Top: Chimney Stack at South Kit Hill mine; Middle: Rock formation, the Cheesewring on Bodmin Moor; Bottom: St Mawes

Top: Torchlit procession through the Eden Project; Bottom: Sun setting at Geevor tin mine

WHAT TO SEE AND DO

On the beach

At low tide, Newquay's central beaches form one long continuous line of sand, but when the tide's in, they become a series of broad coves, each bound by towering cliffs and divided by rocky promontories; each with its own distinct character. For surfing, competitions and crowds of surf posers, **Fistral Beach** is the business – arguably the best known surf beach in Europe (note, novices should stick to the safer North Fistral end). The lovely sandy beach, west facing, is perfect for a sunset stroll, but best avoided in July–August, unless you are surfer. To the east of the headland, the sunny **Harbour Beach** sits inside the harbour's granite piers, and offers safe, sheltered bathing, and close proximity to the ticket booths and departure points for most of Newquay's boat trips (sharking, wrecking and deep-sea fishing trips are the local specialities).

Towan Beach is the closest to the town centre, and one of the most photographed, thanks to an island-like tower of rock linked to the cliffs by a mini suspension bridge (surrounded by water at high tide, Towan Island has a private house and garden on top). Opposite is the **Blue Reef Aquarium**, displaying hundreds of sub-marine creatures seen from an underwater tunnel, turtles, native British sealife, a 'giant ocean' coral reef and a shark lagoon.

BLUE REEF AQUARIUM, Towan Promenade, Newquay TR7 1DU; ☎ 01637 878124; www.bluereefaquarium.co.uk. Entry: adults £9.50, seniors/students £8.50, children £7.30 (under-3s free); open daily 10am–5pm.

CELEBRITY CONNECTIONS

Broad expanses of beach, more or less empty in the winter, make ideal film locations, and North Cornwall's have been seen in some high profile productions. In 1967, **The Beatles** checked into Newquay's Atlantic Hotel while filming scenes for *Magical Mystery Tour* on Towan Beach. In 2002, the beach at Holywell Bay was transformed into a North Korean battlefield for the opening shots of the James Bond movie *Die Another Day* starring **Pierce Brosnan**. And in 2007, C-list soap *Echo Beach*, Cornwall's answer to *Bay Watch*, turned Watergate Bay into fictional Polnarren, a Cornish surfing resort populated with some A-list stars – among them **Jason Donovan**, **Martine McCutcheon** and **Hugo Speer**. The eight-week comedy-drama was complemented by a parallel mockumentary, *Moving Wallpaper*, featuring the fictional producers of *Echo Beach*. Both productions were panned by critics, but with five million viewers apiece, the two series did a sterling job of promoting Cornwall's seaside lifestyle, even though there is nowhere quite like Polnarren. Scenes shot at Watergate Bay were stitched together with footage of Looe beach, 40 miles away.

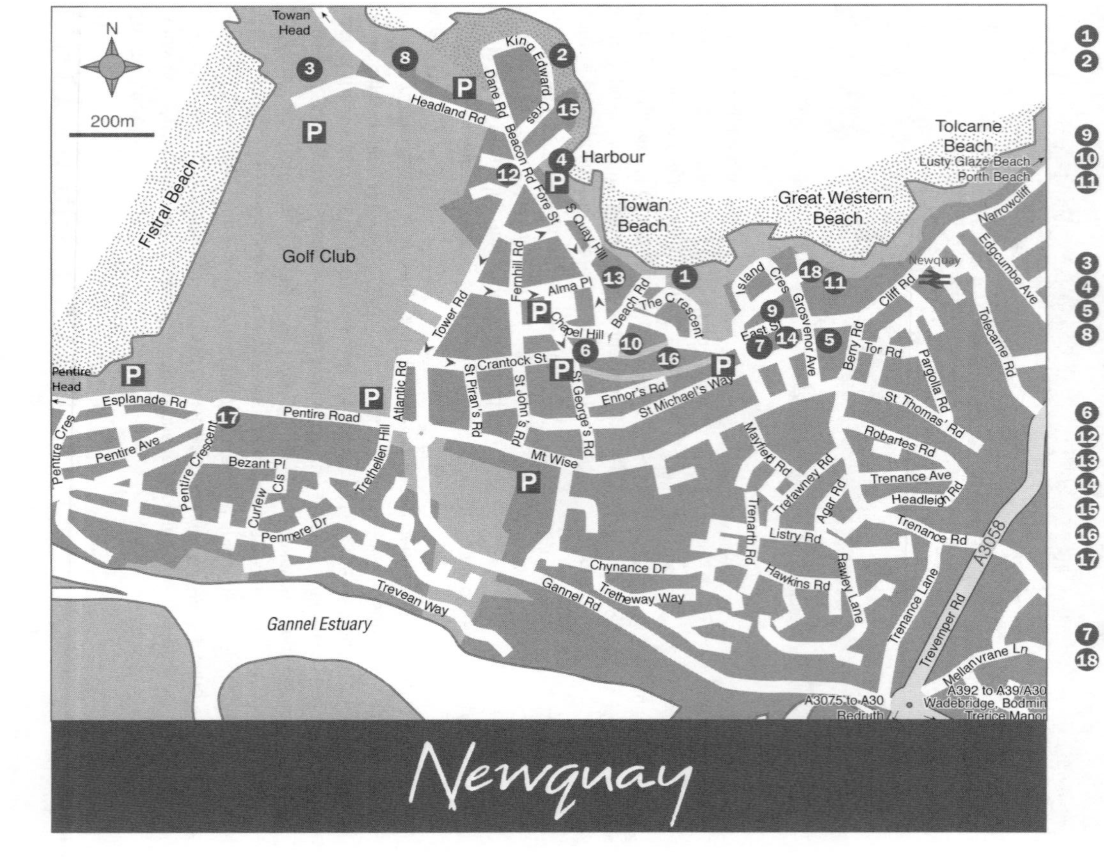

Things to see and do

1. Blue Reef Aquarium
2. Huer's Hut

Entertainment

9. Lane Theatre
10. The Beach
11. Sailor's Nightclub

Places to Stay

3. Headland Hotel
4. Harbour Hotel
5. Reef Surf Lodge
8. The Carnmarth

Eat and Drink

6. Chy Bar
12. New Harbour Restaurant
13. Truscott's
14. Prego Prego
15. The Red Lion
16. The Shack
17. Lewinnick Lodge

Visitor Information

7. Tourist Information Centre
18. Cornwall Surf Academy

Jamie Oliver's Fifteen restaurant at Watergate Bay

Continuing to the east, **Great Western Beach**, just below the station and named after the railway, is marginally quieter than either of its neighbours, though it has a good range of facilities. One of the most popular with families is **Tolcarne Beach**, a length of fine sand tucked beneath 150ft cliffs to the north-east of the town, and reached via 250 steps.

Lovely **Lusty Glaze**, 1.5 miles from the centre, is a relatively quiet all-rounder, privately owned, but open to the public all year. Tucked into the cliffs, there are terraces of beach huts, a restaurant and an adventure centre offering a range of activities including surfing, kite-boarding and 'Baywatch Babes' sea-safety courses for young children (www.lustyglaze.co.uk, ☎ 01637 872444).

There are other, often less crowded, beaches out of town. **Crantock**, 4 miles south of Newquay (or a 2-mile walk along the coast path), is a favourite with locals, with a mile of fine sand and tufted dunes, separated from Pentire Headland by the mouth of the River Gannel. From Crantock it takes 10–15 minutes to walk around West Pentire Head to **Porth Joke**, or 'Polly Joke', as the locals call it, a delightful family beach, but with no facilities. At **Porth**, 2.5 miles north of Newquay, a bay of touristy shops and cafés overlook another good beach. Just over the hill, **Watergate Bay**, a 2-mile stretch of what surfers describe as 'beach break heaven', is home to **Jamie Oliver's Fifteen Cornwall** and the **Extreme Academy**, where you can learn not just surfing but paddle-surfing, kite-surfing and land-boarding among other adrenaline-driven beach sports.

EXTREME ACADEMY, Watergate Bay TR8 4AA; ☎ 01637 860543; www.watergatebay.co.uk

Do you speak surf?

If you've never joined a pack on the line up or been inside a barrel and don't get amped or stoked when you see a bitchin' wave you are definitely a *hoodad* (surf-speak for a non-surfer) or a *kook* (a beginner). In surfing, learning the lingo is as crucial as standing on a board. Like, you get there, and the line up (the place where surfers wait for the next wave) is a zoo (crowded), the sea is full of shark biscuits (body boarders) and then some goofy-footed (right foot forward) grommet (young surfer) on a schlong (old-style single-fin surfboard) drops in (catching a wave when someone else is already on it) and before you know it you're grubbing (falling off) with a ding in your board (damaged surfboard). A *shubee* is someone who buys the gear, talks the talk, but can't surf.

ATLANTIC COAST LINE, Devon and Cornwall Rail Partnership, Plymouth PL4 8AA; ☎ 01752 233094; www.carfreedaysout.com

Getting around

One way of getting from beach to beach is on the **Surf Rider Land train**, a faintly ridiculous but useful fun ride which trundles around town between Bank Street in the centre and Trenance Gardens, leaving on the hour, from 10am. The full circuit includes Great Western Hotel, the Zoo and Hope Terrace (for Fistral beach) and takes 40–50 minutes (all-day tickets costs £4.50, or £1 for children).

On foot, you can avoid the high-street crowds by following the **'old Treffry tramway'**. A tiny section of mining engineer, Joseph Treffry's horse-worked mineral tramway that ran around north-west Cornwall, it runs along the cliffs above Great Western beach from the railway station to the harbour. Stretches of Treffry's original tramway route, which opened in 1849, now form part of the **Atlantic Coast Line**, a coast-to-coast branch railway that runs through the 'wild heart' of inner Cornwall from Newquay to Par on the English Channel.

Hue and cry

On the footpath between the harbour and the Atlantic Hotel, en route to Towan Head, the so-called **Huer's Hut** is one of Newquay's oldest buildings, dating from the 14th century. A rough-stone, white-washed building, rather like a Greek-island chapel, this is where the local **huer** would scan the ocean for shoals of pilchards. The moment he saw the signs – a darkening patch of water, a rippling surface – he would call the fishermen to their boats, by shouting 'hevva, hevva'. He was also responsible for guiding boats into the harbour, and employed a curious form of semaphore using hand-held bushes. In the days when pilchards were everything in the parish of Newquay, the huer's cry could empty a church on a Sunday.

One of the oldest buildings in Newquay, the Huer's Hut

LOCAL KNOWLEDGE

British pro surf champion, **Alan Stokes** (aka Stokesy) moved to Newquay with his parents aged six and was, he says, 'brought up on the beach'. Twice British surf champion, he spends his time travelling the world, competing and training, and is a team rider with the Animal Surf Academy.

Favourite beaches: Well, I'd have to say Fistral Beach. This is where I learnt to surf and I have won some memorable surfing victories here. Out of season it's the place to surf, but when the summer crowds hit town I like to drive down the coast. There are so many hidden beaches and coves around the Newquay area, you can always find your own private surfing playground.

Favourite restaurant: Lewennick Lodge on Pentire Head. I love going when there's a big stormy sea – it's breathtaking and the food is always as awesome as the views.

Favourite bar: The Chy Bar in Newquay. All my friends hang out there, and there's a seamless blend of locals and tourists. The Koola Club next door is good too, and they have some really cool bands on there.

Best walk: From Crantock beach to Pollyjoke and on towards Perran Sands. It takes about two hours and the scenery is not only stunning, but completely unspoilt.

Best view: From the very top of Porth Headland towards Newquay when there is a big swell running. You can see all the in the bay and the town behind.

Favourite shop: The Cornish pasty shop rules! The best ones have big ovens on full view and they smell so good when you walk in. In Newquay, I like Morris's on Gover Lane.

Favourite visitor centre: The Eden Project is fascinating. I travel all over the world, often to exotic places, so I feel really at home in the tropical biome.

Best thing about living here: The beautiful beaches and the wild waves. The beach is my office, but there's always a holiday vibe that rubs off on me – even if I am going to work.

You could at a stretch walk to **Trerice**, the National Trust's petite Elizabethan manor house, set in a peaceful valley, 3 miles south-east of Newquay (on the A3058). Built in 1573 by Sir John Arundell, the house remains remarkably unchanged, having escaped 18th- and 19th-century home improvements. Features include a great hall, lit by a tall bay window with 576 glass panes (some of them original), pretty gardens, an apple orchard and, incongruously, a collection of antique lawnmowers housed in a barn.

TRERICE, Kestle Mill TR8 4PG; ☎ 01637 875404; www.nationaltrust.org.uk. Entry: adults £7, children £3.50; open Mar–Nov (dates may vary), 11am–5pm; in Nov–Dec, Fri–Sun, 11am–4pm..

Wet weather

For keen surfers, there's only one thing to do: get into the wetsuit and out on the ocean waves. An alternative is to dive into the pools at **Waterworld**, Newquay's state-of-the-art leisure centre. There are two pools, a tropical-theme fun pool for sploshing around in and a six-lane 25-metre swimming pool for serious swimmers. There is also a well-equipped gym.

WATER WORLD, Trenance Leisure Park (off Edgecumbe Avenue), Newquay TR7 2LZ; 01637 853828; www.newquaywaterworld.co.uk. Fun pool: adults £6, children £4.60 (under-3s free); swimming pool: adults £3.70, children £2.50 (under-3s free); open daily (times vary); non-members gym sessions, £5.10.

What to do with children

Other than Waterworld (see above) the biggest to-do around here is **Newquay Zoo** or 'environmental park' at Trenance. Cornwall's only proper zoo, it is set in 8 acres of subtropical gardens, 10 minutes from the town centre. Like most modern zoos, it runs captive breeding programmes and research projects, but it's the 'animal encounters' that captivate, and the zoo's 130 species range from the mundane (guinea pigs) to the magnificent (African lions).

NEWQUAY ZOO, Trenance Gardens; Newquay TR7 2LZ; ☎ 01637 873342; www.newquayzoo.co.uk. Entry: adults £10.95, children £8.20 (under-2s free); open Apr to Sept, daily 9.30am–6pm; Oct to Mar, 10am–5pm.

Just outside Newquay (5.5 miles south), you can board the **Lappa Valley Steam Railway**, a narrow gauge railway (on a section of the original Treffry tramway) on which two baby steam locomotives, Zebedee and Muffin, puff around the

LAPPA VALLEY STEAM RAILWAY, St Newlyn East, Newquay TR8 5LX; ☎ 01872 510317; www.lappavalley.co.uk. Entry: adults £10.95, children £8.75 (off-peak: £8.25/£6); trains run roughly every 40 mins, 10.30am–4pm (or until 5.20pm in summer) daily Mar to Oct.

countryside between Benny's Halt near St Newlyn East and East Wheel Rose. The latter, a former silver and lead mine, has been converted into a leisure park arranged around restored Victorian engine houses. The ticket price includes use of the park's facilities, including crazy golf and woodland rides on miniature diesel trains.

DAIRYLAND FARM WORLD, Near Newquay TR8 5AA; ☎ 01872 510246; www.dairylandfarmworld.com. Entry: adults/children, £8.95, under-3s free; open daily 10am–5pm.

Close by, just off the A3058, **Dairyland Farm World** is an interesting farm diversification in the form of a bovine theme park. The main attraction here is agriculture in action, and aside from the farm's dairy herd, there are animals to feed and stroke (cows, pigs, ponies, goats), hayrides, mini tractors, clotted cream and an authentic whiff of dung.

Entertainment

Theatre and cinema

Newquay's **The Lane Theatre** at Marcus Hill (☎ 01637 876945; www.lanetheatre.co.uk) was founded in 1931 and is operated by the Newquay Dramatic Society, which runs a 20-week summer season of amateur dramatics plays. Newquay's Lighthouse Cinema (0871 200 3304, www.wtwcinemas.co.uk) is just off Crantock Street and King Street.

Special events

Newquay has the busiest diary of crowd-pulling outdoor events on Cornwall's summer calendar. Most, such as the **Fat Face Night Surf** on Lusty Glaze Beach (in May or June, times vary) is aimed at the young surfing crowd, but there are other events with wider appeal. One of the biggest and best known is **Run to the Sun** (www.runtothesun.co.uk), a three-day VW fest at Trevelgue Holiday Park at Porth, usually taking place over the Whitsun bank holiday weekend in May. For V Dub enthusiasts, it's a must-do (hundreds of immaculate vintage campers and customised Beetles turn up for the event), but though the car is the star, the music and the

Fifteen Cornwall

The opening of Jamie Oliver's Fifteen Cornwall restaurant in 2006 was deemed the best thing to happen to the county since, well, Rick Stein. In high summer you can wait for literally weeks to get a table. But there's more to Fifteen Cornwall than crab taglierini and Heligan cheese. In association with the Cornwall Foundation of Promise, the restaurant is run as a training ground for budding young chefs, offering places to 20 Cornish students per year, all from disadvantaged backgrounds. The foundation has charity status, and aims to address the problems associated with one of the most deprived areas in the UK. All profits from the restaurant go to the charity. The restaurant also supports Cornish food enterprise by sourcing 80% of the ingredients come from local suppliers.

beach party atmosphere is more important than shiny hub caps. In 2008, the weekend's live acts included Boy George and Fergie.

Newquay Carnival hits the streets in July; in August the surf biggie, **Ripcurl Boardmaster** (www.ripcurlboardmasters.com) unleashes a noisy, laddish surf, skate and music festival on the sands of Fistral Bay; and in September, the high-class Veuve Clicquot **Polo on the Beach** event sees horses and riders thundering across Watergate Bay. The **British National Surf Championships** take place on Fistral Beach in October. Another September event is the more traditional **Newquay Fish Festival** (www.newquayfishfestival.co.uk) which, for once, focuses the attention on the harbour area and celebrates its fishing heritage with cooking demonstrations, produce stalls and entertainment. The big winter party night for Newquay is New Year's Eve.

Nightlife

Nowhere else in Cornwall parties quite like Newquay. The club scene cools in the winter, but in July–August, you can dance until 2am–3am, seven nights a week. The best clubs include:

- **The Beach** – Beach Road; ☎ 01637 872194; www.beachclubnewquay.co.uk. Three floors including a chill-out bar.
- **The Koola Klub** – Beach Road; ☎ 01637 873415; www.thekoola.com. Located in the same space as the Chy Bar; underground sounds, live music, guest DJs, open until 2am.
- **Sailors Nightclub** – Fore Street; ☎ 01637 872838; www.sailorsnightclub.com. Funky club and pub, DJs, four bars, cocktails, free entry before 10.30pm.
- **Berties** – part of Victoria Hotel, East Street; ☎ 01637 870369; www.bertiesclub.com.High energy dance music, guest DJs, and theme nights.

The best... PLACES TO STAY

BOUTIQUE

The Watergate Bay

The Hotel & Extreme Academy, Watergate Bay TR8 4AA
☎ 01637 860543
www.watergatebay.co.uk

This Vic-wardian seaside hotel always had a lot going for it, but it went into fashion overdrive when Jamie Oliver opened up next door. The rooms are all 'beach-chic' wood floors, wallpapers, fun colours and, in some, ocean views and balconies. The Living Space bar is a great place to hang out.

Price: B&B from £110–£415 for a double. Dogs £15 a night.

HOTEL

Scarlet

Tredragon Road, Mawgan Porth TR8 4DQ
☎ 01637 861800
www.scarlethotel.co.uk

Completed in 2009, this is eco-luxe with bells and whistles: a grown-up spa hotel (no kids), all glass, reclaimed timber and shiny white modernism, custom-built in cliff-top gardens that spill down to Mawgan Porth beach, fabulous rooms (all with ocean views), glamorous pool, Ayurveda treatments, seaweed hot-tubs, good food - and kind to the planet too.

Price: from £180–£415 for a double.

Headland Hotel

Fistral Beach, Newquay TR7 1EW
☎ 01637 872211 [check]
www.headlandhotel.co.uk

This Victorian colossus, with 104 rooms, has a bit of a split personality (rich old aunt meets hip young thing) but it's a great family hotel with a relaxed by-the-beach atmosphere, two restaurants and wonderful views over Fistral Bay. The stylish budget rooms are excellent value.

Price: from £89–£389 per room per night.

Bedruthan Steps Hotel

Mawgan Porth TR8 4BU
☎ 01637 860555
www.bedruthan.com

Just along the coast from the beauty spot it's named after, this child-friendly retreat combines rooms, suites and family-size villas and a new 'Ocean spa' (with pool and Turkish-style hammam), set in clifftop gardens. The hotel offers babysitting as well as an Ofsted registered children's club.

Price: from £134–£284 for a double.

The Harbour Hotel

North Quay Hill, Newquay TR7 1HF
☎ 01637 873040
www.theharbour.uk.com

With only five rooms, it's more guest house than hotel and the décor is a tad dated, but it's hard to beat the location: just above the harbour within walking distance of everywhere, and all rooms have balconies and sea views. One-night bookings are not accepted during high season.

Price: B&B from £120–£160 per night (or from £750 per week).

The best... PLACES TO STAY

B&B

The Carnmarth

Headland Road, Fistral Beach, Newquay TR7 1HN
☎ 01637 872519; www.carnmarth.com

Overlooking Fistral Beach (albeit from a slightly oblique angle), the funky new Carnmarth has a choice of economy, standard or balcony rooms. It's also home to the English Surfing Federation, the cool sea view C-Bar, a hair salon and a skittle alley.

Price: B&B from £75–£110 for a double per night.

The Kallacliff

Lusty Glaze Road, Newquay TR7 3AD
☎ 01637 871704
www.kallacliffhotel.co.uk

A civilized retreat away from the madness of Newquay's party zone, it's friendly, family-run and sits on a cliff-top above Lusty Glaze beach. The rooms are bright and modern and most have sea views.

Price: B&B from £76–£100 per night.

SELF-CATERING

270° North

Esplanade Road, Newquay TR7 1PT
☎ 01637 873033
www.newquayselfcatering.co.uk

On Pentire head, just south of Fistral beach, this is one of Newquay's new-generation seaside apartment blocks: all glass and powder-coated steel, decks and terraces. On a quiet beach road, it has great views of the Atlantic.

Price: £375–£995 for a week (sleeps two to four).

Pentowan View

Classic Cottages, Helston TR13 8NA
☎ 01326 555555; www.classic.co.uk

In a Victorian house just above the harbour, this spacious first-floor apartment has stunning views of Newquay's town beaches. Two bedrooms, two fabulous bathrooms, high ceilings, big windows, contemporary furniture and access to communal gardens.

Price: from £429–£1083 for a week (sleeps four).

Headland Village

Fistral Beach, Newquay TR7 1EW
☎ 01637 872211
www.headlandcottages.co.uk

A cluster of modern cottages and apartments in the grounds of the Headland Hotel, this is self-catering with room service, and available by the night. Attractive, spacious and well kitted out, they are billed as luxury, but only really worth the money if you go for the ones with a sea view.

Price: from to £75–£415 per night.

UNUSUAL

Reef Surf Lodge

10–12 Berry Road, Newquay TR7 1AR
☎ 01637 879058
www.reefsurflodge.info

A far cry from the usual doss house, this bunk-bedded surf lodge borrows its style from the boutique hotel. Rooms (for singles, doubles or groups) all have televisions and CD players. There's a funky bar and a stainless steel wave in reception. Oh, yes, and it was voted the cleanest hotel in Britain.

Price: from £15–£29.50 per person per night.

The best... FOOD AND DRINK

Despite the reek of chips and hot bacon fat that scents the air on a sunny day, Newquay has some excellent restaurants, and does a particularly good line in informal Australian-style beach-front café-bars with international dishes and fantastic seaviews. Jamie Oliver raised the stakes when he opened Fifteen Cornwall at Watergate Bay in 2006. Newquay's small surviving fishing fleet, no longer fishes for pilchards, but boats still bring in fresh lobster and crab; and in general, eating out here is cheaper than Padstow.

Staying in

The nearest farm shop is at **Trevilley** (☎ 01637 872310; www.trevilleyfarm.com), a non-intensive, family-run farm, just outside Newquay selling all-Cornish produce (meat, game and loads of deli goodies). A vegetable box delivery service is useful for self-caterers staying within 10 miles of the farm. For barbecue supplies, including homemade lamb and mint sausages, head for the farm shop at the National Trust's Bre-Pen Farm (☎ 01637 860420; www.bre-penfarm.co.uk) at Mawgan Porth. The **New Harbour Restaurant** on Harbour Beach has a takeaway seafood bar selling fresh-from-the-sea lobster and crab.

Takeaways

For fish and chips (eat out or in) try award-winning **Truscott's** on Fore Street, Newquay (☎ 01637 877562). Running for nearly 40 years, it is reckoned to be one of top five fish fryers in Devon and Cornwall. **Prego Prego** on East Street (☎ 01637 852626) does excellent wraps and sandwiches.

Drinking

Drinking in the Surf Capital is more geared towards bars and nightclubs, but there are a few good pubs around, particularly out of town. In Newquay, **the Red Lion** on North Quay Hill, is a proper local with local beers (Skinner's Cornish Knocker, or Sharp's Eden Ale) and great views of Towan Beach. In Crantock, **the Old Albion** (☎ 01637 830243), is a thatched village pub with a whiff of olde smugglers, 'secret' tunnels to the beach, good pub meals and at least two guest ales. Also in Crantock, the **Bowgie Inn** (☎ 01637 830363; www.bowgie.com) is an old pub with a modern vibe, and a terrace out front with ocean views.

Look out for Newquay's own **Atlantic Brewery** organic ales. In an 18th-century farmhouse on the edge of town, the microbrewery (☎ 0870 042 1714; www.atlanticbrewery.com) produces three ales (Atlantic Gold, Blue and Red), all handmade with organic Cornish hops and local spring water. Outlets include **The Shack** in Newquay High Street, the **Beach Bar** at the Watergate Bay hotel and the **Smuggler's Den Inn** in Cubert. The latter runs an annual **Real Ale and Pie Festival** in May as well as regular jazz nights (www.thesmugglersden.co.uk).

EATING OUT

FINE DINING

Fifteen Cornwall

Watergate Bay, Newquay TR8 4AA
☎ 01637 861000
www.fifteencornwall.co.uk

An arm of Jamie Oliver's Fifteen Foundation, this fabulous restaurant right on the beach at Watergate Bay is actually a charity-funded job creation scheme but the food is pukkah, too. Bookings essential, but you can drop in for breakfast. Three-course lunch costs £27, dinner costs £58.

Viners

Carvynick, Summercourt, Near Newquay TR8 5AF
☎ 01872 510544
www.vinersrestaurant.co.uk

Chef Kevin Viner, was the first in Cornwall to win a Michelin Star, but his signature restaurant, set in the grounds of a country club, is neither stuffy nor over-priced. The emphasis is on casual family dining, friendly atmosphere and fresh seasonal local produce. Bar snacks cost from £3.95. Dinner costs around £30 per head.

Odds The Restaurant

Holywell Road, Cubert TR8 5SP
☎ 01637 830505
www.oddstherestaurant.co.uk

A custom-built, grass-roofed restaurant, founded by Adam Coad whose chemical-free Ellenglaze farm provides some of the ingredients. Enjoy Ellenglaze farm beef and lamb, woodpigeon, Crantock Bay lobster and local organic vegetables, great views across farmland towards Penhale dunes, and over 30 wines by the glass. Three courses cost £30 per person. Open Tues–Sat.

RESTAURANT

The Lewinnick Lodge

Pentire Headland TR7 1NQ
☎ 01637 878117
www.lewinnick-lodge.info

With decks of outdoor tables and views of the Atlantic from the cliffs of Pentire Headland, this has one of the best locations in Newquay. The menu includes Mediterranean tapas, seafood, burgers, salads and fabulous puddings. Perfect for sunsets and special occasions. Three-course lunch/dinner costs from £25 per head.

The Terrace

Headland Hotel, Fistral Beach, Newquay TR7 1EW
☎ 01637 872211
www.headlandhotel.co.uk

In a glassy space overlooking Fistral Bay, this is where you sit and watch the surf go by over cocktails and a Cornish crab salad. The food is modern, up-market bistro (pasta, seafood, chargrills, cream teas) and you can sit outside, weather permitting. Starters cost from £5.95, mains from £12.

The New Harbour Restaurant

The Old Boathouse, South Quay Hill, Newquay TR7 1HT
☎ 01637 874062
www.finns2go.com

Right on the harbour beach, within sight of Newquay fishing boats it's lively, informal, with outdoor seating and a menu of Cornish seafood, barbecues and Mediterranean-style dishes: lobster, crab claws, fish, steaks and salads (from £5 to £25). It's a good place for a drink too (serving over 20 wines by the glass).

EATING OUT

GASTRO PUB

Smuggler's Den

Trebellan, Cubert Newquay TR8 5PY
☎ 01637 830209
www.thesmugglersden.co.uk

Local suppliers and fresh ingredients are the keynotes of a hearty menu at this 400-year-old thatched inn on the edge of Cubert, south of Newquay. Prices range from £5 for homemade soup to £12 for a Newlyn cod in Cornish ale batter. You can also enjoy charcoal grills, kids meals, sandwiches and a beer garden.

CAFÉ-BAR

The Chy Bar & Kitchen

12 Beach Road, Newquay TR7 1ES
☎ 01637 873415
www.thekoola.com/the-chy-bar

With a long glass gallery overlooking Towan Beach and a deck for al fresco dining, it's part of the Koola Club and is, indeed, one of Newquay's coolest hang-outs. Imaginative modern British cookery is complemented by contemporary décor and a buzzy vibe. Dishes from £4.95. Open daily from 10am (and Fri/Sat evenings, 6pm–11pm).

Kahuna

Tolcarne Beach
☎ 01637 850440
www.kahunatolcarne.co.uk

Laid-back beach shack right on the sands at Tolcarne beach. Chef Ryan Mather mixes world cuisine with Cornish ingredients (moules frîtes, fish stew, falafel, lamb kofta) at decent prices. Sunday roasts cost £8.95. Beach party barbeques (advance booking) cost £10.95 per person. Under-5s eat for free. Open daily, 10am until late.

CAFÉ

The Beach Hut

Watergate Bay
☎ 01637 860877
www.watergatebay.co.uk

Great place to hang out on the beach, this is the cheaper alternative to Jamie Oliver's neighbouring restaurant. Open for breakfast, lunch and dinner (8.30am until late) serving hot drinks, cakes, cold beers, burgers and fresh seafood dishes (mussels, clam chowder, fish pie). Mains from £8.95. Bookings recommended on summer evenings.

FURTHER AFIELD

To the north of Newquay, beyond Watergate Bay, there's yet another big sandy, surfy beach at **Mawgan Porth**. The opening of the design-conscious, eco-luxe Scarlet Hotel (see page 185) in 2009 adds a bit of glamour, but the village itself is bungalow-land, a little tacky and touristy, with a Butlins-like holiday park, and a row of 1960s-style beach shops. It can become a bottle-neck of traffic in the summer, as cars inch along the B3276 coast road between Padstow and Newquay. But persevere because a little further north the road passes through a stretch of empty clifftop countryside, in its midst the National Trust's **Bedruthan Steps** where a series of rock formations (the stepping stones of the giant Bedruthan, according to legend) rise from the creamy sands of one of Cornwall's most spectacular beaches. You can simply gaze at the views from the top of the cliffs (there's an excellent National Trust tea room next to the car park), or you take a steep cliff staircase down to the beach. Note, that Bedruthan is never safe for bathing, the staircase is closed from November to March, and there is a real danger of getting cut off, so keep an eye on the tide.

Six miles south of Newquay, there's another lovely, duney beach at **Holywell Bay**, popular with families, thanks to the nearby Holywell Bay Fun Park (☎ 01637 830095, www.holywellbay.co.uk).

Visitor Information

Tourist information centre: Newquay Tourist Information Centre, Marcus Hill, Newquay TR7 1BD, ☎ 01637 854020.

Hospitals: Newquay Hospital, St Thomas Road, Newquay TR7 1RQ, ☎ 01637 893600 (small hospital with minor injuries unit). The nearest 24-hour A&E unit is Duchy Hospital, Treliske, Truro TR1 3UP, ☎ 01872 226100.

Doctors: The Health Centre, St Thomas Road, Newquay TR7 1RU, ☎ 01637 872956; Narrowcliff Surgery, Narrowcliff, Newquay TR7 2QF, ☎ 0844 4773307.

Pharmacies: Boots, 15 Bank Street, Newquay TR7 1DH, ☎ 01637 872014; Drury's, 1 Chester Road, Newquay TR7 1RU, ☎ 01637 851844.

Police station: Devon & Cornwall Constabulary, Tolcarne Road, Newquay TR7 1DD, ☎ 0845 2777444.

Supermarkets: Somerfields, Fore Street, Newquay TR7 1EZ, ☎ 01637 876006; Morrisons, Treloggan Road, Newquay TR7 2GZ, ☎ 01637 851328.

Internet access: Cybersurf, Newquay, 2 Broad Street, Newquay TR7 1NE, ☎ 01637 875497; The C-Bar, Carmarth Hotel, Headland Road, Newquay TR7 1HN, ☎ 01637 872519.

Useful websites: For all things surf, check out www.surfnewquay.co.uk. You can check out daily surf conditions anywhere on www.a1surf.com or www.dailysurf.net.

Car hire: United Rental Group, 8A Quintrell Road, Newquay TR7 3DZ, ☎ 0870 1910619; Cornwall Car Hire, the Laurels, Kestle Mill, Newquay TR8 4PJ, ☎ 01637 850971; www.cornwallcarhire.co.uk.; Cornwall Campers (based in Truro) can deliver/collect a hired VW camper van to Newquay Airport, ☎ 01872 571988, www.cornwallcampers.co.uk.

Local radio: Malibu Surf FM (105.4FM), Newquay surfer radio, between mid-July and mid-August.

Surf schools: Freespirit English Surfing Federation Surf School, Carnmarth Hotel, Headland Road TR7 1HN, ☎ 01637 879571, www.englishsurfschool.com; Reef Surf School, Great Western Beach, ☎ 01637 879058, www.reefsurfschool.com; Cornwall Surf Academy, Newquay TR8 5WX, ☎ 0870 240 6693; www.cornwallsurfacademy.com.

Cycle hire: Atlantic Cycle Hire, (☎ 07564 942105, www.atlanticcyclehire.co.uk)

Taxis: BioTravel runs a green taxi and mini-bus service using bio-diesel vehicles, ☎ 01637 880006, www.biotravel.co.uk; A2B Newquay Taxis, Newquay, ☎ 01637 977777; Cubert Taxis, Holywell Bay, ☎ 01637 830819.

HAYLE TO ST AGNES

The Cornish Tourist Board call it 'Mining Country' and throughout the 18th and 19th centuries this was, indeed, Cornwall's industrial heartland. With Redruth its capital, and Hayle its sea port, the region once produced two-thirds of the world's copper. Half of the areas which make up the Cornish Mining World Heritage Site are placed in and around Hayle, Redruth and St Agnes.

History buffs come here to seek out landmarks of industrial archaeology: the remnants of copper-smelting foundries on Hayle harbour, the clifftop engine houses at Wheal Coates, the Methodist preaching pit at Gwennap. But traditionally they come for the sand-sea-and-surf side of things: the beaches as Gwithian, Chapel Porth, Portreath, and Porthtowan are among Cornwall's surfing classics. And the National Trust coastline at Godrevy Point (where you can gaze out across St Ives Bay to Godrevy Lighthouse) is a highpoint of the South West Coast Path.

To the north of Porthtowan, the dunes and broad beaches of the south give way to deep valleys and exhilarating highs; cliffs of dark rock plunging down to craggy coves, wildflowers on windswept hillsides, the whole ensemble pricked with tall brick stacks and ruined engine houses. Mining is never far away.

WHAT TO SEE AND DO

Hayle

In the 19th century, Hayle was a world centre for steam-engine manufacture, a global mining port. These days, the down-at-heel Victorian town is a sprawl of caravan parks on a rather scruffy waterfront, a far cry from nearby St Ives which looks down on it from the opposite side of the Hayle Estuary, but it's on the up. A £175m redevelopment scheme is planned for the harbour area, where remnants of foundries and shipyard wharfs are wrapped around the Copperhouse and Carnsew Pools.

Hayle Sands, all 3 miles of it, is among the most spectacular beaches in Cornwall. To explore the whole length of this glorious beach, you can take the South West Coast Path, across the dunes from **Black Cliff** to **Godrevy Point**, or from **Mexico Towans** to **Gwithian Towans** (the word *towans* simply

Wheal Coates mine

meaning sand hill). Some parts of the journey can be so lonely, you might feel a little like an intrepid explorer on a desert safari, but the effort is often rewarded by sightings of skylarks, orchids or, at dusk, glow-worms, particularly around the nature reserve at **Upton Towans.**

To reach the beach at **Riviere Towans** by road, turn off the B3301 to Phillack and follow the road down through the chalet park – an eccentric community of beach-hut homes scattered among the dunes. To reach the beach at **Gwithian**, continue along the B3301 signposted to Godrevy. Or park in the National Trust car park and follow the footpath around to the dark slate cliffs of the headland at Godrevy Point, the best place to see **Godrevy Lighthouse**. Said to be the inspiration for Virginia Woolf's 1927 novel, *To the Lighthouse*, the white octagonal tower, built in 1859 (and solar powered since 1995), sits on a rocky little island. On the other side of the headland, the secretive little beach at **Fisherman's Cove** is a favourite with naturists.

Portreath and Porthtowan

These two seaside villages, between Hayle and St Agnes, are a funny old mix of faded industry and mass tourism. **Portreath**, for example, was once one of Cornwall's most important mineral ports, all coal, grime and copper ore. There's nothing pretty about the town or the harbour, but the beach is glorious and very popular with locals.

Porthtowan, 8 miles north, has a more resort-like feel, having been established as such by 19th-century day-trippers from Redruth. Surfing is the modern industry here; there is a salt-water bathing pool on the beach, a beach café and, at low tide, you walk along the sands from here to Chapel Porth and on to St Agnes Head.

Redruth and Camborne

They offer shops, banks and post offices and a mainline railway station in Redruth, but these neighbouring towns don't have much in the way of visitor attractions. Camborne in particular clearly demonstrates why Cornwall was identified as a deprived area, deserving high priority European aid. But if you take the time to look beyond the towns' centres, a fascinating inner Cornwall unfolds.

You can't miss **Carn Brea**, the steep ridge of granite and heathland that lies to the south of both settlements and visible for miles, particularly at the point where the **Dunstanville monument** stands. The 90ft granite obelisk was built in 1836 in memory of Francis Bassett (later Lord de Dunstanville), the most philanthropic of a prominent local family that owned most of Camborne district's 300-odd mines. From the south of Carn Brea, you can see the crumbling, overgrown ruins of the engine houses and ore-crushing 'stamps' of the Bassett mines.

The landscape around here is littered with mining heritage sites, but one of the must-dos has to be the National Trust's **Cornish Mines and Engines** at Pool, mid-way between Camborne and Redruth. Aside from a mine-themed discovery centre, what you see is two giant beam engines in a pair of engine houses, and views up a sky-scraping chimney stack from inside a flue tunnel, all beautifully preserved. One of the mighty engines is in working order, though the beam's rise and fall is powered by electricity. Originally, they were driven by high-pressure steam, thanks to the innovation of local-hero engineer, **Richard Trevithick**.

The National Trust's Cornish Mines and Engines

CORNISH MINES AND ENGINES, Pool, Redruth TR15 3NP; ☎ 01209 315027; www.nationaltrust.org.uk. Entry: adults £6.10, children £3.30; open 1 Apr–30 Oct, closed Tues/Sat.

Trevithick's 18th-century home at nearby Penponds is open only on Wednesday afternoons (2pm–5pm, Apr to Oct; ☎ 01209 612154). **Trevithick Cottage** was rescued from dereliction by the Cornish Engines Preservation Trust in the 1900s, and handed to the National Trust in 1967. The house is curated by a live-in family, hence the limited opening hours. Entry is free.

Another worthwhile trip down mining-heritage lane is the **King Edward Mine Museum**, once part of the still-surviving Camborne School of Mines and run, from 1897 until 1974, as a state-of-the-art training college. The school continued to mine and mill tin here until the First World War. As a visitor centre, it's a bit hard-core (unless you're passionate about dipper wheels and frue vanners); nonetheless, this is the oldest complete mining site left in Cornwall, and Grade II listed to boot.

KING EDWARD MINE; Troon, Camborne TR14 9DP; ☎ 01209 614681; www.kingedwardmine.co.uk.

King Edward is right in the midst of what they call the Great Flat Lode, a near- horizontal seam of tin which helped earn the region's reputation as 'the richest square mile in the old world'. Cyclists and walkers can explore its landscapes and legacies on the **Great Flat Lode**

Preaching in the converted pit

A few miles south of Redruth, Gwennap Pit is billed as a cathedral of Methodism, thanks to a series of 18th-century Wesleylian rallies attracting crowds of Cornish miners. The pit was a bowl-like depression, caused by mining subsidence, but it made a natural auditorium – a fact not lost on John Wesley as he faced his Gwennap congregation in a high wind. *'At a small distance was a hollow capable of containing many thousands of people,'* he wrote in his diary in September 1762.

Between then and 1789, Wesley conducted 18 sermons from Gwennap Pit. The largest of these events drew over 30,000 people (though the father of Methodism is thought to have had a bent for exaggeration). In 1806, local mine-owners remodelled the pit in memory of Wesley, cutting 13 terraces into the turf, to form rings of grassy seats. A Whit Monday service has been held there ever since. The freehold of the pit, was secured by the Methodist Church in 1978. A small visitor centre opens daily (closed Sun) in the summer.

Trail, 7.5 miles of track and old tramway, mostly off-road, that loops around Carn Brea through farmland, heathland and dozens of derelict mines. Maps and information points are provided en route.

St Agnes

A neat roses-round-the-door sort of place, full of galleries, craft centres and organic food shops, St Agnes – or 'Aggie' – is set on two levels: the upper is Churchtown (the village centre) and the lower, Peterville (granite cottages and pretty gardens). Between the two, a curious stepped terrace of seafarers' cottages called **Stippy Stappy** follows a sharp incline down Town Hill. In fact, steep hills are a St Agnes speciality. Try the final drop from the car park at the bottom of Quay Road to the sandy beach and harbour walls at **Trevaunance Cove**. Or struggle up to the summit of St Agnes Beacon (the views are worth it). Spectacular views can also be had by following the footpath that runs along the cliffs from Trevaunance to **St Agnes Head** and, continuing south, to the National Trust's mine buildings at **Wheal Coates**.

Chapel Porth beach, 2 miles south of St Agnes, has a National Trust car park, a little café and a bay of white sand which, at low tide, stretches all the way to Porthtowan. The surfing here can be as good as any of Newquay's beaches. To the north of St Agnes, **Trevellas Porth** is a stoney little cove (generally unsafe for bathing), popular with divers, dog walkers and fishermen. You can walk to Trevallas along the coast path from Trevaunance, returning to St Agnes via the wooded **Jericho Valley** and the **Blue Hills Tin Streams**.

The only living, working mine to survive anywhere in Cornwall, Blue Hills is a cottage-industry mine within the deep coastal valley above Trevallas. Owned by the Wills family since the 1970s, it's run as a visitor centre, demonstrating the process of turning mineral to metal – from crushing rocks to casting tin. There is a water wheel, and a little shop selling tin jewellery. Getting there by car is not for the faint-hearted: the narrow roads into the valley drop at a breathtaking angle.

BLUE HILLS TIN STREAMS, Wheal Kitty, St Agnes TR5 0YW; ☎ 01872 553341; www.bluehillstin.com. Entry: adults £6, children £3; open Apr to Oct, 10am–2pm (until 4pm in summer); closed Sundays.

Local legends: Bolster the Giant

He was an ill-tempered bully, so tall that he was able to plant one foot on Carn Brea and the other on St Agnes beacon. He had some nasty habits (such as trampling on crops and lunching on children) but Bolster the Giant was a fool in love. Unable to resist a pretty face, he was easily infatuated, though his ardour was short-lived; having tired of the many wives he had wooed and won, he disposed of them. But Bolster met his match in the beautiful Agnes. Eager to fend off his advances, she asked him to prove his love by filling a hole in a cliff at Chapel Porth with his own blood. Unaware that the tiny hole she picked for him drained into the sea, he obliged, bleeding to death in the process. The cliffs at Chapel Porth, they say, are still stained red with Bolster's blood. Agnes, of course, was heralded a saint.

Wet weather

ST AGNES MUSEUM, Penwinnick Road, St Agnes TR5 0PA; ☎ 01872 553228; www.stagnesmuseum.org.uk. Admission free; open daily Apr to Oct, 10.30am–5pm.

The charming **St Agnes Museum** is worth an hour or so, having an eclectic array of exhibits from the area, including mineral specimens, mining and shipping memorabilia and a leatherback turtle (deceased).

Leatherback turtle at St Agnes museum

What to do with children...

Founded in the 1970s as a tropical bird sanctuary, **Paradise Park** has developed into a small garden zoo housing a variety of birds and animals including otters, red pandas, barn owls, eagles, cockatoos and even penguins. Behind the scenes, the family-owned park is involved in various conservation initiatives (such as the World Parrot Trust and the study of the endangered Cornish Chough), but for children it's all about furred and feathered friends. They will love the Fun Farm (alpacas, pygmy goats and mini donkeys), plus there is an all-weather 'JungleBarn' with an indoor soft-play area and daily free-flying bird shows in the summer.

PARADISE PARK, 16 Trelissick Road, Hayle TR27 4HB; ☎ 01736 753365; www.paradisepark.org.uk. Entry: adults £12.50, children £9.95, under-3s free; open daily 10am–3/4/5pm (depending on season) year round.

Just out of town, **Callestick Farm** offers a great mix of fresh air, farm animals and Callestick's own luxury ice cream. Kids can learn how a dairy farm works and see how the ice cream is made.

CALLESTICK FARM, Callestick, Truro TR4 9LL; ☎ 01872 573126; www.callestickfarm.co.uk. Entry: free; open Mon–Fri, 9.30am–5.20pm; Sat/Sun, 11.30am–5.30pm.

CELEBRITY CONNECTIONS

The so-called 'Mozart of techno', the singular **Aphex Twin** is a local lad, having grown up in Lanner, just south of Redruth. Born Richard David James in 1971, he moved to Cornwall when he was a toddler. The self-taught genius of electronic sound started producing music when he was 12, though his gift for electronics had other outlets: he was suspended from school in Redruth for computer hacking.

'I'm just an irritating, lying, ginger kid from Cornwall who should have been locked up in some youth detention centre,' he later told the *Guardian*. 'I just managed to escape and blag it into music.' At Cornwall College he studied, not music, but engineering.

Richard ventured into the public eye as a teenage DJ, first at the Shire Horse pub in St Ives, and later at the Bowgie Inn at Crantock near Newquay. By that time he was playing tapes of his own music, a fact that drew the admiration of fellow DJ, Grant Wilson-Claridge, with whom he later co-founded the electro music label Rephlex Records – 'the coolest record label in the world' according to NME.

Richard took the name Aphex from a brand of audio equipment, Aphex Systems, while the Twin was an allusion to his older brother, also Richard James, who died at birth. His first recording was the EP *Analogue Bubblebath*, released on the fledgling Cornish Rephlex label in 1991. It was swiftly followed by *Didgeridoo*. Acclaim was almost instant, and a year later, Rephlex had moved to London. Aphex Twin, living in a former bank in south London, has been based in the capital ever since, but Cornwall, and Cornishness, is a recurring theme of his work.

The cover of the 1993 album, *Polygon Window, Surfing on Sine Waves*, features a photograph of Chapel Porth beach. The record *Analogue Bubblebath 3*, came with a poster of Cornwall and a brief tongue-in-cheek guide to places of interest, mostly in and around the Twin's former stomping ground. Gwennap Pit, just outside Lanner, was said to be renowned 'for its fabulous acoustics...a great place for a swift game of tig'.

One of the artist's best known albums is *Drukqs* (2001), on which many of the tracks' names are written in Cornish – jynweythek, for example, can be loosely translated as 'machine music'.

 ... and how to avoid children

PERRANPORTH AIRFIELD, Trevellas, St Agnes Near Truro TR5 0XS; ☎ 01872 552266; www.perranporthairfield.com. Price: scenic flights from £68 per hour up to £285 for a tour of the county; Apr to Oct (weather permitting).

From the privately owned **Perranporth Airfield** you can hop on a Cessna 172 aircraft, and take in the north-coast scenery from above. East of St Agnes, the airport was built in 1942 and remains one of the UK's most complete wartime airfields.

 Entertainment

Theatre and cinema

The Regal Cinema in Redruth (6 Fore Street; ☎ 01209 216278) shows all the usual general release movies, and the local film society shows occasional art films and oldies at the Melting Pot (the Old Grammar School, Krowji, Redruth; ☎ 07915 252757; www.themeltingpotcafe.co.uk).

Special events

Towards the end of April, Camborne hosts **Trevithick Day** (www.trevithick-day.org.uk), a vintage steam fair and street festival in honour of the town's famous son, engineer Richard Trevithick. On May Day, **St Agnes Victorian Fayre** is a nostalgia-themed village street party of stalls and entertainment, culminating in a fancy-dress procession led by St Agnes Silver Band. Another parade of costumes turns out for the **St Agnes Carnival** (www.stagnescarnival.co.uk) in July or August (dates vary), a procession of community floats led by the legendary giant Bolster (see box). In August, the long-established **Hayle Fest** is a week of community events, ending with a carnival procession.

Nightlife

Most of the partying around here goes on in surfer hang-outs right on the beach, notably at **The Blue Bar** at Porthtowan (☎ 01209 890329; www.blue-bar.co.uk) and the **Watering Hole** at Perranporth (☎ 01872 572888; www.the-wateringhole.co.uk), both of which serve live music. Regular live music nights are also a feature of the **Driftwood Spars**, Trevaunance Cove (☎ 01872 552428; www.driftwoodspars.com). The **Salt Kitchen Bar** in Hayle is good for a late-night drink (www.salt-hayle.co.uk). And the **St Agnes Hotel** in Churchtown (☎ 01872 552307; www.st-agnes-hotel.co.uk) is the place for folk, funk, jazz and comedy nights.

The best... PLACES TO STAY

BOUTIQUE

The Aramay

Quay Road, St Agnes TR5 0RP
☎ 01872 553546; www.thearamay.com

Young, fun and funky, the rooms are small or 'intimate', but big on style with a touch of retro Hollywood. And, at the foot of Stippy Stappy, it's just five minutes downhill to Trevaunance Cove.

Price: from £105–£125 for a double per night.

HOTEL

Rose in Vale Country House

Mithian, St Agnes TR5 0QD
☎ 01872 552202
www.rose-in-vale-hotel.co.uk

A creeper-clad Georgian manor house in a wooded valley, offers old fashioned style with modern comforts. The rooms range from standard to sumptuous four-poster suite, most looking through trees at pretty gardens.

Price: from £110 (B&B)–£345 (half board) for a double per night.

FARMSTAY

Treglisson  

Wheal Alfred Road, Hayle TR27 5JT
☎ 01736 753141; www.treglisson.co.uk

There are four charming cottage-style rooms in this farmhouse on the southern edge of Hayle. In the winter, a cosy log-burner warms the dining room; in the summer, there is a heated indoor pool.

Price: B&B from £55–£75 per room per night.

B&B

Calize Country House

Gwithian, Hayle TR27 5BW
☎ 01736 753268
www.calize.co.uk

You can see Godrevy Lighthouse from this homely 1870s villa. It offers four rooms, a self-contained apartment, wholesome breakfast (with homemade bread) and a comfy lounge. The owners subscribe to local sustainable tourism principles where possible.

Price: from £80 per room per night; self-catering from £328–£774.

Driftwood Spars

Trevaunance Cove, St Agnes TR5 0RT
☎ 01872 552428
www.driftwoodspars.com

In a 17th-century inn, minutes from the beach at Trevaunance Cove, there are 15 rooms, decorated with modern nauticalia and in marine colours; all have Wi-Fi, some have sea views, and one has a Victorian half-tester bed. Beware of live music at weekends.

Price: B&B from £86–£102 for a double per night.

SELF-CATERING

Ridgecote

Riviere Towans Chalet Park
☎ 01736 795918
www.coastcornwall.co.uk

Pre-war chalet that has two bedrooms, a bunk-room, French doors opening onto a sandy garden and a whiff of 1930s seaside holidays.

Price: from £235 per week (sleeps six).

The best... FOOD AND DRINK

The region hasn't yet bred the wealth of restaurants that are now synonymous with neighbouring Padstow or St Ives, but it's a rich source of fresh ingredients, particularly meat, vegetables, fruit and dairy. That's partly down to a largely rural community of productive farmers, and partly down to village centres such as St Agnes that have hung onto local family-run shops. There are also lively beach-bum bars and cafés.

Staying in

Trevaskis Farm at Gwinear, Hayle (☎ 01209 713931; www.trevaskisfarm.co.uk) launched The Market in 2008, a one-stop farmshop promising *'the quality of a farmers' market with the convenience of a supermarket'*. The farm's wares include sorbets and ice creams made from Trevaskis-grown fruit, seasonal vegetables (the farm produces around 90 home-grown crops), west country meats, locally caught fish, Cornish cheeses and homemade sausages, jams and ready meals (pies, soups, flans and the like). The farm's produce is served in the **Farmhouse Kitchen Restaurant**, open for breakfast, lunch, dinner and teas.

Also close to Hayle is the **Richards of Cornwall** farmshop at Carwin Farm (Loggans Moor, near the West Cornwall Retail Park; ☎ 01736 757888; www.richardsofcornwall.co.uk). Again, there is a mix of fruit and vegetables, local meat and free-range poultry, Cornish dairy produce and homemade chutneys and sauces.

In Churchtown, St Agnes, there's an excellent butchers, **Batemans** (local and free-range meat, hogs and black pudding), as well as the **St Agnes Bakery** (☎ 01872 552308) and the simply named **Fish Shop** (☎ 01872 553790), good for scallops, Cornish sardines and pre-prepared food such as fish kebabs and crab cakes. To the south-east of St Agnes, you can buy tubs of luxury Cornish dairy ice cream direct from **Callestick Farm** (☎ 01872 573126; www.callestickfarm.co.uk).

Takeaway

With six pasty shops, Hayle is Cornwall's self-proclaimed 'pasty capital', with **Hampsons**, the butchers at Chapel Terrace, and **Warrens** on Foundry Square among the ace pasty makers vying for trade. The undisputed king among Hayle pasties, however, is made by **Philps Bakery**, (www.philpsbakery.co.uk) with shops on Foundry Hill (☎ 01736 753302) and East Quay (☎ 01736 755661). They even sell frozen ready-mades you can cook yourself.

EATING OUT

FINE DINING

The Valley Restaurant

Rose in Vale Hotel, Mithian, St Agnes TR5 0QD
☎ 01872 552202
www.rose-in-vale-hotel.co.uk

An AA rosette is awarded to this hotel eatery, open to non-residents and offering a daily changing menu of seasonal local produce and fresh-catch seafood specials, served on tables with linen napkins and candlelight. Three-course dinner costs £27.50.

RESTAURANT

Carn Brea Castle

Carn Lane, Redruth TR16 6SL
☎ 01209 218358

An odd mix of inexpensive East-meets-Mediterranean cuisine (chilli chicken, garlic butter naan, stuffed vine leaves) is served by a Jordanian host, in a curious little medieval castle set within the walls of an Iron Age hillfort at one of Cornwall's highest points. Make sure you book ahead, and take cash or a cheque book.

Spindrift

Trevaunance Cove, St Agnes TR5 0RT
☎ 01872 552428; www.driftwoodspars.com

This light, lively restaurant overlooks Trevaunance Cove, and serves stylish dishes using Cornish produce. Two courses cost around £18 per head.

GASTRO PUB

St Agnes Hotel

Churchtown, St Agnes TR5 0QP
☎ 01872 552307
www.st-agnes-hotel.co.uk

A 200-year-old inn, and a hotel since 1844, the 'Aggie' is an old-fashioned local, with an atmospheric bar and a relaxed restaurant serving lunch (from £6.50) and dinner (two courses cost £13). All dishes are freshly prepared.

CAFÉ

Salt Kitchen Bar

White's Warehouse, 25 Foundry Square, Hayle TR27 4HH; ☎ 01736 755862
www.salt-hayle.co.uk

In converted warehouse space in a marina backstreet this is the hip side of Hayle. The menu offers reasonably priced brasserie-style meals (gourmet burgers, Cornish rump steak, seafood chowder, herb-crusted cod fillet – all costing around £8.95). Many come just for the cocktails, the live music and industrial-chic décor.

Godrevy Café

Godrevy Towans, Gwithien, Hayle TR27 5ED
☎ 01736 757999
www.godrevycafe.co.uk

In a glorified wooden hut with a double-decker veranda and fabulous views over St Ives Bay, this little gem is a Cornish version of a Sydney-side café (lots of seafood, exotic flavours and bright, seaside décor). Dishes include mezzes, risotto, homemade crab cakes, salads and wraps, priced from £3.95. Open for lunches, afternoon teas, Sunday brunches and some evenings during the summer.

The Blue Bar

Eastclif, Beach Road, Porthtowan
☎ 01209 890329; www.blue-bar.co.uk

A laid-back beach bar and terrace on the sands at Porthtowan with good-quality café food: soups, salads, mezze platters, pizzas, chips and dips, baltis and burgers (all freshly made), Cornish steaks, and seafood specials. Starters cost from £6.50; mains cost from £8.50.

Drinking

The lively bar at **Driftwood Spars** at Trevaunance Cove merits a special place in this section, thanks to its celebrated microbrewery. Following a change of ownership in 2007, the brewery's original Cuckoo ale went out of production, but a year later, it was back in business with Driftwood's own Blue Hills Bitter and Furnace (a fiery, alcoholic ginger beer). The lively bar is popular with locals, surfers and bikers.

More conventional locals include the **Red River Inn** (☎ 01736 753223) at Gwithian, a dog/child-friendly freehouse serving real food and ales, including Sharps ales and not-so-local Adnams Broadside; **the Miners Arms** (☎ 01872 552375) at Mithian (nice old village pub, big on food); or the real-ale **Railway Inn** in St Agnes (☎ 01872 552310). The latter displays an interesting collection of old shoes.

For real-ale takeaways, visit the **Keltek Brewery Shop** on Cardrew Way, Redruth (☎ 01209 313620; www.keltekbrewery.co.uk), for Cornish bottled beers, as well as natural ales made in its own award-winning microbrewery (try Keltek King, Magik or 4K Mild). Another small ale maker is the **Coastal Brewery** in Redruth (☎ 07875 405407; www.coastalbrewery.co.uk). Produced by Alan Hinde (a former British Rail joiner from Crewe), the beers include Golden Hinde, Angelina, Handliner (a traditional session bitter) and award-winning Coastal Sands.

FURTHER AFIELD

The former mining village at **Perranporth**, 4 miles north of St Agnes, is one of the busiest family resorts on the Atlantic coast. With a straggle of post-war bungalows spreading over the clifftops and a brash little beach-shop high street, it's not the most attractive of places, but the beach – **Perran** and neighbouring **Penhale Sands** – is first class. Three miles long and, at low tide, nearly half a mile deep, it's furnished with caves and rock arches, as well as crowds of sand-yachters, surfers and sun-bathers.

It's also the hallowed home of Cornwall's national saint. Among the windblown sandhills behind Penhale, you will find **St Piran's Cross** (an 8ft granite column, *c.* 960AD, thought to be the oldest Celtic cross in Cornwall), alongside the ruined foundations of **St Piran's Old Church** and the site of the 'Lost Church' or **St Piran's Oratory**. One of the most important early Christian sites in Britain, the latter has been buried beneath the dunes since the 10th century. The nearby **Perran Round**, a near-perfect grass circle with an earth rampart, was the medieval theatre where pilgrims would have been entertained with miracle plays in the Cornish language. The protected Ancient Monument, originally an Iron Age hill fort, isn't sign-posted, but you'll find it just off the B3285 between Goonhavern and Perranporth.

Find out more about St Piran at the **Perranzabuloe Museum**, a good place to while away an hour on a wet day. Housed in

PERRANZABULOE MUSEUM, Ponsmere Road, Perranporth TR6 0BW; www.perranzabuloemuseum.co.uk. Admission free; open Apr to Oct, Mon–Fri 10.30am–4.30pm, Sat 11am–1pm.

St Piran: patron saint of Tinners

Cornwall's St Petroc is not only the saint of tin mining, but also its founder. They say he lit a fire on a hearthstone made of granite, and when the tin within smelted in the heat, it formed a cross of white-hot metal ore on the dark stone – thus explaining the origin of Cornwall's black and white St Piran's flag. But the saintly Piran was not a Cornishman. According to legend, he landed on the beach at Perranporth after being thrown off an Irish cliff into stormy seas by a crowd of heathens. Miraculously, the sea calmed and Piran floated across on the millstone they had tied him to.

At Perranporth, he founded his first missionary church, St Piran's Oratory. A place of pilgrimage in medieval Cornwall, the tiny rustic chapel now lies beneath the dunes at Penhale Sands, though you can still see the ruins of St Piran's Old Church at nearby Gear. Built between the 11th and 15th centuries, this too was lost in the shifting sands. But neither the lost oratory, nor the ruined church have been forgotten. The St Piran Trust is dedicated to uncovering the remnants of both. And on St Piran's Day, on 5 March, hundreds of modern devotees make a pilgrimage to these sandy tombs.

the town's Oddfellows Hall, a former chapel, there are displays dedicated to all facets of local Cornish life, from farming to surfing.

Another quite different place of pilgrimage is **Healey's Cornish Cyder Farm** at nearby Penhallow, one of Cornwall's most popular tourist attractions. Billed as *'the nation's favourite farm visit'* it produces Cornish Rattler, among other traditional scrumpies, sparkling cider, country wines and juices, all made from home-grown fruit. Tours of the orchards, the press house and jam kitchen are supplemented by tractor tours and a cider museum.

CORNISH CYDER FARM, Penhallow TR4 9LW; ☎ 01872 573356; www.thecornishcyderfarm.co.uk. Admission free (includes parking and tastings); guided tours: adults £6.50, children £4.50 (under-6s free); tractor tours: adults £4.50, children £3; open daily (times vary) Feb to Dec.

Also worth a look is the **Perranzabuloe Millenium Sundial**, on the cliffs to the south of Perran Sands. Designed by local artist Stuart Thorn, it features a 20ft stainless steel gnomon which casts shadows on a grass and granite clock-face. Set on Cornish time, it runs approximately 20 minutes ahead of GMT.

Visitor Information

Tourist information centres: Hayle Tourist Information Centre, Hayle Library, Commercial Road, Hayle TR27 4DE, ☎ 01736 753 196; Redruth Tourist Information Centre, The Cornwall Centre, Alma Place, Redruth TR15 2AT, ☎ 01209 219048; St Agnes Tourist Information Centre, 5 Churchtown, St Agnes, TR5 0QU, ☎ 01872 554150. Perranporth Tourist Information Centre, Duchy Holidays, 7–8 Tywarnhayle Square, Perranporth TR6 0ER, ☎ 01872 575254.

Hospitals with A&E: Camborne Redruth Community Hospital, Longreach House, Barncoose Terrace, Redruth TR15 3ER, ☎ 01209 881688. The minor injury unit is open 7 days a week, 8am–10pm.

Doctors: New Surgery, Pengarth Road, St. Agnes TR5 0TN, ☎ 01872 553881; Manor Surgery, Forth Noweth, Redruth TR15 1AU, ☎ 01209 313313; Connor Down Surgery, Turnpike Road, Connor Downs, Hayle TR27 5DT, ☎ 01736 756271.

Pharmacies: Alliance Pharmacy, 44–46 Fore Street, Copperhouse, Hayle TR27 4DY, ☎ 01736 752189; Boots The Chemist, 31–32 Fore Street, Redruth TR15 2AE, ☎ 01209 215218; Alliance Pharmacy, 55–56 Vicarage Road, St. Agnes TR5 0TG, ☎ 01872 552340.

Police station: Devon & Cornwall Constabulary, ☎ 08452 777444 have stations at Trecarrel, Drump Road, Redruth TR15 1LU, Sea Lane, Hayle TR27 4DU, or Liskey Hill, Perranporth, Cornwall TR6 0EU.

Supermarkets: Tesco, Tolgus Hill, Redruth TR15 1AZ, ☎ 0845 6779590; Iceland, 25 Fore Street, Redruth TR15 2BQ, ☎ 01209 612642; Costcutter, 4 Churchtown, St Agnes TR5 0QW, ☎ 01872 553991. For chain stores visit Hayle Retail Park on the A30.

Internet access: The Melting Pot, The Old Grammar School, Redruth TR15 3AJ, ☎ 07915 252757.

Car hire: DW Car and Van Rental, 21 Meadowside Close, Hayle, ☎ 01736 754197; MY Motors, East End, Redruth TR15 2EJ, ☎ 01209 214114; 4 U 2 Rent, Scorrier, Redruth TR16 5AW, ☎ 01209 821033.

Surf schools: Breakers Surf School, St Agnes (☎ 07725 842196, www.surf-lessons.co.uk); Gwithian Academy of Surfing (school and accommodation), Prosper Hill, Gwithian, ☎ 01736 757579, www.surfacademy.co.uk.

Bike hire: The Bike Barn, Elm Farm Cycle Hire, Cambrose, Portreath TR16 5UF, ☎ 01209891498 (right on the Mineral Tramways Cycle Network); Bike Chain, Old Conns Works, Bissoe TR4 8QZ, ☎ 01872 870341.

Taxis: St Agnes Taxis ☎ 01872 553795; Alan's Cab, Redruth, ☎ 01209 216990; Hayle Taxis ☎ 01736 753000.

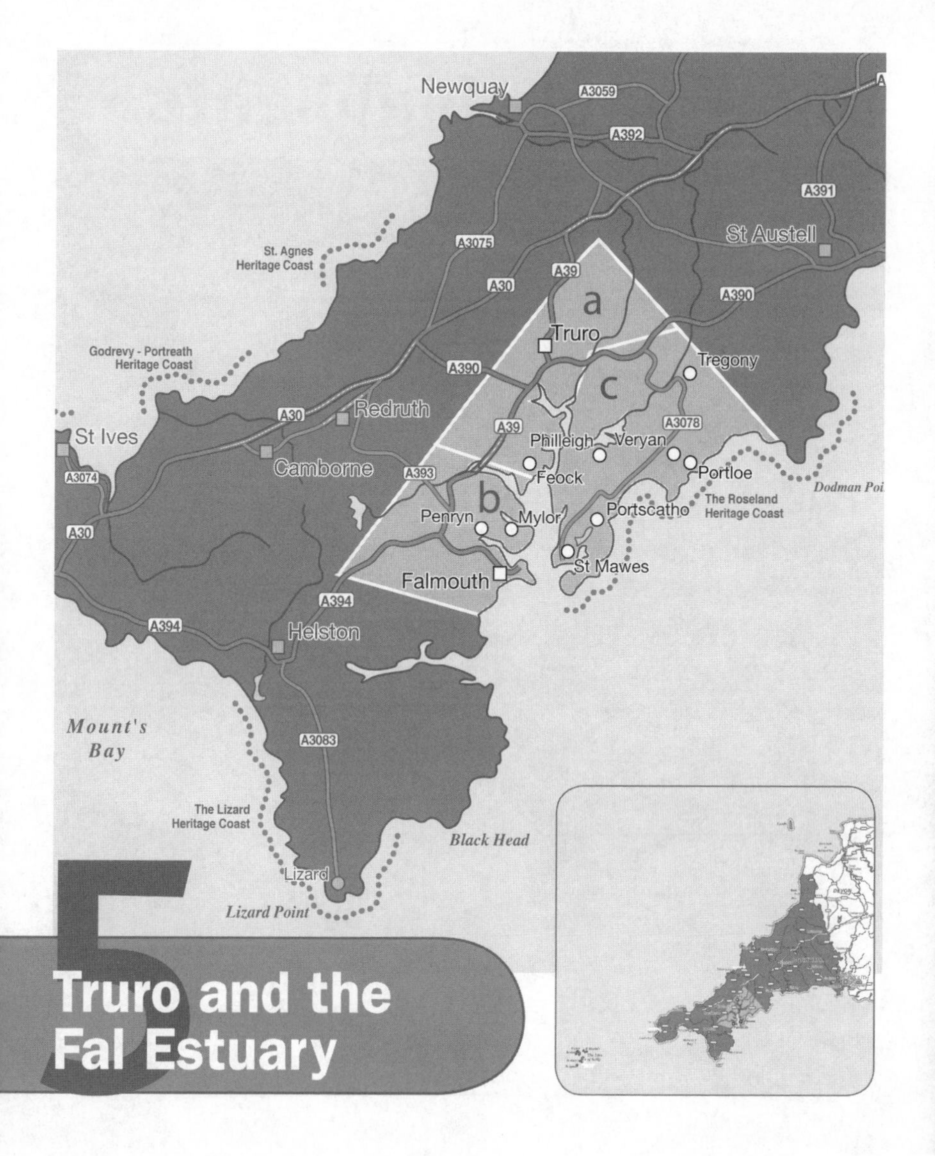

5 Truro and the Fal Estuary

a. Truro and around

b. Falmouth and around

c. The Roseland Peninsula

Unmissable highlights

01 Set sail on dry land at Falmouth's National Maritime Museum on Discovery Quay, p. 220

02 Admire the floodlit spires of Truro Cathedral, the city's Victorian Gothic marvel, p. 208

03 Hang out with the sailing set in swanky St Mawes, the Rock of the south coast, p. 236

04 Roll on, roll off the King Harry Ferry – crossing the Fal Estuary since 1888, p. 211

05 Dine on fresh Falmouth Bay crab, scallops, mussels and lobster at the Wheelhouse seafood café, p. 232

06 Discover Henry VIII's decorative clover-leaf fortress, St Mawes' seaside castle, p. 236

07 Sink your toes into soft sand on the National Trust's beaches at Gerrans Bay, p. 238

08 Shop for Mediterranean olives and mussels, yarg and Cornish pork, at Truro's Lemon Street markets, p. 213

09 From masterpieces to minerals, take a trip around the Royal Cornwall Museum, p. 211

10 Join the boating community – sail in and out of Mylor Yacht Harbour, in a hired boat, p. 226

TRURO AND FAL ESTUARY

With city and sailing capital just a few miles apart, above and below the Fal Estuary's confluence of busy waterways, this is Cornwall at its most cosmopolitan. A former upriver port, Truro is the graceful old lady of the two, with all the pomp and civic ceremony of a traditional county town. On the tidal basin they call the Carrick Roads, down-river Falmouth is the swaggering sea dog. Shipping and rigging are in the blood.

Both are young towns, at least by Cornish standards. Truro was nought but a village until mining struck gold; much of the architecture is 18th and 19th century, and the Cathedral is even younger. In Falmouth, there was nothing much there until the 16th-century castle and the Royal Mail Packet Station. From 1688, the nippy, 40-strong fleet of packet ships, whizzed letters, bullion and even passengers to all corners of the British Empire until the steam ships and railways arrived. Then came the port-related boom that put Falmouth on the map.

These are prosperous places with an urban buzz, colleges and council offices and a life of their own beyond tourism. Indeed, the Maritime Line train that connects Truro to Falmouth gets so busy with commuters the time-table was recently upgraded to offer trains every half an hour. But there's a lot for the visitor: museums, galleries, shops, nightclubs, markets, marinas, boats and beaches... And it's not far to the Roseland Peninsula. A ferry away from Falmouth, St Mawes is another world.

TRURO AND AROUND

Cornwall's only city, Truro is chiefly a centre for government and trade, ever more so since the creation of One Cornwall, the county's unified council. A place of fine civic architecture and municipal buildings, visitors come to see the sky-scraping spires of the Gothic-Revival Cathedral, catch a show at the Hall for Cornwall, eat, drink and shop. Around bustling Lemon Quay, there are antique shops, flea markets, food markets – the latter, among the best in Cornwall. Like most cities, even mini cities such as this one, Truro is cultured, urbane, wealthy and wise.

At the meeting of three rivers – the Truro, Allen and Kenwyn – the city was founded in the 12th century when England's Chief Justice Richard de Luci built a castle, now erased, on a hill above the town. It developed initially as an up-river fishing port, but owes its expansion to the mining trade. As one of Cornwall's Stannary towns, Truro flourished during the 18th and 19th centuries. A new-rich building boom created a legacy of elegant townhouses – for lovers of Regency finery there is nowhere better this side of Bath. Truro soon earned the nickname 'the London of Cornwall'. It was granted city status in 1877.

Truro's mostly a day-trip destination and lacks good places to stay, but it's an excellent touring centre, with easy access to the acres of farmland and garden estates that creep downriver towards Falmouth Bay.

WHAT TO SEE AND DO

Make a beeline for one of Cornwall's most visited buildings, **Truro Cathedral** on Boscawen Street. You can't miss it, the great central tower and spire rise to 250ft, visible almost everywhere in town. Unlike many landmark Cathedrals, this one isn't ancient – a neo-Gothic marvel, it was built between 1880 and 1910, on the site of the 16th-century St Mary the Virgin. The architect John Loughborough Pearson worked the South Aisle of the original parish church into the design, but the rest of the building was a high Victorian interpretation of medieval Gothic. Built of Cornish granite and Bath stone, it was the first Cathedral to go up in England since Salisbury Cathedral in 1220 and it was a colossal undertaking.

'My business is to see what will bring people soonest to their knees,' the architect is quoted as saying. And even if he doesn't quite manage that, his creation will certainly have you looking towards heaven, or the magnificent pointed arches above the nave. Other points of interest are the stained glass and the terracotta Tinworth Panel, by Victorian ceramicist George Tinworth. But the Cathedral's soaring towers and spires are its major feature; less noticeable is the slight bend in its plan, a by-product of fitting an enormous structure into a tight urban space. In 2004, £3.6m was spent on restoring the Cathedral – which is particularly eye-catching at night when its three spires are floodlit.

TRURO CATHEDRAL, 14 St Mary's Street, Truro TR1 2AF; ☎ 01872 276782; www.trurocathedral.org.uk. Admission: free; open Mon–Sat 7.30am–6pm, Sun 9am–7pm.

Truro Cathedral

Having visited the Cathedral, wander the streets and admire the neo-Classical architecture: **Lemon Street**, a gently ascending Regency terrace, or the crescent of Georgian cottages at **Walsingham Place.** Not far from the Cathedral the **City Hall** is a four-square, 19th-century Italianate building that also houses the Mayor's Parlour. For an overview of the city's history, try a guided walk with a Blue Badge Guides (www.alisonstours.com).

Out of town

Enterprise Boats runs a cruise up and down the Fal from Truro to Falmouth or St Mawes, a beautiful stretch of estuary flanked by numerous wooded creeks and teeming with wildlife. Boats leave Truro from Town Quay, where the rivers Allen and Kenwyn join the Truro River.

There's also an optional stop en route at **Trelissick Garden**. Among the wealth of exotic gardens that flourish in this part of the world, the National Trust's Trelissick lies 4 miles south of Truro at Feock. Here, you'll find the National Plant Collection of photinias and azaleas, among other plants. Rhododendrons, hydrangeas, camellias and various species of palm tree are also in abundance. The garden features woodland walks and views over the Fal estuary to the Roseland Peninsula.

ENTERPRISE BOATS, 66 Trefusis Road, Flushing, Falmouth TR11 5TY; ☎ 01326 374241; www.enterprise-boats.co.uk. Tickets: adults from £4.50 to £14, children from £3 to £7; Apr to Oct, 2–4 departures in each direction daily; check website for up-to-date timetables.

TRELISSICK GARDEN, Feock, Truro TR3 6QL; ☎ 01872 862090; www.nationaltrust.org.uk. Entry: adults £7, children £3.50; open daily Feb to Oct, 10.30am–5.30pm; Nov to Jan, 11am–4pm.

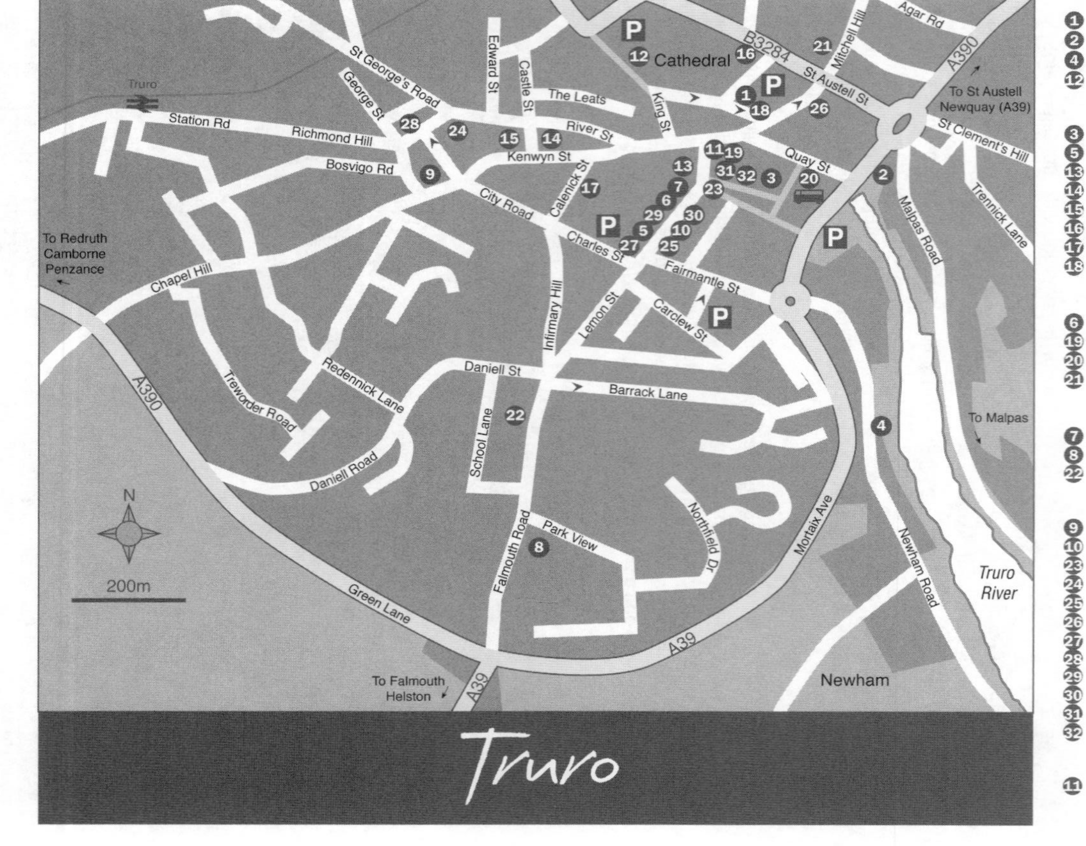

Things to see and do

1. Royal Cornwall Museum
2. Ferry to Falmouth
4. Skinner's Brewery
12. Truro Cathedral

Entertainment

3. Hall for Cornwall
5. Plaza Cinema
13. Manning's Bar and Grill
14. One Eyed Cat
15. Bunters Bar
16. Riverbank
17. L2 Club
18. Bar Qdos

Shopping

6. Lemon Street Market
19. Coinage Hall
20. Artonomy
21. Vitreous Contemporary Art

Places to Stay

7. The Royal Hotel
8. Carlton Hotel
22. The Townhouse

Eat and Drink

9. Tabb's Restaurant
10. Indaba
23. Pannier Market
24. Fine Fettle
25. Scales Fish
26. Grocer on the River
27. Olivio's
28. The Cheese Shop
29. Bustrophers
30. Chantek
31. Saffron Restaurant
32. MI Bar

Visitor Information

11. Tourist Information Centre

Within walking distance of Trelissick is the western dock of the famous **King Harry Ferry** which plies the river from Feock to the village of Philleigh on the Roseland side of the estuary. A recently up-graded vessel is run on ultra-efficient diesel engines, cutting emissions by 75%. Carrying cars bikes and pedestrians, the chain ferry saves 27 miles and over an hour of driving.

Cottages on Walsingham Place

KING HARRY FERRY, 2 Ferry Cottages, Feock, Truro, TR3 6QJ; ☎ 01872 863132; www.kingharryscornwall.co.uk. Price: cars £5 (return £8), bikes 50p; Apr to Oct, ferries depart every 20 minutes from 7.20am (Sun and bank holidays 9am) to 9.20pm. Open daily Feb to Oct, 10.30am–5.30pm; Nov to Jan, 11am–4pm.

The voyage of the King Harry Ferry

One of only five chain ferries still running in England, the King Harry Ferry is something of a classic, having clanked across the Fal Estuary – from Feock to Philleigh – since 1888. A ferry had crossed the upper Fal for centuries, mainly row-boats serving farmers and their livestock – though the latter were expected to swim alongside. But the new King Harry Steam Ferry Company propelled the crossing into a new league, being steam driven and big enough to take carriages and other horse-drawn vehicles. Today, the 'King Harry' plays an important role in the local transport network, carrying 280,000 cars a year and doing 80 crossings a day, every day. In 2006 the company acquired its seventh ferry, a £2.8 million 34-car vessel. The old King Harry ferry, they say, travelled the equivalent of five times around the earth in 32 years of service. Long live King Harry.

Wet weather

As the name suggest, the **Royal Cornwall Museum** is the county's finest. Housed in the former Truro Savings Bank on River Street, it's run by the Royal Institution of Cornwall, founded in 1818 for *'the promotion of knowledge in natural history, ethnology and the fine and industrial arts'*. The Museum's collections cover just about everything from Egyptology to Japanese ivory, but there is a special emphasis on Cornish heritage, geology, archaeology, mythology and nature. Of particular interest, given Cornwall's mining history, is the contents of the Rashleigh Gallery – Philip Rashleigh's world-class collection of 3, 000 minerals, from about 1800.

ROYAL CORNWALL MUSEUM, River Street, Truro TR1 2SJ; ☎ 01872 272205; www.royalcornwallmuseum.org.uk. Admission fee; open 10am–4.45pm, Mon–Sat.

An extensive art gallery, with over 2000 items, includes paintings, drawings, prints and sculptures by Cornish artists, particularly from the Newlyn and St Ives Schools. The collection also includes works by William Hogarth, John Constable, Lord Leighton and Edward Burne-Jones. Visiting exhibitions mix the best of Cornish artists with major touring presentations.

What to do with children…

If it's wet try the 25m swimming pool at **Truro Leisure Centre** on College Road (☎ 01872 261628; www.truroleisurecentre.co.uk). If it's fine, **Boscawen Park**, the city's main area of green space, has a children's play area. Or older kids might enjoy 10-pin bowling at **Truro Bowl** (☎ 01872 222333; www.trurobowl.co.uk) which houses eight lanes as well as a restaurant. It's open daily, 11am–11pm, and Sundays is Family Fun day.

… and how to avoid children

Truro's celebrated **Skinner's Brewing Company**, founded in 1997, is a small, family-run outfit producing award-winning Cornish ales, lagers and ciders in cask and bottle, all named after local legends, places and personalities – from the lazy, ale-loving Betty Stogs to St Piran, the surfing saint. Cornish Knocker Ale was judged Overall Champion in a South West best beer competition in 2008. You can see how they do it on a tour of the state-of-the-art brewhouse, established in a former plumbing centre in 2004. Tours begin and end in the visitor centre, and are rounded off with an opportunity to sample the ales.

SKINNERS BREWING, Riverside, Newham, Truro, TR1 2DP; ☎ 01872 245689; www.skinnersbrewery.com. Entry: £6.50 (no under-14s); Easter to Oct, Mon–Fri, tours at 12pm and 2.30pm.

Entertainment

Theatre and cinema

Truro's **Hall for Cornwall** is the county's premier entertainment venue, hosting an eclectic programme of performing arts. Past performances include Rambert Dance, the Royal Shakespeare Company, Bill Wyman and Coldplay.

HALL FOR CORNWALL, Back Quay, Truro TR1 2LL; ☎ 01872 262466; www.hallforcornwall.co.uk.

Plaza Cinema on Lemon Street (☎ 01872 272894; www.wtwcinemas.co.uk), a cinema since 1938, underwent a refit in 1996, and has wheelchair access and hearing aids.

Truro Cathedral run a programme of music performances, including free Friday lunchtime recitals and there's live music from the bandstand in **Victoria Park** every Sunday afternoon (May to Sept).

Special events

In May/June (dates vary) the annual **Fal River Festival** (www.falriverfestival.co.uk) serves up a vast roster of events of live arts, food and music events, which spreads from the city down the Fal to Trelissick and Falmouth.

September brings the **Cornwall Food and Drink Festival** (www.cornwallfoodanddrink.co.uk) to Lemon Quay: a three-day smorgasbord of food-related events that lures some 20,000 visitors to the Truro quayside. September's **Truro Music Festival** brings a week of music, from jazz and world to rock and opera, to venues including the Cathedral and the Hall for Cornwall.

Truro celebrates the Christmas season with a **Winter Festival**, which includes a paper lantern parade known as the City of Lights Procession, carols at the Cathedral, Christmas markets at Lemon Quay and fireworks on New Year's Eve. Truro also had the distinction of holding Cornwall's first **Gay Pride** event in August 2008.

Nightlife

Truro's blessed with a lively bar scene around Lemon Street and the city centre: try the upmarket **Mannings Bar & Grill** (☎ 01872 247900; www.trurorestaurants.co.uk) at the Royal Hotel; or the **One-Eyed Cat** (☎ 01872 222122; www.oneeyedcat.co.uk), a former chapel on Kenwyn Street with a smart cocktail-bar vibe, open until the small hours.

Bunters Bar on Little Castle Street (www.buntersbar.co.uk) is the place to catch your live music, while a clutch of pubs including the **Riverbank** (☎ 01872 242090; www.theriverbanktruro.co.uk) offer something different nearly every night, be it jazz, funk, soul or acoustic. Clubbers are catered for at the **L2 Club** (☎ 01872 222023; www.l2club.co.uk) and hetro-metro gay bar **Bar Qdos** (☎ 01872 222888; www.barqdos.co.uk) on New Bridge Street.

Shopping

Truro is one of Cornwall's busiest shopping centres but it's not the chain stores around Pydar Street and King Street that attract, but the quirky little independent shops, tucked away down narrow 'opes' (or passageways). Head for **River Street** and **Victoria Square**, or **Lemon Street Market**, where art galleries, crafts, recycled and fair trade goods are sold from stalls shaded by palm trees.

Elsewhere, **the Coinage Hall** on Boscawen Street, where tin was *assayed* and stamped for export, houses an antique centre. Among independent art galleries, **Artonomy** on Green Street (☎ 01872 277733; www.artonomy.co.uk), housed in a beautiful old theological library once belonging to the Cathedral, has a changing exhibitions featuring works by Cornish and national artists. Among independent art galleries, **Artonomy** on Green Street (01872 277733, www.artonomy.co.uk), housed in a beautiful old theological library once belonging to the Cathedral, has a changing exhibitions featuring works by Cornish and national artists.

The best... PLACES TO STAY

HOTEL

The Royal

Lemon Street, Truro TR1 2QB
☎ 01872 270345
www.royalhotelcornwall.co.uk

In a refurbished listed building, the Royal Cornwall on Lemon Quay mixes business with pleasure – all the usual mod cons with a style up-grade. As well as city or executive rooms, there are nine self-contained apartments.

Price: B&B from £99 for a double per night. Apartments from £115 for a night.

Alverton Manor Hotel

Tregolls Road, Truro TR1 1ZQ
☎ 01872 276633
www.alvertonmanor.co.uk

A Grade II listed former convent, Truro's finest has a country house ambience in a town-centre location. The rooms are pleasantly old-fashioned with big beds, and comfortable chairs. Good for afternoon teas in the hotel lounge.

Price: B&B from £130–£160 per night.

Carlton Hotel

Falmouth Road, Truro TR1 2HL
☎ 01872 272450
www.carltonhotel.co.uk

Family-run hotel, housed in a big old house, a 10-minute walk from town. Rooms range in style from spacious Victorian to small modern. The staff are friendly, the location is handy and there is a licensed restaurant, lounges for lounging in and a spa bath/sauna.

Price: B&B from £69.50 for a double; from £99.50 for a family room.

FARMSTAY

Come-to-Good Farm 

Feock, Truro TR3 6QS
☎ 01872 863828
www.cometogoodfarm.co.uk

B&B in a converted barn set in a beautiful valley between Truro and Falmouth. There's one large bright farmhouse room, or a detached family suite that sleeps four. Breakfast features local produce, including the farm's own eggs. Children can feed the ducks and chickens, and babysitting is available on request.

Price: From £60 for a room per night.

B&B

The Townhouse

20 Falmouth Road, Truro TR1 2HX
☎ 01872 273744
www.trurotownhouse.com

Homely budget B&B in central location, with comfortable four-star rooms with king-size beds, decent bathrooms, free Wi-Fi and a nice garden.

Price: B&B from £69 for a double.

Bissick Old Mill

Ladock, Truro TR2 4PG
☎ 01726 882557
www.bissickoldmill.co.uk

Luxury guest house, housed in a renovated 17th-century corn mill. There are three doubles in the mill, with another in the granary just across the courtyard (the latter a house-size self-contained suite with a kitchenette). Hearty breakfasts are a speciality.

Price: from £77.50 for a double.

The best... FOOD AND DRINK

Truro offers one of the best dining centres in the county, particularly good on contemporary cafés, brunch-and-lunch bars and Asian fusion food – the latter, more or less a stranger elsewhere in Cornwall. At the heart of a traditional farming community, Truro is never short of good, fresh meat and vegetables. Hang out on Lemon Street for regular farmers' markets and food events.

Staying in

On Lemon Quay, there's a daily fresh-meat-and-vegetables **Pannier Market** as well as **Truro Farmers' Market** every Wednesday and Saturday. There's also a **country produce market** at the Hall for Cornwall every Tuesday.

There are loads of good specialist food shops, too. A good local butcher is **Fine Fettle** on Frances Street (☎ 01872 320222). For fresh fish head for **Scales Fishmongers** at Lemon Street Market (☎ 01872 277797; www.scalesfishmongers.co.uk). On New Bridge Street, you'll find the **Grocer on the River** (☎ 01872 223068), a pretty deli-counter shop selling Cornish dairy produce, L'Artisan du Chocolat chocolates and Vicky's Breads.

Other goodie shops include the Italian-leaning **Olivio's** at Lemon Street Market (☎ 01872 272555), and **The Cheese Shop** at Ferris Town (☎ 01872 270742) – over 100 British cheeses, many local or organic.

Out of town, there are three farm shops within 5 miles of the centre: **E Watts & Sons** at Penventon (☎ 01872 862308); the **Farm Shop** at Killiewherries, Chacewater (☎ 01872 560481) and **Callestick Farm Shop** (Callestick, ☎ 01872 573126). The latter is the home of the region's finest dairy ice cream.

The region is also home to Pengreep Farm where the **Lynher Dairies Cheese Company** (☎ 01872 870789; www.lynherdairies.co.uk) make Cornish Yarg. The much sought-after semi-hard cheese is hand-made, pressed and brined and wrapped in nettle leaves. The company produces 200 tonnes of the cheese a year.

More unusual is the tea garden on Tregothnan Estate. Chemical-free, English **Tregothnan Teas** and herbal infusions are grown near Truro (☎ 01872 520000; www.tregothnan.co.uk), and available (also online) in classic, afternoon, Earl Grey and green flavours.

EATING OUT

FINE DINING

Alverton Manor

Tregolls Road, Truro TR1 1ZQ
☎ 01872 276633
www.alvertonmanor.co.uk

Winner of two AA Rosettes, the restaurant leans towards traditional cooking, and works with local suppliers, allotments and small growers to ensure supplies of good seasonal produce. The hotel has its own herd of Devon Red cattle and produces its own honey. Three-course dinner costs around £30.

Tabb's

85 Kenwyn Street, Truro TR1 3BZ
☎ 01872 262110
www.tabbs.co.uk

Nigel and Melanie Tabb brought their long-established venture at Portreath to Truro in 2005. And having created a chic dining room in a rejuvenated old pub, they now have two AA Rosettes under their belt. The food is classy, pretty and big on fresh seafood, Cornish meat and Nigel's famous petit fours. Three courses cost around £35. Two course lunch costs £18.50.

RESTAURANTS

Bustophers

62 Lemon Street, Truro TR1 2PN
☎ 01872 279029
www.bustophersbarbistro.com

One of Truro's finest, it manages wine bar, brasserie bar and top-end restaurant all rolled into one, with zingy designer décor and an open-plan theatre kitchen. The food is modern British featuring classics such as River Fal mussels, steak and fries or specials from the daily fish board. Or just pop in for a Cornish tea, or a glass of chilled Chablis and all-day tapas. Two-course dinner costs £15 to £25.

Indaba Fish

Tabernacle Street, Truro TR1 2EJ
☎ 01872 274700
www.indabafish.co.uk

Run by chef Nick Taylor, late of Rick Stein, Indaba is stylish, with an open-plan loft look, and very fishy. For lunch, try Thai fish cakes, crab salad and mussels from a café-style menu; for dinner, Goan fish curry, monkfish, razor clams or fillet steak. There's daily specials and a fish bar. Dinner costs £20 to £25.

Chantek

15 New Bridge Street, Truro TR1 2AA
☎ 01872 225071
www.chantek.co.uk

Asian fusion restaurant/bar with a strong emphasis on fair-trade, organic and local produce. Menu spans Asia and the Pacific Rim, from Thailand and Malaysia via Singapore to Japan and China. Two-course dinner costs £15 to £20, two-course lunch costs £10 to £20.

Saffron Restaurant

5 Quay Street, Truro TR1 2HB
☎ 01872 263771
www.saffronrestauranttruro.co.uk

The emphasis is on seasonal produce and 'made in Cornwall' fare. The lunch menu includes grilled quail with straw potatoes and blueberry vinaigrette (£8) and a Cornish strawberry, Heligan cheese and pinenut salad (£6.20). Seasonal specialities include seafood, game and, in May, local asparagus. Three course kitchen menu, costs £19.50; express lunch, £12.50; two course, pre-theatre supper £10.

EATING OUT

GASTRO PUB

The Old Quay Inn

St John Terrace, Devoran TR3 6ND.
☎ 01872 863142
www.theoldquayinn.com

Old-fashioned boat-like pub overlooking Restronguet Creek, popular with sailors, racers, those-in-the-know locals and cyclists (here ends the coast-to-coast cycle route). Serves real ales, wines by the glass (or bottle) and good unpretentious food using local produce. Meals from around £10.

The Riverbank

Old Bridge Street, Truro TR1 2AQ
☎ 01872 242090
www.theriverbanktruro.co.uk

Relaxed, spacious city-centre pub with a great wine list (plus some good real ales from Cornwall and beyond), regular live music and, of course, some cracking food – chowder, risotto, fresh fish and seafood dishes, steaks, Cornish burgers and more. There's a beer garden by the river.

The Plume of Feathers

Mitchell TR8 5AX
☎ 01872 510387
www.theplume.info

Just a few miles outside town, but worth the trip. 2004's Country Dining Pub of the Year, the Plume mixes British food and European flavours, using local produce – including fruit and vegetables from a fruit farm in the village. Two course lunch costs from £12 to £15. You can also stay the night in a renovated barn conversion next door.

CAFÉ

MI Bar

Back Quay, Truro TR1 2LL
☎ 01872 277214
www.mibartruro.co.uk

Clean, contemporary café-bar in a Grade II listed Cornish inn with an outdoor terrace in the heart of the city. Serves breakfasts, lunch, coffees/teas and kids meals. Try sea bass fillets, fish pie, saffron Cornish mussels or a lamb, rosemary and garlic burger. Also homemade soup (£2.95), bacon, chicken or beef burgers (from £5.75), sausage and mash or the curry of the day (£6.95).

Drinking

The following pubs are strong on their real ales, including local Cornish specialities such as Doom Bar and Tribute, and of course the Truro brewers, Skinner's. Most do good pub food, too.

- **Wig and Pen** – Frances Street; ☎ 01872 273028. Pub-cum-restaurant with a good reputation for food.
- **Crab and Ale House** – New Bridge Street; ☎ 01872 277294. Truro's oldest pub, cosy and traditional.
- **Old Ale House** – Quay; ☎ 01872 271122. Popular bar near the quayside, serving excellent steaks and local ales, Skinner's and others.
- **Bunters Bar** – Little Castle Street; ☎ 01872 241220; www.buntersbar.co.uk. All-ages pub with a large range of beers, big screens for live sport and a friendly atmosphere.
- **City Inn** at Pydar Street; ☎ 01872 272623. A CAMRA award-winning, real ale favourite, serving Skinners, Doom Bar, Exmoor Gold and more.
- **Rising Sun Inn** – Mitchell Hill; ☎ 01872 273454. Up a steepish hill from the city centre, but good food and beers await you at the end of your journey.

Visitor Information

Tourist information centre: Tourist Information Centre, Municipal Buildings, Boscawen Street, Truro TR1 2NE, ☎ 01872 274555.

Hospitals with A&E: Duchy Hospital Penventinne Lane, Treliske, Truro TR1 3UP, ☎ 01872 226100; Royal Cornwall Hospitals Trust Treliske, TruroTR1 3LJ, ☎ 01872 250000.

Doctors: Tregony Surgery 5 Well Street, Tregony, Truro TR2 5RT, ☎ 01872 530483; Chacewater Health Centre Chacewater, Truro TR4 8QS, ☎ 01872 560346.

Pharmacies: Boots 94 Pydar Street, Truro TR1 2BD, ☎ 01872 272810; Alliance Pharmacy 6–7 Lemon Street, Truro TR1 2LQ, ☎ 01872 272823.

Police station: Devon & Cornwall Constabulary Tregolls Road, Truro, TR1 1PY, ☎ 08452 777444.

Supermarkets: Marks & Spencer Lemon Quay, Truro TR1 2LW, ☎ 01872 271511; Sainsbury's Treyew Road, Truro TR1 3XL, ☎ 01872 260881; Somerfield 10–11 Victoria Square, Truro TR1 2RU, ☎ 01872 277379.

Parking: Carrick District Council manages eight pay and displays in town: at Edward Street, Garras Wharf (for Lemon Quay), Old Bridge Street (maximum daytime stay three hours) and Pydar Street. See www.carrick.gov.uk.

Internet access: Truro Library Union Place, Truro TR1 1EP, ☎ 01872 322005. Public access terminals with fast broadband connections.

ATMs: HSBC, 17 Boscawen Street, Truro TR1 2QZ; Barclays, 20–21 Lemon Street, Truro, Cornwall, TR1 2NB; NatWest, St Nicholas Street, Truro TR1 2RN (cashpoint only); Royal Bank Of Scotland, Penhaligon House, Green Street, Truro TR1 2LH.

Car hire: Vospers Ford Rental, Railway Station, Station Road, Truro TR1 3HH, ☎ 01872 223676; Avis Rent a Car Tregolls Road, Truro TR1 1SB, ☎ 01872 262226; Enterprise Rent-a-Car Newham Road, Newham Industrial Estate, Truro TR1 2SU, ☎ 01872 262211.

Bike hire: Bissoe Tramway Cycle Hire, Old Conns Works, Bissoe, Truro TR4 8QZ, ☎ 01872 870341, www.cornwallcyclehire.com.

Local taxis: A1 Taxis, ☎ 01872 275981; City Taxis, ☎ 0800 318708; Truro Taxi Cab Company, ☎ 01872 321321.

FALMOUTH AND AROUND

Falmouth is a two faced sort of town. On its northern, harbour side, the boat's the thing: from the salty waterfront old town and the shiny new Discovery Quay to the boatyards and cruise ships dallying in its deep natural harbour. Said to be the third largest in the world (after Rio and Sydney), it bids farewell to many a transatlantic voyager, and is high on the port hit-list for gatherings of the world's tall ships. The southern, Falmouth Bay side of town is a Victorian-style seaside resort, with promenade gardens, Mediterranean palms and grand hotels. Sheltered and sandy, its town-sized beaches lure holidaying families and an increasingly trendy beach-café crowd.

Running through the middle of town, the Maritime Line railway links Falmouth Docks with Truro and neighbouring Penryn. To the east, on a narrow peninsula, Henry VIII's Pendennis Castle guards the mouth of the Fal Estuary. Pocketed away from the prevailing south-westerly winds, Falmouth's waters have long been drink of the gods for well-heeled yachties. On the national sailing calendar, the regatta in August is second only to Cowes Week. But there's a young, arty crowd, too; their sparkly toenails playing footsie with Falmouth's older, poorer little sister, the port of Penryn. What began as an art school for ladies with a penchant for sketching plants is now University College Falmouth.

WHAT TO SEE AND DO

If you've come for the boats, Falmouth's multi-million **National Maritime Museum**, is a good place to start. Opened in 2002 next to Cornwall's biggest working port, it's a handsome, 21st-century shed wrapped in English green oak by carpenters from a local boatyard. Inside, it's big on small boats and intricate scale models: prototype racing yachts, an 1880s Cornish salmon boat and the very first submarine (a wooden 1620s, four-oared underwater 'rowing machine') hang overhead.

You can find out about the tides, the weather, and Falmouth's 150-year-old reign as packet-ship capital of the UK. Fabulously audiovisual voyages in a night-dark Set Sail gallery simulate electric storms at sea (you might want to hold hands) and adrenaline-fuelled regatta races. Take your camera up the 360° Look Out tower, or look at crabs and

Crabbing at the National Maritime Museum

fish through the huge underwater viewing windows. Out on the museum pontoon, the 100-year-old punts and replica Cape Cod Cats come and go.

Just outside, **Events Square** is studded with high-end bars, shops and summer tourists. Like round-the-world sailor Ellen MacArthur, it's best to arrive by boat, of course and, in season, you can take the wooden-ferried **Park and Float** from Ponsharden to Custom House Quay (your ticket gives discounted entry to the museum).

In winter, the Ponsharden Park and Ride drops you off at bus terminus, **The Moor**, a market square and good starting point for old town, museum and docks. An 111-granite-step climb up **Jacob's Ladder** rewards you with harbour and estuary views that verge on the heavenly. Jacob, however, was merely Mr Hamblen, a mid-1800s tallow chandler and builder. Passenger ferries around the estuary leave from the nearby **Prince of Wales Pier** where the tourist information centre has **Falmouth Town Trail** leaflets, which will talk you through the town's notable landmarks. Further up the hill, the old packet captains' townhouses just stand around elegantly, peering over the estuary towards Flushing.

NATIONAL MARITIME MUSEUM, Discovery Quay, Falmouth TR11 3QY; ☎ 01326 313388; www.nmmc.co.uk. Entry: adults £9.50, children £6.50; open daily 10am–5pm.

PONSHARDEN PARK & FLOAT/RIDE, Ponsharden, signposted off A39 between Penryn and Falmouth; ☎ 01326 319417; www.falriverlinks.co.uk. All-day float pass (parking per car and up to seven passengers) £15.50; boats run May to Sept, Mon--Fri, 10am–5.40pm; Park and Ride by bus to The Moor, daily 10am–6pm; car park closes 9pm.

The pirate queen

The Killigrew family, who ruled the Falmouth roost for most of the 16th and 17th centuries, were a motley crew of smugglers, pirates, murderers and bright sparks. After marrying into a chunk of local land in the middle ages, they rented out a slice to Henry VIII for his Pendennis Castle, then more or less single-handedly dreamed up Falmouth themselves – the inns, boatyards, markets and port that eventually won the town its Post Office Packet Station in the 1680s. Back in the 1500s, Sir John Killigrew was Governor of Pendennis and Vice-Admiral of Cornwall. His other half, Mary, liked to take in sailors, get them drunk, slit their throats and pinch their pocket money. One night, she murdered and pillaged the entire crew of a foreign ship taking refuge in Falmouth's deep harbour, thus incurring the wrath of Queen Elizabeth I. Sentenced to death, Lady Mary was let off the hook at the last minute with just a piffling little spell behind bars. Elizabeth no doubt thought she might need her one day for another of her unofficially sanctioned pirating cruises around the coast.

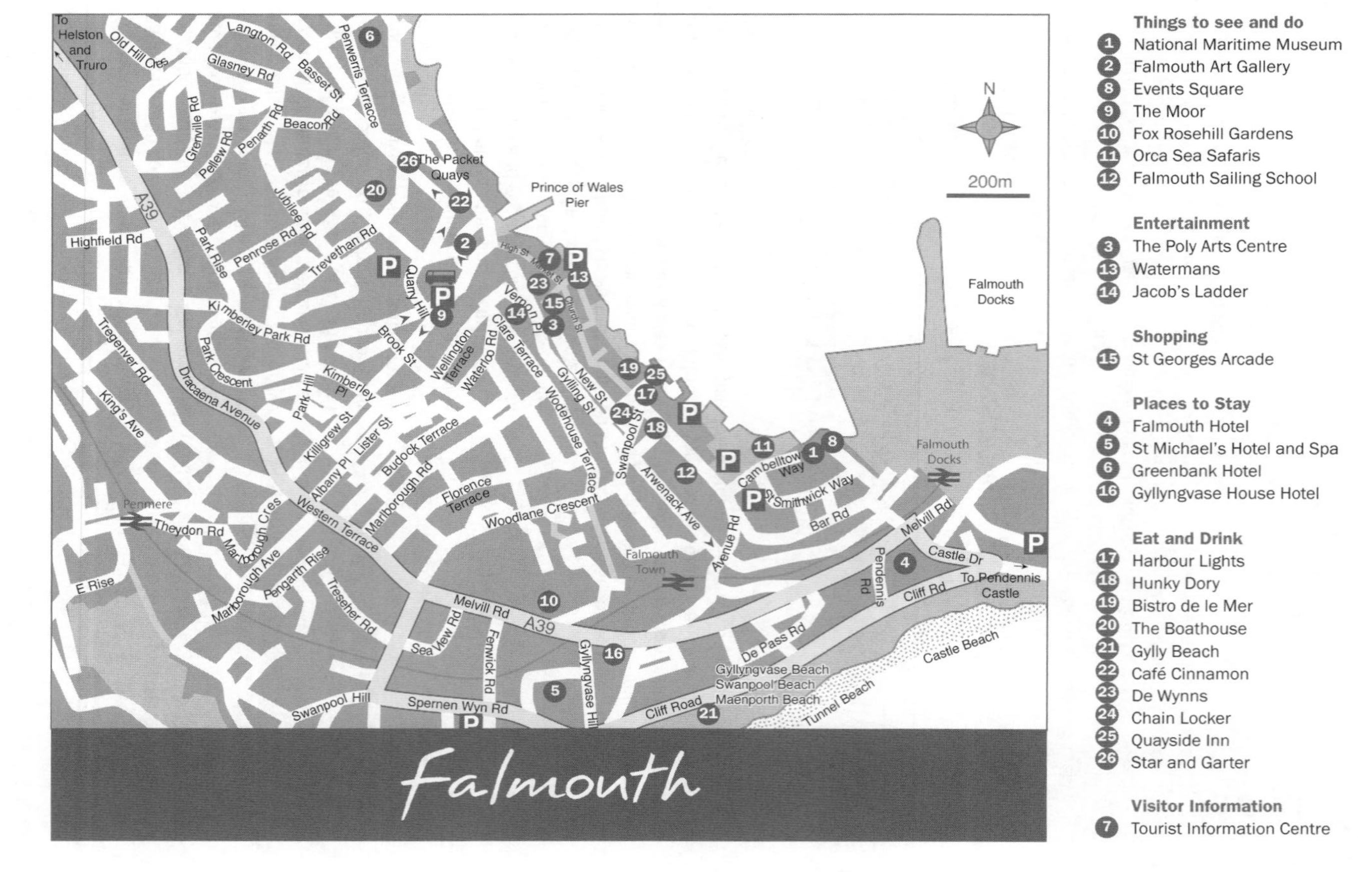

Things to see and do

1. National Maritime Museum
2. Falmouth Art Gallery
8. Events Square
9. The Moor
10. Fox Rosehill Gardens
11. Orca Sea Safaris
12. Falmouth Sailing School

Entertainment

3. The Poly Arts Centre
13. Watermans
14. Jacob's Ladder

Shopping

15. St Georges Arcade

Places to Stay

4. Falmouth Hotel
5. St Michael's Hotel and Spa
6. Greenbank Hotel
16. Gyllyngvase House Hotel

Eat and Drink

17. Harbour Lights
18. Hunky Dory
19. Bistro de le Mer
20. The Boathouse
21. Gylly Beach
22. Café Cinnamon
23. De Wynns
24. Chain Locker
25. Quayside Inn
26. Star and Garter

Visitor Information

7. Tourist Information Centre

Pendennis Castle

> **PENDENNIS CASTLE,** Castle Drive, Falmouth TR11 4LP; ☎ 01326 316594; www.english-heritage.org.uk. Entry: adults £6.30, children £3.80; open daily from 10am, closing times vary (4pm–6pm).

Lurking broodily on Falmouth's easterly jutting headland, **Pendennis Castle** (which mirrors St Mawes Castle across the water) is a collage of changes in foreign policy. Knocked up by Henry VIII to guard the harbour against the threat of marauding French and Spanish, the fortress has been refurbished with everything from Elizabethan bastions to secret Second World War underground tunnels. The views (Lizard, St Mawes, St Anthony Lighthouse) speak for themselves. You can stay in the **Custodian's House** within the ramparts, courtesy of English Heritage. A jaunt around **Castle Drive** throws up fantastic views of both sides of the Falmouth waters. Walk out to **Pendennis Point** to get a feel for lonesome moonlit watches from the semi-circular **Little Dennis Blockhouse**, complete with oven.

Gardens

Falmouth's subtropical gardens, jollied along by its famously mild climate, are a colourwash of spring camellias, rhododendrons and magnolias. The formal **Gyllyngdune Gardens** (www.gyllyngdunegardens.co.uk), with entrances on Melvill and Cliff Roads, have shell grottos, secret tunnels, an Edwardian bandstand and cream teas in summer. In **Fox Rosehill Gardens** (☎ 01872 224377, www.gardensofcornwall.com), off Melvill Road, trophies brought back by Fox

Pendennis Castle

St Anthony Lighthouse

family sea captains include banana, lemon and eucalyptus trees. The 15-acre, privately owned **Penjerrick Garden** (www.penjerrick.co.uk), south of Budock Water, is worth a detour, particularly for its deliciously out of control valley garden.

Beaches

Falmouth isn't blessed with the best beaches in Cornwall, but as town beaches go, they do a splendid job. Brilliantly sheltered, the three main beaches are good for swimming, sunbathing, hanging around on deck chairs chargrilling sausages, but less good for their surf.

At the castle end of Cliff Road (get there early in summer), grand old hotels overlook **Castle Beach**: just a narrow strip of shingly sand at high tide, this is rockpool central, and a south-facing sunspot. Neighbouring, high-walled **Tunnel Beach** is even narrower, with no facilities. The biggest and busiest is crescent-shaped Blue Flag **Gyllyngvase Beach** where soft white sands accommodate watersports, swimmers and headland views. The upmarket beach café is a big draw all year, and there's a little formal garden just behind.

A short stroll along the coast path, the smaller, family-friendly, slightly pebbly **Swanpool Beach** offers a big car park, watersports centre and kids play area. Opposite the beach, walk around **Swanpool Nature Reserve** (www.swanpool.org.uk), a brackish lagoon for jaywalking ducks, swans and the odd kingfisher. Pick up a leaflet in the beach café. A good half-hour's walk from Swanpool along the cliff path (a 10-minute drive from town) wide, sandy **Maenporth Beach** is a decent size. Locals head here to escape summer crowds; small caves and shipwreckage keep young explorers occupied, and dolphin spotting is a favourite pastime. There's a friendly café, and a chilled-out bunch come for sundown.

On the water

The easiest way to get out on the water is aboard a passenger ferry from the Prince of Wales Pier or Custom House Quay, where touted wares include fishing trips. The **St Mawes Ferry** runs a daytime service across to the Roseland Peninsula (see page 237) all year, with evening trips on summer weekends. Or there are trips to **Mylor Yacht Harbour** and **Trelissick Gardens** (see page 209), and on up to Truro if the tides are on your side.

The creek waters can be a blue-green in summer, but it gets busy out there during sailing events, particularly in August. In winter, red-sailed oyster dredgers work the waters. Look out for curlews, herons, oystercatchers and perhaps a little egret. And if you want to share your journey with sharks, dolphins and seals, **Orca Sea Safaris** runs wildlife-watching cruises all year. Operating all year from the National Maritime Museum, the fare includes free museum entry.

ORCA SEA SAFARIS, 01326 214928; www.orcaseasafaris.co.uk. Price: two hours from £39.50 for an adult, children from £28.

CELEBRITY CONNECTIONS

It was a proud day for Falmouth when an exhausted but jubilant **Ellen MacArthur** pulled up alongside Pendennis Port Marina in February 2005 – after 71 days at sea. Ellen had circumnavigated the globe single-handed in world-record time, beating Frenchman Francis Joyon by 32 hours and 36 minutes. The 28 year old received a hero's welcome: with a flotilla of boats, a jostle of press, and thousands of Falmouth folk turning out to greet her.

Sailing legend **Robin Knox Johnston** called her a *'slip of a thing'* but when the trustee of the National Maritime Musuem addressed the crowd he was full of admiration. *'We are immensely proud of you,'* he said. *'You have put Falmouth back on the sailing map, and we are all grateful to you, Dame Ellen.'*

Falmouth has a long history of gallant seafarers. Knox-Johnston's own triumphant sail, the first solo voyage round the world in 1969, began and ended in Falmouth.

A short course at **Falmouth Sailing School** (☎ 01326 211311; www.falmouth-school-of-sailing.co.uk) teaches you a lot of what you need to know about powerboats, keelboats and dinghies. Once you know what you're doing, you can rent one from the school.

Out of town

North-west of Falmouth, past boatyards and chandleries, **Penryn** is as old as they come. Clinging to a steep hill between two creeks at the navigable head of the Penryn river, this ancient fishing village and market town turned international port once exported granite and tin all over the world. By the 1970s, it was a slum, but recent funding injections have re-instilled some charm into the Jacobean and Georgian bits of its frontage. The university's new multi-million-pound **Tremough** campus just outside town is tempting students, wine bars and galleries onto its previously downtrodden **Market Street**. A bijou museum in the Victorian **Town Hall** that straddles the main street gives you the centuries-old lowdown. Down by the water, dilapidated houseboats, the **Jubilee Wharf** eco-development, a jumble of disused coalyards and warehouses are a world away from Falmouth's flashier charms.

Between Islington Wharf and St Gluvias Church, a creekside footpath takes you to the peaceful village of **Flushing** and its small quayside beach (or take the ferry from Falmouth – Flushing's narrow streets were not made for parking) – all Queen Anne-style houses (made for packet-boat captains steering clear of Falmouth's riff-raff) and model boats lurking in front windows. Further up the coast, **Mylor Yacht Harbour** is a hive of nautical industry: sailing school, yacht club, watersports, boat sales and kids crabbing off the pontoon. Built as a tiny dockyard to kit out 19th-century naval vessels, it was recently transformed, complete with picnic spots and holiday cottages, into what's been dubbed

Jubilee Wharf: possibly the UK's greenest building

Flying the flag for a sustainable Cornwall, four astonishingly quiet wind turbines stand tall sentinel over this experimental zero-emissions live-work development on Penryn river, with its studio workshops, community offices and lively café. The man behind its two boatshed-inspired blocks is ZEDfactory's visionary Bill Dunster, the UK's biggest eco-architect and much-lauded pioneer of zero-carbon urban housing.

Jubilee Wharf's squeaky-green credentials include a wood-pellet biomass boiler, solar panels and Ford Mondeo wheel-hub bearings to keep the wind cowls spinning happily. A cheap-zinc-clad roof curving over the public hall, ushers the brisk sea winds up and away from the courtyard and super-insulated maisonettes. It's the kind of place where inventors' conferences go on. *'Inventions do not need to actually work,'* say the posters. *'The more fanciful and outlandish, the better.'*

The Jubilee Wharf building

MYLOR BOAT HIRE, Mylor Yacht Harbour, Mylor TR11 5UF; ☎ 01326 377745; www.mylorboathire.co.uk. Price: family motorboat, gaff-rigged sailing boat or Devon Yawl dinghy, £30 an hour, £100, a day, £400 per week.

'the ultimate self-sufficient Cornish boating community'.

To do it yourself, **Mylor Boat Hire**'s self-drive motorboats carry up to six people or do a bit of creek-crawling on a 16-foot gaff-rigged dayboat.

LOCAL KNOWLEDGE

Helen Gilchrist spent her formative years on the Lizard Peninsula and in 2003 she moved to Falmouth. A year later she set up *Stranger*, Cornwall's lifestyle and media magazine.

Best thing about living here: Spontaneity… a BBQ and a glass of wine on the beach on a sunny Monday evening, a post-work surf, or heading out for a sail at the weekends.

Favourite restaurant: The Quay Inn at Devoran. A stylish gastro pub that serves some of the best food around, in a lovely riverside setting with a beautiful terraced garden out the back. Walk along the river afterwards to burn off their killer desserts.

Favourite beach: Swanpool, just south of Falmouth. Its clear blue water is perfect for swimming, plus you can have a drink and enjoy the view from Indaba on the Beach, perched on the cliff above.

Favourite pub: The Chainlocker, on the old quayside in Falmouth, is a lovely traditional old pub, all real ales and wooden floorboards. A couple of minutes walk away, the Townhouse is the opposite end of the spectrum – a stylish but quirky contemporary bar with comfy sofas and great cocktails.

Best walk: Around Rosemullion Head. This walk takes in beautiful secluded beaches, expansive seascapes, dense pine forests and the mouth of one of the UK's most beautiful river estuaries – the Helford.

Best view: Splash out on a cream tea at St Mawes' famous Hotel Tresanton, and enjoy the views from their terrace.

Best thing to do on a rainy day: Hunker down in one of Five Degrees West's large sofas in front of their roaring log fire. With papers, games and heart-warming beverages, you'll forget what's going on outside.

Favourite visitor attraction: Trebah Gardens still cast their spell on me: a stunning sub-tropical ravine garden tumbling down to a pristine beach on the Helford estuary.

How to get away from the summer crowds: The Roseland Peninsula has gorgeous beaches in abundance. Take the King Harry car ferry and explore the beautiful country lanes and quiet fishing villages.

Wet weather

Falmouth Art Gallery is an absolute delight: small, manageable and winner of family-friendly awards for its simple wooden automatons and life-sized papery gallery attendant. There's one of the best collections in the south-west – maritime, old masters, Victorian British impressionist, contemporary printmakers, and famous Falmouth-based doodlers of the 19th century. These include Henry Scott Tuke, best known for his renderings of fragile sunlight on (young, male) flesh and Charles Napier Hemy, who converted a sizeable yacht into an all-weather floating studio and did a fine line in painted pilchards.

FALMOUTH ART GALLERY, Municipal Buildings, The Moor, Falmouth TR11 2RT; ☎ 01326 313863; www.falmouthartgallery.com. Admission fee; open Mon–Sat, 10am–5pm.

What to do with children

For watersports, **Windsport** cram kayaking, raft building, sailing and windsurfing into their Mylor Yacht Harbour multi-courses.

Similarly energy-expending pursuits are available at **Elemental**'s kids club on Swanpool Beach. They can try taster sessions too, or hire equipment by the hour. Dads with children get special sessions on Friday evenings.

WINDSPORT, Mylor Yacht Harbour, Mylor TR11 5UF; ☎ 01326 376191; www.windsport.co.uk. Price: from £98 per day; week-long courses by arrangement.

ELEMENTAL UK, Swanpool Beach, Falmouth TR11 5BG; ☎ 01326 318771; www.elementaluk.com. Price: half day (9am–12pm) £18, full day (until 4pm) £30. Kids Club runs daily at weekends and school holidays from Apr to Oct. The minimum age is six years old.

Entertainment

Theatre and cinema

Long-serving and much-loved, **The Poly** arts centre and independent cinema on Falmouth's Church Street (☎ 01326 212300; www.thepoly.org) packs film and performance into its upstairs theatre and one-screen cinema. The **Princess Pavilion** in Gyllyngdune Gardens (☎ 01326 211222; www.princesspavilion.co.uk) is the larger, big-name venue for theatre and musicals. The new five-screen cinema, **the Phoenix** (in the town centre's listed Drill Hall), is now open (☎ 01326 313072, www.falmouth.merlincinemas.co.uk). Watch out for repeat summer outings of 2011's classic car-studded **Swanpool Beach Drive-in Movie Night**.

Special events

In mid-June, the town's International Shanty Festival (www.falmouthshout.com/festival) offers a lively weekend of free events in pubs and open-air venues around Custom House Quay and Events Square.

In mid-July, **Stithians Show** (www.stithiansshow.org.uk), north-west of Falmouth, is Cornwall's biggest one-day agricultural knees-up. Falmouth's Pendennis Castle doles out family fun throughout summer, including July's **Grand Medieval Joust**.

Regattas crop up in July and August, but the biggie is the Henri-Lloyd **Falmouth Week** (www.falmouthweek.co.uk) during the first half of August, when the town is shot through with yacht racing, shoreside entertainment, and more yachts. If you want to see Falmouth in its fully-rigged glory, this is when to come.

Kick-starting the harvesting season at one of the last remaining oyster fisheries still dredging with sails (rather than engines), mid-October's **Falmouth Oyster Festival** (www.falmouthoysterfestival.co.uk) brings food events, sea shanties, working boat races and oyster bed jaunts. **Falmouth Beer Festival** (www.carnmenellis.demon.co.uk/html/beerfest.htm) in late October is a low-key affair involving Cornwall's brewing heroes and much friendly banter.

Nightlife

True to its port-town roots, Falmouth nights out revolve around pubs and bars, many of which host live music and DJs, particularly at weekends. Notable venues include **Waterman's** on Market Street (☎ 01326 311158) for rock, chill-out tunes and DJs. The **Prince of Wales** on Market Strand (☎ 01326 311114) gets loud and lively and does good reggae. Mid-week nights at **The Front** on Custom House Quay (☎ 01326 212168) have a folk–acoustic flavour, and live music (Wed–Sun) at friendly local **Jacob's Ladder** on Chapel Terrace (☎ 01326 311010) runs the gamut from folk to punk.

In Penryn, **Miss Peapody's** at Jubilee Wharf (☎ 01326 374424) keeps an eclectic crowd jigging along to middle-Eastern discos and also jazz. Falmouth's fairly cheesy nightclubs aren't much to write home about. **Remedies** on The Moor (☎ 01326 314454) has mid-week live music (Mon, Fri and Sat till 2.30am). The smaller **Shades** on Quay Hill (☎ 01326 311323) provides hip-hop, rock and party nights at weekends.

Shopping

Falmouth's **Market, Church** and **Arwenack Streets** are essentially one continuous cobbled ramble (sadly unpedestrianised, though pedestrians often win), with tempting forays down little passageways to the harbour. Chain stores at **The Moor** end meld into surf shacks, dusty bookends and boho arts and crafts at the other. Halfway along, the 1912 **St George's Arcade**, originally Falmouth's first cinema, is full of hippy clothes, books, maps and CDs.

It's easy to miss the narrow **High Street**, just off The Moor, home to funky boutiques and the pick of the town's independent stores. Artily scruffy music-emporiums-cum-cafés peddle homespun art-student creations, and miniscule boudoirs throw up velvety one-off ballgowns. Antique and junk shops throw up stuffed cats, Hornby model trains and most things in between. Needless to say, for ropes, rigging, maps, deck shoes and sailors' jerseys, Falmouth is the place.

The best... PLACES TO STAY

HOTEL

St Michael's Hotel and Spa

Gyllyngvase Beach, Falmouth TR11 4NB
☎ 01326 312707 www.stmichaelshotel.co.uk

Light-hearted nauticals (like the half-boat reception) ripple through this chic, modern hotel, in subtropical gardens opposite Gyllyngvase Beach. Organic Cornish Spieza goodies litter the spa, and there's a sea-view pool, sauna and gym. The Flying Fish restaurant has an AA rosette.

Price: B&B from £128–£210 for a double.

Greenbank Hotel

Harbourside (bottom end of North Parade), Falmouth TR11 2SR ☎ 01326 312440
www.greenbank-hotel.co.uk

This restored 1700s harbour-front hotel is mazy and dark in places. Kenneth Grahame is said to have dreamed up *The Wind in the Willows* onsite. Rooms are fairly muted, though some have colourful splashes. Really, though, it's all about the wonderful views.

Price: B&B from £145–£215 for a double.

Falmouth Hotel

Castle Beach, Falmouth TR11 4NZ
☎ 0844 502 7587
www.falmouthhotel.com

Falmouth's original grand seafront hotel. Chandeliers and swirling carpets give way to five acres of garden and beach-castle-harbour views. There's a pool, Jacuzzi, sauna, gym, beauty centre, snooker room and restaurant.

Price: B&B from £130–£260.

B&B

Highcliffe

22 Melvill Road, Falmouth TR11 4AR
☎ 01326 314466; www.falmouth-hotel.co.uk

An easy walk to the beaches or the centre, this townhouse gem offers boutique-hotel rooms at B&B prices. There are eight of them, including two dinky singles, three super-king doubles and a penthouse suite in the attic. Expect crisp linens, power showers (or roll-top tubs), smart contemporary décor and a warm welcome.

Price: from £75 to £135 for a double.

SELF-CATERING

Mylor Harbourside

Mylor Yacht Harbour, Mylor TR11 5UF
☎ 01326 372121
www.mylorharbourside.com/cottages.htm

Mylor Yacht Harbour's Admiralty Apartments (Drake, Horatio et al) are conjured from three 200-year-old storeys. Top apartments have balconies and some harbour-view bedrooms; bottom ones have courtyards.

Price: from £285–£1,300 per week.

Number Six

6 Tehidy Terrace, Falmouth TR11 2SZ
☎ 01326 375972
www.creeksidecottages.co.uk/tehidy/index.htm

Rather fine four-bed classic-cum-contemporary townhouse, with a grand, wooden-floored lounge, library-snug and unexpected ethnic touches upstairs. Through French doors, into the suntrap terrace, then up steps to a garden with sunken trampoline. Front bedrooms have river views. The bath is as deep as they come.

Price: from £590–£1,790 per week.

The best... FOOD AND DRINK

Locally caught seafood is the order of the day, from the greasiest chippy to the most expensive fusion restaurant in town. Falmouth Bay oysters, Fal Estuary mussels, crab, lobster, mackerel, monkfish and sea bass all play a starring role in fishmongers' windows. As yet untouched by the hand of a TV chef, Falmouth's beach-café culture is a respectably hip but low-key affair. And there's no shortage of Cornish brews lubricating the creekside taverns and lively town-centre pubs.

Staying in

David Seabourne (yes, that's his real name) flogs choice local seafood at **Seabourne Fish** (Islington Wharf, Penryn; Webber Street, Falmouth) and via his travelling van (☎ 01326 378478). Next door, Rick Stein food heroes the **Cornish Cuisine Smokehouse** (☎ 01326 376244) use Cornish fruitwoods to smoke their line-caught mackerel, crevettes, eel, local cheeses, duck, chicken and game (☎ 01326 376244; www.cornishcuisine.co.uk).

For seasonal vegetables, along with dairy, meat and local preserves, check out **Long Close Farm Shop** on Tregew Road, just before Flushing (☎ 01326 373706, www.tregewfarm.co.uk). The **Cornish Farmhouse Cheese Shop** at Menallack Farm, near Treverva (☎ 01326 340333) harbours more than 40 varieties, many made on site. The local-produce brigade ply their wares at **Falmouth Farmers' Market**, every Tuesday on The Moor, 9am–2pm. Stallholders include **Vicarage Farm**, purveyors of free-range meat, Cornish game and ewe-milk rhubarb yoghurt. The **Natural Store** on Falmouth's High Street (☎ 01326 311507) is a repository of all things organic.

Wine in Cornwall at Kernick Business Park, Penryn (☎ 01326 379426; www.wineincornwall.co.uk), knows most things there are to know about Cornish booze (Camel Valley wine and champagne, Keltek ales, Ninemaidens Mead) and will deliver two cases or more to anywhere in Cornwall.

Takeaways

Harbour Lights, on the corner of Arwenack Street and Custom House Quay (☎ 01326 316934; www.hlfish.co.uk) is hard to beat for top-quality fish and chips. Sustainable fish, cooked in sustainable palm oil, comes in bio-degradable packaging, and is always spot-on.

EATING OUT

FINE DINING

Harbourside

Greenbank Hotel, Harbourside, Falmouth TR11 2SR
☎ 01326 312440
www.greenbank-hotel.co.uk

Under New-Zealand-born head chef Fiona Were, the menu majors on seasonal Cornish produce, ethically-caught fish and Falmouth Bay seafood, served with interesting international twists. Enjoy harbour views and, for a bit of posh, afternoon tea with Roddas clotted cream, smoked salmon and Champagne (at £15.95 per head). Three courses cost around £30. Open daily.

RESTAURANTS

Hunky Dory

46 Arwenack Street, Falmouth TR11 3JH
☎ 01326 212997
www.hunkydoryfalmouth.co.uk

Amid laid-back and super-cool Med-white minimalism in a listed building, local seafood and other local produce get the Euro-Asian treatment. Starters include baked Cornish brie and sushi; mains include sea bass with paella. The steaks are among Falmouth's best. Three courses cost around £30. Open daily from 6pm.

Bistro de la Mer

28 Arwenack Street, Falmouth TR11 3JB
☎ 01326 316509
www.bistrodelamer.com

Two floors of bustling Anglo-French bistro delivering good seafood. Dishes include Cornish crab soup, local free-range Hereford fillet *au poivre*, and rump of herbed lamb with spiced aubergine. They also do snails. Three courses cost around £35. Open Tues–Sat and every evening in the summer (lunch from 12pm, dinner from 7pm).

Indaba Fish on the Beach

Swanpool Beach, Falmouth TR11 5BG
☎ 01326 311886
www.indabafish.co.uk

Perched gloriously just above Swanpool Beach, this bleached-wood, beach-hut-style restaurant with veranda has an anything-goes feel. The emphasis is on quality Cornish seafood: mussels, line-caught seabass, pan-roasted scallops, lobster and crab from the Indaba's own tank, Goan fish curry and classic fish and chips. Three courses cost around £28.

The Wheel House

Upton Slip, Falmouth TR11 3DQ
☎ 01326 318050

The décor is cosy kitchen-diner (with wallpaper and candle-light), the atmosphere is boisterous bistro and the food is wonderfully simple: local shellfish (mussels, crab, prawns, scallops, lobster) served in a Portuguese-style *cataplama* (like a metal clam) with skinny chips and salad. This is one of Falmouth's most popular restaurants, but choose well, and you can eat here for under £15 a head. Open evenings, Wed-Sat. Booking essential.

Rick Stein's Fish and Chips

Discovery Quay, Falmouth TR11 3AX
☎ 01841 532700
www.rickstein.com

Stein's first south Cornwall venture opened on the Fal waterfront in 2010, offering a posh chippy on the ground floor (fish and chips, from £10.80; charcoal roasted fillets from £8.70) and, upstairs, the more expensive Seafood Bar - serving fish and shellfish tapas (from £6.50) and Fowey River oysters (from £9.50) from a kitchen headed up by chef Paul Ripley.

EATING OUT

GASTRO PUB

The Boathouse

Trevethan Hill, Falmouth TR11 2AG
☎ 01326 315425

Up near the Greenbank Hotel, an affable bistro-type pub serving splendid views and modern British food. Local and free-range are of the essence: sea bream on Thai vegetables, Fal Estuary mussels. Cornish real ales rotate, and the rare international spirits range is impressive. Bit of a ciderhouse, too: organic, pear, Hereford and farmhouse.

Five Degrees West

7 Grove Place, Falmouth TR11 4AU
☎ 01326 311288
www.5degreesfalmouth.co.uk

This big-hearted townhouse bistro-bar offers a regular menu of good quality English-Mediterranean dishes at affordable prices (all-day breakfast, £8.95, mezze-style Deliboards, £8.75, or build-your-own burgers, from £6.95), plus home-cooked daily specials, big squashy sofas (a fire in the winter), sea views, tables on the terrace and occasional live music.

CAFÉ

Gylly Beach

Cliff Road, Falmouth TR11 4PA
☎ 01326 312884
www.gyllybeach.com

This mellow, right-on-the-beach café-restaurant dishes up Cornish food in Med-style packages. There's breakfast, tapas, salads, pasta, vegetarian dishes, cocktails and summer barbeques. Main dishes cost from £7–£17.

Café Cinnamon

Old Brewery Yard, High Street, Falmouth TR11 2BY
☎ 01326 211457

There's not much room inside, behind the fairy-lights, but pull up a wooden chair (comfier than they look) in the cobbled, suntrap, olde world courtyard. It's hard not to be healthy here, with homemade organic vegetarian and vegan food, and organic coffees from Origin in Constantine.

Miss Peabody's Kitchen Café

Jubilee Wharf, Penryn TR10 8FG
☎ 01326 374424
www.misspeapod.co.uk

A big, wooden warehouse space with squishy sofa, 1970s sideboard and kids' toys. Coffees are always good, and they do a cool sideline in live music and green gatherings. Drink on deck to watch the Penryn river boat life. Food is organic, free-range, local and vegan-vegetarian, as befits the eco-temple location. Closed on Monday.

TEA ROOM

De Wynns

55 Church Street, Falmouth TR11 3DS
☎ 01326 319259

Switch off your mobile in this refined, old school coffee and tea house. Everything's just so, from the gas lamp (inside) to the old wooden counter. Tregothnan-grown Cornish cream teas come with local Boddington's jam, and they know their coffees. Granny Nunn's Bread Pudding is an institution, but they won't share the recipe.

Drinking

It's not hard to find a good old-fashioned pub in Falmouth. Mind your head on your way into the **Chain Locker** on Quay Street (☎ 01326 311085), which pours Skinner's, Sharp's and St Austell's amid old town photos and quayside tables. Next door at the ridiculously popular **Quayside Inn** on Arwenack Street (☎ 01326 312113) down local brews at sunset by the brick chimney where they used to burn contraband tobacco; there is a special menu for the malt whiskies.

On Custom Quay, **The Front** (01326 212168), is another old salt, and one of the best pubs in town if you like a tot of rum, or your pint of bitter hand-pulled from a cask (there's a choice of ten real ales, and at least half a dozen ciders). It was CAMRA Kernow pub of the year in 2011.

Cornish brews abound (Lizard Organic Brewhouse, Keltek, Skinner's) at the High Street's **Star and Garter** (☎ 01326 318313). The **Seven Stars** on The Moor (☎ 01326 312111), not much bothered by tourists, is a time-warped gem where licensee the Rev. Barrington Bennetts (teetotal, save for the communion wine) and his forebears have administered perfectly served real ales to a loyal congregation since time began. It'd be a tragedy if they got the decorators in.

In Flushing, the traditional **Seven Stars** (☎ 01326 374373) does cask ales, good food and a fine history of flooding, and the **Royal Standard** (☎ 01326 374250) serves hoppy Skinner's Betty Stogs and Heligan Honey. The smallish, contemporary-traditional oak interior fills up quickly on summer evenings, thanks to a top-notch menu.

Castaways wine bar in Mylor Yacht Harbour (☎ 01326 377710) is a good place to watch the boats go by, in a sprawling former boatyard with sofas, dining tables and fairy-lit palms. We would like to recommend the 13th century **Pandora Inn** (☎ 01326 372678, www.pandorainn.com) on Restronguet Creek but, at the time of writing, it was closed due to a fire which destroyed it's thatched roof and most of the upper floor. Hopefully, it will soon be restored to the classic old inn it is, or was: all log fires, low-beamed hidey-holes and maritime memorabilia.

Visitor Information

Tourist information centre: Falmouth Tourist Information Centre, 11 Market Strand, Prince of Wales Pier, Falmouth TR11 3DF, ☎ 01326 312300.

Hospitals with A&E: Falmouth Hospital, Trescobeas Road, Falmouth TR11 2JA, ☎ 01326 434700.

Doctors: Trescobeas Surgery, Trescobeas Road, Falmouth TR11 2UN, ☎ 01326 315615; Westover Surgery, Western terrace, Falmouth TR11 4QJ, ☎ 01326 212120; Penryn Surgery, Saracen Way, Penryn TR10 8HX, ☎ 01326 372502.

Pharmacies: Boots, 47–49 Market Street, Falmouth TR11 3AB, ☎ 01326 312373; Alliance Pharmacy, Trescobeas Surgery, Trescobeas Road, Falmouth TR11 2UN, ☎ 01326 315615; Hendras at Penryn, Penryn Surgery, Saracen Way, Penryn TR10 8HX, ☎ 01326 372233.

Police station: Devon & Cornwall Constabulary, Dracaena Avenue, Falmouth TR11 2ES, ☎ 0845 2777444.

Supermarkets: Tesco, Killigrew Street, Falmouth TR11 3PQ, ☎ 0845 6779267; Iceland Foods, 3 Berkeley Vale, Falmouth TR11 3PL, ☎ 01326 211545; ASDA, Jennings Road, Penryn TR10 9LY, ☎ 01326 378873.

Car hire: Goldmartin Garage, Sampys Hill, Mawnan Smith, Falmouth TR11 5EW, ☎ 01326 250394; DG Self Drive Hire, 31 East Rise, Swanvale, Falmouth TR11 4HN, ☎ 01326 318272; Falmouth Garages Skoda, 9 Church Road, Penryn TR10 8DA, ☎ 01326 377246.

ATMs: Alliance & Leicester, 23 Market Street, Falmouth TR11 3AS, ☎ 01326 311929; HSBC, Market Street, Falmouth TR11 3AA; Lloyds TSB, 25 Market Street, Penryn, TR10 8HT.

Bike hire: Bissoe Tramway Cycle Hire, Old Conn Works, Bissoe, Truro TR4 8QZ, ☎ 01872 870341.

Local taxis: 24/7 Falmouth, ☎ 01326 312470; A1 Xpress Taxis, ☎ 01326 318860; Castle, Penryn, ☎ 01326 313747.

THE ROSELAND PENINSULA

There's something rather exclusive about the Roseland Peninsula; tucked away in a rural backwater, within waving distance of Falmouth on the other side of Carrick Roads. Its harbour-village marinas are the honey pots of the yachting set; its secretive beaches attract brigades of Boden-clad London weekenders; and the real estate is the province of the rich. St Mawes, at its epicentre, is a byword for nautical chic, the Rock of the south coast. Yet, the Roseland, as pretty as its name, remains gloriously unspoiled, rarely crowded.

From Tregony, at its entrance, to St Anthony Head, the peninsula is just 10 miles long. There's not a lot to see other than St Mawes Castle or much to do other than sailing or sitting on beaches. But this seaside playground is one of Cornwall's great escapes. Indeed, there are more boutique hotels per square mile than almost anywhere else in the county. Olga Polizzi's Tresanton Hotel in St Mawes, kicked off the Cool Cornwall tag when it opened back in 1999. Typically, it has its own 48ft racing yacht, and a motorboat for beach picnic parties.

WHAT TO SEE AND DO

Roundhouses in Veryan

There's only one road into Roseland – the lone A3078 which plunges south just short of Truro. On route to salty St Mawes, it travels through the wool town of **Tregony**; the gateway to Roseland, it was an active port until the river Fal silted up in the 16th century – now it is in every sense a peaceful backwater. Further south, a brief detour takes you to the chocolate-box village of **Veryan**, with its five picturesque 19th-century roundhouses.

Once in **St Mawes**, you'll find a line of seafront shops and restaurants overlooking the water, all quickly dispensed with unless you visit the trefoil **St Mawes Castle**, a rugged coastal fortress built by Henry VIII in the 1540s to fend off the French and Spanish. Cross the drawbridge and enter a world of gargoyles, stone carvings and coats of arms – this clover-leaf shaped fort is one of Henry's frilliest castles. Inside you can visit the gun platforms, where suits of armour, canon and artillery are on display, accompanied by almost life-like Tudor mannequins. Unlucky

ST MAWES CASTLE, St Mawes, TR2 5DE; ☎ 01326 270526; www.english-heritage.org.uk. Entry: adults £4.30, children £2.60; open daily from 10am (except Sat, Apr to Sept, and on Tues/Wed/Thurs, 1 Nov to 1 Mar).

The Devil's in the detail

The Roseland village of Veryan is best known for its five white-washed Round Houses – a matching pair at either end of the village, and a slate-roofed loner in the middle, all thatched except the latter. Made of cob – a mixture of clay, earth and straw – they were built between 1815 and 1818 by local squire, the Rev Jeremiah Trist. Local legend has it that with the virtue of his five daughters on his mind, he designed the houses to be devoid of corners where the devil could hide. Each is piously topped by a cross – just to be on the safe side perhaps? The truth is more prosaic: by the time the round houses were built, one daughter had died. And the picturesque roundels were actually designed as estate cottages, and could simply be described as follies. The close proximity of these lodge-like Grade II listed curiosities has ensured that the roads in and out of Veryan can never be widened.

St Mawes Castle

Royalists holed up here in the Civil War soon worked out that while the castle was impenetrable from the sea, it was a pushover if attacked by land, and surrendered without firing a shot. Outside across the waters of the Carrick Roads you can see the castle's larger Falmouth twin, Pendennis.

The **King Harry Ferry** takes people and cars between Philleigh (5 miles north of St Mawes) and Feock, knocking 45 minutes off the drive to Falmouth or Truro (see page 211). And the **St Mawes Ferry** – pedestrians only – takes 25 minutes to ply the route between St Mawes and Falmouth's Prince of Wales Pier or Custom House Quay.

ST MAWES FERRY, 01872 861910; www.stmawesferry.co.uk. Entry: adults single/return £5/£8, children £3.50/£4.50, bikes £1 each way; runs daily all year; June to Sept, roughly every 20 minutes-until 5.15/5.45pm; Jul/Aug evening ferries Fri/Sat until 8.30pm; Oct to May, every hour, 8.30am–4.15/5.15pm.

From May to September a smaller foot ferry makes the 10-minute journey south across the Percuil River between St Mawes and Place Manor (a private 17th-century manor house) in the village of **St Anthony in Roseland**. This is a beautiful area for walks along country lanes and clifftop paths (pick up a leaflet in the tourist office).

A mile south, the **St Anthony Head Lighthouse** guides shipping away from treacherous Manacle Rocks. Built in 1835, its main claim to fame is that it featured in the children's series

St Mawes Ferry

Fraggle Rock. It's not open to the public, but you can stay in the keepers' cottages (www.ruralretreats.co.uk).

Portscatho on Gerrans Bay is a former pilchard-fishing village which now, like so many others, makes its living from tourism. Its beaches, cafés and tiny harbour attract an arty crowd; the Portscatho Society of Artists was formed here in 1984. Five minutes walk away up the hill is the village of **Gerrans**, whose medieval church spire was a useful landmark for passing sailors. On the other side of Gerrans Bay, the National Trust's **Nare Head** rewards visitors with spectacular views of the Roseland coast and Dodman Point. A 6-mile circular walk from Nare Head car park takes you from the headland north along the coastal path to the pretty fishing village of **Portloe**, then back via inland footpaths and lanes. For full details see www.westcountrywalks.com. You don't have to walk that far, but tiny Portloe's wiggly lanes are best approached on foot.

To the east of Veryan Bay, lies **Caerhays Castle**, a castellated mansion designed by Regency architect John Nash for the Trevanion family in 1810. Give or take a few gambling debts, the cost of this extravagant Gothic pile contributed to their financial ruin, and the house – semi-derelict and empty other than a few geese nesting in the drawing room – was seized by creditors and sold at auction to Michael Williams MP in 1855. Still owned by the Williams family, the restored Grade I listed house and its estate is open to the public in spring allowing access to 100 acres of woodland and enchanting gardens. A short downhill walk takes you to the estate's own secluded **Porthluney Beach**.

THE CAERHAYS ESTATE, Gorran, St Austell PL26 6LY; ☎ 01872 501310; www.caerhays.co.uk. Tickets for garden: adults £5.50, children £2.50; for house and garden: adults, £9.50, children £3.50; gardens open daily mid-Feb to Jun (10am–5pm); house open for tours, on weekdays, mid-March to Jun.

Beaches

Roseland's craggy coastline has a number of sandy beaches scattered along its length. St Mawes has two: tiny **Tavern Beach** near the castle, and the larger **Summers Beach** on the other side of the harbour. **Porthbeor**, half a mile from St Anthony in Roseland, isa quiet, remote strip of sand with absolutely no mod cons. **Portscatho** has a small rocky beach with patches of sand, but a better bet is **Porthcurnick**, a wide sandy private beach with rock pools. You can drive there, but it's quicker to walk along the cliff path – 15 minutes or so to the west with ravishing views. On **Gerrans Bay**, south of Veryan, a long lovely stretch of National Trust beach has the sands of **Carne Beach** to the east, and **Pendower** to the west. On Veryan Bay,

Any colour as long as it's magnolia

In 1895, JC Williams, heir of the Caerhays estate, and MP for Truro, left politics and took up gardening. He funded several expeditions by celebrated plant hunter George Forrest to the Orient, and his investment was amply rewarded. The aptly named Forrest supplied him with seeds from hundreds of newly discovered species of rhododendron, camellia, azalea, acer and magnolia. Williams not only successfully grew these species at the gardens at Caerhays, but he and his descendants also undertook an extensive cross-breeding programme to produce brand new hybrids. Today, the garden holds the National Magnolia collection of more than 80 species and 500 hybrids. Early spring is the time to see them.

and part of the Caerhays Estate, sheltered **Caerhays Beach** (also known as Porthluney Cove) is peaceful, thanks to a ban on motorised water craft.

Wet weather

Pack waterproofs and Scrabble because the Roseland doesn't really do indoors. The best bet is to head for Falmouth's National Maritime Museum (see page 220).

Otherwise, you could potter around **Portscatho**'s art galleries. Local artist Chris Insoll runs the **New Gallery** (☎ 01872 580445), specialising in the work of West Country artists. **The Spindrift Gallery** (☎ 01872 580155) on the Quay sells ceramics, jewellery, sculpture, studio glass and seascape watercolours, mostly by local craftspeople. Stained-glass artist Jane Winton runs the **Jellyfish Gallery** (☎ 01872 580075), selling quirky craft items from artists around the UK.

What to do with children

Roseland's beaches are great for children – it's one of the reasons families are so drawn to the place – the majority being clean, sandy and close to supplies of ice cream. Otherwise, St Mawes' **Sit on Kayaks** provides just what it says on the tin, including a Peekaboo option with a transparent bottom, giving a window onto the underwater world. Each kayak seats one adult paddler and one child. The hire fee includes buoyancy aids and a safety briefing – then you're on your own.

SIT ON KAYAKS, 07971 846786; www.stmaweskayaks.co.uk. Peekaboo hire from £15 for 2 hours, or £35 per day; Easter to Oct.

Sailing near St Mawes Castle

Entertainment

Special events

In July, the **St Mawes Town Regatta** (☎ 01326 270953; www.stmawessailing.co.uk) puts on a Saturday morning of children's events followed by an afternoon of sailing races. In October/November, the **Roseland Festival** (www.crbo.co.uk/roseland) celebrates art, literature, poetry, music and dance in an eclectic mix of events in venues all over the peninsula.

The best... PLACES TO STAY

BOUTIQUE

Driftwood

Rosevine, Portscatho, TR2 5EW
☎ 01872 580644
www.driftwoodhotel.co.uk

It has 180° clifftop views, 14 light and airy rooms and a weather-boarded cabin on its own private beach (ideal for honeymooners). The décor is washed-out timber, neutrals, nauticals and starfish – New England with a touch of the Hamptons. There are family rooms and seven acres of coastal gardens.

Price: B&B from £175–£280 for a double.

Rosevine

Rosevine, Near Portscatho, Truro TR2 5EW
☎ 01872 580 206
www.rosevine.co.uk

Rosevine caters for children without compromising on grown-up glamour. The elegant Georgian house is divided into 12 suites, all with mini-kitchens (just the basics), some with balconies or terraces. You can do room service, self-catering or sea-view restaurant. There are play areas, an indoor pool and Portscatho beach just five minutes away.

Price: studios from £145 for a night; suites from £185–£385.

The best... PLACES TO STAY

The Lugger Hotel

Portloe Truro Cornwall TR2 5RD
☎ 01872 501322,
www.luggerhotel.co.uk

This rugged, 17th-century harbour inn was treated to a style makeover under new management in 2008. There's boat-like decks right on the water, a warren of nooks and crannies to nestle into, spa, restaurant and no mobile phone service.

Price: B&B from £115–£235 for a double.

HOTEL

Hotel Tresanton

St Mawes, Cornwall, TR2 5DR
☎ 01326 270 055
www.tresanton.com

This swish former yacht club, with sparkling views over the bay, is one of Cornwall's classics – one hotel survey put it second only to the Ritz. The rooms are understated but classy, with a nautical palette. Owner Olga Polizzi has laid on valet parking, a children's playroom and a 48ft yacht. If you can't afford to stay here, do tea on the terrace instead.

Price: B&B £190–£365 for a double.

B&B

The Nare Hotel

Carne Beach, Veryan-in-Roseland, Cornwall, TR2 5PF; ☎ 01872 501111
www.thenare.com

Set in manicured gardens overlooking Carne beach, this country house hotel is one of the highest rated in the county. A favourite with affluent 60-somethings and quiet families, it has a sea-view pool, spa and jacket-and-tie restaurant.

Double room half board from £262–£720 for a double.

CAMPSITE

Treloan Coastal Farm

Treloan Lane, Portscatho TR2 5EF
☎ 01872 580989
www.coastalfarmholidays.co.uk.

Try to camp nearer the coast than this organic farm's on-the-cliffs perch, and you'll be in the sea. Bring your own tent or caravan, or book the farm's 'Honeycomb Snug', a 12-foot yurt, or a mobile home. A 1926 Eccles caravan with vintage interior is also available.

Price: camping from £13.50–£21.50 for a night.

SELF-CATERING

Philleigh Cottages

Roseland Peninsula
☎ 01872 580751
www.roselandselfcatering.co.uk

Converted from stables in green and pleasant Philleigh, the two cottages, compact and bijou Drift and Harvest, can each sleep six. Outside, all rough Cornish stone; inside, urban chic with pale wood floors and spiral staircases.

Price: from £390–£790 for a week.

Fort House

St Mawes Castle, St Mawes TR2 3AA
☎ 0870 333 1187
www.english-heritage.org.uk

One of English Heritage's recently flaunted landmark holiday cottages in historic buildings. There is nothing historic about the contemporary décor, but you share the cliffs with the castle and surely the best views in St Mawes.

Price: from £800–£1593 for a week.

The best... FOOD AND DRINK

The quality of food in Roseland is generally high. The peninsula's farms supply local restaurants with fruit, vegetables, meat and dairy produce, and the fishing fleets of St Mawes and Portloe land fresh fish and, particularly, shellfish. A high concentration of well-heeled yachties and fashionistas demands a deli kind of shopping. Even the village stores do Prosciutto and Prosecco.

Staying in

St Mawes Bakery on the quayside next to the harbourmaster's office makes exemplary saffron buns and pasties, as well as a mouth-watering range of breads and cakes. If you're planning a picnic, head to **Gills Delicatessen** (☎ 01326 270045) in St Mawes, a popular place with locals in the supermarket-free zone.

For seafood, head for **Curgurrell Farm** (☎ 01872 580243) in Portscatho where fish, lobster and crab straight off the dayboats are sold through the kitchen window. The small fishing fleet in St Mawes also operates a **wet fish shop** (☎ 07792 220 821) on the Harbour Quay. And it doesn't get more local than **Humphrey's Farm Shop** (☎ 01872 530417) in Tregony: 30 varieties of fruit and vegetables grown on the farm, and cheese, milk and ice cream from local dairies.

Drinking

St Mawes Hotel (☎ 01326 270266; www.stmaweshotel.co.uk) describes itself as *'a bar with rooms'*, and its seafront location makes it a popular hang-out. **The Victory Inn** (☎ 01326 270324; www.victory-inn.co.uk/) named after Nelson's flagship at Trafalgar, is the only traditional pub in St Mawes. As well as a range of Cornish Sharp's ales, it stocks 26 wines.

In Portscatho, the 17th century **Plume of Feathers** (☎ 01872 580321) serves St Austell ales from the cask. The popular **Ship Inn** (☎ 01872 501 356) in Portloe was built in the 17th century as a fisherman's cottage, and became a pub in the 1900s. It's full of nautical bric-a-brac. In the heart of the peninsula, the charming and popular **Roseland Inn** (☎ 01872 580254; www.roselandinn.co.uk) in Philleigh is handy for the King Harry Ferry.

The **Kings Arms** in Tregony (☎ 01872 530202) has an open fire for winter, a walled Cornish garden for summer, and St Austell ales on draught all year round.

EATING OUT

FINE DINING

The Quarterdeck (at the Nare Hotel)

Carne Beach, Veryan-in-Roseland TR2 5PF
☎ 01872 500 000
www.narehotel.co.uk

Head chef Malcolm Sparks lifts traditional English food to new heights in this airy yachtie restaurant with decking by a local shipwright, tables on the pool terrace and views of Carne Beach. Specialities include Portloe lobster and crab and Cornish beef. Main courses cost from £12.95.

Hotel Tresanton

St Mawes, Cornwall, TR2 5DR
☎ 01326 270 055; www.tresanton.com

A picture of elegance, all crisp white linen, mosaics, tongue and groove, and yachting blues, Tresanton's is a real treat, with fabulous views and a verdant terrace. Head chef Paul Wadham's eclectic menu is an all-day affair where Cornish produce has a fling with the Mediterranean. A three-course dinner costs around £45.

RESTAURANT

The Lugger

Portloe Truro Cornwall TR2 5RD
☎ 01872 501322; www.luggerhotel.co.uk

Overlooking Portloe's cove and tiny harbour, the emphasis is on unfussy classic cuisine using fresh local ingredients. Try the Portloe crab cakes, Cornish mackerel, or the seafish chowder. Main course dishes from £13.90.

St Mawes Hotel

Marine Parade, Truro TR2 5DW
☎ 01326 270266
www.stmaweshotel.co.uk

Popular reasonably-priced and right on the quayside, the ground-floor Moules Bar serves steaming pots of Moules Mariniere, Moules Frites or mussels with saffron and cider, alongside line-caught fish, fresh king prawns and scallops, Cornish steaks and other local produce.

CAFÉ

Café Chandlers

St Mawes, Truro TR2 5AA
☎ 01326 270998
www.caféchandlers.co.uk

A deli café with an ever-changing seasonal menu of light lunches like charcuterie and local cheese platters, homemade cakes and cream teas, proper Lavazza coffee, fruit smoothies and freshly squeezed orange juice.

TEA ROOM

Smugglers Restaurant

Tolverne, Philleigh, Roseland (near the King Harry Ferry); ☎ 01872 580309

On the River Fal's tranquil eastern bank, and handy for the ferry to Falmouth, this achingly pretty smugglers cottage dates back to the 15th Century. A part of the vast Tregothnan Estate, it's open for lunch or dinner, but the speciality of the house is afternoon tea – served with clotted cream and Tregothnan's own English estate teas. Open daily 12pm–8pm.

Visitor Information

Tourist information centre: Roseland Visitor Centre, Parish Millennium Rooms, The Square, St Mawes, Truro TR2 5AG, ☎ 01326 270440.

Doctors: St Mawes Surgery, Hillhead, St Mawes, Truro TR2 5AL, ☎ 01326 270241.

Pharmacies: St Mawes Pharmacy, 12, Kings Road, St Mawes TR2 5DH, ☎ 01326 270296.

Police station: Nearest is in Falmouth.

Supermarkets: There is a Londis at Veryan, a Spar Shop at St Mawes.

Internet access: Available at the Roseland Visitor Centre listed above; £1.50 for 15 minutes.

ATMs: St Mawes Post Office; Barclays (St. Mawes), 4–5, Marine Parade, TR2 5DW.

Local taxis: Gerrans Bay Taxi (Portscatho), 01872 580673; Roseland Taxis, 01872 501001.

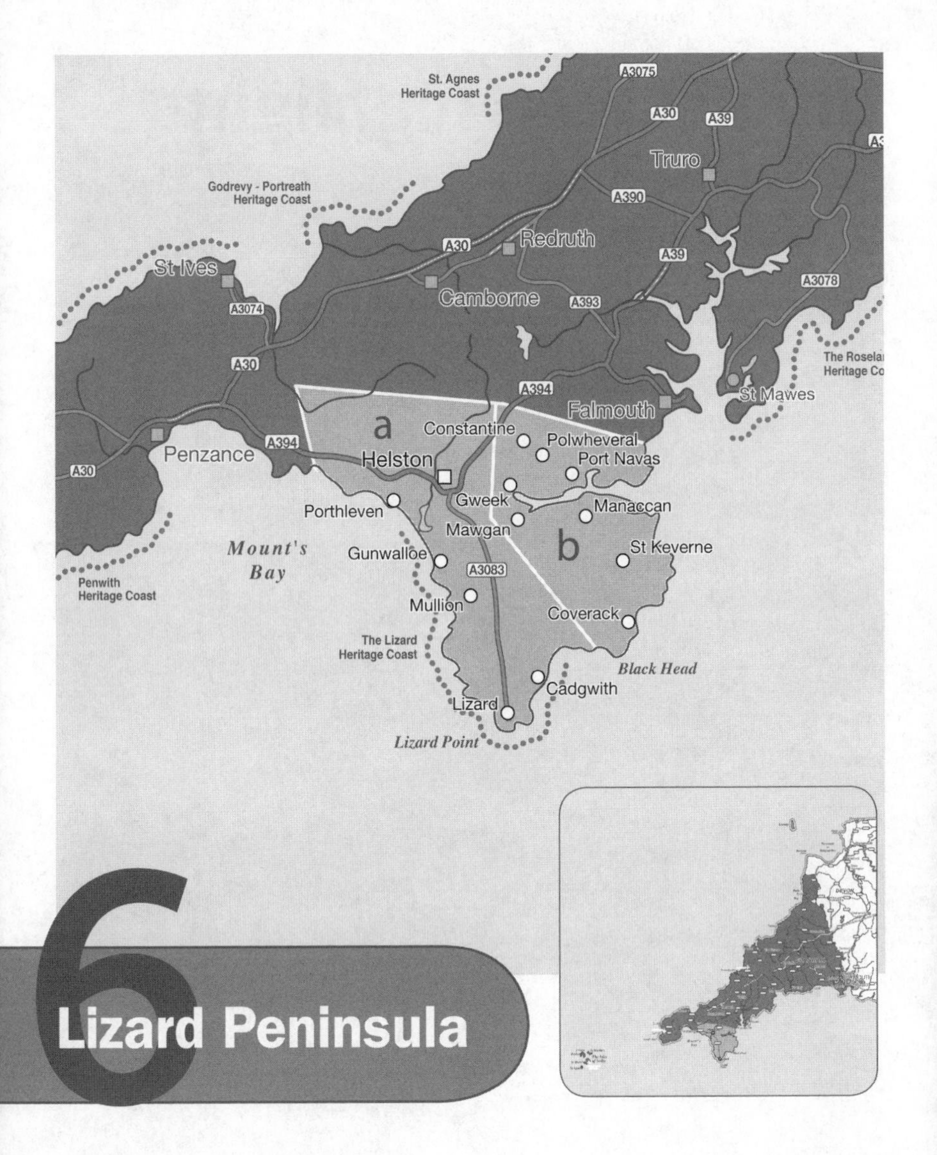

6 Lizard Peninsula

a. Helston and the Lizard

b. Lizard East and the Helford River

Unmissable highlights

01 Take the footpath from the National Trust car park down to ravishing Kynance Cove, where dramatic islands of rock rise from a sheltered bay of white sand, p. 251

02 Explore Trebah Gardens, a sub-tropical paradise with its own Helford River beach, p. 266

03 Meet the legendary Arthur, the world's oldest parabolic satellite dish is now part of Goonhilly Futureworld experience, p. 250

04 Take the foot ferry across the river between Helford and Helford Passage: there has been a crossing here since the 15th century, p. 263

05 Down a pint of Spingo at the 'Old Blue', The microbrewery at Helston's Blue Anchor Inn is behind the bar, p. 260

06 Linger over Sunday lunch at the Halzephron Inn at Gunwalloe, p. 259

07 Wander around the Penrose Estate to Loe Pool and down to the sandbank at Loe Bar, p. 249

08 Try a lick of Roskilly's farm-produced artisan ice cream, marzipan and Sour Cherry perhaps, or Hokey Pokey, p. 267

09 Sit on the clifftop at Lizard Point and enjoy the exhilarating views from the headland where Marconi received the world's first ship-to-shore SOS, p. 251

10 Make sure you're around in May for Helston's Furry Dance, one of the oldest and most colourful of Cornwall's pagan festivals, p. 256

LIZARD PENINSULA

It would be foolish to suggest that the Lizard Peninsula was undiscovered, but the most southerly point of mainland Britain is one of Cornwall's most overlooked regions: loved to bits by those who know it well, but often bypassed by the many travellers that don't make it beyond Flambards theme park.

It does takes a bit of extra effort to get there, wiggling around Truro suburbia, or dropping down B-roads from the A30. This is muddy lanes and tractor country. But that's all part of the Lizard's charm.

The peninsula (the name came from the Cornish *lezou* meaning headland) is said to be a chunk of ancient oceanic crust that rose out of the sea to join the mainland, and it does have a kind of otherworldliness; Cornish to the core, but with a distinct character, an island mentality. Beyond RNAS Culdrose, an extraordinary variety of landscapes unfold, all packed into a knob of land only 12 miles from end to end. To the west, the gloomy beauty of Goonhilly Down, with its heathland, hairy buttercups and retro satellite dishes. To the north-east, the serene wooded valleys of the Helford River; on the coast, serpentine cliffs and smugglers' coves. And it's one of the warmest places in Britain. An early spring brings fields of daffodils and gardens of flowering camellias, and autumn lingers. It's a lingering kind of place.

HELSTON AND THE LIZARD

It is known worldwide as the home of the Floral, or 'Furry', Dance but outside its famous May festival, Helston is a local town for local people: an unpretentious little place, resolutely Cornish and, give or take the odd chain store, barely changed since its 18th-century tin-mining heyday. In the Middle Ages, the former coinage town had its own port, with direct access to the sea via a tidal creek at the mouth of the River Cober. By the 13th century it was landlocked by the Loe Bar, a bank of shingle that silted up the estuary. The Loe Pool, Cornwall's largest fresh-water lake, is now Helston's nearest waterfront.

As gateway to the Lizard, and the region's only market town, modern Helston doesn't bend over backwards to attract visitors. It's an old lady of a town, but if you want something a little racier, the fishing-cum-surfing village of Porthleven – Britain's most southerly working port – is just down the road.

Further south, in Mullion, the Lizard's largest village, a mini high-street of gift shops, galleries and tea shops provides a good base for exploring the sandy beaches around Poldhu Point. Beyond, there is Goonhilly Down, a strange but beguiling heathland where rare plant life meets satellite-technology. And at the far end of the peninsula, the coves at Kynance (one of Cornwall's most ravishing beaches) and Cadgwith (the cutest of fishing villages) sit either side of the dramatic serpentine cliffs at Lizard Point where, looking out across the foaming waves of the Atlantic, anything seems possible.

WHAT TO SEE AND DO

In Helston, head for the **Folk Museum** on Market Place and pick up a copy of the Town Trail (download it from www.helstontc.com). Starting at the Guildhall and meandering around the shopping centre, it provides a good introduction to the town's history. Prominent landmarks include the thatched **Blue Anchor Inn**, a pub since the 15th century and home to **Spingo Ales** (produced in-house by one of the oldest private breweries in the country); the 18th century granite-built **St Michael's Church** (complete with stained glass window depicting Furry dancing angels); and the **Grylls Monument**, a handsome Gothic arch constructed in 1834 in memory of Humphrey Millett Grylls (local solicitor, banker and general good egg).

Blue Anchor Inn

From the foot of Coinagehall Street, beyond the Grylls Monument, and the 18th-century bowling green, you can walk down the beautiful Loe Valley, around Loe Pool to Loe Bar and Porthleven Sands, via a series of footpaths through the National Trust's **Penrose Estate** - over 1,500 acres of farmland, woodland and wildlife. It's about 1.5 miles from the head of the valley down to Loe Bar, or you can circumnavigate the Pool's 5 miles of shoreline.

PENROSE ESTATE, Helston TR13 8GT; ☎ 01326 561407; www.nationaltrust.org.uk.

Stately homes

Three miles north of Helston, the **Trevarno Estate**, former home of the Bickford-Smiths (William Bickford invented the miners' safety fuse) offers several indoor and outdoor visitor attractions within 70 acres of grounds, including a Victorian boathouse on a lake, a sunken Italian garden and three museums - dedicated to soap, toys and gardening. The latter is home to Britain's largest collections of garden tools and memorabilia. Trevarno is owned by Nigel Helsby and Mike Sagin, who bought the estate in 1994 not only to prevent its break up into 33 lots but also to show that a traditional country estate could survive and be viable. They are constantly throwing new elements into the mix and there are plans to add craft workshops, new gardens and more museums. Integral to Trevarno, the **Colin Gregory Toy Museum** presents a colourful collection of vintage toys, dating from 1880 to the present day. According to founder Colin Gregory, the usual response from visitors is 'I had one of them'. *'It may be a toy show, but it is usually the adults who are delighted by the collection,'* he says.

TREVARNO ESTATE, Crowntown, Helston TR13 0RU; ☎ 01326 574274; www.trevarno.co.uk. Entry: £7.50, under-14s £2.50, family, £20 (plus 50p/25p for toy museum); open daily, 10.30am–5pm.

GODOLPHIN HOUSE, Godolphin Cross; Helston TR13 9RE; ☎ 01736 763194; www.nationaltrust.org.uk. Entry: house and garden: adult £7, children £3.50; Garden only, adult £4, children, £2; Estate, free admission. Estate open all year; gardens from Mar to Oct (10am-4pm). House open during selected days from Jul to Sept. With frequent closures during restoration, check opening times on 0844 800 1895).

Godolphin House

Further north, **Godolphin House** is the former country seat of the Godolphins, a prominent West Cornwall family who made a fortune from mineral mines. The original medieval fortified house was developed between the 15th and 17th centuries into a large, elegant, granite mansion. Partial demolition in the mid-18th century reduced it to a farmhouse, though much of its Tudor finery remains: a colonnade of Doric columns, for example, mullioned windows and linen-fold panelling in the dining hall. In 2007, the neglected house was acquired by the National Trust. A sensitive restoration programme is in place, and visitors are likely to see parts of the property in a poor, but atmospheric, state of disrepair for some years to come. The same fragile air of untouched history haunts the grounds, among the oldest and most important gardens in Europe, thanks to some 400 recorded archaeological relics and mine works.

Goonhilly Down

For a different kind of horticultural experience, head for **Goonhilly Down**. At first sight, it looks rather bleak, almost barren, other than an incongruous crop of wind turbines and the vast futuristic dishes of Goonhilly satellite station. But the flora of Cornwall's first nature reserve is internationally important as home to a dozen or so of Britain's rarest plants. The hairy buttercup, prostrate asparagus and Cornish Heath (the latter, only found here on the Lizard), grow alongside lime-loving dropwort, lousewort and milkwort. A 5,000-year-old *menhir* (or Neolithic standing stone), and numerous ancient burial sites, add to Goonhilly's special atmosphere. By contrast, **Goonhilly Satellite Earth Station** is a global centre of high-tech communications, responsible for sending and receiving millions of emails, and telephone calls as well as live television broadcasts such as *Live Aid* and the Olympics. With over 60 satellite dishes pointing into space, it was the largest in the world. However, in 2008, British Telecom decided to close the station (still in use, but operated remotely from Goonhilly's sister station at Madley in Herefordshire), decommission or dismantle some of the antennae and reinvent the centre as the **Futureworld@Goonhilly** visitor attraction.

Segway ride at FutureWorld@Goonhilly

Despite its huge popularity, BT decided to close Futureworld's visitor centre in 2010, without giving any explanation or any clue as to whether it would re-open. But you can still see the station's iconic satellite dishes simply by driving past. They include Merlin (Goonhilly's most powerful antenna, with the largest dish circumference at 32m), Guinevere (built in 1972 by Marconi), Lancelot, Uther and good old Arthur. Grade II listed, and still in use, Arthur was the world's first parabolic satellite dish when it was built in 1962 to track Telstar.

By the sea

From **Porthleven Sands** to **Loe Bar** and on to **Gunwalloe** is one long run of sand and shingle. Like most of the beaches on the Lizard's west coast, they are almost non-existent at high tide, but great for paddling and family picnics – swimmers, however, should take care. Loe Bar is particularly dangerous, thanks to strong, potentially treacherous, currents. It's reasonably safe in the shallows at **Porthleven**, but the beach has a steep shelf and a propensity for big boisterous waves making it unsuitable for young children. For surfers, and surf-watchers, however, this is the business: Porthleven's reef (200m off the northern harbour wall) offers one of the best reef breaks in England, and attracts some of the best surfers. Be warned, though, it's not for the novice and can be risky at low tide.

The only other big stretch of beach on the peninsula is **Kennack Sands**, to the east of Lizard Point; not the most attractive, but one of the most popular, thanks to a generous bay of pebbly sand, decent surf and nearby caravan parks. The rest are tucked into coves of rock, often inaccessible by road. There's the 15th-century church of St Winwaloe right on the beach at **Church Cove**, a short walk across Mullion Golf course from **Poldhu Cove**, the pleasant, sandy and often busy beach where Guglielmo Marconi, the father of wireless telegraphy, sent his first radio transmission across the Atlantic. Neighbouring **Polurrian** is a bit of trek along the cliffs, or a stroll downhill from Mullion, but it's popular with surfers. From Mullion, a narrow road winds down to the National Trust's **Mullion Cove**, a rugged little Victorian harbour, with a fingernail of beach, an old pilchard cellar and views of Mullion island (a bird sanctuary, it's not open to the public).

On foot

The Lizard stretch of the South West Coast Path is one long, lovely walk, easily covered in a couple of days by an enthusiastic walker. For those with less time and energy, there are loads of shorter routes, including the magnificent, and often lonely, stretch of cliff from **Predannack Head** to **Kynance Cove** (roughly 2.5 miles). Park at Predannack Wollas (a National Trust car park), and take the footpath around Ogu Dour Cove, skirting the coastal rim of Predannack Downs and the Lizard Nature Reserve, through seaside farmland, sprinkled with wildflowers and grazed by Dexter cattle. From Soapy Cove, the path drops down into Kynance Cove – where castle-like columns of jagged serpentine rock rise from a spectacularly beautiful beach. Tucked into a ravine, there are caves, a wooden beach-hut café, a tumbling stream and, at the top of a steep stepped path, a clifftop car park. If you are driving to Kynance there is a £2 toll to pay between November and Easter. The beach can get very busy in the summer, but never fails to lift the spirits.

Lizard Point Lighthouse

The Lizard and Cadgwith Cove

Beyond a sprawl of shops and cafés at Lizard village, Britain's most southerly extremity, **Lizard Point** is a place of pilgrimage. But unlike Land's End it's delightfully uncommercialised: just a shack of a gift shop, two cafés, and a shed selling lamp-bases and lighthouses carved from local Serpentine stone. The views are stunning, as are the sunsets, and most visitors just sit on the cliff edge watching distant dolphins or seals playing in the waves.

LIZARD LIGHTHOUSE HERITAGE CENTRE, Lizard Point; ☎ 01326 290202; www.trinityhouse.co.uk. Entry: for Heritage Centre and Lighthouse, adults £6, children £3; Heritage Centre only, adults £4; children £2. Open daily in August, Sun to Thurs/Fri from Feb–July and Sept to Dec; times vary.

You can also take the footpath to the Lifeboat Station at Church Cove, passing the Devil's Frying Pan (a curious bowl of foaming waves, caused by the collapse of a cave) and on to **Cadgwith**. Here, in this raw but picturesque fishing village, you will find thatched cottages, a pub, a gig-racing club and St Mary's (a blue-painted corrugated iron church the size of a room) huddled around two tiny coves, littered with boats, nets and crab-pots, at the bottom of a plunging U-shaped valley.

Lizard lights

When the first privately funded Lizard lighthouse was built in 1619, it was greeted with as much enthusiasm as Gordon Brown's 10p tax band. So many of the locals prospered from the proceeds of wrecked ships, they saw the lighthouse as a threat; and there was public outcry when ship owners were asked to pay a toll to cover its maintenance. The lighthouse closed within three years. Another was built in 1751, though the twin-towered building we see today was the result of alterations made by Trinity House in 1812. Not only is it the most southerly lighthouse in the British Isles, but it was the first to be powered by electricity (1924), and the last in the south-west to be automated (1998). The powerful beam can be seen for 64 miles.

CELEBRITY CONNECTIONS

In Lizard terms, Cadgwith Cove's big claim to fame is as the home of the local gig racing club. Around here, the celebrities are *Buller*, *Rose* and *Socoa*, the village's three pilot gig boats. But in 2003, the tiny fishing village was catapulted to stardom when it landed a leading role in the film *Ladies in Lavender*, directed by Charles Dance and based on a short story by William J. Locke. The venerable dames **Maggie Smith** and **Judi Dench** were cast as the ladies – elderly spinster sisters Jane and Ursula Widdington, living in a lonely clifftop cottage on the windswept coast of Cornwall. Set in fictional Trevannic in 1936, the story revolves around their discovery of a Polish castaway, played by Daniel Brühl, found shipwrecked on their beach. '*They saved a stranger from the sea*,' went the poster catchline. '*... in return he stole their hearts*.' The young man turns out to be a gifted musician. Cadgwith's gig shed was cast as Moyle's Sail Loft, a fact that is proudly proclaimed on the local community website.

Wet weather

Housed in the town's original market house, where eggs, meat and other produce were offered for sale from the mid-19th century, the charming **Helston Folk Museum** offers two floors of relics which reflect the social and industrial history of the area – from shipwrecks and tin mines to fishing and farming. Notable exhibits include a hefty cider press (*c.* 1750), Furry Dance archives and railway memorabilia from the long-redundant Helston branch line (closed in 1964).

HELSTON FOLK MUSEUM, Market Place, Helston TR13 8TH; ☎ 01326 564027. Entry: £2, under-16s free; open Mon–Sat, 10am–1pm.

During really wild weather, you could join the storm-watchers at Porthleven. It faces south-west, right into the prevailing winds that roar across Mounts Bay, and has a reputation for spectacularly rough seas. In winter, people come specially to watch waves breaking over the granite harbour piers or, on rare occasions, the clock tower of the former Bickford-Smith Institute (now the town council offices).

In the Wendron Valley, 2 miles north of Helston, **Poldark Mine** claims to be Cornwall's most popular, and most important, mining heritage site. Unusually, it's independently run by a group of volunteers and enthusiasts who saved the site from receivership in 2000, nearly 30 years after it was first opened to the public. Founder Peter Young took the name Poldark from the Winston Graham novels that formed the basis of the BBC drama series, parts of which were filmed here. Apart from atmospheric tours of the 18th-century mine, 200ft (60m) underground and pumped by a Cornish beam engine, the centre offers a tin-mining museum, various craft workshops, or you can try your hand at a bit of gold panning.

POLDARK MINE, Wendron, Helston TR13 0ES; ☎ 01326 573173; www.poldark-mine.co.uk. Admission free; guided tours, adults £9.50, children £6; Open daily, 10am–5.30pm; closed Sat, from mid-April to mid Jul, and Sept/Oct.

The **Marconi Centre** (☎ 01326 241656) at Poldhu Cove is funded by the National Trust and the Marconi Company, and run by the Poldhu Amateur Radio Club. You can see variety of old equipment, within spitting distance of the original Marconi Transmitting Station, now just a concrete floor, and add to the Marconi story, by visiting the **Lizard Wireless Station** he founded at Lizard Point in 1901. Run by National Trust volunteers, the restored hut is presented much as it was when the station received the first recorded ship-to-shore SOS signal in 1910.

LIZARD WIRELESS STATION, Lizard Point TR12; 01326 561407; www.lizardwireless.org. Admission free (donations invited); open from Jun–Sept, on Sun, Tues, Wed and Thurs, from 12pm–3pm (weather permitting). Days/times subject to change.

What to do with children…

Flambards, on the southern edge of Helston, is one of Cornwall's oldest and best known theme parks. It began in the early 1980s as the Cornwall Aircraft Park, and gradually expanded, adding a life-size walk-through Victorian Village, the Britain in the Blitz experience and a variety of classic theme-park attractions. It also has a 'Tots Zone' play area, a programme of high-season live entertainment and a hands-on Science Experience. All these elements are indoors or undercover, so perfect for miserable weather.

FLAMBARDS EXPERIENCE, Culdrose Manor, Helston TR13 0QA; ☎ 01326 573 404; www.flambards.co.uk. Entry: £19.50, children (under 15) £12.95, infants (under 3) free; open Apr to end of Oct (times vary, but last admission 3.30pm).

Children, particularly boys, love watching the comings and goings of **RNAS Culdrose**. The largest naval air station in Europe with 3,000 personnel and over 100 fixed and rotary wing aircraft including Westland Merlin and Sea King helicopters and Hawk jets, the base provides a search-and-rescue service to the whole of the south-west, and is occasionally called out to assist in newsworthy dramas. **Culdrose Viewing Enclosure** offers parking, a shop and café, for those who want to watch the action (for free) from just outside the perimeter fence. To get closer, take a guided bus trip around the base, which takes visitors into hangars, the cinema and right up to aircraft.

RNAS CULDROSE: viewing enclosure, Helston, TR12 6BB; ☎ 01326 565085; www.royal-navy.mod.uk. Entry: adults £6.50, children £3.75, under-5s free; guided tours (1 hour 45 min), 2pm daily (except Friday); booking advisable.

 ... and how to avoid children

Explore the Lizard in style, by borrowing a sleek vintage soft-top from **Helston Classic Car Hire**. The small fleet of immaculately restored 1950s–1960s vehicles include a 1966 Austen Healey Mk III (in sporty chrome-trimmed Colorado red), a 1967 Triumph TR5, and a 1952 MG TD Sports (a soft-top two-seater).

HELSTON CLASSIC CAR HIRE, Castle Green Garage, Castle Green, Helston TR13 8EZ; ☎ 01326 565700; www.helstonclassiccarhire.co.uk. Price: day rates £220 (Triumph TR5) to £285 (Jaguar E-type); weekly rates from £880 to £1010.

 Entertainment

Theatre and cinema

The small **Flora Helston** cinema on Wendon Street (☎ 01326 569977; www.merlincinemas.co.uk) is the only standard entertainment venue on the whole Lizard peninsular. At Flambards, the **Kingsford Venue** (☎ 01326 573404; www.kingsfordvenue.co.uk) is a domed, 400-seater marquee-style music/theatre venue offering a regular programme of concerts (typically, a Queen tribute band, a local youth music festival or a DJ-driven 1970s night).

Special events

Helston's **Flora Day**, and the famous Furry Dance (see box overleaf), is held on 8 May, unless that date falls on a Sunday or Monday, in which case it takes place on the previous Saturday. RNAS Culdrose run an annual aviation-fest **Air Day** at the end of July (www.royal-navy.mod.uk). In July or August (dates vary), Cadgwith Gig Club's **Buller Day** races (named after the oldest of the club's three pilot gigs) takes place in the village harbour and on the beach (www.cadgwithgigclub.co.uk). A gig is a West Country rowing boat, designed to pilot larger boats intro tricky harbours (see page 34). One the best-known fixtures in the gig-racing calendar, this is a lively community event but with limited parking you'll have to get there early, or walk from, say, Kennack or Lizard Point.

Nightlife

Helston has one nightclub, **Trelawneys** (25 Coinagehall Street, ☎ 01326 573323), open until 2am at weekends. Also on Coinagehall Street, **The Beehive Bar** (☎ 01326 565636), a former run-down pub transformed into a contemporary bar, is open late-ish. The Cadgwith Singers do a turn around 10pm every Friday at the **Cadgwith Cove Inn** (01326 290513) which also has a Folk Club night on Tuesdays.

Dancing in the streets – Flora Day

Helston's Flora Day, one of Britain's oldest folk customs, is traditionally held on 8 May, and although it coincides with the Feast of the Apparition of St Michael's (Helston's patron saint), it's believed to be an ancient rite of spring that pre-dates Christianity. The town is dressed for the occasion with bluebells, gorse, laurel, hazel and flags.

The day starts early with the first of four processional dances, swiftly followed by the Hal-an-Tow, a song (possibly derived from an old sea shanty) sung to the crowds by local youths waving sycamore branches: '*Hal-an-Tow, Jolly rumble O, For we are up as soon as any Day, O...*'. The dancers, togged up in their finest, weave in and out of houses and gardens, and down streets crowded with onlookers – and all accompanied by the distinctive (and somewhat repetitive) Furry Dance tune, pumped out by the Helston Town Band.

Shopping

The local speciality is **serpentine** stone, a dark green-to-black or brownish stone, streaked and veined with red and white; it looks a little like snakeskin, and was all the rage during the latter part of the 19th century. Particularly prevalent between Kynance and Cadgwith coves, it is still quarried locally before being carved and polished into gift items.

If visiting the Trevarno Estate, near Helston, check out **Trevarno Organic** (☎ 01326 574282; www.trevarnoskincare.co.uk), a range of local organic skincare products, handmade on the estate without using harsh chemicals or animal testing. The products include wonderful natural soaps, creams and bath oils made from herbs and plant extracts. Visit the workshops in Trevarno's garden and you can see how the products are made.

Queen of pasties

According to Anne Muller, serving chips with a pasty is '*ignorant*'. A good-quality pasty, '*proply made*', is a meal in itself, she says. And she should know. The doyenne of the authentic Cornish pasty, her savoury pastry parcels have been lauded as the world's best, and though the accolade may be a little overblown (it's a pasty after all), she certainly knows her stuff: a classic mix of chopped meat, potato, onion and swede, encased in crimped short-crust pasty. Before becoming a full-time pasty chef, the former art student's only experience of catering was as a waitress in a vegetarian restaurant in Notting Hill. When she returned to Cornwall, she was called on to help her mother produce a batch of pasties for an agricultural fair. The positive response inspired a stall at Helston market, followed by a shop in Porthleven, and finally, the celebrated Lizard Pasty Shop, housed in a converted garage behind Anne's home in Beacon Terrace. Aside from hot, fresh pasties, you can pick up a copy of *The Pasty Book*, a short history written by Anne's mother, Hattie Merrick.

The best... PLACES TO STAY

HOTEL

Polurrian Hotel

Mullion Cove TR12 7EN
☎ 01326 240421; www.polurrianhotel.com

The ambience is akin to a traditional country house hotel, and the rooms are a bit Holiday Inn, but the hotel's recent facelift has taken years off it, and it would be hard to improve the location: in 12 acres of cliff-top gardens overlooking Mounts Bay.

Price: £110–£170 for a double per night.

INN

Top House

The Lizard TR12 7NQ
☎ 01326 290974
www.thetophouselizard.co.uk

The pub is a traditional old timber, but the refurbished rooms (in an annexe to the rear) are bright young things, simple, uncluttered, newly decorated in pale seaside colours and good value. Go for the top floor for the best views.

Price: B&B from £70 for a double.

B&B

Halzephron House

Gunwalloe TR12 7QD
☎ 07899 925816
www.halzephronhouse.co.uk

In a walled garden, high on a blustery headland overlooking Mount's Bay, Lucy and Roger Thorp's castellated white villa has three stylish, self-contained guest rooms: the Tower Room (with its own lounge and verandah), the Cabin (dinky little hideaway for two) and the Observatory (overlooking the garden).

Price: from £80 to £130 for a double.

SELF-CATERING

Kynance Cove Cottage

Kynance Cove, The Lizard TR12 7PJ
☎ 01326 290941
www.kynancebeachcafe.co.uk

The location is an escapist's dream – just you, the beach and the café next door. The cosy little cottage has one-bedroom, a wood-burner and eco-friendly solar roof tiles.

Price: from £330–£695 for a week (sleeps two, or a family of four in one bedroom).

The Old Ration Shop

Gunwalloe
☎ 01326 561282
www.theoldrationshop.co.uk

This dinky cottage for two, offers a light open-plan living space, a rustic-modern kitchen, double bedroom and wet room bathroom, all beautifully decked (think pale Farrow and Ball colours, granite worktops and travertine mosaics). There's a quaint little courtyard garden, too.

Price: from £350 to £550 a week.

UNUSUAL

Wolf Rock Cottage

Lizard Lighthouse
☎ 01326 240333
www.cornishcottagesonline.com

One of six former keepers' cottages at Lizard Lighthouse, this one includes the unused West Tower – which has 32 stone steps leading up from a round dining room to an observatory with breathtaking views. The cottage sleeps six.

Price: from £437–£1137 for a week.

The best... FOOD AND DRINK

Predominately rural, the Lizard is very much an agricultural economy meaning there's a lot of good, fresh produce around, with many enterprising producers (meat, dairy and even brewery) going organic. Fishing has declined, but fishing boats still bring crab, lobster and crayfish into Porthleven and to a lesser extent Mullion and Cadgwith. Eating out is more fish and chips than fine dining, and the nearest the Lizard gets to a celebrity chef is a master (or mistress) pasty maker.

Staying in

Helston's centre is a good place to buy fresh food, though note some of the shops are closed on Wednesday. For fresh meat and cheeses, head for **Oliver's Deli** (65, Meneage Street, ☎ 01326 572420; www.oliverscornwall.com). A butcher since 1860 (the deli was added in the 1950s), Oliver's also sells jams, pickles, olives, deli-counter meats and Cornish produce, including honey, marmalade, bottled Spingo beer and Lizard bitter.

The Natural Store (3 The Parade, ☎ 01326 564226) sells health foods, plus Vicky's Breads – from the organic bakery just outside Helston. Started by a lawyer turned 'artisan baker', **Vicky's Breads** are hand-finished and made without improvers or preservatives. To buy direct, you can visit the bakery (7am–12pm, Tues–Fri) at Unit 5, Treprison TR13 0QD (☎ 01326 572084). For fresh fish, go for the **Quayside Fish Centre** on the quay at Porthleven (☎ 01326 562008). For meat and dairy produce, check out the organic farmshop at **Rosuick Farm** at St Martin, near Helston (☎ 01326 231302; closed Sun/Mon/Wed).

Pick up bags and boxes of high quality handmade chocolates (plain, milk, white and honey-flavoured) from **Trenance Chocolate** at the Mullion Meadows Craft Centre just outside Mullion village (☎ 01326 241499; www.trenancechocolate.co.uk). You can also watch them being made in the kitchen-like factory behind the shop. In Porthleven, **Billy Goat Stuff** (www.billygoatstuff.co.uk) produces goats milk chocolate, developed by Sarah Williams, originally as a response to her son's intolerance to both cows' milk and soya. You can buy the chocolates at Celtic Signs (The Square, Porthleven).

Takeaway

For traditional fresh-baked pasties, Helston's best are made by the **Horse & Jockey** bakery in Meneage Street (☎ 01326 563534); for fish and chips, try **Hutchinsons** (also in Meneage Street). In the centre of Mullion, the **Cornish Curry Company** (☎ 01326 240016) produces a range of homemade takeaway curries (opens only on Tues and Thurs 5.30–8.00pm). In Lizard village, **The Smugglers** is best the local chippy, and around the corner, on Beacon's Terrace, you'll find Anne Muller's **Lizard Pasty Shop** (☎ 01326 290889; closed Sun/Mon); just follow the lurid yellow signs. The day's batch of fresh-cooked pasties are usually sold out by lunchtime.

EATING OUT

RESTAURANT

Kota

Harbour Head, Porthleven TR13 9JA
☎ 01326 562407
www.kotarestaurant.co.uk

Celebrated restaurant, specialising in fresh organic produce (such as Falmouth Bay scallops and Cornish wood pigeon). Accents of Asia characterise many of the dishes (chef Jude Kereama is part Chinese, part Malaysian), and the wine list includes over 60 wines. A meal costs around £25 per head (early bird lunch-dinner menus available, from £15). Closed in Jan and Feb (dates vary).

High Point

Polurrian Hotel, Mullion TR12 7EN
☎ 01326 240421
www.polurrianhotel.com

A recent refurbishment has given a fresh contemporary look to the restaurant at the otherwise traditional Polurrian hotel. The menu is bistro style, not too pricey, and mainly British (Cornish pork, rack of lamb, sausage and mash, seafood platter) with vegetarian options. But the big attraction here is the views of the sea from the terrace. Dinner from £25 per head.

Crab Pot Bistro

Harbour Road, Porthleven TR13 9JD
☎ 01326 573355

Unpretentious little café-cum-restaurant overlooking Porthleven harbour, serves simple, inexpensive fish and seafood dishes (prawn and lobster chowder, for example) all freshly cooked in a theatre kitchen, plus cream teas with home-baked scones.

GASTRO PUB

Halzephron Inn

Gunwalloe TR12 7QB
☎ 01326 240406
www.halzephron-inn.co.uk

An inviting mix of maritime antiques, jolly chequered tablecloths, open fires and sea views, this traditional inn wins awards for its food (twice winning Cornwall Dining Pub of the Year). The emphasis is on 'real' Cornish produce, with local meat, fish, game and cheeses featuring on an adventurous menu with Mediterranean leanings. Three courses cost £20–£25. Booking advisable particularly at weekends and Sunday lunch.

CAFÉ

Polpeor Café

Lizard Point
☎ 01326 290939

Perched on the edge of the cliff overlooking the sea, its looks like an old-fashioned café but not only does it have one of the best locations in Cornwall, it serves great food at café prices: homemade pies, fish, salads, ices, cream teas. There is a terrace of outdoor tables and you can bring your own wine and beer. Open every day in July/Aug (last orders, 7.30pm), until 4pm for the rest of the summer, and only on Sundays during the winter (Nov to Feb).

Barefoot Kitchen

Halzephron House, Gunwalloe TR12 7QD
☎ 01326 240517
www.barefootkitchen.com

On the coast path between Porthleven and Church Cove, this welcoming cafe offers all-day log fires, homemade soups, light lunches, teas and delicious cakes. Open: Wed - Sun, 11am-5pm, and for occasional pop-up restaurant evenings.

EATING OUT

Kynance Beach Café
Kynance Cove, The Lizard TR12 7PJ
☎ 01326 290941
www.kynancebeachcafe.co.uk

On a grassy rock ledge on the beach, this wooden café-cum-shop does a good line in snack-style lunches, local bakery pasties, ploughmans, crab sandwiches, homemade cakes and cream teas with Rodda's clotted cream. The café is powered by solar roof tiles and has Bio Bubble waste-treatment system. Closed in winter.

TEA ROOM

Porthmellin Tea Rooms
Mullion Cove, Helston TR12 7ES
☎ 01326 240941

Overlooking the harbour and the cove, the traditional café serves crab sandwiches, cream teas, homemade cakes and ice cream. Open Easter to October.

Drinking

Helston's **Blue Anchor** (50 Coinagehall Street, ☎ 01326 572293) is one of the best pubs in Cornwall, a big favourite with the CAMRA crowd, thanks to its own strong Spingo Ales (IPA, Middle, Bragget and Special) brewed in the oldest ale-house brewery in the country. The 'Old Blue', as it's known, was a monastic rest home, before becoming a tavern in the 15th century. The quaint thatched pub is a genuine, atmospheric local, featuring an old-fashioned barrel alley with a bar either side, dark wood, history, open fires in the winter, an 18th-century skittle alley, and a behind-the-bar brewery which you can visit.

We've already recommended the **Halzephron Inn** (www.halzephron-inn.co.uk, ☎ 01326 240406) as a great place to eat, but the former smuggler's hang-out is also a friendly watering hole with low beams, lots of cosy corners, outdoor tables for sunny days, and a choice of ales including Sharps Doom Bar and Halzephron Gold. Described as *'generously hopped with hints of passion fruit'*, the latter is brewed especially for the pub by the **Organic Brewhouse** at Cury Cross Lane in Mullion (☎ 01326 241555). The first in Britain to brew only organic ales, the one-man microbrewery produces Charlie's Pride, Wolf Rock, Serpentine and Lizard Point ales, all using fresh malt and whole hops. You can try a pint of Lizard Point or, another bespoke-original, Witch Ball at the **Witch Ball Inn** in Lizard village (☎ 01326 290662; www.witchball.co.uk). For atmosphere, local colour, seafaring history and good food you can't beat the **Cadgwith Cove Inn** (☎ 01326 290513; www.cadgwithcoveinn.com).

Visitor Information

Tourist information centres: Helston Tourist Information Centre, the only one on the Lizard, has now closed, but a limited service is provided by Helston Customer Services Office, Isaac House, Tyacke Road TR13 8RR, ☎ 01209 614000. Open Mon–Fri, 9am–4.30pm (Wed, 10am–4.30pm). Some information is also provided by Helston Folk Museum on Market Place, ☎ 01326 564027.

Hospitals with A&E: Community Hospital, Meneage Road, Helston TR13 8DR, ☎ 01326 435800 has a minor injury unit (open daily 8am–8pm). The nearest hospitals with 24-hour A&E is West Cornwall, St Clare Street, Penzance (30 minutes), ☎ 01736 874000.

Doctors: Helston Medical Centre, Trelawney Road, Helston TR13 8AU, ☎ 01326 572637; Helston Health Centre, Trengrouse Way, Helston TR13 8AX, ☎ 01326 435869.

Pharmacies: Steven Hall Pharmacy, 77 Meneage Street, Helston TR13 8RB, ☎ 01326 561400; Alliance Pharmacy, Churchtown, Mullion TR12 7BY, ☎ 01326 240238.

Police station: Helston Police Station, Godolphin Road, Helston TR13 8QE, ☎ 0845 2777444.

Supermarkets: The only ones on the Lizard are Tesco on Clodgey Lane in Helston (TR13 8PJ) and the new Sainsbury's (also on Clodgey Lane, TR13 0QA). There's a licensed convenience store in Mullion village, Hatton's Spar, ☎ 01326 240271.

Car hire: Castle Green Garage, Castle Green, Helston TR13 8EZ, ☎ 01326 564411; www.helstonclassiccarhire.co.uk; Hertz Rent A Car, Trenethick Business Park, Water-Ma-Trout, Helston TR13 0LW, ☎ 01326 574873.

Bike hire: Lizard Bike Hire, Mullion, ☎ 01326 241613.

Local taxis: Abba Cabs, Helston, ☎ 01326 573000; Auto Cabs, Helston, ☎ 01326 573773; Peters Taxis, Helston, ☎ 01326 561139.

LIZARD EAST AND THE HELFORD RIVER

The scenery around the Helford River could have been dreamed up for an old-fashioned children's story book. Its tiny lanes weave in and out of dense wooded valleys, beneath arches of foliage, from one picture-postcard village to another. Clusters of thatched cottages sit among fields of spring flowers. At the river's edge, forests of oaks dip branches into their own watery reflections. And though summers can be busy, you can always find a place where you can hear nothing but ducks and grey herons, droning insects and the put-put-put of a single motor dinghy, and smell nothing but marsh gas and wild garlic.

Tucked into the right armpit of the Lizard Peninsula, the 4-mile tidal estuary, or *ria* (it's actually a drowned valley), runs from the boat-building quay at Gweek down to Falmouth Bay, passing en route a complexity of creeks and inlets: to the north, Porthnavas and Polwheveral, to the south, Mawgan, Gillian and Frenchman's Creek (the inspiration behind Daphne Du Maurier's novel of the same name). South of the cliffs of Nare Point, at the mouth of the river, a succession of beaches line the Lizard's east coast.

Inland, you can explore the ancient woodland of Trelowarren Estate, the UK's leading green resort. By the sea, you can hunt for basalt and serpentine on Coverak beach. The main attraction around here is nature, and in a sense there is nothing else; in one of the best places in Cornwall for messing about in boats, it's all about the great outdoors.

WHAT TO SEE AND DO

Explore the **Helford River** on foot, by boat, bike or by car. Just wander around as the mood takes you; every bend in the river, every hilltop view, every village is a delight. The prettiest and, in the summer, one of the busiest, villages is **Helford** itself. Traffic-free from mid-March to the end of October, it's a huddled community of thatched cottages, sitting on the water's edge, or on either side of a shallow ford. Hard to imagine now, but it was once an important port, with ships bringing rum, lace and tobacco from across the channel. Now, its only industry is tourism, and though it's a hub of boat-related activity in the summer, it virtually empties in the winter.

Helford is a good starting point for some of the excellent riverside walks. On the South West Coast Path, you can follow the riverbank to the little harbour at **St Anthony-in-Meneage** with its stone cottages and candlelit church. From there, you can continue, along the road that runs alongside **Gillian Creek** up to the charming hilltop village at **Manaccan**, where a fig tree grows out of the walls of the church. On a longer walk, you can cover river valley, woodland, farmland and Lizard coast on a 4.5-mile route from Gillian to **Porthallow** (known as *P'raller* to the locals) either across country or on the coast path, via **Nare Point**: at the mouth of the Helford, the perfect place to watch ships slip in and out of Falmouth Bay. The Helford's creeks

Trelowarren Estate

reach into countryside north and south of its drowned valley. Above **Mawgan Creek**, the **Trelowarren Estate**, home to the Vyvyan family since 1427, offers 1,000 acres of woodland walks (open to the public between April and October). Surrounding the Vyvyans' Georgian mansion, the grounds include a Rococo pleasure gardens (currently under restoration), the Lizard's highest point and the curious **Halliggye Fogou**, a tunnel-like burial chamber dating from the late Iron Age.

To the north of the river, **Port Navas**, a former granite-shipping port tucked up Porthnavas Creek, is a haven of holiday homes for the yacht-club set. And **Constantine** (beyond Polwheveral, where the quarries were) is a well-heeled village with a heritage centre, local history museum and arts centre. To the south of the Helford, the largest village is **St Keverne**, a charming little place with shops and pubs arranged around a central square. St Keverne's Church of St Akeveranus was once voted the best church to visit in Britain. Some of the SS *Mohegan* shipwreck victims - lost when the ship hit the treacherous Manacles rocks in 1898 - are buried in the churchyard.

On the water

The Helford is internationally recognised as one of the best sailing areas in Britain, with sleek yachts sliding in and out of the estuary, and there are some seriously expensive houses around here. But you don't have to be rich, or even to have a boat of your own, to enjoy a little of what life is all about in this watery neck of the woods. At the very least you can cross the river via a pedestrian ferry service between Helford and **Helford Passage** on the northern bank (where there's a small sandy beach, a few posh shops, and the Ferry Boat Inn). In continuous use since the 15th century, the ferry makes the 10-minute crossing on demand (or by request out of hours) between April and the end of October. The ferry's operator, **Helford River Boats** (based in a kiosk next to the Ferry Boat Inn) also runs the Garden Ferry, which does a continuous round trip from Helford village, Helford Passage, Trebah Gardens, Gendurgan Garden and Budock Vean Hotel. You can also hire a variety of self-drive boats, by the hour, the day or the week. And if you are bringing your own boat, Helford River Boats can arrange moorings.

HELFORD RIVER BOATS, The Kiosk, Helford Passage TR11 5LB; ☎ 01326 250770; www.helford-river-boats.co.uk. Ferry crossings on demand, from Easter to Oct: £5.50 return, children £2 (under-4s free). Garden Ferry service £5 return; self-drive motor boats from £40 per hour (or £420 per week), rowing boats £15 per hour (£150 per week), sports kayaks £10 per hour (or £150 per week).

Boats at Helford

SAILAWAY ST ANTHONY, Manaccan TR12 6JW; ☎ 01326 231357; www.stanthony.co.uk. Kayaks from £10.50 per hour (£115 per week), 15–18ft motorboats and Longboat day cruisers from £24.50 per hour (£231 per week), sailing dinghies, from £18.50 per hour (£178.50 per week) and row boats from £13.50 (£133 per week); sailing tuition from £47 per two hours.

You can also hire boats from **Sailaway St Anthony** at Manaccan. A choice of boats includes chugging diesel launches (suitable for families and groups), longboat cruisers, Toppers and Lasers, rowing boats and kayaks. To hire a sailing boat, you will need to show that you have some experience, though tuition is offered for beginners.

Once on the water you can explore the creeks and the riverbank villages, enjoying the scenery or, as Daphne du Maurier put it, '*ploughing in and out of the shadows, a prawning net in hand*'. You will see the Oyster Farm at the entrance to Porthnavas Creek, the eel grass beds off Grebe, the river beaches at Durgan and Bar, Merthen Wood, Tremayne Quay and dozens of other fellow boaters.

Thatched cottages at Helford Village

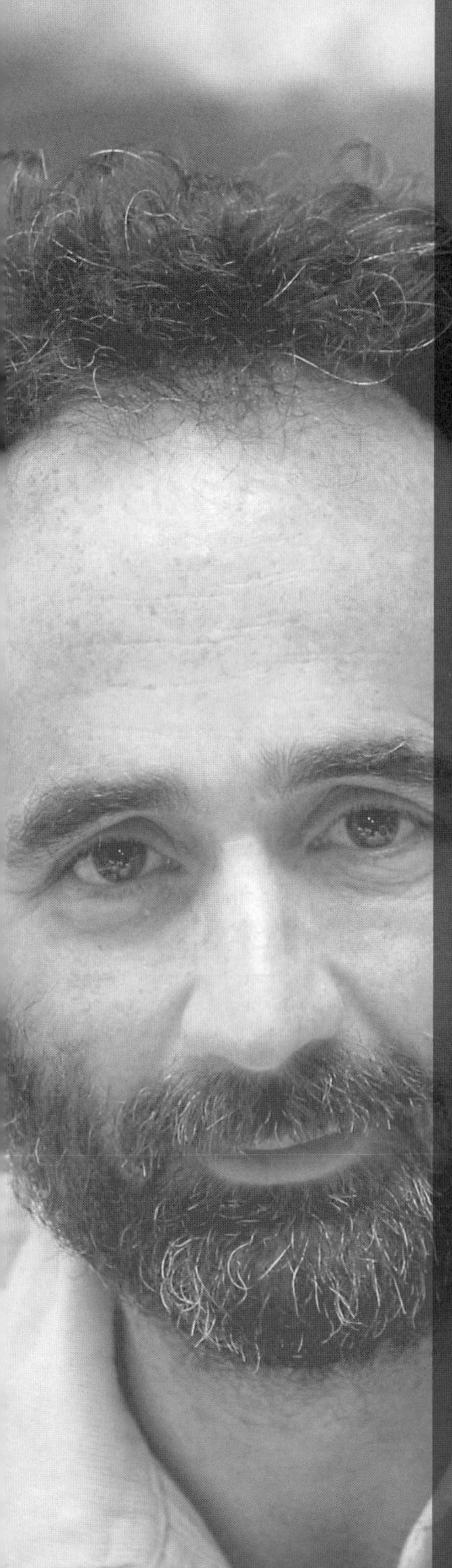

LOCAL KNOWLEDGE

Sir Ferrers Vyvyan inherited the Lizard's Trelowarren Estate in 1997 (his family have been there since the 15th century). He has since undertaken an extensive programme of estate restoration, including the creation of a zero-carbon, eco-friendly holiday village – now one of the world's greenest resorts. In 2008, at the age of 48, Ferrers was appointed High Sheriff of Cornwall one of the youngest people to hold the post.

Favourite restaurant: South in Manaccan. It's in a converted antiques shop, nicely gothicised, very clean and contemporary. They serve lots of local fish and beef, and it's very smart and professional.

Favourite pub: For me the quirkier the better, and one of my favourites is the bar at the Cadgwith Hotel. It's always full of local people, there's no pretentious food, and overlooks a little beach at Cadgwith Cove – perfect.

Quirkiest attraction: The Dry Tree standing stone on Goonhilly Down. It's right next to the satellite station, where five parishes meet. It's a bit spooky because they used to hang people there, but it puts you in touch with prehistoric landscape.

Favourite café: Roskilly's in St Keverne. Or Polpear Café, right on Lizard Point. It's a great place to watch a storm, have a flapjack and a cup of tea, while ships scud around the headland, in and out of Falmouth Bay.

Favourite pasty: The Horse and Jockey Bakery in Helston. They are made with short crust, not flaky, filled with skirt not steak – all very important in a good pasty.

Favourite activity: Swimming in the sea. When we can we go to Lankidden. One of the Lizard's hidden beaches, it's very hard to find, and at the end of a long walk you have to get down the last bit by rope.

Why here: Nowhere else I know, anywhere, has such a varied landscape, from downs and beaches to hidden river valleys. Even in high summer, it's very easy to get away from people.

> **COVERACK WINDSURFING CENTRE,** Cliff Cottage, Sunny Corner, Coverack TR12 6SX; ☎ 01326 280939; www.coverack.co.uk; 2–14 day courses, Apr–Oct 30.

On the coast

With its sand, rock pools and safe bathing, the best local beach is **Coverack**. A river runs down to the beach, and there are shops, restaurants, thatched cottages and a small picturesque harbour; and aside from all the usual seaside activities, the beach can provide an elementary geology lesson: just sort through all those pretty pebbles and decide which are made of basalt or gabbro, and which are troctolite or serpentine. A seafront information board helps identify them. Coverack is also home to one of Cornwall's best windsurfing schools. **Coverack Windsurfing Centre** offers holidays and courses for all levels, providing all the equipment, including dryland simulators for novices.

Mears Beach, a 10-minutes walk heading south towards Chynhalls Point, is where the locals like to swim; there are no facilities. The east Lizard coast is well known to divers, particularly drawn to the so-called **Manacles Rocks**, a treacherous reef, a mile off Godrevy Cove. **Porthkerris Cove** a gritty little beach of derelict loading jetties near a former quarry, is said to provide some of the best shore dives in Britain.

Gardens

On the south bank of the Helford, **Trebah** is one of the most magical gardens in Cornwall, not least because its 26 acres of subtropical plants slope gently down to its own private beach. Trebah (which means House on the Bay), was first recorded in the 11th century as home of the Bishop of Exeter. It belonged to clergy and yeoman farmers until 1831, when it was bought by the quaker Fox family of Falmouth.

Charles Fox was responsible for creating the pleasure garden; so meticulous, he instructed his head gardener to construct a rudimentary scaffolding tower to represent each tree before it was planted. A garden boy would be sent up the tower with a white flag while Charles, armed with a megaphone and telescope, gave orders ('left a bit... right a bit') from an attic window. A ravine garden, run by the Trebah Garden Trust, it features a tinkling stream which cascades over rocky waterfalls, an extraordinary Gunnera Passage (gunnera being a large otherworld plant also known as 'giant rhubarb') and glades of sub-tropical ferns. It has some record-beaters including the tallest magnolia (at 29.16m). And for the kids, there is a Tarzan's Camp adventure playground. Whatever time of year you visit, it looks stunning, but go in the spring for the rhododendrons, in the summer for the blue and white hydrangeas. Make a day of it, picnic on the beach or have lunch in the Planters café.

> **TREBAH GARDEN, TREBAH,** Mawnan Smith TR11 5JZ; ☎ 0136252200; www.trebah-garden.co.uk. Summer prices (Mar to Oct): adults £8, seniors £7.70, children £2.75 (under-5s free); winter prices: adults £4.40, seniors £3.85, children £1.10; open daily, 10am–5pm.

Close to Trebah (walking distance), The National Trust's **Glendurgan Garden** is another wonderful sheltered valley garden with views of the Helford and access to a beach. The highlight is the laurel maze, the 'Giant's Stride' rope swing, and sandy beach at **Durgan**. Actually, there are two beaches, both pebbly-shingle, one known locally as Grebe, and both open to the public. A free National Trust car park is a 10-minute walk to the mouth-of-the-river village of Durgan.

GLENDURGAN GARDEN, Mawnan Smith, TR11 5JZ; ☎ 01326 252020; www.nationaltrust.org.uk. Entry: adults £6.30, children £3.20, family £15.90; open 10.30am–5.30pm; open Feb to Oct, Tues–Sat, in Aug, Mon–Sat.

Wet weather

A good option is the **Cornwall Craft Centre**, a converted Georgian stable block in the grounds of the Trelowarren Estate. You can see the work of the Crafts Association, in a permanent but ever-changing selling exhibition of ceramics, jewellery, furniture, textiles and other handmade things of beauty.

CORNWALL CRAFTS ASSOCIATION, Trelowarren TR12 6AF; ☎ 01326 221567; www.cornwallcrafts.co.uk. Admission free; open daily Mar to Nov, 10.30am–5pm.

What to do with children

Aside from making great ice creams, **Roskilly's at Tregallast Barton** offers a day-out on a working organic farm. The 40-acre farm welcomes visitors to watch the cows being milked, talk to the calves, wander around the ponds, the meadows, the orchards and the Wetland Withy Woods. The farm supports a free-grazing Jersey herd, donkeys, ducks and moorhens.

ROSKILLY'S ORGANIC FARM, Tregellast Barton, St Keverne TR12 6NX; ☎ 01326 280479; www.roskillys.co.uk. Admission and parking: free; open all day, every day.

Just outside Gweek, the **National Seal Sanctuary**, turned 50 in 2008 and is dedicated to the rescue, rehabilitation and release of seals. It began in 1958 when founder Ken 'the Seal Doctor' Jones took pity on a abandoned two-day-old grey seal pup that couldn't be persuaded to return to the sea. He has since rescued around 2,000 lost pups. The permanent residents or 'guests' include grey seals, common seals, Cape Fur seals and Patagonian and Californian sea lions.

NATIONAL SEAL SANCTUARY, Gweek TR12 6UG; ☎ 01326 221361; www.sealsanctuary.co.uk. Entry: adults £11.50, children (3–14) £8.50; open daily from 10am (closing times vary).

Ice cream from Roskilly's Organic Farm

 Entertainment

Theatre and cinema

The only venue in the region is the **Tolmen Centre**, on Fore Street in Constantine (01326 341353; www.constantinecornwall.com). A community arts centre cum theatre, it holds regular film nights in the summer, showing classics and golden oldies.

Special events

August is regatta season around the Helford River. One of the largest is Helford Regatta, organised by **Helford River Sailing Club**, but there are regattas at Coverack and Port Navas. Other events, take the form of local community customs: at low tide on Good Friday, families turn out en masse to do a bit of 'trigging' (collecting cockles) from the muddy river banks around Bar Beach, Gillan and Treath. And on **Christmas Day**, around 50 or so brave souls do a charity swim in the sea at Coverack harbour, cheered on by a large crowd.

The best... PLACES TO STAY

HOTEL

Budock Vean Hotel

Mawnan Smith, TR11 5LG
☎ 01326 250 288
www.budockvean.co.uk

Set in 65 acres of subtropical gardens right on the Helford River, this traditional four-star hotel, or 'resort', has a health spa, indoor pool, comfortable lounges for hanging out, snooker room and cocktail bar, a nine-hole golf course and a private foreshore.

Price: B&B from £82–£169 per person.

B&B

The Hen House

Tregarne, Mannacan TR12 6EW
☎ 01326 280236
www.thehenhouse-cornwall.co.uk

Award-winning guest house at the top of the Porthallow Valley, has ethnic-style rooms in a former piggery and hen house, plus wholesome breakfasts, holistic therapies, tai chi classes, a dog house, 2 acres of flower meadow and a brood of resident chickens.

Price: B&B from £80–£90 for a double.

The best... PLACES TO STAY

Old Temperance House

The Square, St Keverne TR12 6NA
☎ 01326 280986
www.oldtemperancehouse.co.uk

A pretty Georgian house in St Keverne's village square, with four guest rooms (Baileys, Champagne, Cointreau and Pimms) all with fresh sunny décor, en suite baths or power showers, and Wi-Fi. A one-bed self-catering cottage (Ginentonic) is also available.

Price: B&B from £82 for a double.

Tremayne House

St Martin-in-Meneage TR12 6DA
☎ 01326 231618
www.tremaynehouse.com

A member of Wolsey Lodges (all private houses with guest rooms), Tremayne is elegant, Georgian and tucked away in 3 acres of wooded riverbank. The rooms are traditional, but the beds are super-comfortable, the food is fresh, generous and home-cooked. Bring your own wine.

Price: B&B from £45 per person.

SELF-CATERING

Trelowarren

Trelowarren, Mawgan TR12 6AF
☎ 01326 222105
www.trelowarren.co.uk

A community of historic cottages and new green-build eco lodges, featuring biomass heating, rainwater harvesting, low-energy appliances and organic paints, Trelowarren is deemed one of the world's leading green resorts. The houses are luxurious as well as responsible, and guests have use of the estate's gardens, woodlands and heated outdoor pool.

Price: from £465–£2,650 for a week.

The Sea House

Coverack, Lizard Peninsula Holiday Cottages
☎ 07867 551137
www.lizardholidaycottages.co.uk

Not your usual twee holiday cottage, this was built in 2000 and designed to look like a Cape Cod sea house. An upside-down layout puts the living space on the top floor to capitalise on the ocean views. There are three bedrooms, including a master double with its own balcony.

Price: from £462–£1,245 for a week.

UNUSUAL

Goongillings Farm

Constantine TR11 5RP
☎ 01326 340630
www.goongillings.co.uk

Stay in a restored antique 'showman's wagon' (gypsy caravan). You get your own little meadow corner, a double bed, and camping loo. Showers are in the adjacent summerhouse. The organic farm, half a mile from Constantine, has woodland and a tidal quay.

Price: £200 for a week, £30 for a night (sleeps two + small child).

Lovelane Caravans

Tregallast Barton Farm, Saint Keverne TR12 6NX
☎ 01326 340406
www.lovelanecaravans.com

From an array of classic caravans (the last word in retro glamping) choose from a pink 1958 Sterling tourer, a glitzy 1970s fairground caravan (complete with chandeliers) or a vintage Airstream. The vans are all kitted out with appropriate stuff (from kitchen utensils to knick-knacks) and set in glorious countryside.

Price: from £180 for three nights to £435 for a week.

The best... FOOD AND DRINK

A high propensity of well-heeled visitors and a complete absence of supermarkets has helped spawn a niche-market foodie economy and provided the impetus behind home-grown but nationally known brands such as Roskilly's at St Kerverne, Cornish Sea Salt (www.cornishseasalt.co.uk) at Porthkerris and the Lizard Leaf Company (www.lizardleaves.com) at Gear Farm, which supplies salads leaves, field crops and fresh herbs to restaurants and gastro pubs all over Cornwall. Clams and oysters are among the fruits of the river. And quality ingredients is a selling point for many the good local restaurants, cafés and pubs.

Staying in

Roskilly's famous artisan ice creams (www.roskillys.co.uk) includes 40 delicious flavours and can be bought direct from Tregallast Barton Farm at St Keverne, alongside jams, chutneys, apple juice, frozen yoghurts and mustard. At St Martin, near Mawgan, **Gear Farm Shop** (☎ 01326 221150) supplies organic produce (meat and vegetables), ready meals and delicious steak pasties. The best local butcher is **Retallack's** in St Keverne (☎ 01326 280252). A favourite village shop is the deli-style **Manaccan Stores** in Manaccan (☎ 01326 231365), which sells ready-meals from Helston-based Caroline's Country Cooking, and Vicky's Breads (see page 258).

The Helford River's **Duchy of Cornwall Oyster Farm** (☎ 01326 340210; www.duchyoysterfarm.com) at Port Navas is managed by Ben Wright, co-owner of Wright Brothers Oyster Merchants (which also runs the Oyster and Porter House in London's Borough Market). The molluscs, which have been farmed here for centuries, are collected in August by iron-frame dredges. **Porthallow Vineyard** (☎ 01326 280050) produces robust port-like wines made from flowers, vegetables and honey. There is a **farmers' market** in the parish hall at Keverne, first Wednesday of the month, 9.30am–12.30pm.

Takeaway

If you see a notice at Manaccan saying 'Fish and Chips every Tuesday, 4.30am–7.30pm' don't assume that this is some lazy, crazy chippie that only opens once a week. You will find similar notices in St Keverne, Ruan Major and Gweek. For this is the **Rosevear mobile fish and chip shop**, run by Sid and Dorothy Rosevear. Objective One funding in 2003 helped them expand by buying the means to grow their own spuds. In Coverack, look out for **Elizabeth's** thatched cottage near the harbour, well-known locally for pasties and fruit pies baked in her own kitchen.

EATING OUT

FINE DINING

The New Yard Restaurant

Trelowarren Estate, Mawgan TR12 6AF
☎ 01326 221595
www.trelowarren.co.uk

The best place to eat on the Lizard with one of the grandest approaches (a long wooded drive), and the finest wine lists outside London. In a former carriage house, it's posh without being snooty, cosy but contemporary. And award-winning chef Olly Jackson (two AA rosettes) sources 90% of his ingredients from within 10 miles of the estate. The restaurant also serves morning coffee, lunches and cream teas. Three-course set dinner from £19.50 per head; Sunday lunch, £17.95 for two courses. Evening bookings essential. Closed Sunday evening.

RESTAURANT/CAFÉ

The Greenhouse Restaurant

6, High Street, St Keverne TR12 1NN
☎ 01326 280800
www.thegreenhouse-stkeverne.co.uk

Modern rustic cooking is the mainstay of this attractive village restaurant, which cooks up simple but delicious food (hand-raised pies, terrines, fresh bread, fish, game, Cornish cheeses and home-made desserts and ice creams) using organic produce, where possible, local and seasonal. Vegetarian and gluten-free dishes available. Three courses cost around £22. Dinner from Tuesday to Sat, and Sun lunch.

South

Manaccan TR12 6HR
☎ 01326 231331
www.south-cafe.co.uk

In Manaccan village, this attractive eatery is a really good all-rounder offering lunches, afternoon teas, dinners, a children's menu, a wine list, woodburner in winter and a courtyard for sunny days. The daily specials designed to make the best use of local, seasonal produce. Evening dishes cost from £8.

The Lifeboat House Café & Bistro

Coverack TR126PE
☎ 01326 280899
www.lifeboathouse.com

As the name suggests, it's Coverack's old lifeboat station and perched on a slipway above the harbour, with wonderful views from the terrace. Fish and local seafood is the speciality of the house, but steaks and vegetarian dishes are also featured on the menu.

GASTRO PUB

The New Inn

Manaccan TR12 6HA
☎ 01326 231323
www.newinnmanaccan.co.uk

Good quality pub food at reasonable prices (lunch costs around £7, evening meals costs around £10), in an atmospheric thatched pub. The menu features crusty-bread sandwiches, soups (eg crab bisque), fish, salads and other fresh-cooked dishes. The pub welcomes children, dogs and muddy boots and there are tables in the garden.

CAFÉ

The Croust House

Tregellast Barton Farm, St Keverne TR12 6NX
☎ 01326 280479
www.roskillys.co.uk

In an old milking parlour and calving shed, on the farm best known for Roskilly's ice cream, this licensed café serves home-made pizzas, pies, pasties, salads, cakes and even ciders. You can eat inside (by a log fire in the winter) or outside in the former dairy yard. Open Sun-Wed, 9am–6pm, Thurs–Sat, 9am–9pm.

Drinking

The two best-known pubs in the area sit on opposite sides of the Helford River – at either end of the ferry-boat crossing. On the southern bank, the **Shipwrights's Arms** (☎ 01326 231235) at Helford is a delightful thatched pub with a terrace of outdoor seating right on the river, and a dark, low-beamed bar serving draught beers (Whitbread Castle Eden and Flowers). The fact that you can only get there by boat or on foot in the summer, when the village is closed to traffic, adds to its charm. On the north bank, the **Ferryboat Inn** (☎ 01326 250625) has a deck of seating right on the water at Helford Passage, and is a great spot for watching the world go by while downing a pint of St Austell ale.

The Gweek Inn at Gweek (☎ 01326 221502; www.gweekinn.co.uk) reckons it has the Lizard's largest selection of real ales on tap. On the coast the **Five Pilchards** at Porthallow has an interesting collection of shipwreck relics and offers a seafood-based bar menu, local brewery ales (Sharps Doom Bar, Abbott Bitter) and regular guest ales. **The White Hart** in the Square at St Keverne (☎ 01326 280325; www.whitehartcornwall.co.uk), serves hand-pumped real ales. And for great seaviews, try the bar at the **Paris Hotel** at Coverack (☎ 01326 280258; www.pariscoverack.com), where you can catch the setting sun from outdoor tables within yards of the quay.

Visitor Information

Doctors: St Keverne Health Centre, Polventon Parc, St Keverne TR12 6PB, ☎ 01326 280761; Mawnan Surgery, Goldmartin Square, Mawnan Smith TR11 5EP, ☎ 01326 250861.

Supermarkets: On the south side of the Helford, the nearest is Tesco, Clodgey Lane, Helston TR13 8PJ. To the north Tesco, Killigrew Street, Falmouth TR1 3PQ, ☎ 0845 6779267.

Parking: Narrow roads and close-knit villages make parking tricky. Helford, for example is closed to vehicles from March to September. In Coverack, there's a car park at North Corner (from 40p for one hour). At Helford Passage, there's a pay-and-display on the hill before you reach the village.

Internet: Online Centre at The Wave café (next to the Post Office) in Coverak, internet access available daily, 10am–11am, and 3pm–4pm, £1 per half hour.

Useful websites: www.helfordriver moorings.co.uk; moorings and anchorage, piloting, and Helford river etiquette); www.helfordriver.net (a general guide to river valley villages and local wildlife); www.helfordmarineconservation.co.uk (all about the region's marine life).

Village stores and post offices: A dying breed elsewhere in rural Britain, but here in the B-road backwaters, the local village shop and Post Office is a lifeline. You will find them at Helford, Manaccan and Coverack. St Keverne has a Londis.

River moorings: The Moorings Office is next to the Ferry Boat Inn in Helford Passage, ☎ 01326 250749; open daily, 9am–5pm.

Car hire: Alanco Motor Services, Goldmartin Garage, Mawnan Smith TR11 5EW, ☎ 01326 250394, www.alanco.co.uk.

Local taxis: Cove Cars Taxi Service, Coverack, ☎ 07980 814058.

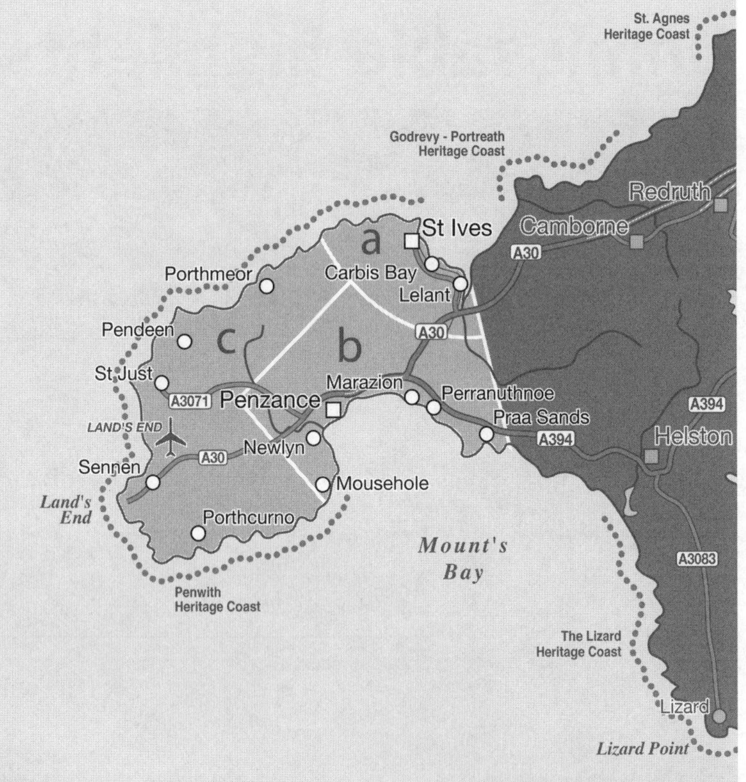

7 Far West

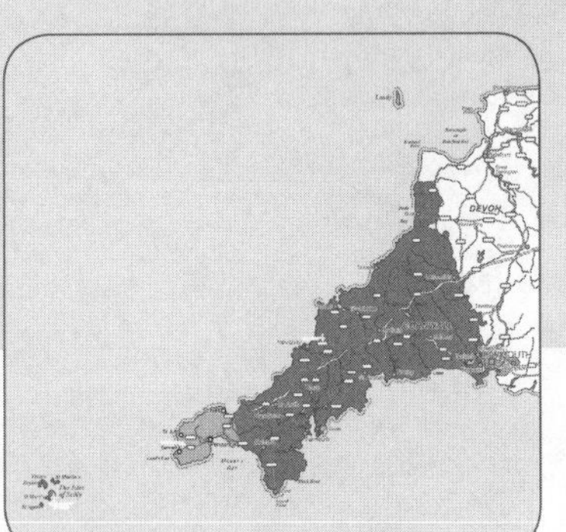

a. St Ives and Carbis Bay
b. Penzance and Mount's Bay
c. Land's End and surrounds

Unmissable highlights

01 Walk across the sea to St Michael's Mount, the iconic island castle-on-a-rock, p. 296

02 Be inspired by Tate St Ives, where art galleries and architecture hit the beach, p. 280

03 Discover the white sands of Porthcurno – the unlikely birthplace of global communications, p. 311

04 Immerse yourself in the jazz-age at the Art Deco Jubilee Lido on Penzance seafront, p. 283

05 Leave the car, and board the St Ives Bay Line, one of Britain's most scenic branch-line railways, p. 277

06 Dine on seafood Australian-style, on the sun decks of the Porthminster Beach café, p. 288

07 Surf the waves at Sennen Cove, within skanking distance of Land's End, p. 310

08 Immerse yourself in old Penzance, on a stroll down historic Chapel Street, p. 291

09 Delve into the underground world of Geevor Mine, where mining comes to life, p. 308

10 Hang out at the Gurnards Head, first walk to the headland and then to the pub, p. 316

FAR WEST

Penwith, or *Penwyth* (meaning 'extremity') is as far west as you can go, the end of the line. Even from the Cornwall-Devon border, it's a long trek (another hour and a half, at least) but the wild beauty of this nose-shaped Atlantic peninsula make it worth every mile.

Barely 10 miles across from coast to coast, it offers two must-do Cornish towns, St Ives and Penzance, set in an extraordinarily diverse landscape: to the south wooded valleys and fields of springtime daffodils, gardens of camellias, winding down to miniature fishing harbours; to the west rough heathland and high granite cliffs; to the north crescents of yellow sand, a froth of surf and Godrevy lighthouse in the distance.

Stretching from Lelant to Praa Sands, Penwith's 60 miles of rugged coast lays claim to some of the best known landmarks in the west: Tate St Ives, St Michael's Mount, Newlyn harbour, the Minack Theatre and Land's End. Inland Penwith Moor claims the most concentrated collections of ancient monuments in Europe. Add smugglers, tinners, mining relics, boats, beaches and, in recent years, some of the best restaurants in Cornwall. Nowhere else in the county packs so much into such a small space. The exposed Land's End coast can be bleak, windswept and drenched in sea mists. But when the sun's out, it's all brilliant colour: ferns, pink sea thrift and mauve heathers, dashed with yellow gorse, the white-fringed breakers of a peacock sea. Facing due west, across the Atlantic, from the top of a rocky headland, the sunsets are truly magnificent.

ST IVES AND CARBIS BAY

One of the West Country's top tourist hotspots, St Ives is the complete package – everything you could possibly want in a Cornish seaside town, plus waves, cliff walks, wonderful scenery and Tate St Ives: there is a proper Cornish fishing harbour, its granite piers jutting into the blue Atlantic waters of St Ives Bay; a tight-knit community of white-washed fishermen's cottages; swathes of sandy beach tucked into sheltered bays either side of the so-called 'Island' (a mini-peninsula topped by a little granite chapel). 'Downalong' is all narrow cobbled streets that dive down steps and alleyways (look out for Salubrious Place and Teetotal Street). From 'Upalong', with its terraced rows of solid Victorian houses, the views are sublime.

Founded in the 6th century by St Ia, an Irish missionary princess who arrived, so the story goes, on a floating leaf, St Ives was built on pilchard fishing and tin mining. When the first tourists arrived with the railway in the 1870s, hotels sprung up along the clifftops, spreading into Carbis Bay. Many of the early visitors were painters. And by the 1900s, St Ives was a thriving artists' colony, a little corner of bohemia which continued to flourish until the late 1970s. The opening of the Tate St Ives in 1993 kick-started a renaissance but what really hits the spot for most visitors is the urban beach experience: the surf-and-sand holiday with fashion, culture and boutique hotels on the doorstep. The only downside, perhaps, is the town's popularity. In high season, you can hardly move for people shuffling along Fore Street, the salt air reeking of pasty.

As a general rule, St Ives is best-served off season, and best explored on foot. And for many of its overnight guests, it also best seen from a distance. Neighbouring Carbis Bay may look like a New World suburb but it has a good hotels and a great beach within walking distance of St Ives Harbour. A mile or two further east, the little village of Lelant offers a quieter, more traditional alternative.

WHAT TO SEE AND DO

By the sea

The obvious thing to do is to hit the beach, and in St Ives there are four stunning beaches to choose from and two more within hiking distance. For surf, head for **Porthmeor**, one of Cornwall's favourite winter surfing beaches, it's just below the Tate Gallery, offering fine yellow sand, a beach café and the BSA-approved **St Ives Surf School** (☎ 01736 793366).

Porthgwidden is the baby of the town's beaches – smaller, safer, more sheltered, it's tucked into a bay between the Island headland and the harbour. Below the St Ives Museum and the remnants of Wheal Dream tin mine, secluded **Bamaluz** is barely there at high tide, but provides shade and shelter in a tiny, rocky cove which occasionally offers good surf. The **Harbour Beach** (right in the thick of things, below a curve of seafront shops and restaurants) is a good place to sunbathe, paddle, picnic or just sit on the sand and watch the world go by when the tide's out. And to the east of the town, popular **Porthminster** (just below St Ives's branch-line station) offers a Blue Flag beach, great for families, complete with beach huts, mini golf, a shop and café.

Just over a mile east of St Ives, the big and beautiful sandy beach at **Carbis Bay** is one of the area's favourite beaches, and offers safe bathing in clean waters, a café-takeaway, and a shop with deck-chair hire. A good way to travel between beaches is to take the **St Ives Bay Line** train which takes three minutes from St Ives station to Carbis Bay, or seven minutes from Carbis to Lelant Saltings.

ST IVES BAY LINE, First Great Western; ☎ 08457 000 125; www.firstgreatwestern.co.uk. Ranger tickets: adults £4, children £2; cheap day return: £2.90/£3. Services run every half-hour in summer (times vary).

An alternative is to walk: using the coast path, Porthminster to Carbis Bay is an easy 20 minutes along coast footpath between the railway track and the sea. At Carbis Bay, you can continue onto **Lelant Church**, a 30–45-minute walk (1.25 miles) along a much narrower, prettier, cliff path, which winds around the Carrack Gladden headland, through woodland, and lush subtropical gardens to **Porth Kidney** beach. From the headland, the view across this vast stretch of sand and dunes, around the Hayle Estuary to Godrevy is breathtaking. A flat walk through sand dunes (wave at the train as it trundles past) takes you to Lelant's 15th-century church of St Uny, where a cemetery, its lichen-clad granite headstones and garden of brambles and daffodils, meets the manicured greens of the **West Cornwall Golf Club**. The oldest golf club in UK, it's open to non-members, subject to providing a handicap card.

WEST CORNWALL GOLF COURSE, Church Lane, Lelant TR26 3DZ; ☎ 01736 753401; www.westcornwallgolfclub.co.uk. Green fees: weekday £37, or weekend £42; 5-day or 7-day season tickets available.

Out to sea

A variety of boat trips are available from St Ives harbour including daily excursions to **Seal Island** (a little hump of rock, 3 miles west of St Ives, it's home to a colony of Atlantic grey seals). The **St Ives Pleasure Boat Association** run three of St Ives' six pleasure boats. One of them, *The Dolly Pentreath* is a replica of *The Godrevy*, a late 19th-century Cornish fishing lugger built in St Ives in 1993 from plans housed at the British Science Museum.

ST IVES PLEASURE BOAT ASSOCIATION, (Outside the Lifeboat Station); ☎ 0777 300 8000; www.stivesboats.co.uk. Seal Island trips (one hour): adults £10, children (under-14s) £8; fishing trips (two hours): adults £15, (under-14s) £10; Easter to Sept, subject to weather conditions.

There is also good **diving** in the clean, clear waters of St Ives Bay. Around Porthminster reef (or the Carracks), about half a mile south of Porthminster beach, you might see triggerfish Conger Eel and the occasional sunfish among other marine life. Further out, the St Chamond, also known as the 'Train Wreck' (loaded with steam engines, it was sunk in 1918 by a German U-boat) lies on the seabed. As well as the outline of the St Chamond's hull, you can see trains lying on their sides, some of them eerily intact. These and other dives can be organised by **Dive St Ives** (☎ 01736 799229).

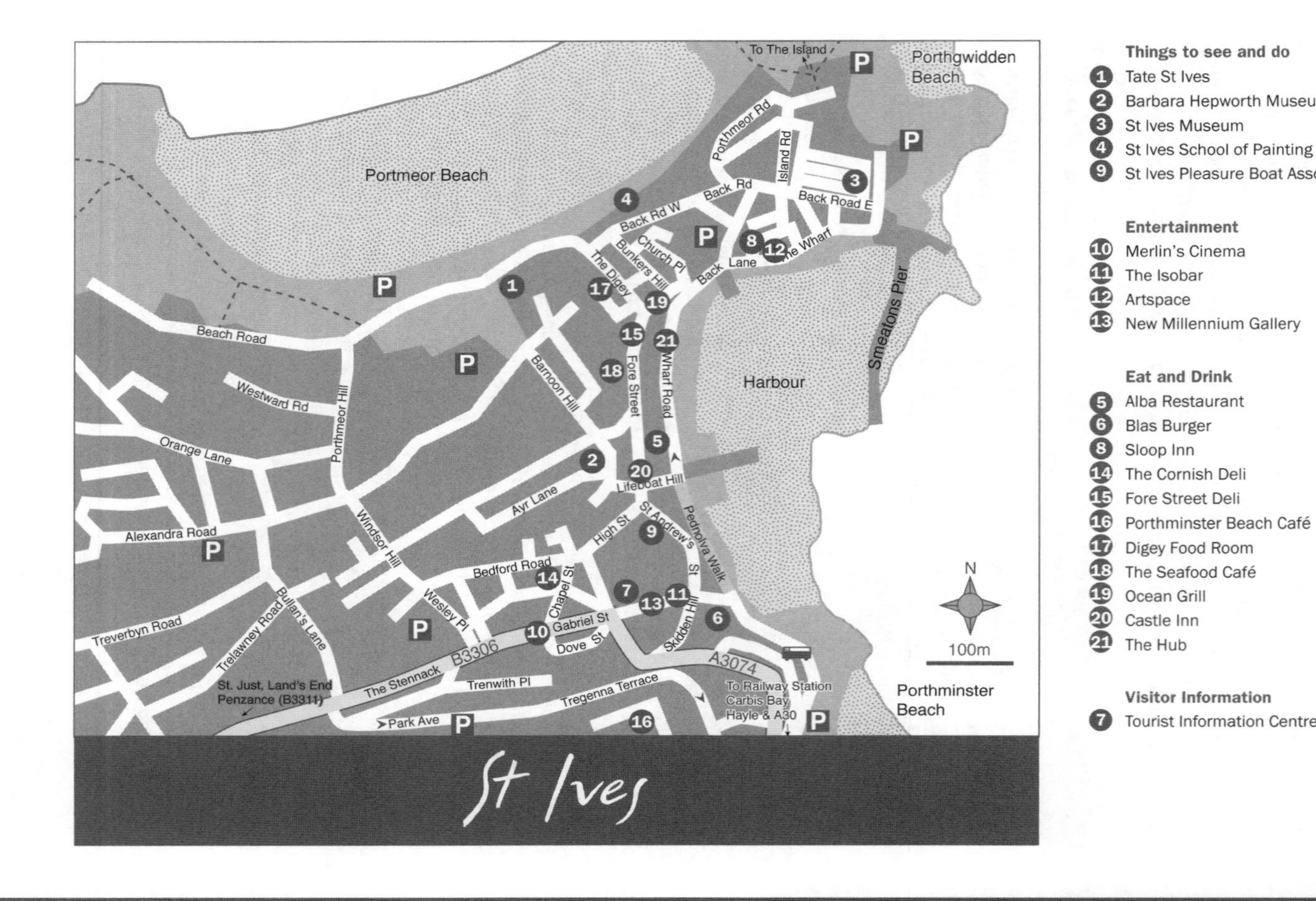

Things to see and do

1. Tate St Ives
2. Barbara Hepworth Museum
3. St Ives Museum
4. St Ives School of Painting
9. St Ives Pleasure Boat Association

Entertainment

10. Merlin's Cinema
11. The Isobar
12. Artspace
13. New Millennium Gallery

Eat and Drink

5. Alba Restaurant
6. Blas Burger
8. Sloop Inn
14. The Cornish Deli
15. Fore Street Deli
16. Porthminster Beach Café
17. Digey Food Room
18. The Seafood Café
19. Ocean Grill
20. Castle Inn
21. The Hub

Visitor Information

7. Tourist Information Centre

Wreck of the Alba

At low tide in St Ives Bay, you can just see the of boiler of the SS *Alba*, the Panamanian steamer, carrying coal from Barry in South Wales, which ran aground in a stormy sea just off Porthmeor beach one January night in 1938. St Ives leapt to the rescue, and quickly evacuated the crew from the stricken ship. But en route to the harbour, the lifeboat, overcome by a powerful wave, capsized and was sent crashing into the Island headland. Hundreds of people turned out to help, risking their lives on treacherous rocks to reach the men. The lifeboat was lost, but its crew and all but two of the 23 *Alba* men survived. You can see memorials to *Alba* engineers Ernest Stipanovi and Gyula Szabo in Barnoon cemetery, overlooking Porthmeor beach.

Galleries

You can't leave town without visiting **Tate St Ives**, even if you just wander down to Porthmeor beach and admire the building: a vision of white geometry, all curves and clean-cut modernism, it is Cornwall's contemporary equivalent of Bexhill's De La Warr Pavilion. Designed by Eldred Evans and David Shalev and built in 1993 on the site of a demolished gasworks just north of Downalong, its inspirations, according to the architects, were part gas cylinder, part Ben Nicholson painting.

Set into a cliff, the building spirals around a glazed central rotunda with a rooftop restaurant which opens onto a terrace. Inside, are light, white galleries with wonderful views (and we don't just mean the paintings). The exhibitions, the collections, reflect the history of St Ives artists, both past and present (Naum Gabo, Peter Lanyon, Alfred Wallis) though the focus is national and, indeed, international.

Tate St Ives on Porthmeor Beach

Change at St Erth for St Ives

Hugging the Atlantic coast, cutting through cliffs and skirting sand dunes, it is said to be the most scenic train ride in branch-line Britain, but First Great Western's *St Ives Bay Line* is as practical as it is pretty. Connecting the town to the mainline Paddington to Penzance route, it helped turn a struggling 19th-century fishing village into a busy holiday resort, and still provides a lifeline for a town that suffers traffic congestion and a shortage of parking.

The last railway in Britain built to Brunel's broad gauge, the line was constructed for the West Cornish Railway between May 1874 and March 1877, a marvel of Victorian engineering that entailed blasting a cutting through the headland cliffs of Carrack Gladden (meaning 'rocks on the brink') and building a four-arch viaduct across the Carbis Valley. The first service chuffed out of St Erth's station, steamed around the western edge of the Hayle Estuary, to Lelant Satlings and Carbis Bay, before swinging into St Ives station. The trains themselves have changed, but the route, the ride and the ocean scenery, remain unspoilt. This lovely little line was almost lost during the savage Beeching cuts of the 1960s, but it lives on, the busiest branch-line railway in Cornwall; the best way to arrive.

Recent exhibitions have explored the work of artists Rose Hilton, Bryan Pearce, Francis Bacon and Roger Hilton, sculptor Nick Evans and jeweller Helen Feller. But it's not just the art that excites the eye. Look, too, at the Patrick Heron stained glass panel in the foyer and the Cornish slate floors (often sprinkled with a light dusting of sand – there is nothing formal about this seaside gallery); stand on the mezzanine inside the curve of the rotunda and see a mirror image of the sea, the waves, the weather, reflected in the glass.

TATE ST IVES, Porthmeor Beach, St Ives TR26 1TG; ☎ 01736 796226; www.tate.org.uk/stives. Entry: £6.25, Tate members and under-18s free, or £9.75 to include the Hepworth Museum; open daily Mar to Oct, 10am–5pm. Nov to Feb, Tues–Sat, 10am–4pm; guided tours 2.30pm daily (except Sun).

Around the corner, the Tate-run **Barbara Hepworth Museum and Sculpture Garden** celebrates the life and work of the St Ives art-colony doyenne, who moved to the town with her husband, the artist Ben Nicholson, in 1939. For nearly 30 years, until her death in a fire in 1975, Hepworth lived and worked at Trewyn Studio, where she sculpted her distinctive monolithic forms in stone, carved wood and cast bronze. In accordance with her wishes, the studio and much of her work were left to the nation, and has been in the care of the Tate since 1980. Aside from her sculptures, the museum houses photographs, letters, drawings, and other personal effects, which provide an intriguing insight into the life of one of our greatest 20th-century artists. The verdant garden, where works of art lurk among flowering shrubs, is a delight.

BARBARA HEPWORTH MUSEUM AND SCULPTURE GARDEN; Barnoon Hill TR26 1AD; ☎ 01736 796266; www.tate.org.uk/stives. Entry: £5.25, Tate members and under-18s free, or £9.75 if combined with Tate St Ives; open daily Mar to Oct, 10am–5.20pm; Nov to Feb, Tues–Sun, 10am–4.20pm.

Sculpture garden at the Barbara Hepworth museum

Aside from the dozens of private galleries in the town, you can also visit the **St Ives Society of Artists**, founded in 1927, by marine artist George Fagan Bradshaw. In the Mariners Gallery, housed in a former Methodist Chapel in Norway Square, the society runs regular seasonal exhibitions including members' shows.

The venerable **St Ives Art Club** (on the corner of the Warren and Westcott Quay) has occasional open days (www.stivesartsclub.org). And the new **Bernard Leach Pottery** opened in March 2008, provides a study centre, museum and gallery in the cottage and workshop he established in 1920. Leach was one of the founding fathers of the early 20th-century Studio Pottery movement, and is probably Britain's best known ceramicist. He and a group of associates produced what was known as 'Standard Ware', a range of utilitarian stoneware vessels that remained in continuous production until his death in 1979.

BERNARD LEACH POTTERY; Higher Stennack, St Ives TR26 2HE; ☎ 01736 799703; www.leachpottery.com. Entry: £5.50, concessions £4.50, under-18s free; Mar to Oct, Mon–Sat, 10am–5pm; Sun, 11am–4pm; Nov to Feb, Mon–Sat, 10am–5pm.

Artists in residence

St Ives has attracted artists since the early 19th century. JMW Turner was one of the first (he painted the harbour during a tour of Cornwall in 1811). Whistler and Sickert followed and by the time the Arts Club was founded in 1884, the declining fishing port was fast becoming Cornwall's Chelsea-on-sea. They came not just for the quality of the light and the vivid marine landscapes, but also for the supply of cheap, empty property: redundant net lofts and fish stores, north-facing, with seaviews, made wonderful studios.

In 1895, Julius Olsson founded the town's first school of painting. In 1927, marine artist George Fagan Bradshaw formed the St Ives Society of Artists. By 1930, St Ives' own Alfred Wallis was enjoying the first glimmer of fame as Britain's finest primitive painter. But the golden years of the St Ives' School belong to the 'moderns' of the mid-20th century. It began when Barbara Hepworth and Ben Nicholson moved from London to St Ives in 1939, and continued through to the 1970s with a new generation of abstract artists: Terry Frost, Peter Lanyon, Patrick Heron and Bryan Winter among others. And still they come, adding the contemporary and the conceptual to the tapestry of artistic endeavour that is now central to the culture of West Cornwall.

Wet weather

The **St Ives Museum** at Wheal Dream has an interesting collection of mining, fishing and farming artefacts, vintage toys and art-world memorabilia. There is also a replica of an olde worlde Cornish kitchen, and a room devoted to the Hain Steamship Company, St Ives' very own international shipping line.

ST IVES MUSEUM, Wheal Dream, St Ives, Cornwall TR26 1PR; ☎ 01736 796005. Entry: adults £2; children 50p; open Apr to Oct, Mon–Fri, 10am–5pm; Sat 10am–4pm.

View from Porthminster Beach Café

ST IVES SCHOOL OF PAINTING, Porthmeor Studios, Back Road, West, St Ives TR26 1NG; ☎ 01736 797180. www.stivesartschool.co.uk. Drawing classes, workshops and courses (3–5 days); life classes are available on Mon, Wed (evening), Sat all year round.

If St Ives' plethora of art galleries inspires you to have a go yourself, the **St Ives School of Painting** runs regular courses in drawing, painting and print-making in a former Downalong sail loft used by artists since the 1900s. Drop-in life-drawing classes are taught by artists in a paint-splattered studio at the top of a narrow flight of stairs.

What to do with children...

PLAY ZONE, Carbis Bay Holiday Park, Laity Lane TR26 3HW; ☎ 01736 799499; www.play-zone.co.uk. Entry: adults, £1.50, children £6.95, under-3s £3; open Wed–Fri 11am–7pm; Sat/Sun 10am–7pm.

Children are well catered for at **Tate St Ives** with a range of fun activities on offer to help them understand and enjoy the exhibits and the setting. During holidays and half-terms, you can pick up an Art Safari 'activity bucket' (an art kit, including crayons and sketch pads); or join one of the gallery's family-friendly beach workshops (weather permitting). **Play Zone** at the Carbis Bay Holiday Park, has a 'soft adventure playground' including ball pools and corkscrew slide.

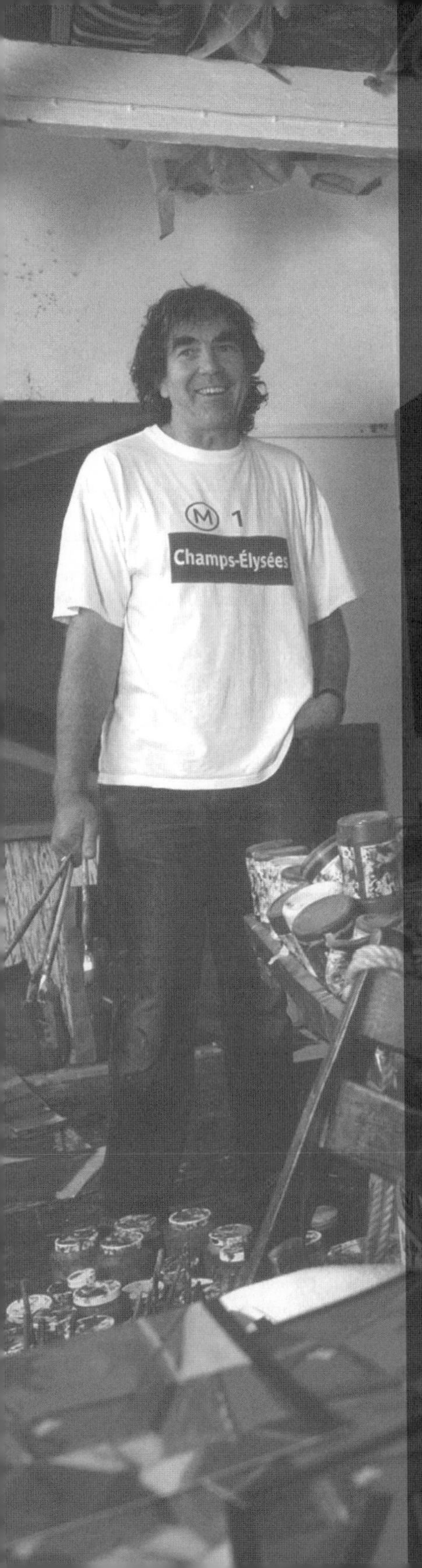

LOCAL KNOWLEDGE

Abstract painter, **Anthony Frost,** son of Sir Terry (one of the leading modernists of the post-war St Ives School) is the most colourful of Penwith's contemporary artists. Born in St Ives, he left Cornwall for art college in the 1970s but returned to make a life within sight of the West Penwith coast. A self-confessed 'music freak', he paints to a soundtrack of Captain Beefheart in a studio above the Exchange Gallery in Penzance. His vibrant paintings (acrylic on canvas, sacking, netting, sailcloth and an onion bag, among other materials) have been shown in galleries all over the country – as well as reproduced on album covers for the Fall.

Best thing about living here: Being surrounded by the sea – and the thriving art scene. There's always something to look at, something going on.

Favourite restaurant: The Porthminster Café. Right on the beach, they serve beautiful food, cooked by an Australian chef – and the walls are always crowded with my paintings.

Favourite beach: St Ives' Harbour beach. For me it's full of childhood memories, playing cowboys and Indians and go-karting down the slipway. We would stay there until the light faded – and the sand is beautiful.

Favourite café: The Swanpool beach café in Falmouth – for lovely views of a lovely bay, a desert-island beach and flapjacks with tea.

Favourite pub: The Sloop Inn – especially after a private view, or a Wednesday evening drawing class, at the St Ives Art School. It's a great place for a Guinness and a gossip.

Best view: From our bathroom window – the cliffs, the sea, and fantastic end-of-the-world sunsets.

Secret tip for lunch: My mother used to take a bottle of chilled champagne packed in a cool bag. I remember us drinking one in the car park at Porthminster beach before walking down to the café.

How to get away from the summer crowds: I visit my friends in Gorran Haven near Mevagissey. It's busy there too, but the crowds are their crowds, not mine.

Barnoon Cemetery overlooking Porthmeor Beach

 ... and how to avoid children

Put on your hiking boots and set off towards **Zennor Head**. From the chapel of St Nicholas (on the Island), cross Porthmeor Beach and pick up the demanding but beautiful section of the South West Coast Path which meanders along high cliffs past Clodgy Point, Pen Eny Headland and up Tregenna Cliff to the little village of Zennor (see page 308). Rough, rugged footpaths and strenuous ascents, are rewarded by spectacular views of Godrevy and Pendeen lighthouses. On the return, you can head inland via the Tinner's Way (see page 308). Taken at a leisurely pace, the 12-mile round trip could take the best part of a day.

Entertainment

Theatre and cinema

Merlin's Royal Cinema on Royal Square (☎ 01736 796843; www.merlincinemas.co.uk) is a three-screen 'picture house' showing all the usual general-release movies, plus regular art-film nights hosted by the Penwith Film Society. The **Kidz-R-Us Youth Theatre** Company (www.kidzrus.net) does occasional shows, pantos and musicals in its own 321-seat theatre housed in a converted Wesleyian chapel at Lower Stennack.

Special events

St Ives' annual **Literature Festival** (www.stiveslitfest.co.uk) kicks off in May. And later, the larger **September Festival** (www.stivesseptemberfestival.co.uk) offers a two-week celebration of music, literature, theatre and art. Music concerts (folk, jazz, reggae, world music), take place in the St Ives Guildhall, alongside dozens of street events, art exhibitions, and performances staged in pubs, galleries and other venues all over town.

In February, you might also catch the **Hurling of the Silver Ball**, a curious St Ives custom that takes place on Feast Monday in February (the day before Shrove Tuesday). This ancient rite starts at 10.30am when the mayor hurls a silvery ball over the wall of the Parish Church (St Ia's on Market Place) to a waiting crowd. The ball is then passed from person to person, with teams battling for possession, along the streets and beaches of the town.

The Knill Will

The Knill Steeple, a curious three-sided obelisk rising 50 feet from the top of Worvas Hill, a mile or so inland from Carbis Bay, is home to one of the oddest rituals in Cornwall. The granite steeple was built in 1872 as the mausoleum of St Ives' former mayor and collector of customs, John Knill. It was never actually used as such, but before his death Knill drew up a will asking his townspeople to commemorate his life with a ceremony on the site of his granite monument.

According to his stipulations, 10 white-clad maidens (daughters of fishermen, tinners or seamen aged under 10), two widows, and a fiddler, were required to prance around the obelisk three times, overseen by the local mayor, the customs officer and the vicar, before singing the Old 100th Psalm. Knill himself was present at the first outing which took place 10 years before he died in 1811. And the Knill Day congregation continues to this day, on 25 July, the Feast of St James the Apostle, every five years. The ceremony celebrated its 200th anniversary in 2001.

Nightlife

St Ives doesn't do late nightlife in a big way, though there is a cool, surf-crowd nightclub the **Isobar** on Street an Pol (☎ 01736 799199) with dance floor and café-bar, open until late. **St Ives Jazz Club** (www.stivesjazzclub.com), billed as *'the last jazz club before New York'*, holds regular Tuesday-night gigs at the Celtic Craic Bar, at the Western Hotel, in Royal Square (☎ 01736 795277; www.westernhotel-stives.co.uk). The hotel also hosts acoustic folk evenings (every Wednesday) and regular blues nights during the summer. The **St Ives Arts Club** at Westcott's Quay (www.stivesartsclub.org) runs a regular programme of 'bring-your-own-drinks' events from comedy or cabaret to live music, poetry and jazz evenings and regular **Café Frug** nights.

Shopping

St Ives is packed with small shops – and barely a chain store in sight. What it lacks in everyday stuff, it more than makes up for in independent outlets selling everything you can think of from books, prints and local crafts to handmade candles, decorative nick-nacks and clothing (surf and beach wear a speciality).

Among a crowd of galleries (at least 30), check out **ArtSpace** (The Wharf, ☎ 01736 799744; www.artspace-cornwall.co.uk), run by a seven-member artists cooperative and the **New Millennium Gallery** (Street an Pol, ☎ 01736 793121; www.newmillenniumgallery.co.uk). Also worth a peep is **St Ives Ceramics** (1 Fish Street, ☎ 01736 794930): owner John Bedding, former apprentice of Bernard Leach, specialises in the work of 20th-century master potters. At **Tremayne Applied Arts** (Street an Pol, 01736 797779) you can see, and buy, 20th century design classics.

The best... PLACES TO STAY

BOUTIQUE

Blue Hayes Hotel

Trelyon Avenue, St Ives TR26 2AD
☎ 01736 797129
www.bluehayes.co.uk

This small luxury hotel is a breath of fresh air, with its bright white exterior, Mediterranean seaside colours (warm corals, cool blues), lush gardens, cocktail bar and sea-view terrace. The five suites, have giant beds and deluxe bathrooms; most have ocean views and two have a private terrace. No children under 10.

Price: B&B from £140–£230 for a double (open Mar to Oct).

Headland House Hotel

Carbis Bay TR26 2NS
☎ 01736 796647
www.headlandhousehotel.co.uk

A big, stone-clad Edwardian house set back from the sea, completely refurbished to provide seven light, spacious rooms, all with king or super-king beds, crisp white linens and stylish décor with a subtle nautical flavour. Downstairs there is a homely lounge and bar, a decked terrace and garden. No children under eight.

Price: B&B from £85–£125 for a double.

HOTEL

The Boskerris Hotel

Boskerris Road, Carbis Bay TR26 2NQ
☎ 01736 795295
www.boskerrishotel.co.uk

All silks, smiley staff and soothing seaside colours, the look is New England meets Provence; the rooms are light and comfortable and most have seaviews; as does the fabulous decked terrace. Carbis Bay station (and the beach) is a five-minute walk.

Price: B&B from £115–£240 (open Mar to Oct).

Primrose Valley Hotel

Porthminster Beach, St Ives TR26 2ED
☎ 01736 79493
www.primroseonline.co.uk

The first hotel in Cornwall to win Green Tourism accreditation, this revamped Edwardian villa offers bright contemporary design in a seaside location. There are nine bedrooms and a luxury suite (two have sea-view balconies). Owners Sue and Andrew Biss are big on Cornish produce. Closed Dec/Jan (dates vary).

Price: B&B from £105–£240 for a double.

B&B

Salthouse

Venton Road, St Ives TR26 2AQ
☎ 01736 791857
www.salthousestives.co.uk

A timber-clad modernist cube, this swish contemporary house has two uber stylish guest rooms, both kitted out with oak floors, floor-to-ceiling windows, cool contemporary furniture, complimentary goodies in the mini bar and free wi-fi. Big indulgent bathrooms feature walk-in showers and double-ended tubs. Both rooms have private terraces with to-die-for views over St Ives Bay and Godrevy Lighthouse.

Closed Dec-Apr. Price: from £170-£220 for a double.

The best... PLACES TO STAY

SELF-CATERING

Mermaid's Purse

Carbis Bay Apartments, Carbis Bay
☎ 01326 555555
www.classic.co.uk

One of two luxury apartments offered by Classic Cottages in a block of purpose-built holiday flats, three minutes walk from the beach. Mermaid's Purse has two bedrooms, two bathrooms, a modern open-plan living space with all mod cons, a generous decked terrace and fantastic views of the sea.

Price: from ££531–£1422 for a week (sleeps four).

The Sail Lofts

☎ 01736 448545
www.thesaillofts.co.uk

Not just one Sail Loft property but a dozen of them; a portfolio of five-star townhouses, studios and apartments dotted around the town; all crisp white-washed décor, brushed with colour, smart tiled bathrooms and open-plan space. Driftwood, Surf and Lighthouse are designed for two; Harbour and Island sleep four, Sail Lofts Cottage sleeps six, and luxurious Bay has room for eight.

Price: from £299–£3149 for a week.

Gonwin Manor

Gonwin Manor Drive, Lelant (2 miles from St Ives) TR26 3GN
☎ 01736 798858
www.gonwin-manor.co.uk

The architect-designed conversion of a group of granite barns, has created six luxury cottages set in 8 acres of clifftop countryside with direct access to Porthkidney beach. The rooms, the facilities are hotel standard, and include Jacuzzis, bathrobes, wood-burning stoves. There is an on-site gym and a baby-sitting service.

Price: from £575–£2100 for a week.

The best... FOOD AND DRINK

Modern St Ives is a foodie heaven full of great places to eat, good quality produce, seafood restaurants and cool cafés, many with fabulous seaviews (the café at Tate St Ives, or Alba, on the Wharf) or terraces on the beach. There are a few too many pasty shops (at least six, at the last count), but there is barely a vestige of a greasy spoon. No restaurant worth its salt would dare serve anything but local organic meat and fresh St Ives Bay seafood (mackerel, crab, sea bass, straight from the harbour boats).

Staying in

Such is the march of the gift shop and gallery, that St Ives is not the best place to shop for food, especially fresh produce. However, there is a small farmers' market every Friday (9am–2.30pm) at the Parish Rooms. **The Cornish Deli** on Chapel Street (☎ 01736 795100; www.cornishdeli.com) is a good place to buy Cornish cheeses, local meats and deli-style groceries, as is the **Digey Food Room** (see restaurants below). In the middle of town the **Fore Street Deli** (☎ 01736 794578) combines world foods and Cornish deli with a bakery, fruit and vegetables, an off-licence and 'basic provisions'. They also provide welcome packs for self-caterers (phone orders can be delivered to your accommodation). At Trevarrack, just outside Lelant, **Bill and Flo's Farm Shop** (☎ 01736 798885) sells fruit and vegetables, local jams, chutneys and other produce.

EATING OUT

RESTAURANT

Alba Restaurant

Old Lifeboat House, The Wharf, St Ives TR26 1LF
☎ 01736 797222
www.thealbarestaurant.com

In a converted lifeboat station on the seafront, Alba specialises in fresh, seasonal produce and line-caught fish, straight off the boats. The menu is modern European, served with style, and the odd South-East Asian twist. Rick Stein recently picked it out as one of Cornwall's top five. Tall double-height windows afford views of the harbour. Three courses cost around £30 per head; set menus available from £15.50.

Porthminster Beach Cafe

Porthminster Beach
☎ 01736 795352
www.porthminstercafe.co.uk

A St Ives favourite, right on the beach, this place has a relaxed Australian-style café atmosphere and a deck of outdoor tables, plus Mediterranean seafood (including Cornish oysters, crab, scallops and mussels). You can drop in for coffee, cakes and cold drinks (if you can find a table), but in the evenings it's all sophisticated at high-end restaurant prices. Two courses cost around £30 per head. Open all year round.

EATING OUT

Blas Burgerworks

The Warren, St Ives TR26 2EA
☎ 01736 797272
www.blasburgerworks.co.uk

A contradiction in terms perhaps, but this is the home of the 'ethical burger'. Served on rough, reclaimed-wood tables, the burgers are made from 100% Cornish free-range meat and served in a local-bakery bun with salad and mayo (from £6.50). Open, evenings only, all year, except a few weeks in winter.

The Seafood Café

Fore Street, St Ives TR26 1HE
☎ 01736 794004
www.seafoodcafe.co.uk

It boasts a 'new concept in dining' and this is how it works: first choose your dish (local fish, shellfish, Cornish meat, free-range chicken), then choose your sauce and side orders. There is also a choice of classic dishes (fish and chips, sausage and mash, gourmet burger) and a busy, buzzy wine-bar atmosphere. Lunch costs £6–£12, three-course dinner costs around £25.

CAFÉ

The Digey Food Room

6, The Digey, St Ives TR26 1HR
☎ 01736 799600
www.digeyfoodroom.co.uk

Tucked down a back-street between Porthmeor Beach and the Harbour, this little café-cum-deli serves, breakfast, lunches and teas, using Cornish produce, including local-smoked salmon, Cornish bacon, cream teas with home-made scones and Trewithin clotted cream, Cornish cheddar and Crellow chutney and Callestick Farm ice cream. There are tables outside during fine weather.

Tate St Ives Café

Porthmeor Beach, St Ives TR26 1TG
☎ 01736 796226
www.tate.org.uk/stives

On the top deck of the gallery, all white walls, light and ocean views, the café commits to sourcing the majority of ingredients from Cornish growers and suppliers (including cider and wine). It serves breakfast, lunch (hot main courses, at £9.50) and afternoon tea during gallery opening times. Needless to say, it gets mega busy. During the summer, an evening Sunset Café runs from Thurs–Sat.

Ocean Grill

Wharf Road, St Ives TR26 1LG
☎ 01736 799874
www.ocean-grill.co.uk

On an upper floor, right on the seafront, this is a favourite with locals for a breakfast special, thanks to friendly staff and views of the harbour, plus a choice of full English, vegetarian, smoked salmon and scrambled eggs or blueberry pancakes. The Grill also serves lunch and dinner (mains from £9.95).

The Bean Inn

St Ives Road, Carbis Bay TR26 2RT
☎ 01736 795918

High quality vegan and vegetarian food served by staff in Beans Don't Scream T-shirts. Part of the Coast B&B (you can stay there too), it overlooks the sea at Carbis Bay. Check for opening times, as off-season it's only open on Friday and Saturdays. Expect tofu stir-fry with lime and ginger, or stuffed pepper with salsa dip. Three courses around £20.

Drinking

The local pubs tend to be traditional boozers or tourist traps, and in the summer most are a bit of both. The **Sloop Inn** (☎ 01736 796584; www.sloop-inn.co.uk) is the oldest (*c.* 1312) and has the best location on the Wharf, overlooking the Harbour beach. All low-beams and flag-stone floors, the former fishermen's pub, used to be a favourite of the art-club set (and still is off-season) and, aside from traditional cask ales and good pub food, it offers free surfboard storage, Wi-Fi and a gallery of original drawings by Hyman Segal. On Fore Street, **The Castle Inn** (☎ 01736 796833) is a good town-centre option, serving Adnams Broadside, Skinners ale, Cornish Orchards Farm Cider and occasional live music. For a more contemporary feel and wine-bar atmosphere head for **The Hub** (cocktails and lounge music on the harbour; ☎ 01736 799099).

In Carbis Bay, the **Boskerris Hotel** has a pleasant little bar with tables on a decked terrace and great views towards Godrevy Lighthouse. In Lelant, the **Badger Inn** (☎ 01736 752181), serves local-brewed Cornish ales and good pub grub in a traditional village pub with a pretty garden.

Visitor Information

Tourist information centre: The Guildhall, Street an Pol, St Ives TR26 2DS, ☎ 01736 796297.

Hospitals with A&E: St Ives' Edward Main Memorial Hospital, 1 Albany Terrace, ☎ 01736 795044, has a small casualty department but can only deal with minor injuries. The nearest A&E is at West Cornwall Hospital, St Clare Street, Penzance, ☎ 01736 362382.

Doctors: The Old Stennack School, Stennack, St Ives, ☎ 01736 796413.

Pharmacies: Leddra Chemist. Fore Street, St Ives, ☎ 01736 795432; Boots, 3 High Street, St Ives, ☎ 01736 795072.

Police station: Royal Square (behind Royal Cinema), ☎ 0870 577 7444.

Supermarkets: Tesco, St Ives Road, Carbis Bay; Co-op, Royal Square, St Ives.

Internet access: The Sloop Inn on St Ives Quay has a Wi-Fi connection.

Car hire: St Ives Car Hire; ☎ 0845 0579 373, www.stivescarhire.co.uk; Meet-and-greet service and little red Ford Kas from £20 per day; St Ives Motor Company, ☎ 01736 795156.

Local taxis: Les Cars, Dove Street, St Ives, ☎ 01736 796633; Jon's Cab, Ellis Close, St Ives, ☎ 01736 799888; Greg's Taxis, Carbis Bay Holiday Village, ☎ 01736 799999.

PENZANCE AND MOUNT'S BAY (MARAZION TO MOUSEHOLE)

The last stop on the Paddington to Penzance railway line, the administrative 'capital' of Penwith is a proper, working Cornish town; a little rough around the edges, but a sunny, cheerful place that crosses market town and medieval port with a dash of Victorian holiday resort. Palm trees wave in the breeze on the mile-long seaside promenade which follows the curve of Mount's Bay from Penzance quay's Lighthouse Pier all the way to Newlyn harbour. And always in the background there is the iconic St Michael's Mount. A fairytale castle on an island of rock, it's one of Britain's best-loved coastal landmarks.

In recent history, Penzance has tended to be looked down on as St Ives' poorer neighbour but a century or so ago, it was the other way around. Old Penzance was awash with cash. The bankers, merchants, and 'mineral lords' who fed off the lucrative mining industries in the 18th and 19th centuries built splendid houses with exotic seaside gardens. The streets that slope gently down from Market Jews Street to the harbour, have barely changed since those better days (colourful Chapel Street remains one of the most unaltered streetscapes in Britain). And if you enjoy looking at architecture, Penzance has everything from 17th-century inns and rugged granite chapels to Regency terraces and an Art Deco classic (the fabulous Jubilee Pool).

For some, it's still merely a gateway to Land's End, or a stopover en route to the Isles of Scilly, but an increasing number of visitors are coming here for longer. On one side, Newlyn, Cornwall's largest and most commercial fishing port; on the other, pretty Marazion, one of the of country's oldest towns. And 3 miles south, the harbour village of Mousehole – all cats, pilchards and Christmas lights – enriches the mix.

WHAT TO SEE AND DO

On dry land

Exploring Penzance on foot is a pleasant way to while away a couple of hours. You could start at the **Victorian station** (c. 1880), head up Market Jews Street, take a left at the old Market House, amble down **Chapel Street** and, turning left again, stroll along the Quay, past the harbour marina and docks (where *Scillonian III* sails for the Scilly Isles) and back to the station. This short route provides a tour of some of the town's finest buildings, but for a longer walk, pick up a free 'Walk around Historic Penzance' guide from the tourist information centre in the station car park.

One of the most prominent buildings is the **Market House** (*c*. 1835) at the top of Market Jews Street (a corruption of *Marghas Yow*, meaning Thursday Market). Like a mini St Paul's,

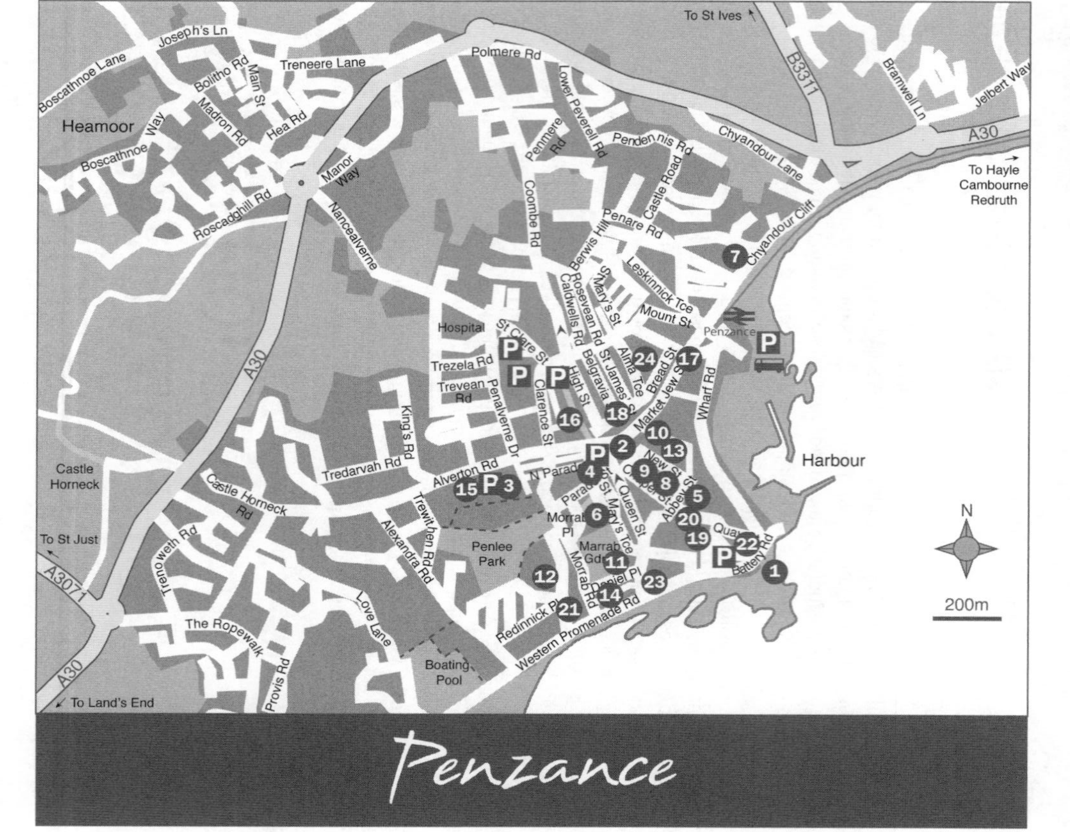

Things to see and do

1. Jubilee Bathing Pool
2. Exchange Gallery
3. Penlee Gallery
8. Admiral Benbow
9. Turks Head
10. Egyptian House
11. Morrab Gardens
12. Mermaid Pleasure Trips
13. Morrab Library
14. Penlee House Gallery and Museum
15. Alexander Playsite

Entertainment

4. Acorn Arts Centre
16. Savoy Cinema
17. Club 2K
18. Studio Bar
19. Penzance Arts Club

Shopping

20. Kitts Couture

Places to Stay

5. Abbey Hotel
6. Morrab Hotel
21. The Summer House
22. Dolphin Tavern

Eat and drink

23. Captain's
24. Archie Browns

Visitor Information

7. Tourist Information Centre

you can see its leaded granite dome from all over town (it is thus rather disappointing to find that the bulk of the building, the former Guildhall, is now a Lloyds TSB bank). Below the impressive portico, the statue of gifted chemist Sir Humphry Davy, looks east down Market Jews Street where he was born in 1778. A former president of the Royal Society, he was credited, among other things, with discovering laughing gas and inventing the miners' safety lamp.

The oldest pub in Penzance, the Admiral Benbow

The jewel-box of Penzance is quirky **Chapel Street**, a narrow thoroughfare, leading from the town centre down to St Mary's Church (a Victorian Gothic landmark, built in the 1830s, on the site of a medieval chapel). The street's assortment of 17th- and 18th-century buildings includes the **Turks Head**, the town's oldest pub, the **Admiral Benbow** (note the smuggler sneaking across the roof) and the **Union Hotel**, the former assembly room where victory at Trafalgar, and Admiral's Nelson's death, was first announced in 1805 (to the rear of the building there are the unrestored remnants of a Georgian theatre). And opposite is the extraordinary **Egyptian House**, a colourful evocation of the *faux* Egyptian style which flourished, briefly, around the time of Napoleon's campaign in Egypt in 1798. All lotus-bud columns and stylised hieroglyphics, this late example was built in around 1835 by John Lavin, a local geology enthusiast, who used the ground floor shop as a museum devoted to his collection of minerals. In 1968, the building was acquired by the Landmark Trust in a dilapidated state, and converted into three holiday apartments available to rent.

The Landmark Trust's Egyptian House

On the seafront, you can stride along Cornwall's only promenade, from the harbour all the way to Newlyn (just over a mile), but first take a look at the **Jubilee Bathing Pool**, an Art Deco classic that adds a touch of cruise-ship glamour to Penzance's Victorian prom. Like the prow of an ocean liner heading out to sea, it consists of blue and white linear sundecks wrapped around a triangular pool. Designed by borough engineer, Captain F Latham in 1935 (to celebrate George V's Silver Jubilee), it remains one of the largest open air pools still in use in the UK – though it was almost closed in 1992 due to structural

The Spanish invasion

The last foreign invasion of British soil was a Spanish raid on West Cornwall in July 1595. A hostile fleet of four Spanish galleys landed at Mousehole, followed by Newlyn and then Penzance. Firing on the retreating Cornish, the Spaniards (or 'Turks') torched all three towns (little more than villages at the time), and might have done more damage had Drake not sent ships to Cornwall's aid. The Turks Head in Chapel Street, Penzance, is among the very few surviving buildings that pre-date this brief but destructive 16th-century attack on Mount's Bay.

JUBILEE BATHING POOL, The Promenade, Penzance; ☎ 01736 369224; www.jubileepool.co.uk. Entry: adult bather £4.30, junior bather, £3.20, £1.65 half price entry after 4pm; open daily from May to early Sept (dates vary), 10.30am–6pm.

TREWIDDEN GARDEN, Buryas Bridge; Penzance TR20 8TT; ☎ 01736 363021; www.trewiddengarden.co.uk. Entry: adults £5.50, children free; open 10am–5.30pm, closed Mon/Tues (all week in Jul/Aug).

TRENGWAINTON GARDEN, Madron, Penzance TR20 8RZ; ☎ 01736 363148; www.nationaltrust.org.uk. Entry: adults £5.90, children £2.90; open Feb–Oct 30, 10.30am–5pm; closed Fri/Sat.

problems. Funding was found to save it, and it is now Grade II listed – a rare survivor among a generation of Art Deco lidos. The million gallons of tidal seawater that fills the pool is chemically treated but unheated and can be a little bracing on a cool day.

To enjoy the fruits of the region's mild climate, take a stroll around **Morrab Gardens** (entrance is free). Between the town centre and the seafront, it originally formed the grounds of a private house (now the Morrab Library). Acquired by the council in 1889, it was developed as a municipal pleasure garden and still provides a delightful urban haven, planted with tender subtropical plants. At Buryas Bridge, 2 miles west of Penzance, **Trewidden Garden**, is another horticultural heaven. Planted in the late 19th century by Thomas Bolitho, former MP for St Ives, the 10-acre garden is laid out on the site of an old tin mine. Paths meander from 'burrow' (or old mining excavation) to bluebell wood taking in an array of exotic plants, rare trees and beautiful displays of flowers: camellias and magnolias in spring and rhododendron and azalea in May.

More rare plant species and giant tree ferns, plus views of Mount's Bay, are part of a visit to the National Trust's **Trengwainton Garden** at Madron, 2 miles north-west of Penzance. You get a reduced rate if you arrive by bike, on foot or by public transport.

For a slice of ancient Cornish life, wander around the remnants of the 2,000-year-old Iron Age settlement at **Chysauster** on the edge of Penwith Moor (3 miles north of Penzance). Behind an enigmatic gate, the ruins of eight stone-built courtyard houses, a type of dwelling peculiar to the Land's End peninsula and the Isles of Scilly, line the ghost of a village street, on a hilltop with wonderful rural views. Chysauster's community of lowly native houses is a

The Neolithic tomb, Lanyon Quoit

rare survivor of the Roman occupation; their legacy is seen by archaeologists as remarkable because they clearly continued a Celtic way of life, untouched by Roman influences. A little younger is the easy-to-find **Lanyon Quoit** (a Neolithic tomb shaped like a three-legged table) which sits on the side of road between Madron and Morvah.

CHYSAUSTER, Badger's Cross TR20 8XA, ☎ 07831 757934; www.english-heritage.org.uk. Entry: adults £3.40, children £2; open daily 1 Apr to 31 Oct, 10am–5pm (or until 6pm in Jul/Aug, 4pm in Oct).

Galleries

Tucked down a side street, between Market Jew Street and Chapel Street, **The Exchange** gallery is Penzance's answer to Tate St Ives and together with its older sibling, the modernised **Newlyn Gallery**, succeeds in presenting a credible rival, providing the region with an international showcase for the best of contemporary art. Both are the work of Muma (Mcinnes, Usher and McKnight Architects), the Scottish firm that won an international architecture competition in 2003 to design The Exchange (a converted 1950s telephone exchange) and add a contemporary extension to Newlyn's 1890s building – dating from the days when the Newlyn School of artists was as important and as influential as St Ives'.

THE EXCHANGE, Princes Street, Penzance TR18 2NL; ☎ 01736 363715; www.newlynartgallery.co.uk. Admission free; open Mon–Sat, 10am–5pm; Sun 11am–4pm; in winter, closed Sun–Mon.

NEWLYN ART GALLERY, 24 New Road, Newlyn TR18 5PZ; ☎ 01736 363715; www.newlynartgallery.co.uk. Admission free; open Mon–Sat, 10am–5pm. In winter, closed Sun–Mon.

The Exchange, with its white-cube galleries (the largest art space west of Bristol) is a little clinical inside, and lacks substance, but check out the exterior's wave-like panel of glow-in-the-dark glass – a permanent installation by Penwith artist Peter Freeman. The rippling LED light sculpture responds to weather, or passersby.

ST MICHAEL'S MOUNT, Marazion TR17 0HS; ☎ 01736 710507; www.stmichaelsmount.co.uk; www.national-trust.org.uk. Entry: adults: £7, children £3.50; plus an extra £3.50/£1.50 for entry to the garden; open Mar–Oct, 10.30am–5pm, Jul to Aug, 10.30am–5.30pm (closed Sats), subject to tides and weather conditions; last admission 45 mins before closing.

Marazion and St Michael's Mount

Five miles east of Penzance, charming **Marazion** is one of Cornwall's oldest market towns (a port since the Bronze Age, it was granted a charter by Henry III in 1257). A line of pretty cottages follows the curve of Mount's Bay; there is a decent beach, shops, galleries, pubs, and a small museum, but the big attraction is **St Michael's Mount**.

One of Cornwall's must-see sites, the iconic island – a crag of rock crowned by an enchanting medieval castle – lies 400m off Marazion. Owned by the National Trust and managed by the resident St Aubyn family (who have lived there since 1659), it is open to the public from spring to autumn, offering a chance to explore its rich history: a tale of miracles and mythology, politics and religion that spans over 1,000 years. At the core of the castle, is the remnants of a Benedictine monastery; founded in the 12th century, it was once a dependency of the island's French twin, Mont St Michel.

If you time your visit right (when the tide's out), you can walk across on a cobbled causeway that links Marazion beach to the island's rocky 18th-century harbour. It costs nothing to visit the island's village (a tiny picturesque community of lived-in cottages, plus a couple of shops and restaurants) but there is a fee to visit the church, castle and hanging gardens which cling to its summit. It's a steep climb to the top, but worth the effort for the views alone – and there's the added thrill of being cut off by an incoming tide. In reality, you will be ushered off the island just in time. In the summer (weather permitting) you can get there by boat from three Marazion departure points, depending on conditions.

Marazion also provides easy access to two of the area's most popular south-coast beaches: **Perran**, and **Praa Sands**. The road to Perran winds down from the A394, through Perranuthnoe, an unspoilt seaside village, between Marazion and Prussia Cove. From the car park, a short walk takes you down to a sandy, often surfy, beach, sheltered by low cliffs. From

Local legends: Jack the giant killer

As you make your way up to the castle on St Michael's Mount, look out for a heart-shaped stone set into the cobbles. According to legend it belonged to Cormoran, a mythical giant who not only built the Mount but terrorised his mainland neighbours by wading across the bay to steal their livestock. When a reward was offered for his killing, the challenge was taken up by a Land's End lad called Jack. First he dug a deep pit and camouflaged it with straw. Then he lured Cormoran to the spot by blowing his horn. When the enraged giant stumbled into the hole, Jack delivered a fatal blow. Quite how the boy came to remove his enemy's heart, doesn't seem to feature in the story, but there it is, among the stones on the pilgrim's path. Stand on it, so they say, and you can hear the giant's heart beat.

Perran, you can take the coast path to **Kenneggy Sands**, a quieter, smaller beach with sand at low tide.

The Blue Flag beach at **Praa Sands** (pronounced *Pray*) is one of the best surfing spots on the south coast (when the conditions are right, body boarders like it, too).

Out to sea

From Penzance, there are several boat-excursion options, ranging from adventurous wildlife-spotting trips to leisurely cruises to St Michael's Mount. **Marine Discovery** offers trips in a speedy jet RIB, including sea safaris (in search of seals, dolphins, porpoises, sunfish and basking sharks) en route to Land's End or the lonesome Wolf Rock Lighthouse.

As well as coast-hugging scenic cruises, family-run **Mermaid Pleasure Trips** (☎ 07901 731201; www.cornwallboattrips.com) does fishing trips aboard the **Mermaid II**, including experienced crew to show you how it's done. You can also board the *Scillonian III* for a daytrip to the **Isles of Scilly** (see page 19). The 28-mile journey to St Mary's takes roughly 2 hours 40 minutes each way and costs £30 per person (children £18). You will need to book in advance (☎ 0845 710 5555).

MARINE DISCOVERY, Penzance Harbour (Albert Pier or South Pier) ☎ 01736 874907; www.marinediscovery.co.uk.
Trips: from £35 per person/£25 per child.

Ripple effect

The *Ripple SS.19* was one of dozens of tarred black luggers, with tall masts and dark brown sails, that ran in and out of Newlyn harbour in the 19th century. She was built in St Ives around 1895; a double-ended pilchard driver, owned by Betsy Barber and her two fisher sons. The *Ripple*'s career was cut short in 1933, when a fire broke out as she was about to sail out of St Ives, and she spent over 50 years as a houseboat moored in the Fal estuary. Rescued in 2003, she was brought back to Newlyn, and following a four-year restoration by the Newlyn Marine Heritage Project has been returned to seaworthy condition. The oldest boat on the UK Fishing Vessel Register, the *Ripple* is now a local tourist attraction and may one day provide enthusiasts with a taste of life on a sailing lugger in the good old days of sustainable fishing.

Wet weather

If you fancy delving into a bit of local history or researching your Cornish roots, take out a day's membership to the **Morrab Library**, one of the oldest independent libraries in the country. Housed in a 19th-century villa in the centre of Penzance, its collections include

MORRAB LIBRARY, 62 Morrab Road, Morrab Gardens, Penzance; ☎ 01736 364474; www.morrablibrary.org.uk. Entry: daily memberships available at £5; open Tues–Fri 10am–4pm, Sat 10am–1pm.

around 40,000 books (many of them pre-1801), and over a century of Cornish newspapers, plus photography, manuscripts and memorabilia.

Nearby **Penlee House Gallery and Museum** presents an eclectic collection of art and artefacts relating to Penwith culture and social history: flint heads, mining equipment, costume, pottery, photography and Newlyn Copperware are represented as well as a permanent collection of paintings by Newlyn and Lamorna School artists. The house was built in 1865 in the Italianate style for Penzance merchant John Richards Branwell. Both house and gardens (or Penlee Memorial Park) were bought by the borough in 1946, to serve as a memorial to all those who lost their lives during the Second World War.

PENLEE HOUSE GALLERY & MUSEUM, Morrab Road, Penzance TR18 4HE; ☎ 01736 363625; www.penleehouse.org.uk. Entry: adults £4.50, children, free; open all year, Mon–Sat; Easter to Sept: 10am–5pm; 1 Oct to Good Friday, 10.30am–4.30pm.

What to do with children...

The Jubilee Pool in Penzance has a small 'baby pool' and further west down the Promenade, the public **Alexander Playsite** right on Marine Terrace provides a collection of swings, seesaws, roundabouts, model boats and other novelty playthings all laid out on a floor of soft sand. On a wet day, head for the Victorian Village at **Flambards** theme park near Helston (see Lizard Peninsula, page 254).

... and how to avoid children

Join a Ghost night at spooky **Pengersick Castle** near Praa Sands. Privately owned, the fortified Tudor mansion hosts regular Saturday night vigils in which groups of ghost-hunters are guided around the castle's most haunted corners, to do a bit of spirit-dowsing and watch video footage of Pengersick's paranormal. These dark evenings are far too scary for children, though the castle and its ancient gardens is also open in daylight by appointment.

PENGERSICK CASTLE, Praa Sands, Penzance TR20 9SJ; ☎ 01208 832846; www.pengersickcastle.com. Entry: check with castle for times and prices.

Entertainment

Theatre and cinema

The **Acorn Arts Centre** on Parade Street (☎ 01736 365520,www.acornartscentre.co.uk) is the main performance venue for Penzance, and offers an all-season programme of theatre, music, dance, and film events (including live bands). At the time of writing the Acorn was under threat of closure, but was campaigning for survival. See website for details.

Penzance's only cinema, the former Picture Theatre (opened in 1912, it is said to be the UK's oldest continuous running cinema), is the **Savoy** in Causewayhead (☎ 01736 363330; www.merlincinemas.co.uk) a modern triple-screener showing all the usual general releases, plus art films and oldies screened on Sun/Mon by the award-winning **Penwith Film Society** (www.penwithfilmsociety.co.uk).

Special events

Towards the end of June, Penzance celebrates Midsummer with one of Cornwall's largest community arts festivals: **Golowan** (www.golowan.org). The 10-day feast of street entertainment, music, story-telling, film shows and the like, involves local schoolchildren as well as artists, writers and performers from around the region, culminating with the Mazey Day street parade. The **Newlyn Fish Festival** (☎ 01736 364324, www.newlynfishfestival.org.uk) takes place around the harbour and fish market every year, on August bank holiday, offering fish dishes, local crafts and entertainment.

Nightlife

There are bigger, rowdier nightclubs such as **Sound** (www.soundpenzance.com) and **The Barn** (www.thebarnclub.com), but the coolest late-night hangout is the **Studio Bar** (behind Bread Street Studio in Market Place; www.studiobar.com). A bar, live music venue and 'groove lounge' it provides free live entertainment every night until 1am (acoustic, electric jam and Swing band nights among other offerings). Elsewhere, **Penzance Arts Club** boho bar on the foot of Chapel Street (www.penzanceartsclub.co.uk) holds Salsa nights, Bob Devereux's Café Frug (Thursday evening sessions of poetry and song) and an OUTabout Gay Night on a Sunday (subject to temporary club membership from £2).

Shopping

Most of the interesting shops in Penzance are found in the pedestrianised Causewayhead, or down Chapel Street. In the latter, look out for **Penzance Art and Antique Centre**, a warren of collectables in a two-storey arcade; **Kitts Couture** (among the UK's top five vintage clothes shops, according to *Tatler* magazine), and **Pure Nuff Stuff** in the Egyptian House, for natural skincare products, soaps and toiletries, made in Penzance (www.purenuffstuff.co.uk).

The best... PLACES TO STAY

BOUTIQUE

Abbey Hotel

Abbey Street, Penzance TR18 4AR
☎ 01736 366906
www.theabbeyonline.co.uk

It's owned by 1960s supermodel Jean Shrimpton, but a room at the Abbey is a bit like staying with a kindly, rather eccentric, old aunt. In a sky-blue, 16th-century townhouse, just above the harbour, the rooms and suites are stylishly quirky, with quilts, rugs, granny prints and comfortable armchairs. There is a panelled dining room and a walled garden.

Price: B&B from £105–£210 for a double.

The Summer House

Cornwall Terrace, Penzance TR18 4HL
☎ 01736 363744
www.summerhouse-cornwall.com

A few steps inland from the sea is a Regency townhouse (painted a happy shade of blue), a pretty tropical garden and Mediterranean-style restaurant. The five-star rooms combine original features and antiques with modern comforts and fresh, vibrant colours.

Price: B&B from £105–£120 for a double (open Apr to Oct).

HOTEL

Mount Haven Hotel

Turrnpike Lane, Marazion TR17 0DQ
☎ 01736 710249
www.mounthaven.co.uk

The comfortable contemporary lounge, the decked terrace (perfect for a seafood lunch) and most of the rooms have amazing views of St Michael's Mount. The rooms are functional rather than glamorous, but there is a good restaurant, relaxed bar and a healing room offering holistic de-stress treatments.

Price: B&B from £130–£220 for a double room (open Feb to Dec).

The Old Coastguard Hotel

Mousehole TR19 6PR
☎ 01736 731222
www.oldcoastguardhotel.co.uk

Acquired in June 2011 by the Inkin brothers (who also run the popular Gurnards Head near St Ives), this seaside hotel has changed for the better on all fronts, and the location is, as always, sublime. Set in sub-tropical gardens, on a hill looking down on Mousehole Harbour, it has stunning views of Mount's Bay from most of its light, airy rooms.

Price: B&B from £120 to £195 per double.

INN

Dolphin Tavern

Quay Street, Penzance, TR18 4BD
☎ 01736 364106
www.dolphintavern.co.uk

The pub is old and ultra traditional (and boasts a ghost or two), but the rooms are newly decorated in contemporary style, and provide big beds, sofas, harbour views and sound-proofing (it can get a bit noisy down here on the quay). The bar downstairs serves good, fresh-cooked meals and local ales (Newlyn fish, Cornish cream teas, St Austell ales).

Price: B&B from £70–£85 for a double, children £15 a night, under-2s free.

The best... PLACES TO STAY

FARMSTAY

Kerris Farm

Paul, Near Mousehole, Penzance TR19 6UY
☎ 01736 731309
www.kerrisfarm.co.uk

On a working beef and dairy farm, a handsome Victorian farmhouse owned by the Giles family since 1947. There are three elegant rooms (big comfortable beds, private bathrooms, bathrobes, rural views), plus big Cornish breakfasts, pretty gardens, four cats, three dogs, and Celtic standing stones on the land.

Price: B&B from £80 for a double.

B&B

Ednovean Farm

Perranathnoe TR20 9LZ
☎ 01736 711883
www.ednoveanfarm.co.uk

A converted granite barn with three deluxe rooms, sumptuously furnished with rich colours and fabrics, arranged around a parterre garden. All have their own private terrace, roll-top or slipper baths, amazing beds, and distant but beguiling views of St Michael's Mount.

Price: B&B from £100–£115. No reductions for single occupancy.

The Cornish Range

6 Chapel Street, Mousehole TR19 6SB
☎ 01736 731488
www.cornishrange.co.uk

Just around the corner from the pilchard-factory restaurant, a cottagey space with three simple, tasteful chintz-free rooms, all with super-king or king-size beds and named after artists (Pender, after Jack Pender who used to have a studio here).

Price: B&B from £65 - £95 per double.

Ennys

St Hilary, Penzance TR20 9BZ
☎ 01736 740262
www.ennys.co.uk

A historic Georgian estate, offering five-star rooms in the main house or two-bedroom suites in a Grade II listed barn (for groups of friends, or families with children over 5). Clean, bright modern décor furnished with king-size beds and power showers, plus landscaped gardens and a 12m swimming pool.

Price: B&B from £105–£195 for a double (including afternoon tea).

SELF-CATERING

The Fish Store

St Clements Terrace, Mousehole TR19 6SJ
☎ 01637 88194
www.uniquehomestays.com

Owned by food writer Lindsey Bareham (and the inspiration behind her *Fish Store* cook book), it's a former pilchard factory, with three picture windows looking out to sea, an industrial-size open-plan living space, with wood floors and high beams, three double bedrooms, a small yard, lots of quirky seaside details and free Wi-Fi.

Price: from £745 (for 4) to £2950 (for 10) for a week.

The best... FOOD AND DRINK

With Britain's premier fish market at Newlyn and lots of small neighbouring farms (raising everything from beef to broccoli) in the surrounding countryside, it's not surprising that the area has bred a fair number of excellent restaurants.

Staying in

Penzance is well-served with everyday shops: butchers, bakers and greengrocers and the like. The best of the butchers is **Ian Lentern**, at the top of Chapel Street (☎ 01736 363061). A butcher shop for over 100 years (and in the Lentern family for 30), it specialises in Cornish meat and native breeds. There is another branch in Newlyn. For fresh fish and seafood head for Newlyn harbour (the market supplies some of the best restaurants in Cornwall, including Rick Stein's). **Trelawany Fish** has a shop and deli on The Strand (☎ 01736 361793; open 9am–5pm, Mon–Sat). **The Pilchard Works** at Tolcarne (☎ 01736 332112; www.pilchardworks.co.uk) supplies sardines fresh, frozen, tinned or salted (the tins feature prints by Newlyn artist Walter Langley). Newlyn fish wholesalers W. Stevenson & Sons has a **Fish Boutique** in the Wharfside Shopping Centre in Penzance (☎ 01736 331459).

Higher Trenowin Farm at Nancledra (☎ 01736 362439; www.highertrenowin.co.uk) is mid-way between Penzance and St Ives and has a shop in a converted cowshed, selling free-range eggs, seasonable vegetables and herbs, joints of Trenowin beef and homemade cakes and jams.

Takeaways

On New Road in Newlyn, sample **Jelberts** vanilla ice cream (*'possibly the finest ice cream in Britain'*, according to the *Guardian*). Using a secret recipe, handed down from the owner, Jim Glover's grandfather, the ice cream is made daily in small batches and is designed to be eaten fresh, not frozen. For good fresh-fried fish and chips, try **Captain's** at Daniel Place in Penzance (eat in or out). Or for great pizzas, head for **Pizza Patio** (www.pizzapatio.co.uk, 01736 363446) in Newlyn. It doesn't deliver but you can order ahead and pick up a fresh-cooked 11-inch pizza made with a choice of classic Mediterranean toppings.

EATING OUT

FINE DINING

Untitled by Robert Wright

Abbey Street, Penzance TR18 4AR
☎ 01736 448022
www.untitledbyrobertwright.com

Affiliated to the Abbey Hotel (but independently run), chef Robert Wright's classy contemporary restaurant has a split personality: The Untitled Lounge on the ground floor has a drop-in, wine-bar vibe and majors on tapas (Helford oysters, fried little octopus, goats cheese and thyme tortilla) all at £3 each; while the bright sea-view Dining Room upstairs, is a more formal affair, offering an à la carte menu of interesting dishes (Falmouth Bay scallops, plaice with crab butter, lamb loin and anchovy) priced from £14.50 for a main course. Overall, the emphasis is on fresh, seasonal Cornish ingredients or, as the chef puts it, 'real food for real people'.

Harris's Restaurant

46 New Street, Penzance TR18
☎ 01736 364408
www.harrissrestaurant.co.uk

Falmouth estuary mussels, Tywardreath pork sausages, Newlyn crab, local-smoked salmon, West Country goats cheese and interesting desserts are all on the menu in this long-established, award-winning Penzance favourite – a flower-decked red and white building in the town centre. Two-course dinner costs around £25.

The Old Coastguard

Mousehole TR19 6PR
☎ 01736 731222
www.oldcoastguardhotel.co.uk

Head chef, Bruce Rennie (who also oversees the kitchen at the Gurnards Head) presents a concise menu of simple but delicious food dishes served in great surroundings (you can dine out on the terrace, and the views are to die for). From the seasonal menu, try crab cakes, pea and mint risotto, steamed hake or grilled plaice. Lunch dishes cost around £8; two-course supper, costs around £22.

RESTAURANT

2 Fore Street

Mousehole, TR19 6QU
☎ 01736 731164
www.2forestreet.co.uk

The *Daily Telegraph* put this French Bistro-style restaurant, right on the harbour, at number 14 in Britain's top 30 coastal restaurants – thanks to a great mix of contemporary Cape Cod-style décor, sea views, shingle garden (with al fresco tables) and an ever-changing menu of local seafood dishes and Cornish produce (including fish and hand-cut chips). Three-course dinner costs around £25.

The Cornish Range

6 Chapel Street, Mousehole TR19 6SB
☎ 01736 731488
www.cornishrange.co.uk

In a former pilchard processing factory, with wood floors and sturdy wooden tables, the warm, friendly restaurant specialises in seafood (delivered fresh every day from Newlyn) plus local meat, vegetables and cheeses. Three-courses cost £27.50.

La Luna Rossa

Chapel Street, Penzance TR18 5BQ
☎ 01736 350222

This big, bright Italian restaurant – decked out in scarlet, black and aubergine – gets mixed reviews for both food and service, but it's excellent value. Try pasta, risotto and seafood dishes from £12.50 and budget lunches at only £5.

EATING OUT

GASTRO PUB

Victoria Inn

Perranuthnoe TR20 9NP
☎ 01736 710309
www.victoriainn-penzance.co.uk

In the oldest recorded inn in Cornwall, dating from the 12th century, you get fresh-cooked food (Cornish beef, local crab, St Buryan pork, hog's pudding, real chips and Carn Brea goats cheese); the chef trained with Raymond Blanc and Michael Caines. Food can be served inside or outside (there is a subtropical garden). Light lunches cost from £5.50.

CAFÉ

Poolside Café

Jubilee Bathing Pool, Wharf Road, Penzance TR18 4HH; ☎ 0777 9998590
www.poolside-indulgence.co.uk

The views across Mount's Bay from a deck of the art deco lido would be enough, but the food is great too. In the day, the Mediterranean-style menu offers a great selection of homemade food. In the evening, there are tapas, hot specials, wines and delicious puddings. Weather permitting, you can sit outside.

Archie Browns

Bread Street, Penzance TR18 2EQ
☎ 01736 362828
www.archiebrowns.co.uk

Fresh wholefood, vegan and vegetarian dishes served in a small café space above a healthfood shop. Local fruit and vegetables, local eggs, milk and cheeses. Also good for food intolerances.

Sandbar

Praa Sands TR20 9TQ
☎ 01736 763516
www.sandbarpraasands.co.uk

Hip, happening café-bar right on the beach, popular with surfers. The food is Asian-fusion meets Mediterranean, plus local seafood, Cornish bangers and mash, all-day breakfasts, children's meals, Sunday lunch, wines, beers and cappuccino. Pool table, table football, and occasional live music make it good place to hang-out on a rainy day. Main courses cost from £8.95.

TEA ROOM

The Old Pilchard Press

8 Old Quay Street, Mousehole TR19 6RY
☎ 01736 731154

In a whitewashed cottage close to the harbour, this family-run traditional tea room does delicious Cornish cream teas and homemade cakes, as well as hot lunches, sandwiches and salads, largely prepared with local produce. Closed in January.

Drinking

If it's history you're after, then head for Chapel Street: the **Admiral Benbow** promises a '*unique experience.....[with] a vast array of seafaring antiques*', and the neighbouring **Turks Head** claims to be the oldest pub in Penzance. Both can be a little crowded and a little touristy. If you want Cornish ales, local colour and good pub food, check out the **Fountain Tavern** in St Clare Street (at the top of Causewayhead), **the Crown Inn** on Victoria Square (Otter Ale, or Skinner's Heligan Honey), or the **Dolphin Inn** on Quay Street (all in Penzance, the latter claiming to be the first place where tobacco was smoked on British soil).

Visitor Information

Tourist information centre: Station Road (in the car park next to the station), Penzance TR18 2NF, ☎ 01736 362207.

Hospitals with A&E: West Cornwall Hospital, St Clare Street, Penzance TR18 2PF, ☎ 01736 874000. Operates a 24-hour casualty service.

Doctors: Bellair Clinic, Alverton Road, Penzance TR18 4TA, ☎ 01736 575500.

Pharmacies: Boots, 100–102 Market Jew Street, Penzance TR18 2LE, ☎ 01736 361246; Newlyn Pharmacy, 5 The Strand Newlyn TR18 5HH, ☎ 01736 362324.

Police station: Penzance Police Station Penalverne Drive TR18 2NS, ☎ 08452 777444.

Supermarkets: The Co-op, Chapel Street, Penzance; Morrisons, Long Rock, Penzance TR18 3RF; Tescos, Branwell Lane, Penzance TR18 3DU.

Parking: The main car park in Penzance is the big pay-and-display right next to the station. There is also free short-stay parking on the promenade (if you can find a space). In Mousehole use the car park just before you enter the village, though off-season you can park right on the harbour (at a price).

Car hire: Tucker Car Hire Longrock Industrial Estate, Longrock, Penzance TR20 8HX; www.tuckercarhire.co.uk, family-run company, offers cars from £21.50 a day including delivery and collection.

ATMs: Barclays, 8/9 Market Jew St TR18 2TW; Natwest, 31 Alverton St TR18 2QQ; Abbey, 37 Market Place, TR18 2SE; Lloyds TSB, Market House TR18 2TN.

Bike hire: Pedals Bike Hire, The Wharfside Shopping Centre, Penzance TR18 2GB, ☎ 01736 360600; Mount's Bay Cycle Hire, Station House, Marazion, ☎ 01736 363044.

Local taxis: Penzance Taxi Company, ☎ 01736 366366; Stone's Taxis, Newlyn, ☎ 01736 363400.

FURTHER AFIELD

Mousehole

With its teeny beach, dinky harbour and dolls-house fishing cottages, Mousehole (pronounced *Mowzel*), has a lot going on for such a small place. Nothing much in the way of nightlife, of course, but art, folklore, award-winning restaurants and one of the best displays of Christmas lights this side of Oxford Circus. It rose to fame in 1990, when Antonia Barber's classic children's story of Mowzer, *The Mousehole Cat* gave the village a kind of mythic status. And in the summer, it's like a mini St Ives, its narrow streets gridlocked with people.

Dylan Thomas reckoned it was *'the prettiest village in England'*, and it's true that most of Mousehole's visitors come here just to have a look; to amble around the 13th-century harbour, climb up to the top of Raginnis Hill (for bird's-eye views of the village from the clifftop footpath), peer into the windows of its little shops and galleries or seek out a genuine Mousehole cat. Finish up with a fish-and-chip supper sitting on the granite walls of the almost circular harbour, enjoying the views of St Michael's Mount and St Clements Isle, a rocky islet due south of Mousehole.

The closest Mousehole gets to a visitor centre is the low-key **Wild Bird Hospital** on Raginnis Hill (☎ 01736 731386; www.mouseholebirdhospital.org.uk). A sanctuary for sick, orphaned or injured birds – plus a live-in community of budgies, blackbirds and a cockerel called Big Boy – it was founded in 1928 and relies on charitable donations (entrance is free). Down in the village, among the old (mostly converted) fish stores and pilchard presses, look out for Mousehole's oldest building, the 14th-century **Kelgwin Arms**: the former home of Squire Jenkyn Kelgwin, who died defending the harbour from an invasion of Spaniards (see page 294). The **Mousehole Harbour Lights** (www.mouseholelights.com) show at Christmas (an annual fixture since 1965) is one of Cornwall's big-crowd pullers (from mid-Dec to early Jan) and it is a magical spectacle, the quays festooned with an array of illuminated shapes and strings of coloured lights – all reflected in the waters of the harbour.

Fish to feed the hungry

On the day before Christmas Eve, Mousehole celebrates **Tom Bawcock's Eve**, in memory of the heroic fisherman who, according to the stories (the basis for *The Mousehole Cat*), saved the village from starvation by braving a tempestuous sea to fish for food. He returned with seven varieties of fish to feed the hungry villagers. Central to the celebrations is Mousehole's very own stargazy pie. Made with whole gutted fish (herring, mackerel or pilchards) their heads protruding from a pastry lid, the dish is served on the night, particularly in the **Ship Inn**: a genuine but often crowded local right on the harbour.

LAND'S END AND SURROUNDS

This is Cornwall's wild west, the toe of Britain; a gloriously remote headland of high granite cliffs and rugged coves pounded by Atlantic breakers. A mosaic of heathland, and ancient pasture, crowned by the brooding hills of Penwith Moor, it's romantic, wild, and to a large extent free: people who love this far-flung corner of England come for the exhilarating clifftop views, the rocks, the walks, the primitive landscapes, the sounds of the sea.

There is one small town, St Just (a former mining centre, now colonised by artists), one mass-market tourist attraction in the Land's End visitor centre, one long surf-and-sand beach at Whitesand Bay. Elsewhere, the region is almost entirely rural, dotted with tiny villages and huddled communities of solid granite farm cottages.

The moorland slopes, which roll down to the west coast, are riddled with prehistoric settlements, stone circles, 'quoits' and megalithic tombs. The pattern of the fields, the low granite walls, are of Celtic origin. The villages around St Just (Pendeen, Carnyorth, Botallack), were once a heartland of tin and copper mining, and the legacy is plain to see: from engine houses to the Tinner's Arms in Zennor, all strung along the course of the B3306 (the best Sunday drive in the country, according to the AA).

WHAT TO SEE AND DO

Pendeen Lighthouse

Walking

In this part of the world they call it 'skanking', and there are few better places for a good skank than this part of the world. A network of footpaths provides routes to suit a range of abilities, but though you don't have to be superfit the longer walks are not for softies. The Far West stretch of the **South West Coast Path** is all roller-coaster dips and steep ascents on rocky paths which occasionally skirt the edge of sheer cliffs. Inland, more rough paths meander across grassland and heathland and over **Penwith Moor**, cutting through dry bracken and spiky gorse. You will need stamina, an OS map (number 203), and sensible clothing. But you will be justly rewarded for your efforts: one of the most dramatic coastal landscapes in Britain, there's a picture-perfect view at every turn.

Between St Ives and Penzance, there is roughly 40 miles of coastal footpath at your disposal. Keen walkers often do the entire route, taking three to four days, or longer, stopping off at guest houses and farmstays on the way. Otherwise, simply divide the route into manageable chunks, and pick a walk. Local tourist offices will help plan routes; and a series of downloadable, round-trip guides are available from **Penwith Access and Rights of Way** (www.parow.org.uk).

One of the most scenic south-coast options runs from **Porthcurno** up to the spectacular rock formation and Iron Age cliff fort at **Logan Rock** and on to **Penberth**, the National Trust's miniature fishing village (an ancient granite slipway, a stony beach, four fisherman and few picture-postcard cottages). The more energetic could try all or part of the 10-mile **Tinner's Way**, a classic walk following ancient paths used for centuries to transport tin and copper from the west-coast mines to the harbour at St Ives. The path heads inland from Cape Cornwall, across Penwith Moor, and down to the north coast. For some of the best of the ancient sites, do the **Ding Dong Moor** route, a 3-mile walk following the footpath from **Bosullow** to **Men-an-tol** (see box), up to the atmospheric ruins of Ding Dong Mine and on to the standing stones known as the **Merry Maidens** (19 granite pillars, said to be a gaggle of girls who were turned to stone for dancing on a Sunday).

The healing stones of Men-an-Tol

On a clear day you can see all three coasts from the curious moorland monument, Men-an-Tol near Madron (OS map reference: SW426349). The unique arrangement of standing stones consists of a doughnut-like granite circle, or Crick Stone, and two vertical stones, which can be aligned by eye if you stand in the right place. There are various theories about its origin: the entrance to a tomb, perhaps, or a megalithic lunar observatory. And centuries of superstitious locals have imbued the stones with curative powers. Haul your sick, naked child through the stone three times to treat tuberculosis and rickets. And if you want to get pregnant, walk backwards through the hole, seven times, during a full moon.

Visiting **Land's End** is a symbolic gesture (have your photograph taken under the First and Last signpost) – but the visitor centre, a dispiriting collection of buildings with all the charm of a motorway service station, is best avoided. You can visit the Land's End headland for free, but there are lovelier, lonelier places on this coast: **Cape Cornwall** (the only cape on the British coast), **Zennor Head** and **Gurnard's Head** are favourites among dozens of headlands and lookouts, all accessible from the B3306 between St Ives and St Just. On the same route, check out the charming, privately owned **Wayside Museum** (☎ 01736 796945) at Zennor. In a series of themed areas, spread around the outbuildings and gardens of a 16th-century miller's cottage and granite water mill (the wheel still turns), there are crowded displays of some 500 artefacts, representing Cornish history from 3000BC to the 1950s. The museum is open daily from May to the end of September.

Further south, at Pendeen, the museum at **Geevor Tin Mine** is one of the most interesting on the peninsula. The largest preserved mining site in the UK, it was designated a scheduled

First and Last signpost at Land's End

Local legends: fish tales

In the Church of St Senara at Zennor, there is a gnarled oak seat made from medieval bench ends. On one carved panel, there is a mermaid holding a comb and mirror. This is the legendary Morveran, the bewitching she-creature, who won the love of a curate's son, Mathew Trewella. She heard the sweet-voiced Mathew singing the closing hymn at Evensong. Enchanted, she dragged herself on to dry land and up to the church. The moment the young man set eyes on the beautiful fish-girl, he was besotted. Losing all reason, he followed Morveran into the sea and disappeared, presumed drowned, beneath the waters of Pendour Cove.

monument in 2006, and made an important contribution to the Cornish Mining area's World Heritage status. But unlike most of mining's legacy, it was in use until 1991. Its closure ended 300 years of Penwith mining. This is no ordinary museum – remaining more or less as it was when the last miner left, it is a ramshackle collection of rusting industrial sheds which takes you on an indoor and partly underground journey through the tin-mining process. The guides are ex-miners, with first-hand experience of the hardships of their now redundant industry. Geevor's underground works had 21 levels stretching half a mile out to sea. The miners, we are told, worked in unbearable heat, and could hear rocks rolling on the seabed above their heads.

GEEVOR TIN MINE, Pendeen TR19 7EW; ☎ 01736 788662; www.geevor.com. Entry: adults £9.75, children/students, £5 (under-5s free); open daily except Sat, Easter to Oct, 10am–5pm (in winter until 4pm).

There is another opportunity to go underground at the National Trust's **Levant Mine** at Trewellard, where you can also see winding and pumping shafts and an active steam-powered Cornish beam engine (the oldest in Cornwall). Steam buffs love the place, but the evocative clatter of old machinery, the glorious sea views, belie the harsh realities: Levant remains a poignant

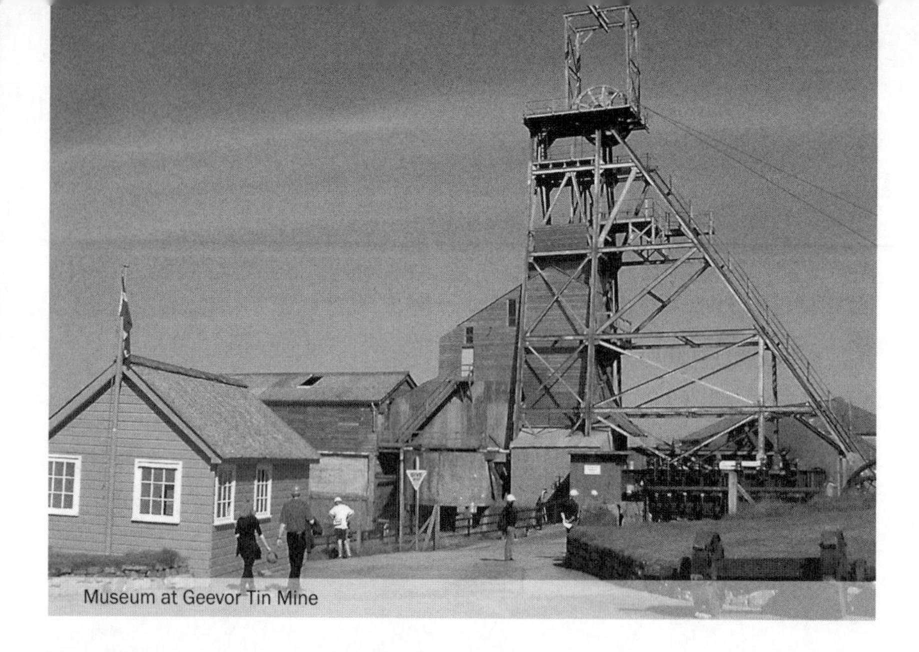
Museum at Geevor Tin Mine

LEVANT MINE, Trewellard, Pendeen TR19 7SX; ☎ 01736 786156; www.nationaltrust.org.uk. Entry: adults £6.10, children, £3; mid-May to Sept (Tues–Fri, Sun), Apr–mid-May/Oct (Wed/Fri), 11am–5pm; Jan–Mar/Nov–Dec, 11am–4pm.

memorial to the 31 miners who lost their lives in a lift failure in 1919. The mine closed in 1930. Both Geevor and Levant are now flooded to sea level.

The best preserved, and most photogenic of the many remaining tin-mining relics include two Crowns Mine engine houses and associated workings perched on the cliffs at **Bottallack**. The easiest to find are the remains of **Carn Galver** Mine, right on the B3066 coast road near Rosemergy. It's a great place to watch a sunset, and there's handy parking right next to the ruined engine houses.

By the sea

Although the coast is visible from almost every corner of this elevated peninsula, most of its beaches are small, rocky coves, often difficult to get to, or even difficult to find. An example is the lovely little cove at **Treen**. A steep climb down precarious cliff paths, it is only accessible during low tide – and it's popular with nudists. Park at the car park at Treen village and follow the signs for Logan Rock. On the west coast, **Portheras Cove** (a mile from Pendeen) is a favourite with locals, offering a lovely sandy beach and off-shore seals.

The largest, most popular beach in the region is at **Sennen** (a crescent of surfing beach at the southern end of the aptly named Whitesand Bay, a mile from Land's End). At one end is Sennen Cove, a small fishing harbour, at the other a line of surf shops, pubs and cafés looking west over the Atlantic, which often delivers spectacular waves. Less well-known is **Gwenvor**, a mile north-east of Sennen (walk along the coast path, and clamber down the cliffs). Some surfers reckon it offers the best, or at least the most consistent, surfing conditions in Cornwall.

On the gentle southern side of Land's End, you'll find a completely different seaside experience in **Porthcurno**: a dream of a beach with a deep bay of powdery white sand accessed down a sloping dune, or down steep steps from the clifftop **Minack Theatre**.

Sun, shade, shelter, a beach café and lots of parking all contribute to the summer crowds, but visit off-season and you can have the place more or less to yourself. To the west, tiny rocky **Porthgwarra**, in the lea of Gwennap Head, has a slipway leading down to small strip of sand, but the cove is best known for the tunnels which have been carved through rock to provide an easy passage from the village to the beach. They seem to reek of old smugglers, but actually they were used by donkeys carrying seaweed to nearby farms (for use as fertiliser). To the east of Porthcurno, there's a stoney beach at **Lamorna Cove**, a former quarry, reached via the beautiful Lamorna Valley, where a stream, banked by trees and pretty gardens, meanders through a village, once an outpost of the Newlyn School artistic colony.

A dog's life

He's an international star, a Crufts regular; he's even had a book written about him, but Bilbo, Britain's first and only 'beach safety dog', belongs in Sennen Cove. The 14-stone chocolate Newfoundland, patrols the beach wearing a canine lifeguard jacket printed with the message 'Swim between the flags', but he is occasionally required for active service. The specially trained dog won praise in August 2007, when he prevented a swimmer from entering dangerous waters.

Wet weather

It's hard to imagine the Porthcurno Valley as a world centre for international telecommunications, but from 1870 Porthcurno was connected to Mumbai via the 'victory internet', the first submarine telegraph cable. As the network grew, it became the epicentre of global Cable and Wireless communications and it still is. A fibre-optic cable system lies buried beneath Porthcurno's fine sandy beach.

The **Porthcurno Telegraph Museum**, a short walk uphill from the beach, tells the full story in a fascinating display of vintage hardware housed in a series of bomb-proof tunnels built to protect the centre during the Second World War. This is a journey around the world of communications, from needle telegraph to buzzer Morse, but it's the authentic 1940s atmosphere that really makes this place. In the Instrument Room, looking much like it would have would have done when it first opened in 1941, you can see an operational telegraph cable network using original 1920s–1930s equipment, and send a telegram. Ironically, there is no mobile phone signal in Porthcurno village.

PORTHCURNO TELEGRAPH MUSEUM, Eastern House, Porthcurno TR19 6JX; ☎ 01736 810966; www.porthcurno.org.uk. Entry: adults £6, children £3.40; open daily from Apr to Oct/Nov (dates vary), 10am–5pm; May to Sept, late nights (until 7.30pm) every Wed.

Doing an 'end to end'

The route to Land's End, from John O'Groats is a trail of human endeavour. Around 3,000 people a year attempt the 874-mile journey, and it takes all sorts: one of the first was Robert Carlyle, the Cornishman who walked to John O'Groats pushing a wheelbarrow in 1879. The first to do the journey by bicycle were Harman and Blackwell who made it in 12 days in 1880. More recently (1999), 53-year-old businessman Martyn Bracegirdle ran the route as a double-ended marathon (there and back), getting through eight pairs of shoes, 500 cans of beans, 1,000 Mars Bars and 500 litres of cranberry juice. In June 2003, Steve Gough did it naked; the following month, Barrie Walker carried a door on his back. Other curious modes of transport include a mobile skip, a fire engine, a wheelchair and a motorised garden shed. All are awarded honorary membership of the End to Enders Club (www.endtoenders.co.uk) based at Land's End.

What to do with children...

LAND'S END VISITOR CENTRE, Sennen TR19 7AA; ☎ 0871 7200044; www.landsend-landmark.co.uk. Entry: all-inclusive tickets: adults £10, children £7; family saver £25. Parking £5. Open daily in summer from 10am–5pm; in winter from 10.30am–3.30pm.

The **Land's End** visitor centre is the only theme-park-style indoor attraction in the area, and children do enjoy the Doctor Who Up Close exhibition or the Return to the Last Labyrinth 'sensory' theatre show (smugglers, wreckers, witches and the lost land of Lyonesse).

... and how to avoid children

WESTWARD AIRWAYS, Land's End Airport; ☎ 01736 788771. Price: £32–£82 per person, depending on route; or £270 an hour for tailor-made off-route flights; scenic flights available daily from Mar to Sept and by arrangement Oct to Feb.

Take to the skies in a Cessna light aircraft from Land's End airport. **Westward Airways** run frequent scenic flights (weather permitting) with a choice of three standard routes: A quick Land's End circuit, a Newlyn route (covering the south-west corner of the peninsular) and the longer Penwith route (from Penzance to St Ives, round Cape Cornwall and back to Land's End). The views from above are unforgettable.

CELEBRITY CONNECTIONS

Author **Helen Dunmore**, who has a home in St Ives, is among a string of well-known writers whose stories have been inspired by the landscapes of coastal Penwith. Cornishman **Winston Graham** made tin-mining sexy with the series of novels which formed the basis of 1970s cult TV drama *Poldark*, filmed at Botallack among other places. **Rosamund Pilcher's** autobiographical novel *The Shell Seekers* (based on her own Cornish upbringing in Lelant, near St Ives) was the best-selling paperback of the 1990s. The film of the same name, starring Patricia Hodge and Angela Lansbury, was filmed at Land's End, Lamorna Cove, Porthgwarra and Marazion.

Dunmore's more literary early novel *Zennor in Darkness* fictionalised DH Lawrence's bitter-sweet Cornish journey (he wrote most of *Women in Love* while staying in Zennor in 1916). And her celebrated trilogy of books for children (*Ingo, The Tide Knot, The Deep*) create a magical, mythical Mer world of an underwater Cornwall.

Entertainment

Theatre

A Romanesque amphitheatre in a clifftop gully on the south side of Porthcurno beach, the **Minack** is one of the most remarkable of English theatres. It was planned and developed by Derbyshire lass, Rowena Cade, who moved to Cornwall with her mother in the 1920s. The gully was in the seaside garden of a house they built at Minack on a crag of rock bought for £100. She begun the project in 1931, initially to provide a make-shift stage for a production of *The Tempest* by a local amateur dramatics group. The magic of this first performance inspired her to develop the theatre further, and she, her gardener and his apprentice built the auditorium, an access road and a flight of 90 steps linking the theatre to the beach, virtually by hand. Rowena not only carried bags of sand on her back, but she also etched intricate Celtic designs into the cement she used to build

Minack Theatre on the clifftop

the terraces. The project was to consume the rest of her life until she died aged 89 in 1983. Seven years earlier she had insured the theatre's future by handing it over to a charitable trust.

Shakespeare is still the maintstay of the Minack's programme of live events, which spans the summer months from May to September. There is a visitor centre and café, and non-theatre-goers can visit during the day.

MINACK THEATRE, Porthcurno, Penzance TR19 6JU; ☎ 01736 810181; www.minack.com. Entry: adults £4, children £2 (under-12s free); open daily: 9.30am–5.30pm (or until 11.30am on performance days).

Special events

St Just's community arts festival, the **Lafrowda Festival** (☎ 01736 888160; www.lafrowda-festival.co.uk) takes place in July, culminating in a Lafrowda Day parade. It is a week-long festival of the performing arts, each year adopting a theme (Faraway Places, Space, Legends and Playtime), expressed not only in the performances but in costumes and street decoration.

The best... PLACES TO STAY

BOUTIQUE

The Cove

Lamorna, Near Penzance TR19 6XH
☎ 01736 731411
www.thecovecornwall.com

In the heart of the valley, this contemporary complex of seaview apartments is billed as five-star self-catering, but the feel of the place is more luxury boutique hotel. There is a restaurant, bar, heated outdoor pool, children's play area and room service.

Price: from £115–£375 for a night, or from £1365 to £2625 for a peak week.

INN

Tinner's Arms/The White House

Zennor, St Ives TR26 3BY
☎ 01736 796927 www.tinnersarms.com

Right next door to the pub, in a Grade II listed building. Simple, light cottage-style rooms, hearty breakfasts using local produce which are cooked on the Aga downstairs.

Price: B&B from £95 for a double.

FARMSTAY

Tregiffian Farm

St Buryan TR19 6BG
☎ 01736 810243 www.tregiffianfarm.co.uk

Between Lamorna and Penberth Coves, a family-run dairy and beef farm with two comfortable guest rooms in a traditional farmhouse, both with pretty décor and views across fields to the sea. You also get a welcome tray and fresh farm eggs for breakfast.

Price: B&B from £90 for a double (children 5–12, £25).

SELF-CATERING

Nancy's House

Classic Cottages
☎ 01326 555555 www.classic.co.uk

On a working organic farm, on the St Ives side of Pendeen, this one-bedroom eco-friendly cottage sleeps two (babies up to six months are welcome). The decor is modern rustic, the rooms are dinky, and the electricity is powered by a wind turbine.

Price: From £279–£600 per week.

Kymaurah and Dovecote Cottages

Lamorna Cove ☎ 01736 732266
www.2lamorna.co.uk

Close to the beach with sea views, these are two barn cottages, both treated to an interior design makeover. Kymaurah has three double bedrooms, a gallery-like open-plan living space and a garden. Romantic Dovecote has a luxury 'contemporary gothic' look, a four-poster double, and an al fresco hot-tub.

Price: from £395–£995 per week.

Pendeen Lighthouse

Pendeen Watch
☎ 01386 701177 www.ruralretreats.co.uk

Vestal, Argus and Solebay are three original keepers' cottages which are available as holiday lets. Beautifully furnished, each has two bedrooms, a walled patio and all mod cons.

Price: from £441–£917 per week.

EATING OUT

RESTAURANTS

The Cove
Lamorna, Near Penzance TR19 6XH
☎ 01736 731411
www.thecovecornwall.com

Open to non-residents, the contemporary restaurant and pool-side terrace is a good place for a romantic meal. The Cornish-Mediterranean menu includes hand-dived scallops, Newlyn crab, local lamb and beef and a children's menu. Three courses cost around £30. Open daily Apr to Oct (and in the winter, Fri–Sun evenings, and Sunday lunch).

RESTAURANT/CAFÉ

The Beach Restaurant
Sennen Cove TR19 7BT
☎ 01736 871191
www.thebeachrestaurant.com

This multi award-winning café-style restaurant by the sea overlooks Sennen beach from a light, lofty timber building with wide deck of outdoor tables. There's a fixed day menu (salads, soups or homemade burgers) and a more expensive evening menu (Pina Colada pork, Cornish steak, scallops, marinated monkfish). It's great for summer evenings; perfect for sunsets. Lunches from £6.95; home-made pizzas from £8.25. Closed in winter (dates vary).

GASTRO PUB

Gurnard's Head
Near Zennor, St Ives TR26 3DE
☎ 01736 796928
www.gurnardshead.co.uk

'The Gurn' as the locals call it, was bought by the Inkin brothers in 2006 (they also own Felich Fach Griffin in Wales), and was transformed into a gastro pub with rooms. Keeping the old-pub atmosphere, they added a lick of Mediterranean paint, rustic refectory tables and a gastro menu (spring lamb, grilled langoustine, crab and fish stew, homemade pork pie) created by a Kiwi chef. There is a garden and lovely country views. Dishes cost from around £6.50 to £16.50. Also offers B&B.

CAFÉ

Geevor Mine Café
Pendeen TR19 7EW
☎ 01736 788662
www.geevor.com

It's basically a functional caféteria, but it has fantastic views of the coast to Pendeen Watch, and possibly the best pasties in the region – home-cooked by café franchisee, Margaret Burford. It's open to non-mine museum visitors and there's plenty of parking. Open all year, daily except Sat.

The best... FOOD AND DRINK

The Land's End peninsula is a natural larder of fresh produce and local-grown vegetables. There are no supermarkets (other than a small convenience store in St Just) and little in the way of shopping facilities – providing a good incentive to seek out local suppliers rather than trek to a superstore. With few hotels, and only one town, most of the best places to eat in the area are traditional pubs, of which there are many.

Staying in

In St Just, try **McFaddens** (☎ 01736 788136) in Market Square, for local meats, cheeses, homemade pies and delicious but high-in-calories steak pasties. Try neighbouring **Warrens Bakery** (☎ 01736 788538), founded in 1860, for Cornish saffron cake.

Bosavern Farm (☎ 01736 786739) at Kelynack, just outside St Just, has a little farm shop selling organic vegetables, naturally reared meat, free-range eggs and other produce. Further south, the shop at **Chegwidden Farm** near St Levan (☎ 01736 810516; www.chegwiddenfarm.com) sells rare-breeds pork (sausages, bacon, pork and apple burgers), Hereford beef and fresh vegetables.

Drinking

There are some genuinely old and largely unaltered country pubs in this area, and many form a convenient pub trail along the course of the B3306 coast road, between Zennor and St Just. Start with Zennor's atmospheric **Tinners Arms** (☎ 01736 796927; www.tinnersarms.com). Dating from 1271, DH Lawrence's former local is all low beams and dark wood; there is a warm fire in the winter and in the summer you can sit out in the pleasant seaview garden and enjoy a pint of Tinners or Sharp's Special (the latter labelled Zennor Mermaid). Next up is the **Gurnard's Head**, or 'the Gurn' (☎ 01736 796928; www.gurnardshead.co.uk) which not only serves a selection of Skinner's ales (Betty Stogs, Ginger Tosser) and Cornish ciders, but also good world wines (around 10 of them available by the glass).

At Pendeen, **The North Inn** (☎ 01736 788417; www.thenorthinnpendeen.co.uk) was CAMRA Pub of the Year in 2003, and continues to serve St Austell beers and hearty, homemade food at 'fair pub prices'. The attractive creeper-clad inn is lined with mining memorabilia (it was a tin-miners' local from the 19th century until nearby Geevor mine closed in 1990); and if you want to make a night of it, the pub has its own little campsite. There are more real ales on offer at the **Queens Arms** at Botallack (☎ 01736 788318), including Lizard Organic and Ales of Scilly. And finally in St Just, the St Austell Ales' **Star Inn** (☎ 01736 788767) is another traditional, no-frills pub, serving cask ales, seasonal beers, occasional live music and late-night openings at the weekend.

On the southern coast, near Porthcurno, the 400-year-old **Logan Rock Inn** at Treen (☎ 01736 810495) is a friendly, popular St Austell inn with bags of character. Or at Lamorna Cove, the **Wink Inn** is said to have started out as an illegal drinking den, where sprits were banned but a wink could produce a glass of smuggled brandy.

Visitor Information

Tourist information centre: The Library, Market Street, St Just TR19 7HX, ☎ 01736 7886699.

Hospitals with A&E: West Cornwall Hospital (see Penzance, page 305).

Doctors: Cape Cornwall Surgery, Market St, St Just TR19 7HX, ☎ 01736 788306.

Pharmacies: Ramsay Pharmacy, 42 Fore Street, St Just TR19 7LJ.

Police station: See Penzance information (page 305) or St Ives (page 290).

Supermarkets: Co-op, Market Square, St Just TR19 7HE; Tesco/Morrisons in Penzance (see page 305).

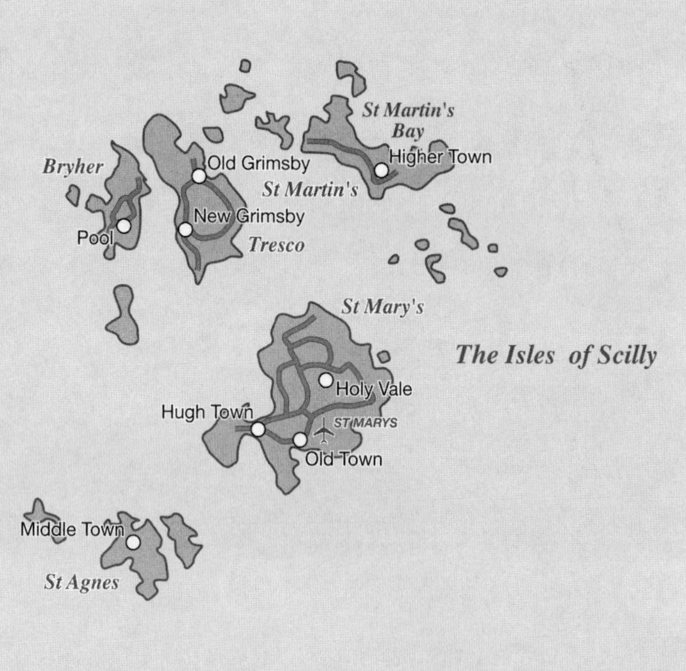

8 The Isles of Scilly

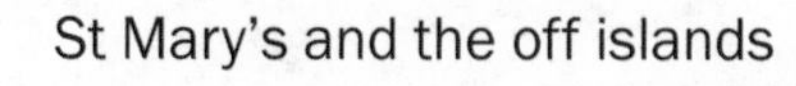

St Mary's and the off islands

Unmissable highlights

01 Enjoy a pasty, a pint and a perfect sunset on an evening cruise to the Turks Head on St Agnes, p. 335

02 From South Africa to the Med, take a horticultural tour of the world's sub-tropics at Abbey Gardens on Tresco, p. 324

03 Hire a bike and pedal around St Mary's: in a day you can do the entire island – more than once, p. 324

04 Play Robinson Crusoe on one of St Martin's dreamy white beaches – all yours most of the time, p. 328

05 Cruise around the rocky islets of the Eastern Isles, where you can meet the puffins or snorkel with seals, p. 324

06 Watch a pilot gig race – St Mary's hosts the World Championships in May, p. 331

07 Splash out of a Michelin-star meal at St Martin's Hotel's Tean restaurant, p. 336

08 Take a boat trip to the foot of the mighty Bishop's Rock lighthouse, a pillar of strength in these shipwrecking isles, p. 324

09 Walk across Bryher's lonely Shipman Head Down to stormy Hell Bay, p. 328

10 Buy a home-baked lunch made with home-grown ingredients at St Martin's award-winning bakery, p. 334

THE ISLES OF SCILLY

If you were teleported, blindfolded, to an Isles of Scilly beach on a summer's day, you could be forgiven for thinking that you'd washed up on a Caribbean island. The natural colour scheme leans towards the Aegean: a dappled palette of sapphire deeps and turquoise shallows, decorated with sea pinks and subtropical palms. The beaches are dazzling white, glittering with sea shells and more or less empty. Can this really be England?

The so-called Fortunate Isles are not always sunny of course; in fact they do a nice line in ship-tossing Atlantic storms; sea mists, common in early summer, can hide the entire archipelago behind a veil of white vapour for days on end; and the sea is much chillier than it looks. But the climate has a Mediterranean tang. Autumn hangs around for longer, and frost is unheard of. No wonder the islands' principal industry is growing flowers.

Just 28 miles to the south-west of Land's End, the Scillies are 56 islands – 200 if you count all the little islets of rock which rise from the sea like fairy castles. Only five are inhabited; the entire population runs to no more than 2,000 people, the majority living on St Mary's, the rest scattered across Tresco, St Martin's, Bryher and St Agnes. The smallest unitary authority in the UK, it's part of the Duchy of Cornwall and has been entitled to the Prince of Wales since 1337. What really governs this maritime community, however, is the weather and the tides – a factor which plays a large part in the islanders' laid-back approach to life. Nobody's in a rush, there's no crime and no traffic jams. The air is clean, the water pristine, there are no fast-food chains, and no nightlife other than starry skies. The attractions are mostly natural: the birds, the silence, the scent of wild garlic. And if we say that the Scillonians are warm and friendly, it's not just one of those things that people say in guide books.

ST MARY'S AND THE OFF ISLANDS

Around 80% of Scillies' visitors stay in Hugh Town, the village-like 'capital' of St Mary's, but the largest island remains one of the least explored. A crowd of day-trippers queuing on the quay for boats to the 'off islands' is a morning routine. There's another rush-hour when the boats return late in the afternoon, but though people eat, drink and shop in Hugh Town, they don't tend to see much of what the locals call 'Up Country'. Still, some complain that the place has become over-commercialised of late. And, yes, it has changed (more deli than dairy, more sailing clobber, more gift shops) but it's still at least a decade behind the mainland. Even by Cornish standards, St Mary's is delightfully backward.

A trip to one of the off islands is like winding the clock back yet another few years. Stand on the garrison above the harbour and you can see them laid out before you: to the east St Martin's, to the north, Tresco and Bryher, and right over to the west, tiny St Agnes. This is what most people come for: the scatter of jewel-like islands, each trimmed with a bracelet of white sand, each quite different than the other. Everyone has their favourite, but provided the weather's on your side, you can see them all in a few days.

WHAT TO SEE AND DO

St Mary's

Hugh Town, St Mary's capital, the islands' only town, is roughly the size of a Cornish fishing village, but in Scillonian terms, all life is here: shops, pubs, one supermarket, one bank. The airports sit above the town, a mile or so to the north. The drone of aircraft and helicopters flying in and out is part of St Mary's daily routine.

The town's centre sits within a narrow isthmus, at the south-west corner of the island, with the harbour and **Town Beach** on one side, **Porthcressa** beach on the other. A good place to start a day is outside the tourist information centre on Hugh Street which gives a chalk-board weather forecast and a time-table of the day's boat trips. Another good start is the **Wildlife Trust Visitor Centre** on the quay. The Trust, a registered charity, was formed in 1986 to protect the islands' wildlife and maintain its delicate balance of nature. Here, you can fill up on information about Scillies' flora, fauna and marine life, book snorkelling and diving trips, and get directions for walks.

WILDLIFE TRUST VISITOR CENTRE,
St Mary's Quay, High Town; ☎ 01720 422988; www.ios-wildlifetrust.org.uk.

Half a mile to the east of Hugh Town, is the **Old Town** – not a town at all, but a seaside hamlet on a nook of a bay. On the seafront, note the tiny **Old Town Church**, which holds candlelit services on Sunday evenings between April and September. The footpath from Hugh

Town to Old Town via the lighthouse on **Penninis Head** is one of St Mary's most popular walks, but there are dozens more.

Less than 3 miles across at its widest point, St Mary's is easily explored in a day, either on foot or by bike (car hire is almost unheard of). At a brisk pace, you can circumnavigate the entire island – around 10 miles of coastal footpath – in a few hours. Among shorter walks, follow the footpath from **Porthmellon** beach, on Hugh Town's northern outskirts, up to **Porthloo** beach and, ultimately to the café at **Juliet's Garden**. The route will take you past the **Porthloo Studios**, home to artists, craftspeople and the **Isles of Scilly Perfumery**, which makes soaps and scents from Scillonian flowers.

For magnificent views, particularly at sunset, take a stroll around the **Garrison**, a circle of fortifications around the island-like headland to the west of Hugh Town. You can start and finish at the 18th-century Garrison Gate next to the **Star Castle**. Built in 1593, in the form of an eight-pointed star, the castle has ramparts 18ft thick and a dry moat. The star-shaped quarters inside the fortress walls were converted into a hotel in the 1930s. In the summer, you can do these and other walks by joining local guide Katherine Sawyer's **Scilly Walks**; not only does she lead the way but her walks throw shafts of light on the archaeological and historical landscapes of the Scillies.

SCILLY WALKS, St Mary's; ☎ 01720 423326. Price: half-day walks: adults £5, children £2.50; full day walks: adults £10, children £5; Apr to early Oct.

Another way to see the island is to take a bus tour with **Island Rover**. One of the buses is the cranky vintage coach, a 1948 KT Austin, often seen parked on the Strand by the Town beach. In summer, they also run an open-top red bus, a bit like an old London Routemaster. The tours include a lively commentary and the odd unscheduled stop when the driver dallies in a lane to have a quick chat with someone he knows – and like everyone here, he knows everyone.

Island Rover bus tour on St Mary's

There's also a community bus service, which does a 17-minute island circuit around seven times a day, making it easy to plan walks around the time-table. Another good way of getting around is by bike. With just 3 miles of metalled roads, very few hills and hardly any traffic, it's hard to think of a safer place to cycle. Within a half-day's hire you can cover all the main roads – just country lanes – two or three times. But once you've done the obvious routes, there are miles of bumpy

ISLAND ROVER, The Nook, Church St, St Marys TR21 0JT; ☎ 01720 422131; www.islandrover.co.uk. Tours from £7 per person.

ST MARY'S BIKE HIRE, The Strand, ☎ 01720 422289. Half-day bike hire around £5; full-day £8.
BOOK A BIKE ON SCILLY, ☎ 01720 422786, www.bookabikeonscilly.com. Mountain bike hire, £12 for a day.

ST MARY'S BOATMEN'S ASSOCIATION, ☎ 01720 423999, www.scillyboating.co.uk. Price: adult return tickets from £8, children from £4; full service April to Oct; limited service Nov to Mar.

tracks to explore; roll downhill to the beautiful sandy beaches at **Pelistry Bay, Watermill Cove** or **Bar Point**; explore the Iron Age village at **Halangy Down**, or the pretty subtropical gardens at **Carreg Dhu** (where a notice invites visitors to a do a bit of weeding, with a bag of tools left behind a stone wall). You can hire bikes at reasonable cost from **St Mary's Bike Hire** or **Book A Bike**.

Boats trips

Most of the hotels work with a favourite boatman, making it easy to book your trip over breakfast; otherwise, head down to the quay and see what's on offer. The day's trips depend on the tides, but will usually include at least one daily trip to each of the four off islands – though poor weather can scupper all boat movements for days at a time. An association of 10 independent boatmen form the **St Mary's Boatman's Association** with a booth on the quay. The morning boats leave between 7.45am and 10.15am, and you can book tickets the night before.

Each of the off islands has its own boat service running independent trips between islands. And aside from inter-island services, there are numerous sight-seeing trips around the far-flung uninhabited islets. On a trip to lonely **Samson**, to the south of Bryher, you will see the eerie ruins of 19th-century houses, seabirds, seals and the lovely beach at Bar Point. Other trips will take you around the bird sanctuary at **Annet**, the seal colonies and peregrine falcons of the **Eastern Isles**, or to the shipwreck sites and puffin islands of the treacherous **Western Rocks**, up to **Bishop's Rock Lighthouse**. Courtesy of **Island Sea Safaris**, you can also do 'snorkelling with seals' trips, riding out to the seal colonies on an 8m high-speed RIB.

ISLAND SEA SAFARIS, Old Town, St Mary's; ☎ 01720 422732; www.islandseasafaris.co.uk. Price: Shipwrecks, Seals and Seabirds trip (2 hour): £31 per person, under-12s £21; Snorkelling with Seals £38 (including equipment).

Tresco

Tresco is the crowd-pleaser, the subtropical beauty, leased by the Duchy of Cornwall to the Dorrien-Smith family, and best known for its **Abbey Gardens** (*'Kew with the roof off'*), a world-class global garden of around 20,000 exotic plants. Here you'll find a jungle of bananas, Himalayan Ginger, New Zealand Flame Trees, cacti, palms, paper plants, prickly pears – plants that would struggle to survive on the mainland – thriving in a beautifully landscaped setting.

The gardens were begun by Hertfordshire squire, Augustus Smith, who took up the lease of Tresco in 1834. At its heart is the scant remains of the 12th-century St Nicholas priory, alongside the home of present incumbents, Robert and Lucy Dorrien-Smith. The gardens are

Wreckers ball: from Colossus to Cita

With over 500 recorded wrecks lying off the Scillies, the islands have a fearsome reputation as a seaman's graveyard. A map of the archipelago is dotted with the names of foundered ships and every island has a litany of tragedies on its conscience. For example, in October 1707, *HMS Association* sank on Gilstone Reef, along with three other ships *Firebrand*, *Eagle* and *Romney*, with the loss of 2,000 lives. But it's not just lost souls that make shipwreck headlines: among centuries of drowned cargoes, Scillies' seas are littered with goods ranging from gold bullion and Chinese porcelain to elephants tusks and pianos.

One of the most legendary of shipwreck treasures is that of the 74-gun warship, *HMS Colossus*, sunk in a storm off the coast of Samson in 1798. As well as wounded men from Nelson's fleet, the ship was carrying eight crates of Sir William Hamilton's Greek antiquities. Some of the pottery from this precious cargo was recovered in 1974 and is now in the British Museum.

Much later, the loss of *MV Cita* in 1997 left a wreckers' feast of a more prosaic nature. The Antiguan container ship ran aground at Newfoundland Point, to the south of St Mary's. Tyres, trainers, doors, kitchen scales, baby clothes and 2,400 miles of polyester tape were among the tons of goods that washed up on the islands' shores.

TRESCO ABBEY GARDENS, ☎ 01720 424108; www.tresco.co.uk. Entry: £10, under-16s free; open daily 10am–4pm.

not huge, but the wealth of plant life, the statuary, the walks and the vistas warrant a half-day visit. Laid out on terraces that slope down to Abbey Green, it is divided into themed zones: Bamboos, Mediterranean, South Africa Cliff, Pebble Garden, Palm Ring and East Rockery among others.

Included in the ticket price is the **Valhalla Museum**, a remarkable collection of ships' figureheads, begun by Augustus Smith and dating from the mid-19th century. Around 30 carved and painted figureheads show a craft tradition which died with the age of sail, all salvaged from merchant vessels shipwrecked off the isles. Typical is the sword-waving figurehead from the *Palinurus* wrecked on Lion Rock, off the northern tip of St Martin's, en route from Demerara in 1848, with the loss of all 17 crew.

The gardens sit on the southern end of the long narrow island, only a mile across at its widest point and 2 miles long. There are two freshwater pools, **Abbey Pool** and **Great Pool**, both attractive to bird-watchers. To the west lies **New Grimsby**, where the recent **Flying Boat Club** development has added a snazzy new timeshare and holiday resort to the shoreline.

To the east of Tresco is one long, continuous, white beach, running from the quay at **Old Grimsby**, just below the Island Hotel's private beach at **Raven's Porth**, down to the south end of **Pentle Bay**. Most of the land is gentle, green fields, criss-crossed by a network of lanes (used only by farm vehicles and golf buggies) and dotted with holiday cottages, a church, a school and the **New Inn** pub. The storm-battered North End is more rugged, and furnished with the ruins of a 17th-century tower, **Cromwell's Castle**; at the northern tip, the impressive

Ruins of Cromwell's Castle on Tresco

cave at **Piper's Hole**, was the haunt of smugglers and, so they say, mermaids. The island is, in essence, an independent resort and with its own helipad and direct helicopter flights from the mainland, some of its visitors never see beyond Tresco. A pity, because it's not typical of Scilly. There's something slightly unreal about the place; with its clean-cut rather corporate air; you half expect the cows to be stamped with a Tresco logo. Do visit, but not at the expense of the other islands.

Duchy of Cornwall

The Isles of Scilly have been part of the Duchy of Cornwall since its creation in 1337 by Edward III for his son Prince Edward, also known as the Black Prince. Ever since, the ruling of the Duchy's lands has been handed down to the eldest son of the British monarchy, currently the Prince of Wales.

As a whole, the Duchy is spread around 23 counties, with the highest concentration of landholdings in the south west, but in no other region does it have more sway than in the Scillies, where it owns the freehold of large swathes of land and a third of the houses. In his role as Duke of Cornwall, Prince Charles is not entitled to profit from the sale of these assets, only from the income they generate, but there is more than a hint of medieval feudalism about the Duchy's power over Scillonian properties and its tenants.

Tresco has a different story. In 1834, the Duchy leased the islands to Hertfordshire merchant banker, Augustus Smith, one of the few Lord Proprietors to have made the islands his home. The Local Government Act of 1988, resulted in a new democratic Isles of Scilly government but the Smith family's long lease still applies to Tresco. Everything on the island is owned and run by current incumbents, Robert and Lucy Dorrien-Smith, heirs of the Tresco Estate.

Bryher

Bryher is the smallest of the inhabited islands, with a community of 100 residents, a single road, a 'Town' (a handful of cottages and a church), a tea room, a café-bar, a post office and the **Hell Bay Hotel**. There are two quays, both on the east shore: **Anneka Quay** (built for the television show *Challenge Anneka* in 1992) and **Church Quay**. Other than that it's just rolling

LOCAL KNOWLEDGE

James Francis manages the Star Castle Hotel alongside his father, Robert and wife Ella. The family have moved to the Isles of Scilly – twice; first as the founders of St Martin Hotel in the 1980s, and then in 2003 to take over the historic Star Castle. They live in Hugh Town on St Mary's, making the most of the sea at every opportunity, regularly fishing, boating and enjoying the outdoor life.

Best thing about living there: Being out of the rat race. The lack of traffic and crime adds hugely to the laid-back atmosphere and there's a sense of community that I haven't felt anywhere else. The natural beauty of the place is awesome.

Favourite restaurant: Blues opposite the Bishop and Wolf pub in Hugh Town serves a very good standard of modern French-English food using fresh, local produce.

Favourite beach: Great Bay on St Martin's. Or just St Martin's – the whole island is one big gorgeous, white-sand beach.

Favourite café: The tea rooms at Carnvean near Pelistry Bay on St Mary's – it's a lovely spot, as is the Coastguards on St Agnes. I also like Dibble and Grub on St Mary's, for superb views and very good food.

Favourite pubs: The Mermaid and The Atlantic, both in Hugh Town. For lunch, I also like The Turks Head on St Agnes. It's right by the sea, sheltered from the prevailing wind, and serves great food and good beer.

Best walk: Walking all the way round any of the off-islands is entirely manageable and a great pleasure. The walks tend to be quite flat and you can always see the sea and over to the other islands.

Best thing to do on a rainy day: Go to the pub! The joy of the Scillies is that it hasn't caught up with modern-day living and there are no theme parks, nor manufactured activities.

Best boat trip: Mark Groves' Sea Safaris which bounce out to the outlying islets on a fast RIB looking at seals, puffins and shipwrecks. The boats are equipped with underwater cameras, making it easy to see all the marine life, too.

downs of wildflowers and hillocks of heathland trimmed by the islets and sandy beaches of **Green Bay** on the eastern shore, and **Great Porth** to the west. You can easily stroll around Bryher in half a day.

To the south of the island lies unpopulated Samson, the cursed isle of author Michael Morpurgo's classic children's book *Why the Whales Came*, which is set on Bryher. At the wild north end, stand on **Badplace Hill**, for views of **Shipman Head** and **Hell Bay**, the names of which come into their own in an Atlantic storm. On a few days a year, when the tide is at its lowest, you can walk, or wade, across sand and shallow water, from Bryher to Tresco, or vice versa.

St Martin's

In the north-east corner of the archipelago, St Martin's is noted for its fabulous beaches, in particular the long stretches of fine white sand at **Great Bay**, on the north shore and **Lawrence Bay** and **Par Bay** on the south. Aside from the few people that spill out of St Martin's Hotel by the Lower Town Quay, you will mostly have these beaches to yourself.

St Martin's is a gentle isle, like a large flowery market garden, all stone cottages, verdant hedgerows, meadows of wildflowers and vivid colour. A hilly spine runs through its middle, where a single road links the hamlets of Lower Town, Middle Town and Higher Town – where you'll find the post office, bakery, tea rooms, two galleries and **Little Arthur Farm** (☎ 01720 422457). The latter is run as a 'green enterprise' self-sufficiency scheme and invites you to follow a series of trails around the 8-acre farm. You can see the best of the island on foot in three or four hours, taking in the 17th-century Daymark at **St Martin's Head**, to the far east, **Cruthers Hill** (for Bronze Age rubble and views of the Eastern Isles), or **Rabbit Rock** at the western tip, for views of White Island. Add extra time for lunch at the **Seven Stones Inn**, or a tour of **St Martin's Vineyard**, Britain's most southerly winery, producing small quantities of a palatable red and crisp white wines.

ST MARTIN'S VINEYARD, St Martin's TR25 0QL; ☎ 01720 423418; www.stmartinsvineyard.co.uk. Price: self-guided tour £1, 1 hour guided tour £3 (with tasting £4.50); weekdays in summer, 11am–4pm.

Seven Stones Inn on St Martin's

Flowers from Churchtown Farm on St Martin's

The award-winning **Scented Island Flowers** ('Scent from the Islands'; ☎ 01720 422169; www.scillyflowers.co.uk) at Churchtown Farm is also based on St Martin's. Owners Andrew and Hilary Julian send out around 75,000 mail-order presentation boxes of flowers a year. In 2007 they won the Farming Family of the Year award in recognition of this expanding island enterprise. You can buy flowers direct from the farm office, which is open daily.

St Agnes

Only one-mile across, unspoilt St Agnes is the prettiest, most remote, most Scillonian of the islands; essentially a flower-farming community, with moorland-like landscapes at one end and fields of spring daffodils, at the other. Next door is **The Gugh** (pronounced *gew* as in few) which you would call an island were it not for a sand bar that connects the two at low tide. St Agnes has a population of just 72 people (at the last count) and no cars, other than a couple of quad bikes; its doll-house cottages are connected by footpaths and its cricket team, fire brigade and gig crew are more or less the same people. But despite its size, it manages to pack a lot in.

The village sustains three cafés, a post office and a flower shop. To the west, **Troy Town Farm** runs a small herd of Jersey and Ayshire cows (and a Hereford bull called Ding Dong). To the east, the **Turks Head** pub, overlooks the Old Quay. At the island's centre, **St Agnes Lighthouse**, is one of the oldest in England, the lighthouse tower dating from the 1680s. Closed in 1911, it's now privately owned, though there is a self-catering cottage in its grounds.

Walk the gorse-and-heather sprigged wilds of **Wingletang Down** with its fox-gloves and craggy rocks leading up to **Horse Point** at the island's southern tip; take a peek inside **St Agnes Church**, the most enchanting little chapel, said to be built on the proceeds of wrecking. At **Porth Coose** – among other sheltered bays – sit on a perfect crescent of glittering white sand and listen to the sound of oystercatchers on the wind. Or cross the sandbar to Gugh at low tide; the views across St Mary's Sound from **Kittern Rock** are among the best on the islands.

Calf from Troytown Farm, St Agnes

Wet weather

The Scillies holiday is all about the outdoor life, and most of its visitors are prepared to take the rough with the smooth, striding out across islands in the most inclement of weathers. One of the few indoor visitor centres, is the delightful **Isles of Scilly Museum**, open since 1967, after gales on the Eastern Isles exposed a cachet of Romano-British treasures – enough to warrant a small museum. As well as archaeological finds, the collection represents the island's history, industries and traditions with an eclectic mix of ancient jewellery, ship-building, smuggling and wrecking relics, wild flowers, local art, sea shells and stuffed birds.

ISLES OF SCILLY MUSEUM, Church Street, St Mary's; ☎ 01720 422337; www.iosmuseum.org. Entry: adults £2, children 50p. Open Mon-Fri, 10am-4.30pm, Sats 10am-12pm.

There's another folk museum at the **Longstone Heritage Centre**, right in the middle of St Mary's near Holy Vale. The charmingly amateur centre tells the story of the islands and its people in a village-hall style display of photographs and artefacts.

LONGSTONE HERITAGE CENTRE, Longstone, St Mary's TR21 0NW; ☎ 01720 423732; Entry: adults £2, children 50p; open daily Apr to Nov, 9.30am–5.30pm.

What to do with children...

Shrimping, crabbing, combing beaches for shells and driftwood, building sand castles and sploshing about in clean shallow water, are the simple activities that make the Scillies so popular with families. Among the best child-friendly beaches are **Porthcressa** on St Mary's, **Par Beach**, or **Lawrence's Bay** on St Martin's (particularly at the sheltered end close to the quay), **Rushy Bay** on Bryher, **the Cove** at St Agnes and almost any beach on Tresco.

Riding tour from St Mary's Riding Centre

World Pilot Gig Championship

The islands are virtually crime-free and there's no traffic to worry about. Even the horses are 'gentle and well-mannered'; so says Claire Morley of **St Mary's Riding Centre**, which offers short guided hacks over gentle terrain, perfect for young novices.

ST MARY'S RIDING CENTRE, Maypole, St Mary's TR21 0NU; ☎ 01720 423 855; www.horsesonscilly.co.uk. Price: from £16 half-hour lead rein ride for beginners (minimum age four).

 ...and how to avoid children

By prior arrangement, you could spend an hour or so looking around Mark Praeger's micro brewery, **Ales of Scilly**, on the Porthmellon Industrial Estate (01720 423233). The former deputy head at St Mary's primary school started the brewery in 2001 and has since expanded three times, eventually moving to his current premises on the outskirts of St Mary's where he brews two regular ales, both best bitters, and a variety of seasonal brews, such as Chaplain of the Ales, made to celebrate the arrival of a new vicar. The little brewery is not technically open to the public but, as Mark says, he's always happy to *'show off my baby'*.

 Entertainment

Special events

The biggest event of the year is May's **World Pilot Gig Championship** (☎ 01720 422000; www.worldgigs.co.uk), involving some 200 teams of oarsmen (and women), from all over the West Country and beyond. At no other time do the islands get so crowded, nor indeed, so rowdy. It's all very good humoured but there's a lot of late-night drinking involved, particularly on the last day of the Friday-to-Monday event. Every room on the island is booked, every table taken.

In April (times vary) the annual **Walk Scilly** festival (☎ 01720 422603; www.walkscilly.co.uk) encourages off-season visitors to enjoy the Scillies' early spring. The festival features over 40 guided walks ranging from a Narcissi Flower Walk on St Martin's to a late evening Astronomy Walk on St Mary's, the event is timed to coincide with the **Isles of Scilly Folk Festival** (www.scillyfolkfestival.org.uk).

Tresco marathon

The best... PLACES TO STAY

BOUTIQUE

Hell Bay Hotel

Hell Bay, Bryher; ☎ 01720 422947
www.hellbay.co.uk

This micro resort sits on the west coast of Bryher, and offers a cluster of studio-style rooms close to the beach at Great Porth. Expect Lloyd Loom, seaside art, boat-shed beams and Caribbean colours. The restaurant is excellent, too.

Price: half board from £270 for a double.

St Mary's Hall

Church Street, Hugh Town, St Mary's TR21 0JR
☎ 01720 422 316
www.stmaryshallhotel.co.uk

In a house built in the 1920s by Count Leon de Ferrari (from Tuscany) for his Scillonian wife Enid, on the outer edge of Hugh Town. It has a bit of a split personality with leather, wood and fire-engine reds in the bright new brasserie-bar and traditional frills in the rooms.

Price: half board from £190 for a double.

HOTEL

Star Castle

The Garrison, St Marys TR21 0TA
☎ 01720 422317
www.star-castle.co.uk

The best hotel on St Mary's by a mile, and in one of the islands' oldest, most interesting buildings. Choose between castle rooms or garden suites. The décor is light and modern, and some have private terraces with views of the off islands.

Price: half board from £85 per person.

St Martin's Hotel

St Martin's Isle
☎ 01720 422090
www.stmartinshotel.co.uk

Built in 1989, with Prince Charles' blessing, and designed to look like a row of stone cottages, it's right on the island's quay, with what seems like its own beach at the foot of seaside gardens. There's a fresh ocean-breeze look to the décor, though the luxury rooms are quite chintzy.

Price: half board from £150 per person (look out for last-minute specials).

Island Hotel

Tresco Estate
☎ 01720 422883
www.tresco.co.uk

The décor is a tad dated, a shade too bright, but this is the classic of the Tresco hotel colony. There's a range of room types, including luxury suites and family rooms, but most have verandas or a garden terrace and sea views that really couldn't be bettered.

Price: half board from £135–£350 per person.

INN

Atlantic Hotel

St Mary's TR21 0PL
☎ 01720 422417
www.atlantichotelscilly.co.uk

Right in the middle of 'town', this St Austell Brewery inn has been welcoming guests since the 1860s. Spruced up rooms, some with four-poster beds, have all the usual mod cons, and most have great views of the harbour. Downstairs is the Ocean Bar and Tide Reach restaurant.

Price: B&B from £75 per person.

The best... PLACES TO STAY

B&B

Shearwater Guest House

The Parade, Hugh Town, St Mary's TR21 0LP
☎ 01720 422402
www.shearwater-guest-house.co.uk

Traditional terraced cottage in central Hugh Town, with five simple but comfortable guest rooms with a nautical look. Evening meals available four nights a week.

Price: B&B from £68 for a double.

Covean Cottage

St Agnes
☎ 01720 422620

There are seaviews from every room in this homely stone-built guest house on St Agnes. Home-cooked meals are available in a conservatory dining room. And there is also a 'Little House' self-catering cottage available.

Price: B&B £85 for a double.

Polreath Guest House

Higher Town, St Martin's TR25 0QL
☎ 01720 422046
www.polreath.com

Family-run guest house in a traditional stone-built house and pleasant garden on St Martin's with seaviews from each of its three four-star rooms. The owners also run the Polreath tea rooms – except hearty breakfasts and cream teas.

Price: B&B from £95 for a double.

CAMPSITE

Troy Town Campsite

St Agnes TR22 0PL
☎ 01720 422360
www.troytownscilly.co.uk

Part of Troy Town dairy farm, you can camp right on the beach at this seaside site, with views across the Atlantic to the island of Annet and Bishop's Rock Lighthouse.

Price: from £7.50–£8.50 per person per night, plus £1–£7 for each tent (depending on size).

SELF-CATERING

The Flying Boat Club

New Grimsby, Tresco
☎ 01720 422883; www.tresco.co.uk

The latest addition to the Tresco community, this posh time-share-cum-holiday complex has the feel of an exclusive sailing club. The weekly rental entitles you to use the club facilities (indoor pool, gym, bar, restaurant). The sea views are stunning.

Price: from £1,445 for a week (for six people).

The Sandpiper

Peninnis Farm, St Mary's TR21 0NA
☎ 01720 422122
www.sandpiper-scilly.co.uk

Contemporary, open-plan all mod-cons apartment with views of the quay and harbour and sleeping four in two bedrooms. Available all year, it's one of a collection of self-catering holiday homes in St Mary's.

Price: from £650 per week.

The best... FOOD AND DRINK

Eating out on the Scillies is a shade more expensive than on the mainland, as food production is costly. There is, for example, no abattoir on the islands; animals have to be shipped to the mainland for slaughter, and the meat shipped back for consumption. Seafood is, of course, plentiful, particularly lobster, crab and crawfish, line-caught hake, turbot, pollack and John Dory – all brought in by small family-run fishing boats. The off islands produce, among other goodies, jams, chocolates and, on St Martin's, wine. St Mary's even has its own Ales of Scilly microbrewery at Porthmellon Industrial Estate.

At the budget end of eating out, head for the pubs (see drinking) and cafés. Most of the best restaurants are part of high-end hotels. In 2007, St Martin's Hotel's restaurant won the Scillies' first Michelin star. But home-cooked food is standard on the islands; McDonald's and Pizza Express haven't made it this far.

Staying in

In summer, there's a **local produce market** at Holgates Green (in fine weather) or undercover in St Mary's Town Hall, usually on the first Thursday of the month. This is where you'll meet the majority of the Scillies' farmers and food producers.

In Hugh Town, there are several high street food shops: **The Deli** on Hugh Street (☎ 01720 422734) is housed in former butcher's shop Woodcock and Mumford (the sign survives), and sells a range of fresh-made salads and pizzas to eat in or takeaway, as well as local deli fare, like Cornish cheeses, **Little Island Chocolate Company** chocolates and **Wendy & Mollie's** marmalade (both products of St Agnes). For meat, **S Griffin and Son** the butchers on Garrison Lane (☎ 01720 422626) sells fresh local meats including Cornish and Scillonian (when available) and pies. **Longstone Farm** on St Mary's has its own small beef herd. For fish, you can buy fresh from the **Gallery Fish and Chip** shop in Hugh Street between 9am and 12pm; or **Martin Bond Fish** (☎ 01720 423113) does deliveries in his back-of-a-van mobile shop.

On St Agnes, **Troytown Farm** (☎ 01720 422360; www.troytown.co.uk) is home to the Scillies' only dairy, and the place for fresh butter cream and delicious Troytown ice cream. The farm will deliver milk and other produce to self-catering cottages on the island on a quad-bike, or you can visit the farm's little shop for supplies of sausages and home-grown poly-tunnel vegetables – whatever happens to be growing at the time.

The islands' only bakery is **St Martin's Bakery** at Higher Town (☎ 01720 423444; www.stmartinsbakery.co.uk) on St Martin's. Aside from delicious traditional loaves, it churns out cakes, pastries, pasties, savoury tarts, salads and picnic food. Much of the ingredients are either home-produced (eggs, pork, home-dried tomatoes) or local, a factor which won the title 'Best UK Food Retailer' in BBC Radio 4's Food and Farming Awards in 2002. In winter you can join the bakery's holiday baking courses.

Much of the Scillies' home-grown fare is presented at **Tresco Stores** (☎ 01720 422806) by the quay at New Grimsby. A bit like a mini Waitrose, it's bigger than Hugh Town's Co-op, and stocks just about everything you could possibly want on a self-catering holiday including groceries, wines, Cornish cheeses and Tresco's own grass-fed beef.

Baking course at St Martin's Bakery

Drinking

There are four pubs on St Mary's, all in Hugh Town, and one on each of the three off islands – Bryher doesn't have a pub, unless you count the bar at the **Hell Bay Hotel**, or the licensed **Fraggle Rock** café-bar. All are traditional inns, all of them patronised by regular Scillonian folk, all serve food and some offer accommodation, too.

If you arrive by boat, the first stop is **The Mermaid Inn** (☎ 01720 422701) almost on the quay. The large, salty, boaty bar to the fore offers a good selection of real ales, including **Ales of Scilly** brews. It's particularly lively during gig racing events. On Hugh Street, the **Atlantic Inn** (☎ 01720 422323) has a big, busy St Austell Brewery bar with views of the harbour to the rear. Regular quiz nights (usually Thursdays) and live music make it one of the most popular with locals. Get there early, or book, if you want to eat there in high season. The **Porthcressa Inn** (☎ 01720 422405) serves Sharp's and Ales of Scilly beers and has a south-facing terrace of tables overlooking Porthcressa beach. The **Dungeon Bar** at the Star Castle Hotel, is also open to non-residents. The bar manager, an affable Scouser called Dave, has done the equivalent of a life sentence in the castle's Tudor dungeons and rarely forgets a face.

Among the Scillies' finest is the **Turks Head** on St Agnes – the UK's most south-westerly pub. Aside from a wonderful location, looking down on the Old Quay and the island of Gugh, it's warm, friendly and does great food. A homemade pasty and a pint in the Turks sea-view garden is one of the Scillies' must dos. Look out for sunset cruises to the Turks Head from St Mary's. The gastro pub **New Inn** on Tresco (☎ 01720 422844; www.tresco.co.uk) is furnished with nautical memorabilia, has tables in a seaview garden and serves Tresco Tipple (brewed in Cornwall) and local brew Natural Beauty alongside Michelin-listed pub food. On St Martin's, the **Seven Stones Inn** (☎ 01720 423560) is a low stone building perched on Tinklers Hill to the west of the island among meadows of wild flowers. The bar is decked with flags, there is a deck of refectory-style tables outside and the pub's partnership with St Martin's Bakery ensures excellent food. The **Round Bar** at St Martin's Hotel is a good place for a chilled sundowner.

EATING OUT

FINE DINING

Tean

St Martin's Hotel
☎ 01720 422092
www.stmartinshotel.co.uk

Named after the island it overlooks, the upper floor restaurant at St Martin's Hotel was awarded a Michelin star in 2007, the first on the island. It's a slick, no-T-shirts sort of place, serving simple but beautiful dishes using mainly local ingredients: Scillonian pollack, Newlyn sea bass, Bude venison and the like. Three-course dinner costs £39.50. For lunch try the hotel's less formal Round Bar and Bistro, which has seaside tables in the garden. Open daily Easter to October.

Star Castle

The Garrison St Marys TR21 0TA
☎ 01720 422317
www.star-castle.co.uk

The castle's two restaurants tend to get overshadowed by the more famous off island hotels, but the food and service here are seriously good. If you ate here every day of the week, you would be unlikely to see the same dish twice. For wet or winter nights, try the cosy castle dining room, with the meatier of the two menus; or for summer evenings, go for the fish-and-seafood conservatory in the garden. Both do a three-course dinner at around £30. The restaurant grows its own vegetables and herbs, and runs a lobster/crab boat, the *Gallos*.

RESTAURANT

Chez Michel

Nornour, Hugh Town, St Mary's TR1 111
☎ 01720 422871

It has the aura of cheap French bistro but what looks a little dingy by day is bijou by evening, and the home-cooked food is among St Mary's best. Swiss chef-patron Michel's seasonal menu might include Cornish fillet steak, rack of lamb, baked sea bass and St Agnes ice cream. Lobster requires 24-hour notice. Three courses cost around £25.

Blues Restaurant

The Cornerhouse, Hugh Street, St Mary's TR21 0LL
☎ 01720 422221
www.bluesrestaurantscilly.co.uk

Fresh blue-and-white décor, and seasonal produce is the order of the day in this central Hugh Town bistro-bar. Expect a daily specials board (lots of fish, local asparagus and Scilly vegetables) and the signature dish, roasted monkfish on crab and saffron risotto. Mains cost from £13.50. Open Easter to end of October.

Boat Shed

Porthmellon, St Mary's TR21 0JY
☎ 01720 423881
www.the-boatshed.co.uk

Sunny and jolly with the beach literally on the doorstep (you walk across sand to get there) it is, as the name suggests, an old boat house. The food is local with an emphasis on seafood, and a dash of Mediterranean (mains cost from £10.95), though we found it a little militant about portion control. Closed in winter.

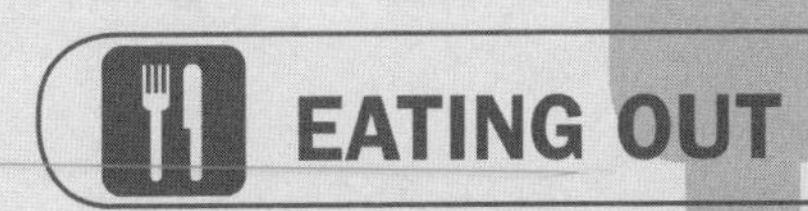

EATING OUT

Juliet's Garden Restaurant

Seaways Flower Farm, St Mary's
☎ 01720 422228
www.julietsgardenrestaurant.co.uk

On an elevated spot above Porthloo, this is good food with breathtaking views of St Mary's harbour from a lofty, woody barn conversion. Serving everything from cream teas to à la carte dinners, the menu includes crab salads, homemade soups, fish, meat and vegetable dishes (from £12.95). You can sit outside on the terrace, but the views are just as good indoors. On foot from Hugh Town takes about 20 minutes.

CAFÉ

Dibble and Grub

The Old Fire Station, Porthcressa Beach, St Mary's
☎ 01720 423719

Overlooking the beach at Porthcressa, this feels like a little corner of the Med – particularly if you manage to grab an outdoor table on a sunny day. Warm paninis, tapas, fish and vegetarian dishes are served with wines and beers. Lunches cost from £5.

Tolman Café

St Mary's Old Town
☎ 01720 423060

Smart contemporary décor, affordable bistro-style food and a handy location, just above the beach at Old Town, this friendly café is popular with locals, and is open all day every day (except January). Dishes include classic English breakfast, crab soup with homemade bread or steak. Hot meals from £7.50.

Coastguards Café and High Tide

St Agnes TR22 0PL
☎ 01720 422197
www.hightide-seafood.com

Home-cooked food using island produce served on driftwood tables in a cottage-café with wonderful views over the Western Rocks. By day, it's all toasties, teas, cappuccinos and cakes; in the evening, it transforms into High Tide, an informal fish restaurant. Dine on St Agnes crab sushi rolls, red mullet, wild sea bass with steamed samphire, or wood pigeon risotto. Three courses around £25 per head. Open Wed–Sat, Apr–Oct.

Little Arthur Café

Higher Town, St Martin's TR25 0QL
☎ 01720 422457

Little Arthur Farm's organic produce makes it straight to the table in this rustic little café-bistro overlooking the Eastern Isles. Bistro meals (from £8) are served most evenings and on Tues/Thurs it's open for fresh fish and chips (from £6). Check for opening times.

TEA ROOM

Vine Café

Vine House, Bryher, TR23 0PR
☎ 01720 423168

In a little hut of a building within yards of Annneka's Quay, this is the Women's Institute school-room style of catering, the staples being home-made scones, cakes and cream teas. Opening times can be erratic but it's generally open daily for snack lunches and for home-cooked dinners five nights a week: two courses cost £15 (bring your own wine). Closed in winter.

Visitor Information

Tourist information centre: Isles of Scilly Tourist Information Centre, Hugh Street, St Marys TR21 0LL ☎ 01720 424031, www.simplyscilly.co.uk.

Hospitals with A&E: St Mary's Hospital, Hospital Lane, St Mary's TR21 0LE, ☎ 01720 422392.

Doctors: The Health Centre, King Edward Lane, St Marys TR21 0HE, ☎ 01720 422628.

Pharmacies: The Health Centre, King Edward Lane, St Marys TR21 0HE, ☎ 01720 422 628.

Police station: Isles of Scilly Police Station, Garrison Lane, Hughtown, St Marys TR21 0JD.

Supermarkets: The Co-op in Hugh Town is the islands' only supermarket.

Internet access: Available at the tourist information centre, listed above; £1 for 15 minutes.

ATMs: Lloyds Bank, Hugh St TR21 0LL.

Local taxis: Q Cabs, St Mary's, ☎ 01720 422260; St Mary's Taxis ☎ 01720 422555.

INDEX

C

D

E

F

G

H

S

T

This second edition published in Great Britain in 2011 by
Crimson Publishing, a division of Crimson Business Ltd
Westminster House
Kew Road
Richmond
Surrey
TW9 2ND

First published 2009

A catalogue record for this book is available from the British Library

ISBN: 978 1 78059 041 7

Printed and bound by Ashford Colour Press Ltd., Gosport, Hants.

Series editor: Guy Hobbs
Layout design: Nicki Averill, Amanda Grapes, Andy Prior
Typesetting: Nicki Averill
Cover design: Andy Prior
Picture editor: Holly Ivins
Production: Sally Rawlings
Town map design: Linda M Dawes, Belvoir Cartographics & Design and Angela Wilson, All Terrain Mapping, using source material from Ordnance Survey.
Regional map design: Linda M Dawes, Belvoir Cartographics & Design and Angela Wilson, All Terrain Mapping, using source material: © Maps in Minutes™/Collins Bartholomew, 2009.

Acknowledgements

The author would like to thank the following writers for their tireless support and invaluable contributions: Honor Peters (St Austell Bay and Roseland, plus large chunks of the Background section), Jo Renshaw (Falmouth) and Steve Wright (Truro). Thanks too to Anna Rice and Kitty Wheeler Shaw (for their help in researching and compiling information) and, in Cornwall, Rhona Gardner at Excess Energy, Sir Vyvyan Ferrers at the Trelowarren Estate, the Francis family at Star Castle, the Earl and Countess of St Germans, Julia Cox at Visit Cornwall, Anthony Frost, Mike Parnell at Carruan Farm, Helen Gilchrist of Stranger magazine, Alan Stokes, Deborah Boden and the team behind the Cornish Mining World Heritage Site.

Help us update

While every effort has been made to ensure that the information contained in this book was accurate at the time of going to press, some details are bound to change within the lifetime of this edition: phone numbers and websites change, restaurants and hotels go out of business, shops move, and standards rise and fall. If you think we've got it wrong, please let us know. We will credit all contributions and send a copy of any *The Best of Britain* title for the best letters. Send to: The Best of Britain Updates, Crimson Publishing, Westminster House, Kew Road, Richmond, Surrey TW9 2ND.

Cornwall picture credits

Front cover: Fisherman's Cove, www.britainonview.com; **Inside flap:** Greenaway Beech just outside St Moritz Hotel, David Loftus, St Moritz Hotel; **Back cover:** Padstow Boats, www.britainonview.com; Wheal Coates mine, B. Gamble © Cornwall County Council, www.cornishmining.co.uk; **Inside cover:** Pentle Bay, Tresco Estate; **Contents:** Kite surfers at Watergate Bay, www.britainonview.com/Martin Brent; **Introduction double page:** Ding Dong Mine in Penwith, B. Gamble © Cornwall County Council, www.cornishmining.org.uk; **Introduction:** Sailing at Tresanton, Tresanton Hotel; **Introduction:** Sunset at Island Hotel, Robert Sanger, Blue Planet images; **Unmissable Highlights: 1.** B. Gamble © Cornwall County Council, www.cornishmining.org.uk; **2.** www.britainonview.com/Eden Project; **3.** English Heritage; **4.** www.britainonview.com/ Martin Brent; **5.** National Trust/David Norton; **6.** Visit Cornwall/Trevor Burrows; **7.** www.britainonview.com; **8.** www.britainonview.com; **9.** Sam Morgan Moore; **10.** Minack Theatre; **Local Recommendations: 1.** Bob Berry; **2.** Stephen Wolfenden; **3.** Kristin Prisk; **6.** Visit Cornwall; **7.** Devon and Cornwall Rail Partnership; **9.** Council of the Isles of Scilly; **Factfile:** www.britainonview.com/ Martin Brent; **p.57:** www.britainonview.com; **p.57:** Chris Leather/www.cornwalls.co.uk; **p.58:** www.britainonview.com; **p.59:** Morwellham Quay; **p.60:** Lesley Gillilan; **p.66:** Chris Leather/www.cornwalls.co.uk; **p.68:** Kristin Prisk; **p.69:** Catherine St Germans; **p.71:** Tamar Cruising & Cremyll Ferry; **p.73:** Smeaton Farm; **p.84:** Paul Wattes/Visit Cornwall; **p.85:** www.britainonview.com; **p.87:** Bodmin and Wenford Railway; **p.95:** The Castle Heritage Centre and Gallery, Bude-Stratton Town Council; **p.98:** Bangor's Organic; **p.107:** www.britainonview.com; **p.108:** Rock Water Taxi; **p.109:** Mike Parnell; **p.110:** Alison Avery, www.beautifulengland.net; **p.112:** David Loftus, St Moritz Hotel; **p.123:** Paul Corin's Magnificent Music Machines; **p.125:** Looe Life Boats; **p.126:** www.britainonview.com; **p.127:** © The Monkey Sanctuary, registered charity number 1102532; **p.135:** www.britainonview.com; **p.137:** Deborah Boden; **p.138:** Roger Hamlin; **p.139:** Nanadobbie; **p.146:** Visit Cornwall; **p.147:** Square Sail Shipyard Limited; **p.148 and 149:** Ben Foster; **p.152:** St Austell Brewery; **p.162:** The Seafood Restaurant; **p.163:** Mr and Mrs Peter Prideaux-Brune; **p.166:** Dominic Boothroyd; **p.174:** The John Betjeman Centre; **p.175:** www.britainonview.com; **p.176:** www.britainonview.com; **p.179:** Ben Rowe; **p.180:** Visit Cornwall; **p.181:** Animal; **p.192:** www.britainonview.com; **p.194:** National Trust/Paul Harris; **p.196:** St Agnes Museum; **p.209:** www.britainonview.com; **p.211:** Visit Cornwall; **p.220:** National Maritime Museum Cornwall; **p.223:** www.britainonview.com; **p.224:** King Harry's Cornwall/www.kingharryscornwall.co.uk; **p.226:** www.zedfactory.com; **p.227:** Helen Gilchrist; **p.236:** David Hastilow/ Visit Cornwall; **p.237:** www.britainonview.com; **p.238:** King Harry's Cornwall/www.kingharryscornwall.co.uk; **p.240:** Hotel Tresanton; **p.248:** Chris Leather/ www.cornwalls.co.uk; **p.249:** National Trust/Aerial-Cam; **p.250:** Images courtesy of Future World; **p.252:** Trinity House; **p.263:** Trelowarren Estate; **p.264:** www.britainonview.com; **p.264:** www.britainonview.com; **p.265:** Sir Ferrers Vyvyan; **p.267:** Roskilly's Ltd; **p.279:** www.britainonview.com; **p.281:** www.britainonview.com; **p.282:** Porthminster Beach Café; **p.283:** Simon Cook, www.cornish-images.com; **p.284:** www.britainonview.com; **p.293:** Chris Leather/www.cornwalls.co.uk; **p.293:** www.britainonview.com; **p.295:** www.britainonview.com; **p.307:** Trinity House; **p.309:** www.britainonview.com; **p.310:** Geevor Tin Mine; **p.313:** Minack Theatre; **p.323:** Lesley Gillilan; **p.326:** Tresco Estate; **p.327:** James Francis; **p.328:** Seven Stones Inn; **p.329:** Churchtown Farm; **p.329:** Troytown Farm; **p.330:** St Mary's Riding Centre; **p.331:** Council of the Isles of Scilly; **p.331:** Tresco Estate; **p.335:** St Martin's Bakery.

Colour Section: The Cornish Coast: St Martin's: Council of the Isles of Scilly; Kite Surfing at Watergate Bay: www.britainonview.com/ Martin Brent; St Mawes dolphin, King Harry's Cornwall/ www.kingharryscornwall.co.uk; Porthtowan Beach: Visit Cornwall/ Ingrid King; Towan Beach: www.britainonview.com: Hell Bay Hotel Bedroom: Ben Rowe/ Tresco Estate; Aerial view of Tresco: Tresco estate; Gwithian Towans: Visit Cornwall/ Ingrid King; St Michael's Mount sunset: www.britainonview.com; Sunset over the Fowey Estuary: www.britainonview.com.

Colour Section: Cornish Culture and Heritage: St Ives boats: www.britainonview.com; Wheel Pit: The Friends of Luxulyan Valley (www.luxulyanvalley.co.uk); Trevarno Estate boat house: Trevarno Estate; St Germans Viaduct: Kristin Prisk; Kit Hill Sunset: B. Gamble © Cornwall County Council, www.cornishmining.org.uk; Cheesewring: Visit Cornwall/ Trevor Burrows; St Mawes: www.britainonview.com; Eden Project: www.britainonview.com/ Eden Project; Geevor Tin Mine: Geevor Tin Mine.

Garfield's

Guide
To
BEING A COUCH POTATO

JiM DAViS

RR
RAVETTE PUBLISHING

This edition first published by Ravette Publishing Limited in the Year 2000.

Printed and bound for Ravette Publishing Limited
Unit 3, Tristar Centre
Star Road, Partridge Green
West Sussex RH13 8RA

by Gutenberg Press Ltd, Malta.

ISBN: 1 84161 039 9

WELCOME TO "TRUTH IS STRANGER THAN FICTION THEATER"
© 1990 PAWS, INC.

THE FOLLOWING STORY YOU ARE ABOUT TO SEE IS ABSOLUTELY TRUE

EXCEPT, OF COURSE, FOR THE STUFF WE MADE UP TO MAKE IT MORE INTERESTING
I LOVE TELEVISION
JIM DAVIS 1-3-90

HERE I SIT, WASTING TIME WATCHING TELEVISION
© 1990 PAWS, INC.

WHILE OTHERS ARE BUCKLING DOWN, WORKING HARD AND GETTING THINGS DONE

JIM DAVIS 10-18

BOY, IT'S COLD IN HERE!
JIM DAVIS 11-7

BETTER TURN THE HEAT ON
CLICK

WELCOME TO MONSTER THEATER!

TONIGHT'S FEATURE... "CURSE OF THE VAMPIRE GOLDFISH"

RALPH!..THERE'S A FISH ON YOUR NECK!
I LOVE THE CLASSICS
JIM DAVIS 12-12

DON'T DELAY!....
© 1991 PAWS, INC.

ACT NOW!!

FAST ENOUGH FOR YOU?
CLICK
JIM DAVIS 2-12

CLICK

THIS LOOKS LIKE AN INTELLIGENT AND INFORMATIVE PROGRAM
© 1991 PAWS, INC.

FORTUNATELY, THERE ARE OTHER THINGS ON
CLICK
JIM DAVIS 4-8

...AND SO WE END ANOTHER PROGRAMMING DAY. UNTIL TOMORROW, GOOD NIGHT

Z
© 1991 PAWS, INC.

TURN THE SET OFF!!!
JIM DAVIS 4-10

ARF!
WHAT IS IT, BOY?
© 1991 PAWS, INC.

ARF! ARF!
HE SAYS HE'S HUNGRY

YOU SAY TIMMY FELL DOWN THE OLD MINE SHAFT?
ARF!
HE WANTS PIZZA
JIM DAVIS 4-11

LET'S SEE... NINE O'CLOCK, CHANNEL SIX...

Movie: "The Mummy's Curse"

"Mummy rises only to be hit with five thousand years of back taxes"

THIS SHOW IS REALLY DULL

I DON'T KNOW WHY YOU LIKE IT

Z
OH

THIS BULLETIN HAS JUST BEEN HANDED TO ME!
JIM DAVIS 5-24

POLICE REPORT THAT SOMEONE IS GOING AROUND HANDING BULLETINS TO NEWSCASTERS!

...AND HERE'S ANOTHER BULLETIN!
© 1991 PAWS, INC.

MEOW*
*CATS OF THE WORLD UNITE!

MEOW MEOW*
*SCRATCH THE FURNITURE!
© 1991 PAWS, INC.

WHAT ARE YOU WATCHING, GARFIELD?
CLICK!
NOTHING!
JIM DAVIS 6-5

COMING UP NEXT, "THE CAT, NATURE'S SMART ALECK"

WHAT'S ON?

NOTHING THAT WOULD INTEREST YOU, BEAN BRAIN
JIM DAVIS 7-12

WELCOME TO "CATS WATCHING TELEVISION"
JIM DAVIS 8-27

HI, MOM!
WBOR
TV

I LOVE THIS SHOW!
JIM DAVIS 9-17

YOU DO?

CLICK

I'M STUCK ON ONE CHANNEL!
CLICK
CLICK
CLICK
CLICK

WHAT COULD BE WORSE?

WELCOME TO THE LASSIE FILM FESTIVAL
AARRRGHH!
JIM DAVIS 10-4

TODAY ON "ANIMAL KINGDOM," WE GO IN SEARCH OF...

THE HOUSE CAT
© 1991 PAWS, INC.

HEEERE KITTY, KITTY, KITTY...
THERE'S NOTHING WORSE THAN A LOW-BUDGET ANIMAL SHOW
JIM DAVIS 11-16

THIS IS THE ALL PET NETWORK
JIM DAVIS

AND NOW IT'S TIME FOR EVERY CAT'S FAVORITE SHOW...
© 1992 PAWS, INC.

"HARASS THE DOG!"
FINALLY... QUALITY TELEVISION
2-3

DON'T CHANGE THE CHANNEL

WE KNOW WHERE YOU LIVE...

THE RATINGS WARS ESCALATE
JIM DAVIS 2·4

JUST WHEN YOU THINK THEY HAVE TELEVISED EVERY SPORT...

YOW!

THERE'S BLINDFOLDED DARTS
JIM DAVIS 2·5

WELL, GARFIELD, WE CAN GET A GOOD NIGHT'S SLEEP...
JIM DAVIS 2-6

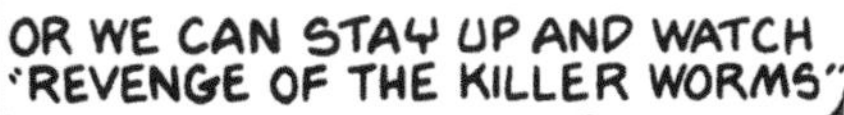
OR WE CAN STAY UP AND WATCH "REVENGE OF THE KILLER WORMS"

© 1992 PAWS, INC.

"BAIT STORE OWNER LEARNS NOT TO TEASE THE INVENTORY"
I'LL MAKE THE POPCORN

HMMPH, ANOTHER MOVIE ABOUT THE HEROIC FEATS OF A KIND-HEARTED, LOVABLE DOG
JIM DAVIS 2-7

WHY IS IT YOU NEVER SEE ANYTHING LIKE THAT ABOUT KIND-HEARTED, LOVABLE CATS?
© 1992 PAWS, INC.

MOVE OR DIE, BEAN BRAIN

ONLY AN IDIOT WOULD WATCH A SHOW THIS BAD

CLICK!
© 1992 PAWS, INC.

IT WAS A RERUN ANYWAY
JIM DAVIS 2-8

WE'VE RUN OUT OF SHOWS!
© 1992 PAWS, INC.

YOU'LL JUST HAVE TO GO OUT AND LIVE YOUR LIVES INSTEAD OF SITTING THERE WATCHING US!

JUST KIDDING!
WHEW!
JIM DAVIS 4-27

THIS STORY JUST IN!

KING KONG IS CLIMBING UP THE OUTSIDE OF THE EMPIRE STATE BUILDING!

APPARENTLY, HE WOULDN'T FIT INTO THE ELEVATOR! HA! HA!
THAT HAPPENED TO ME!
JIM DAVIS 5-2

WE HAVE A VERY SPECIAL GUEST TODAY

THE INVENTOR OF THE REMOTE CONTROL!

JIM DAVIS 5-7
CLICK

CLICK

HOW DO YOU LIKE THIS SUIT, GARFIELD?

JIM DAVIS 7-10
© 1992 PAWS, INC.
CLICK

SO, DOCTOR, ARE DOGS MORE INTELLIGENT THAN CATS?

WELL, DOGS SCORED VERY HIGH IN TESTING
...AND CATS?

© 1992 PAWS, INC.
WELL, THEY WOULDN'T TAKE THE TEST
WE HAVE NOTHING TO PROVE
JIM DAVIS
8-3

YOU ARE WATCHING THE NATIONAL DOG CHANNEL

AND NOW THE HEADLINES...
© 1992 PAWS, INC.

CATS SPREAD DISEASE!
I HATE BIASED REPORTING
JIM DAVIS 8-12

TODAY ON "WILDLIFE," MY ASSISTANT, BUBBA, WILL FORD THIS RIVER

AIEEEEE!!
© 1992 PAWS, INC.

MY, AREN'T THOSE PIRANHA BUSY LITTLE FELLAS!
I NEVER LIKED BUBBA
JIM DAVIS 8-18

BILLY WRITES TO ASK PROFESSOR ASTRONOMY, "HOW MANY STARS ARE THERE IN THE UNIVERSE?"

EXCELLENT QUESTION, BILLY!
© 1992 PAWS, INC.

LET'S SEE... ONE... TWO... THREE... FOUR...
I HOPE THIS ISN'T ONE OF THOSE TWO-PARTERS
JIM DAVIS 8-19

I'M WATCHING TELEVISION WITH A CAT
JIM DAVIS
8-29

IT'S SATURDAY NIGHT
I'M WATCHING TELEVISION WITH A CAT!
© 1992 PAWS, INC.

AND REALITY REARS ITS UGLY HEAD
I'M WATCHING TELEVISION WITH A CAT!!

JIM DAVIS 9·29

© 1992 PAWS, INC.

WHERE'S THE TV?
YOU DON'T WANT TO KNOW

GARBAGE... JUNK... GARBAGE... JUNK... GARBAGE... JUNK...
CLICK CLICK CLICK CLICK CLICK CLICK CLICK
© 1992 PAWS, INC.

AH!

TRASH!
JIM DAVIS 10·22

THIS IS THE NATIONAL CAT NETWORK

NOW BACK TO OUR FEATURE PRESENTATION...
© 1993 PAWS, INC.

"LASSIE CROSSES THE FREEWAY"
I'M ROOTING FOR THE TRUCKS
JIM DAVIS 1-8-93

NOW THIS FRIDGE HAS A 19" TV INSTALLED RIGHT IN THE DOOR

AND FOR THE HOPELESSLY DECADENT...
JIM DAVIS 1-16
© 1993 PAWS, INC.

A ROLL AWAY BED!
WHAT? NO HOT TUB?

JOIN US AGAIN NEXT TIME FOR "MACRAMÉ AND YOU"!
Z
JIM DAVIS 2-3

Z
© 1993 PAWS, INC.

GARFIELD!
Z

AND NOW IT'S TIME FOR...
© 1993 PAWS, INC.

BOWLING FOR BEAN DIP!
JIM DAVIS 4-28

BROUGHT TO YOU BY...
GARFIELD, WHEREVER YOU ARE, LEAVE THE REMOTE CONTROL ALONE!

SOME PEOPLE ACTUALLY BELIEVE TELEVISION CAUSES STUPIDITITY...

STUPIDIDDLE... STUPIDDY...
© 1993 PAWS, INC.

NOT SMARTNESS!
NO KIDDING
JIM DAVIS 7-19

MEOW!
WHAT IS IT, BOY?
© 1993 PAWS, INC.

MEOW!
TIMMY FELL DOWN THE OLD WELL?

YOU PUSHED HIM, DIDN'T YOU?
MEOW!
YOU WANNA HERO?! GET A DOG!
JIM DAVIS 7-20

CLICK

AND NOW, BOWLING FOR GEEKS!
JIM DAVIS 7-21

AH HA!
JUST FLIPPING THROUGH THE CHANNELS!
CLICK CLICK CLICK
© 1993 PAWS, INC.

YES, IT SLICES, DICES, CHOPS AND SHREDS!
JIM DAVIS 7-22

IT CUTS AND CUBES!
© 1993 PAWS, INC.

IT PULVERIZES!
SELLING CATS?
YES

HIDEY-HO, EARLY BIRDS!
GROAN
© 1993 PAWS, INC.

NOW, THE FARM REPORT

DOUG, THERE'S A DEAD COW ON ROUTE FOUR...
I HATE EARLY MORNING TELEVISION
JIM DAVIS 7-23

CLICK CLICK CLICK CLICK
© 1993 PAWS, INC.

CLICK CLICK CLICK CLICK CLICK CLICK CLICK CLICK

I KIND OF ENJOY IT WHEN THERE'S NOTHING GOOD ON
JIM DAVIS 7-24

I CAN'T BELIEVE THEY'RE SHOWING THIS MOVIE ON TV!

"THE MAN WHO STUBBED HIS TOE"

I UNDERSTAND THERE'S A LOT OF ADULT LANGUAGE IN IT
JIM DAVIS 10-19

I CAN'T DECIDE WHAT TO WATCH
CLICK
CLICK
CLICK

CLICK
CLICK
CLICK
CLICK

WHICH IS PRETTY ENTERTAINING
CLICK
CLICK
CLICK
JIM DAVIS 11-15

DO YOU WATCH TOO MUCH TELEVISION?
WAY, WAY TOO MUCH?
IF SO, THANK YOU FROM THE BOTTOM OF OUR HEARTS
YOU'RE WELCOME
© 1993 PAWS, INC.
JIM DAVIS 11-16

ARF! ARF!
WHAT IS IT, BOY?
JIM DAVIS 11-17
DID TIMMY FALL DOWN THE WELL AGAIN?
ARF!
LEAVE HIM DOWN THERE
© 1993 PAWS, INC.
LEAD ME TO HIM!
ARF!
GOOD THINKING! YOU CAN TOSS THE DOG IN TOO!

SAY, FRIEND, ARE YOU CONSIDERED AN IDIOT?
JIM DAVIS 11-18

THEN WE HAVE JUST THE PRODUCT FOR YOU!

I HAVE THREE OF THOSE
FIGURES

JIM DAVIS 11-20

PET FOOD COMMERCIAL

CLICK

COMING UP NEXT: HELP FOR THOSE OF YOU WITH SHORT ATTENTION SPANS

CLICK
JIM DAVIS 11-19

HERE WE SEE THE COMMON SPARROW
JIM DAVIS 1-17

DELICIOUS PLAIN, OR WITH A LITTLE KETCHUP

WHAT ARE YOU WATCHING ?
THE ALL-CAT CHANNEL

STAY TUNED

OR DON'T. WE DON'T CARE...

FOR APATHY THEATER
JIM DAVIS 1-18

AND NOW... THE JUGGLING RIGATONI BROTHERS

OOPS
OUCH!
OUCH!
OUCH!
OUCH!

OUCH!
OUCH!
OUCH!
THE FLAMING BATON MAY NOT BE A GOOD IDEA
JIM DAVIS 1-19

CATS ARE MORE POPULAR THAN EVER

AND OUR HIDDEN CAMERA SHOWS WHY!
JIM DAVIS 1-21

PAYOFFS TO PET OWNERS FROM THE POWERFUL CAT LOBBY!
LIES! ALL LIES!
© 1994 PAWS, INC.

OH, BROTHER
CLICK
© 1994 PAWS, INC.

GIMMIE A BREAK
CLICK
JIM DAVIS 1-22

WHAT'CHA WATCHING?
I WENT WITH THE "OH, BROTHER"

THEY SAY WATCHING TOO MUCH TV MAKES YOU PASSIVE

JIM DAVIS 1-31
© 1994 PAWS, INC.

NOT THAT I'M COMPLAINING
NOT THAT WE CARE

AND HERE'S TONIGHT'S EDITORIAL COMMENT
ARF ARF BOW-WOW BARK
JIM DAVIS 2-1
© 1994 PAWS, INC.

AND NOW, A REBUTTAL

MEOW MEOW PURRRR MEOW
THAT'S TELLING HIM!

STAY TUNED FOR WHATEVER IT IS WE'RE SHOWING NEXT
© 1994 PAWS, INC.

AS IF YOU HAD ANYTHING BETTER TO DO ANYWAY...

IN LIGHT OF YOUR DREARY, EMPTY EXISTENCE
SOUNDS GOOD TO ME
JIM DAVIS 2-2

IS YOUR CAT FAT AND LAZY?

DOES HE DO NOTHING BUT EAT AND SLEEP?
© 1994 PAWS, INC.

SO WHAT?!
JON! YOU'RE MISSING A GOOD SHOW!
JIM DAVIS 2-3

THE BANK'S SECURITY CAMERA TOOK THIS PICTURE OF THE CULPRIT
JIM DAVIS 2-4

© 1994 PAWS, INC.

I THOUGHT IT WAS A BAKERY!

STAY TUNED FOR "WATCHING PAINT DRY"
JIM DAVIS 2-5

RATS!
© 1994 PAWS, INC.

THEY PREEMPTED "WATCHING GRASS GROW"

AND NOW, THE STORY OF A WARM AND LOVING CAT
JIM DAVIS 5-20

...ON "SCIENCE FICTION THEATER!"
© 1994 PAWS, INC.

WEIRD
CLICK

DOCTORS REPORT THAT YOU SHOULDN'T-
CLICK

STUDIES FIND THAT IT'S HARD TO-
CLICK

NEXT-A SALUTE TO BACON!
NOW WE'RE TALKING
JIM DAVIS 9-6

BOOKS ARE VERY IMPORTANT

© 1994 PAWS, INC./Distributed by Universal Press Syndicate

I'M SITTING ON ONE TO GET A BETTER VIEW OF THE T.V.
JIM DAVIS 10-3

WOW. THE SAME THING IS ON EVERY CHANNEL!
CLICK CLICK
© 1994 PAWS, INC./Distributed by Universal Press Syndicate

CLICK CLICK CLICK CLICK
JIM DAVIS 11-28

THE REMOTE IS BROKEN
GET REAL! WHAT ARE THE CHANCES OF THAT?
CLICK CLICK CLICK CLICK

COMING UP NEXT: SHOWS THAT ARE THREE SECONDS LONG...

FOR THOSE WHO LIKE TO CHANGE CHANNELS...

BUT ARE TOO LAZY TO PRESS THE BUTTONS!
FINALLY!
JIM DAVIS 11-29

TODAY ON "COOKING FOR CATS"...HEALTHY SALADS!

WE HAVE OUR LETTUCE, OUR CARROTS, OUR TOMATOES...

AND NOW WE ADD OUR SQUIRREL
I LIKE ORGANIC FOOD
JIM DAVIS 11-30

THE FOLLOWING PROGRAM CONTAINS SCENES NOT SUITABLE FOR CATS
© 1994 PAWS, INC./Distributed by Universal Press Syndicate

ARF!

WHAT'S THIS WORLD COMING TO?
CLICK!
JIM DAVIS 12-1

THE CAT CHANNEL PRESENTS EVERYONE'S FAVORITE GAME SHOW...

"SLEEPING FOR DOLLARS!"
© 1995 PAWS, INC./Distributed by Universal Press Syndicate

Z
Z
Z
Z
Z
I LOVE SPORTS
JIM DAVIS 2-7

THAT CONCLUDES TONIGHT'S PROGRAM

NEXT ON "NATURE WORLD"...
JIM DAVIS 3-10

THE BEAR... FRIEND OF MAN? OR VICIOUS KILLER?

Z

CLICK!
Z

HEY! I WAS WATCHING THAT!
JIM DAVIS 3-17

IT'S TIME FOR THE WEATHER!

BUT, THERE WAS NO WEATHER TODAY!

HEY! THIS JOB IS EASY WHEN YOU DON'T GET OUT OF YOUR CHAIR
TELL ME ABOUT IT
JIM DAVIS 4-13

THE NEWS IS TOO DEPRESSING

SO TONIGHT I'LL READ A COMIC BOOK INSTEAD!

ZOMBIES FROM VENUS ARE INVADING EARTH?!
FILM AT ELEVEN
JIM DAVIS 4-28

HOW HAVE I BEEN? I'M FINE, THANK ME

WELL, I LOOK GOOD. THANK ME FOR SAYING SO

TELL ME, WHAT HAVE I BEEN UP TO?
I HATE IT WHEN HIS GUESTS DON'T SHOW UP
JIM DAVIS 5-4

THE NATIONAL NONVIOLENT NETWORK...

PROUDLY PRESENTS...

"BALLOON TOSS AT THE O.K. CORRAL"
I CAN'T WATCH!
JIM DAVIS 5-23

COMING UP NEXT...

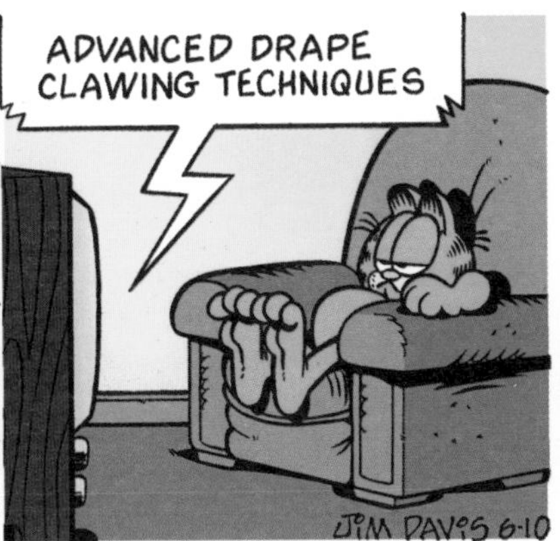
ADVANCED DRAPE CLAWING TECHNIQUES
JIM DAVIS 6-10

EDUCATIONAL T. V. !

TONIGHT THE NATIONAL CAT CHANNEL PRESENTS...

AN UNWANTED DOG'S TRAGIC JOURNEY...

"OLD DROOLER MEETS THE ELECTRIC FENCE"
I SHOULD BE TAPING THIS
JIM DAVIS 7-7

TONIGHT'S MOVIE CONTAINS MATERIAL OF A GRAPHIC NATURE

VIEWER DISCRETION IS ADVISED

JIM DAVIS 7-31

CLICK
CLICK
CLICK
CLICK
CLICK

NOTHING GOOD ON

DOGS ARE STUPID!
HOLD ON
JIM DAVIS 9-13

LASSIE, COME HOME!

MAKE ME

THE TRUE STORY
JIM DAVIS 2-15

OW! I CUT MYSELF!

OUCH! NOW I BURNED MY FINGER!

I THINK I'LL ORDER A PIZZA
"COOKING FOR KLUTZES"
JIM DAVIS 2-28

THE NATIONAL CAT CHANNEL PRESENTS...

ED THE WONDER CAT, IN THE ACTION ADVENTURE...

"HAIRBALLS FROM OUTER SPACE!"
NOT EVERY CAT CAN WEAR TIGHTS
JIM DAVIS 3-13

THE ADVENTURES OF ED THE WONDER CAT!

ED! ED! I'M SINKING IN QUICKSAND! GET HELP!

NO, ED! DON'T GO TO SLEEP!
MY HERO
JIM DAVIS 3-29

TODAY I'LL BE PREPARING MY SPECIAL "SOUP SURPRISE"

PEOPLE ASK, "WHAT'S SO SURPRISING ABOUT SOUP"?
© 1996 PAWS, INC./Distributed by Universal Press Syndicate

YOU SEE, THERE'S A LITTLE MAN INSIDE THE POT...
GUESS WHO'S BEEN HITTING THE VANILLA EXTRACT?
JIM DAVIS 4-18

AND NOW TO DISCUSS MAN-EATING PLANTS, OUR GARDENING EXPERT, STEVE!
© 1996 PAWS, INC./Distributed by Universal Press Syndicate

HELP! IT'S GOT ME!
RUSTLE RUSTLE RUSTLE
JIM DAVIS 5-15

BURP
THAT SHOULD HELP THE RATINGS

CLICK
CLICK
CLICK
CLICK
CLICK

HEY!
CLICK
CLICK
CLICK
CLICK

HE GETS MORE CHANNELS THAN WE DO!
CLICK
CLICK
CLICK
JIM DAVIS 7-25

ANOTHER SATURDAY NIGHT WITH NO DATE

MAYBE I'LL WATCH TELEVISION
JIM DAVIS 8-10

FOR ABOUT A YEAR!
HE'S WORKING OFF A BACKLOG OF REJECTIONS

CATS ARE SMARTER THAN DOGS!

AND NICER, TOO!
JIM DAVIS 9-7

SO DON'T HURT ME!
WE KNOW WHERE HE LIVES

TODAY THEY ALL STARED INTO SPACE FOR A WHILE...

THEN THEY LICKED THEMSELVES AND TOOK NAPS

CAT NEWS
JIM DAVIS 9-28

GET OUT OF MY WAY!
© 1996 PAWS, INC./Distributed by Universal Press Syndicate

JIM DAVIS 10-1

HAVE A NICE WALK?
YUP

JIM DAVIS 10-24
© 1996 PAWS, INC./Distributed by Universal Press Syndicate

CANARY SHORTAGE HITS CITY!
GARFIELD!

THERE'S NO NEWS TODAY

BECAUSE EVERYBODY EVERYWHERE SPENT ALL DAY WATCHING TV
JIM DAVIS 1-25

LOOKS LIKE WE'RE GOING TO HAVE TO START TAKING TURNS

LOOK, GARFIELD!
JIM DAVIS 5-5

IT'S THE 24-HOUR SOCK DRAWER CHANNEL!

WELCOME TO "DARNING FOR DOLLARS"!
ALL RIGHT!
I THINK I'LL GO DUST OFF THE RADIO

FIRST WE CARESS THE MEAL WITH OUR EYES...

THEN WE ALLOW THE SCENT TO PERMEATE THE ROOM...

THEN WE SHOVE OUR FACE IN THE PLATE AND INHALE!
I KNEW SHE'D CRACK
SNORT! GRUNT! GULP!
JIM DAVIS 5-6

SO ONE ACCOUNTANT SAYS TO THE OTHER, "YOU'RE SO ACCRUAL, YOU DON'T DEPRECIATE ME ANYMORE!"

HA! HA! HA! HA! HA!
I DON'T GET IT
JIM DAVIS 5-7

THIS HAS BEEN "INSIDE JOKE THEATER"
FIGURES

NOW IT'S TIME TO PLAY "NAME THAT PAIN"! LISTEN CAREFULLY, CONTESTANTS...

OUCH! EEECH! YAAACH! YEEECH! OIIIIEEE!
BZZZT
JIM DAVIS 5-8

PAT, THAT'S A GUY WHO FORGOT TO TAKE ALL THE PINS OUT OF HIS NEW SHIRT!
I KNEW THAT ONE!
GO FIGURE

SLAP SLAP SLAP SLAP SLAP SLAP

SLAP SLAP SLAP SLAP SLAP SLAP SLAP SLAP SLAP SLAP SLAP SLAP SLAP SLAP SLAP SLAP

"NINJA SISSIES" WILL RETURN IN A MOMENT
WHERE'S THE REMOTE?
JIM DAVIS 5-9

WELCOME TO "ED, THE WONDER CA-...
CLICK

...THE ADVENTURES OF "LOTHAR: MOUSE WARRIOR"!
JIM DAVIS 5-10

I HOPE THOSE BATTERIES WEAR DOWN SOON

HERE KITTY, KITTY

GOOD KITTY!

WHOA. A SURPRISE ENDING
JIM DAVIS 7-30

WELCOME TO "QUANTUM PHYSICS AND YOU"

CLICK
CLICK
CLICK
WHOA! LOOK OUT!

WHEW! I ALMOST SAW SOMETHING WORTHWHILE
JIM DAVIS 9-8

WELCOME TO "THE LOUD SHOW"
JIM DAVIS 9-9

WE'RE LOUD, WE'RE PROUD...

AND WE'RE MEAN, TOO!!

IT'S TIME TO OPEN THE DOOR...
HERE COMES THE SCARY PART

CREEEEEEEEK...
I CAN'T LOOK!

AHHH, A PERFECT SOUFFLÉ!
WHEW!
JIM DAVIS 9-10

HERE WE SEE A LION EATING AN ANTELOPE

JIM DAVIS 9-11

PRETTY ICKY, HUH?
I'LL SAY. NO TABLE LINEN!

MY NEXT GUEST IS A PREHISTORIC MONSTER

WHO ROSE FROM THE DEPTHS OF THE EARTH TO STOMP ON TOKYO

AND HAS WRITTEN A BOOK ABOUT HIS EXPERIENCES
OF COURSE
JIM DAVIS 9-12

I'M GETTING THE TV FIXED, GARFIELD

I CAN'T STAND WATCHING YOU STARE OUT THE WINDOW...
JIM DAVIS 9-13

CLICKING THE REMOTE
CHANGE! DARN YOU!
CLICK
CLICK
CLICK
CLICK

HELP! HELP!
THIS LOOKS LIKE A JOB FOR SUPER DOG!
© 1997 PAWS, INC./Distributed by Universal Press Syndicate
WHACK!
FLEW INTO A FIRE HYDRANT
JIM DAVIS 10-20

JON WANTS ME TO WATCH THIS TAPE
CLICK
© 1997 PAWS, INC./Distributed by Universal Press Syndicate

HI! UH, THIS IS JON ARBUCKLE, AND I'D LIKE TO PRESENT THE GARFIELD WORKOUT VIDEO!
JIM DAVIS 10-21

Z
YOU'RE A FUNNY MAN, JON ARBUCKLE!

JIM DAVIS 10-22

WHY ARE YOU TRYING TO CHANGE THE CHANNEL WITH A CANDY BAR?

BURP
UH-OH

HERE COMES THE OLD SLOWPOKE, MISTER THREE-TOED SLOTH...

AND WHO'S THIS? WHY, IT'S MISTER ANACONDA!
JIM DAVIS 10-23

MY, THAT DIDN'T TAKE LONG
I'LL BET THEY'RE DARN TASTY, TOO

WOOF! WOOF!
JUST LIKE A DOG
JIM DAVIS 10-24

UH, WOOF?
FORGOT HIS LINES

COMING UP NEXT, "THE CAT: NATURE'S PERFECT PREDATOR"

HA!
JIM DAVIS 1-26

WHAT'S WITH HIM?

CLICK
CLICK
CLICK
CLICK
CLICK
RATS! THE CHANNEL CHANGING BUTTON IS STUCK!
JIM DAVIS 6-29
www.garfield.com

CLICK
CLICK
CLICK
CLICK
CLICK

CLICK
CLICK
CLICK
CLICK
CLICK
sAAAAAY....

THE ALL-CAT CHANNEL PRESENTS "THE BUDGET CHEF"!

TODAY: HOW TO MAKE YOUR RAT LAST A WHOLE WEEK!
JIM DAVIS 6-30
www.garfield.com

THAT STEW HAS WHISKERS
AND ONLY THREE GRAMS OF FAT!

THE ALL-CAT CHANNEL PRESENTS "THE PIECE OF DANGLING STRING SHOW"!

HERE, A PRIDE OF LIONS PREPARE TO GORGE THEMSELVES

THEY ROAR IN TRIUMPH OVER THEIR PREY

NOW WE SEE THEM PASS OUT LINEN NAPKINS AND FINGER BOWLS
SISSIES!

OH, CECILE MY DARLING... I LOVE YOU MADL-MAD-MAAAAAACCK!
AND I LOVE YOU, REGINALD! WITH ALL MY HEAR...HEAR-HAAAARRRK!
© 1998 PAWS, INC./Distributed by Universal Press Syndicate
JIM DAVIS 7-3
www.garfield.com

HAAAACK!
HAAARRK!
HAIRBALL THEATRE

CLICK
www.garfield.com

"CLICK" YOURSELF!
© 1998 PAWS, INC./Distributed by Universal Press Syndicate

HOW WAS TV TONIGHT?
TOUCHY
JIM DAVIS 7-4

FIDO, HERE'S YOUR FINAL "PET QUIZ" QUESTION
© 1998 PAWS, INC./Distributed by Universal Press Syndicate
HOW MUCH IS ONE PLUS ONE?
WOOF, WOOF...
www.garfield.com
JIM DAVIS 8-20
WOOF?
DOGS

IT'S WONDER DOG! FLYING THROUGH THE AIR...
© 1998 PAWS, INC./Distributed by Universal Press Syndicate
SEARCHING OUT EVIL WHEREV...
SMACK!
www.garfield.com
JIM DAVIS 8-22
HARD TO DO FROM THE WINDSHIELD OF A 747
TURN THE WIPERS ON, DOUG

SOMEDAY, INSTEAD OF JUST SITTING THERE...

YOU'LL ALL BE INTERACTING WITH YOUR TELEVISIONS!

WHO CAME UP WITH THAT STUPID IDEA?
JIM DAVIS 10-19
www.garfield.com

THE ALL-CAT CHANNEL PRESENTS "COOKING WITH CATNIP"

AND NOW YOUR HOST, CHEF FLUFFY

Whooo-Peee!
I THINK CHEF FLUFFY'S BEEN RAIDING THE OL' PANTRY
JIM DAVIS 10-20
www.garfield.com

WELCOME TO
"MOO LIKE FRED"

MOO
MOO
MOO
MOO
YOU GOTTA
BE KIDDING!
CLICK
www.garfield.com
JIM DAVIS 10-21

WELCOME TO
"CLUCK LIKE CHUCK"

WHAT AN
AWFUL SHOW

WHY IN THE WORLD
DID WE WATCH THAT?
www.garfield.com

BECAUSE WE COULDN'T
REACH THE REMOTE
JIM DAVIS 10-23